W9-CEF-191

Research
in Education

fifth edition

Research
in Education

John W. Best
Butler University, Emeritus

James V. Kahn
University of Illinois at Chicago

Prentice-Hall, Englewood Cliffs, N.J. 07632

Library of Congress Cataloging-in-Publication Data

Best, John W.
  Research in education.

  Includes bibliographies and index.
  1. Education—Research. I. Kahn, James V.,
[date]. II. Title.
LB1028.B4 1986   370′.7′8   85-12445
ISBN   0-13-774035-2

Editorial supervision and
  interior design by **Lisa Halttunen**
Cover design by **Diane Saxe**
Manufacturing buyer: **Barbara Kelly Kittle**

PRINTED IN THE UNITED STATES OF AMERICA

10 9 8 7 6 5 4 3 2 1

ISBN 0-13-774035-2   01

PRENTICE-HALL INTERNATIONAL (UK) LIMITED, *London*
PRENTICE-HALL OF AUSTRALIA PTY. LIMITED, *Sydney*
PRENTICE-HALL CANADA INC., *Toronto*
PRENTICE-HALL HISPANOAMERICANA, S.A., *Mexico*
PRENTICE-HALL OF INDIA PRIVATE LIMITED, *New Delhi*
PRENTICE-HALL OF JAPAN, INC., *Tokyo*
PRENTICE-HALL OF SOUTHEAST ASIA PTE. LTD., *Singapore*
EDITORA PRENTICE-HALL DO BRASIL, LTDA., *Rio de Janeiro*
WHITEHALL BOOKS LIMITED, *Wellington, New Zealand*

Contents

Preface   xi

1   The Meaning of Research   1

The Search for Knowledge   2
Science   5
The Role of Theory   8
The Hypothesis   9
Sampling   11
Randomness   12
What Is Research?   17
Purposes of Research   21
Assessment, Evaluation,
    and Descriptive Research   23
Types of Educational Research   24
Summary   25
Exercises   26
References   27
Additional Readings   28

2   Selecting a Problem and Preparing a
    Research Proposal   29

The Academic Research Problem   31
The Research Proposal   37

Ethics in Human Experimentation   41
Using the Library   46
Finding Related Literature   46
Note Taking   47
The First Research Project   51
Submitting a Research Proposal
    to a Funding Agency   54
Summary   55
Exercises   56
References   57
Additional Readings   57

3   Historical Research   59

The History of American Education   61
History and Science   63
The Historical Hypothesis   66
Sources of Data   68
Historical Criticism   70
Writing the Historical Report   74
Summary   75
Exercises   76
References   76
Additional Readings   77

4   Assessment, Evaluation, and Descriptive Research   78

Assessment Studies   80
Evaluation Studies   86
Assessment and Evaluation
    in Problem Solving   87
The Follow-up Study   88
Descriptive Research   90
Ex Post Facto or Explanatory
    Observational Studies   98
Replication and Secondary Analysis   101
The *Post Hoc* Fallacy   104
Summary   105
Exercises   106
References   107
Additional Readings   108

5 Experimental and Quasi-Experimental
   Research   110

   Early Experimentation   111
   Experimental and Control Groups   113
   Variables   114
   Controlling Extraneous Variables   116
   Operational Definitions of Variables   118
   Experimental Validity   118
   Experimental Design   123
   Summary   140
   Exercises   141
   References   142

6 Methods and Tools of Research   143

   Reliability and Validity
     of Research Tools   144
   Quantitative Studies   145
   Qualitative Studies   147
   Psychological Tests and Inventories   148
   Qualities of a Good Test or Inventory   154
   Observation   158
   Inquiry Forms: The Questionnaire   166
   Inquiry Forms: The Opinionnaire   179
   The Interview   186
   Q Methodology   188
   Social Scaling   190
   Simple Data Organization   194
   Limitations and Sources of Error   200
   Summary   201
   Exercises   202
   References   202
   Additional Readings   203

7 Descriptive Data Analysis   204

   What is Statistics?   206
   Parametric and Nonparametric Data   207
   Descriptive and Inferential Analysis   208
   The Organization of Data   209
   Statistical Measures   210
   Normal Distribution   219

Measures of Relative Position:
   Standard Scores   225
Measures of Relationship   229
Interpretation of a
   Correlation Coefficient   239
Standard Error of Estimate   243
A Note of Caution   246
Summary   247
Exercises   248
References   252

8   Inferential Data Analysis   253

Statistical Inference   254
The Central Limit Theorem   255
Parametric Tests   258
Testing Statistical Significance   258
Decision Making   262
Student's Distribution (*t*)   267
Homogeneity of Variances   268
Analysis of Variance (ANOVA)   275
Analysis of Covariance (ANCOVA)
   and Partial Correlation   280
Multiple Regression and Correlation   282
Nonparametric Tests   285
Summary   293
Exercises   294
References   297
Additional Readings   297

9   Computer Data Analysis   298

The Computer   299
Data Organization   301
Computer Analysis of Data   304
Summary   313
Suggested Readings   314

10   The Research Report   315

Style Manuals   316
Format of the Research Report   316

The Thesis or Dissertation 322
Style of Writing 322
Typing the Report 323
Reference Form 324
Pagination 326
Tables 327
Figures 329
Evaluating a Research Report 333
Summary 334
References 335
Additional Readings 335

APPENDIXES

A Statistical Formulas and Symbols   336

B Percentage of Area Lying between the
   Mean and Successive Standard Deviation
   Units under the Normal Curve   341

C Critical Values for Pearson's
   Product-Moment Correlation (*r*)   342

D Critical Values of Student's Distribution (*t*)   344

E Abridged Table of Critical Values for CHI
   Square   345

F Critical Values of the *F* Distribution   346

G Research Course Report Evaluation   350

H Answers to Statistics Exercises   351

I Selected Indexes, Abstracts, and Reference
   Materials   354

Index
Author Index 373
Subject Index 376

Preface

The fifth edition of *Research in Education* has the same goals as the previous editions. The book has been written for use as a research reference or as a text in an introductory course in research methods. It is appropriate for graduate students enrolled in a research seminar, for those writing a thesis or dissertation, or for those who carry on research as a professional activity. All professional workers should be familiar with the methods of research and the analysis of data. If only as consumers, professionals should understand some of the techniques used in identifying problems, forming hypotheses, constructing and using data-gathering instruments, designing research studies, and employing statistical procedures to analyze data. They should also be able to use this information to interpret and critically analyze research reports that appear in professional journals and other publications.

No introductory course can be expected to confer research competence, nor can any book present all the relevant information. Research skill and understanding is achieved only through the combination of coursework and experience. Graduate students may find it profitable to carry on a small-scale study as a way of learning about research.

This edition expands and clarifies a number of ideas presented in previous editions. Additional concepts, procedures, and examples have been added, and a few have been deleted. The order of the chapters has been modified so that Chapters 3, 4, and 5 proceed from historical to descriptive to experimental research. A number of experimental designs and threats to experimental validity have been added in Chapter 5. The statistics chapters (Chapters 7 and 8) have been expanded, and a new chapter (Chapter 9) has been added on using computers to analyze data.

This edition has been rewritten to conform to the guidelines of the American Psychological Association's (APA) *Publications Manual* (3rd. ed.). The writing style suggested in Chapter 10 is also in keeping with the APA manual. Many of the references listed in Chapter 9 of the previous edition are now in Appendix I.

Many of the topics covered in this book may be peripheral to the course objectives of some instructors. It is not suggested that all of the topics in this book be included in a single course. It is recommended that instructors use the topics selectively and in the sequence that they find most appropriate. The portion of the book not used in those courses can then be used by the student in subsequent courses, to assist in carrying out a thesis, and/or as a reference.

The second author takes full responsibility for the additions and deletions from the previous edition. This revision benefited from the comments of my students who had used the fourth edition of this text. To them, to Ernest Pascarella, and to the anonymous manuscript reviewers, I express my appreciation. I wish to acknowledge the cooperation of the University of Illinois at Chicago Computer Center, SPSS, Inc., and SAS Institute, Inc. I am indebted to Mike Korenchan for typing Chapter 7, to Penelope Witte for typing the other nine chapters, and to Merry Mastney for programming the word processor. Their patience, persistence, and cooperation made it possible to complete this project in a timely manner. Finally, I wish to thank my wife, Kathleen Cuerdon-Kahn, for her assistance, encouragement, and support.

James V. Kahn

Research
in Education

Chapter 1

The Meaning
of Research

THE SEARCH FOR KNOWLEDGE

Human beings are the unique product of their creation and evolution. In contrast to other forms of animal life, their more highly developed nervous system has enabled them to develop sounds and symbols (letters and numbers) that make possible the communication and recording of their questions, observations, experiences, and ideas.

It is understandable that their greater curiosity, implemented by their control of symbols, would lead them to speculate about the operation of the universe, the great forces beyond their own control. Over many centuries, people began to develop what seemed to be plausible explanations. Attributing the forces of nature to the working of supernatural powers, they believed that the gods, at their whims, manipulated the sun, stars, wind, rain, and lightning.

The appearance of the medicine man or priest, who claimed special channels of communication with the gods, led to the establishment of a system of religious authority passed on from one generation to another. A rigid tradition developed, and a dogma of nature's processes, explained in terms of mysticism and the authority of the priesthood, became firmly rooted, retarding further search for truth for centuries.

But gradually people began to see that the operations of the forces of nature were not as capricious as they had been led to believe. They began to observe an orderliness in the universe and certain cause-and-effect relationships; they discovered that under certain conditions events could be predicted with reasonable accuracy. However, these explanations were often rejected if they seemed to conflict with the dogma of religious authority. Curious persons who raised questions were often punished and even put to death when they persisted in expressing doubts suggested by such unorthodox explanations of natural phenomena.

This reliance on empirical evidence or personal experience challenged the sanction of vested authority and represented an important step in the direction of scientific inquiry. Such pragmatic observation, however, was largely unsystematic and further limited by the lack of an objective method. Observers were likely to overgeneralize on the basis of incomplete experience or evidence, to ignore complex factors operating simultaneously, or to let their feelings and prejudices influence both their observations and their conclusions.

It was only when people began to think systematically about thinking itself that the era of logic began. The first systematic approach to reasoning, attributed to Aristotle and the Greeks, was the deductive method. The categorical syllogism was one model of thinking that prevailed among early philosophers. Syllogistic reasoning established a logical relationship between a *major premise*, a *minor premise*, and a *conclusion*. A major premise is a self-evident assumption, previously established by metaphysical truth or dogma, that concerns a relationship; a minor premise is a particular case related to the major premise. Given the logical relationship of these premises, the conclusion is inescapable.

A typical Aristotelian categorical syllogism follows:

Major Premise . . . . All men are mortal.

Minor premise . . . . Socrates is a man.

Conclusion . . . . Socrates is mortal.

This deductive method, moving from the general assumption to the specific application, made an important contribution to the development of modern problem solving. But it was not fruitful in arriving at new truths. The acceptance of incomplete or false major premises that were based on old dogmas or unreliable authority could only lead to error. Semantic difficulties often resulted from shifting definitions of the terms involved.

Centuries later, Francis Bacon advocated direct observation of phenomena, arriving at conclusions or generalizations through the evidence of many individual observations. This inductive process of moving from specific observations to the generalization freed logic from some of the hazards and limitations of deductive thinking. Bacon recognized the obstacle that the deductive process placed in the way of discovering new truth: It started with old dogmas that religious or intellectual authorities had already accepted and thus could be expected to arrive at few new truths. These impediments to the discovery of truth, which he termed "idols," were exposed in his *Novum Organum*, written in 1620.

The following story, attributed to Bacon, expresses his revolt against the authority of the written word, an authority that dominated the search for truth during the Middle Ages:

> In the year of our Lord, 1432, there arose a grievous quarrel among the brethren over the number of teeth in the mouth of a horse. For thirteen days the disputation raged without ceasing. All the ancient books and

chronicles were fetched out, and wonderful and ponderous erudition was made manifest. At the beginning of the fourteenth day a youthful friar of goodly bearing asked his learned superiors for permission to add a word, and straightway, to the wonder of the disputants, whose deep wisdom he sorely vexed, he beseeched them in a manner coarse and unheard of, to look in the mouth of a horse and find answers to their questionings. At this, their dignity being grievously hurt, they waxed exceedingly wroth; and joining in a mighty uproar they flew upon him and smote him hip and thigh and cast him out forthwith. For, said they, "Surely Satan hath tempted this bold neophyte to declare unholy and unheard-of ways of finding truth, contrary to all the teachings of the fathers." After many days of grievous strife the dove of peace sat on the assembly, and they, as one man, declaring the problem to be an everlasting mystery because of a dearth of historical and theological evidence thereof, so ordered the same writ down. (Mees, 1934, pp. 13–14)

The method of inductive reasoning proposed by Bacon, a method new to the field of logic but widely used by the scientists of his time, was not hampered by false premises, by the inadequacies and ambiguities of verbal symbolism, or by the absence of supporting evidence.

But the inductive method alone did not provide a completely satisfactory system for the solution of problems. Random collection of individual observations without a unifying concept or focus often obscured investigations and therefore rarely led to a generalization or theory.

The deductive method of Aristotle and the inductive method of Bacon were fully integrated in the work of Charles Darwin in the nineteenth century. During his early career his observations of animal life failed to lead to a satisfactory theory of man's development. The concept of the struggle for existence in Thomas Malthus' *Essay on Population* intrigued Darwin and suggested the assumption that natural selection explains the origin of different species of animals. This hypothesis provided a needed focus for his investigations. He proceeded to deduce specific consequences suggested by the hypothesis. The evidence gathered confirmed the hypothesis that biological change in the process of natural selection, in which favorable variations were preserved and unfavorable ones destroyed, resulted in the formation of new species.

The major premise of the older deductive method was gradually replaced by an assumption or *hypothesis* that was subsequently tested by the collection and logical analysis of data. This deductive-inductive method is now recognized as an example of a scientific approach.

John Dewey (1938) suggested a pattern that is helpful in identifying the elements of a deductive-inductive process:

A METHOD OF SCIENCE

1. Identification and definition of the problem
2. Formulation of a hypothesis—a hunch, an assumption, or an intelligent guess

3. Collection, organization, and analysis of data
4. Formulation of conclusions
5. Verification, rejection, or modification of the hypothesis by the test of its consequences in a specific situation

Although this pattern is a useful reconstruction of some methods of scientific inquiry, it is not to be considered the *only* scientific method. There are many ways of applying logic and observation to problem solving. An overly rigid definition of the research process would omit many ways in which researchers go about their tasks. The planning of a study may include a great deal of exploratory activity, which is frequently intuitive or speculative and, at times, a bit disorderly. Although researchers must eventually identify a precise and significant problem, their object may initially be vague and poorly defined. They may observe situations that seem to suggest certain possible cause-and-effect relationships and even gather some preliminary data to examine for possible relevancy to their vaguely conceived problem. Thus, much research begins with the inductive method. At this stage, imagination and much speculation are essential to the formulation of a clearly defined problem that is susceptible to the research process. Many students of research rightly feel that problem identification is one of the most difficult and most crucial steps of the research process.

Frequently researchers are interested in complex problems, the full investigation of which requires a series of studies. This approach is known as *programmatic research* and usually combines the inductive and deductive methods in a continuously alternating pattern. The researcher may begin with a number of observations from which a hypothesis is derived (inductive reasoning). Then the researcher proceeds deductively to determine the consequences that are to be expected if the hypothesis is true. Data are then collected through the inductive method to verify, reject, or modify the hypothesis. Based on the findings of this study, the researcher goes on to formulate more hypotheses to further investigate the complex problem under study. Thus, the researcher is continually moving back and forth between the inductive method of observation and data collection, and the deductive method of hypothesizing the anticipated consequences to events.

SCIENCE

The term *science* may be thought of as an approach to the gathering of knowledge rather than as a field of subject matter. Science, put simply, consists of two primary functions: (1) the development of theory and (2) the testing of substantive hypotheses that are deduced from theory. The scientist, therefore, is engaged in the use, modification, and/or creation of theory. The scientist may emphasize an empirical approach in which data collection is the primary method, a rational approach in which logical and deductive reasoning are primary, or a combination of these approaches, which is most common. Regardless of the emphasis, the scientist begins with a set of ideas that direct the effort and with a goal that entails the development or testing of theory.

By attempting to apply the rigorous, systematic observation and analysis used in the physical and biological sciences to areas of social behavior, the social sciences have grown and have advanced humanity's knowledge of itself. The fields of anthropology, economics, education, political science, psychology, and social psychology have become recognized as sciences by many authorities. To the extent that these fields are founded on scientific methodology, they are sciences. Some reject this concept, still defining science in terms of subject matter rather than methodology. Historically their position can be readily explained. Since scientific methods were first used in the investigation of physical phenomena, tradition has identified science with the physical world. Only within the last century has the methodology of science been applied to the study of various areas of human behavior. Since these are newer areas of investigation, their results have not achieved the acceptance and status that come with the greater maturity and longer tradition of the physical sciences.

The uniformity of nature is a reasonable assumption in the world of physical objects and their characteristics, but in the area of social behavior such assumptions are not warranted. Human nature is much more complex than the sum of its many discrete elements, even if they could be isolated and identified. Because human nature is so complex, it is much more difficult to develop sound theories of human behavior than to predict occurrences in the physical world. Research on human subjects has numerous problems.

1. No two persons are alike in feelings, drives, or emotions. What may be a reasonable prediction for one may be useless for another.
2. No one person is completely consistent from one moment to another. Human behavior is influenced by the interaction of the individual with every changing element in his or her environment, often in a way that is difficult to predict.
3. Human beings are influenced by the research process itself. They are influenced by the attention that is focused on them when under investigation and by the knowledge that their behavior is being observed.
4. The behavioral sciences have been limited by a lack of adequate definition. Accurate operational definitions are essential to the de-

velopment of a sophisticated science. Such traits as intelligence, learning, hostility, anxiety, or motivation are not directly observable and are generally referred to as "constructs," implying that they are constructions of the scientist's imagination. Constructs cannot be seen, heard, or felt. They can only be inferred by test scores or by observed hostile or aggressive acts, skin responses, pulse rates, or persistence at a task.

But even constructs for which useful descriptive instruments are available account for only limited sources of variation; they yield only partial definitions. For example, intelligence, as defined by a score on an intelligence test, is not a satisfactory measure of the type of intelligence that individuals are called upon to demonstrate in a variety of situations outside a formal academic environment.

In the physical sciences, many complex constructs have been more effectively defined in operational terms. Time is one such construct: Time is a function of the motion of the earth in relation to the sun, measured by the rotation of a hand on the face of a circular scale in precise units. Weight is a construct involving the laws of gravitation, measured by springs, torsion devices, levers, or electronic adaptations of these instruments.

The instruments which measure such constructs are devised so that they are consistent, to a maximum degree, with known physical laws and forces, and yield valid descriptions in a variety of situations. An international bureau prescribes standards for these devices so that they may provide precise operational definitions of the constructs.

Although the problems of discovering theories of human behavior are difficult, they may not be insolvable. Behavioral scientists need to carry on their investigations as carefully and rigorously as have physical scientists. However, one must not overestimate the exactness of the physical sciences, for theoretical speculations and probability estimates are also inherent characteristics.

Today we live in a world that has benefited greatly from progress made by the biological and physical sciences. Infant mortality is decreasing, and life expectancy continues to increase. Surgery is now performed on fetuses *in utero* to correct such conditions as hydrocephalus. Children born prematurely weighing less than 1000 grams (approximately 2 pounds) survive and generally thrive. The Salk and Sabin vaccines promise to rid the world of poliomyelitis. Many forms of cancer are being conquered by early detection and chemotherapy. Improved nutrition, antibiotics, innovative surgical techniques, and countless other accomplishments allow us to lead longer, healthier lives. Automation and computerization touch every aspect of our lives reducing our physical labor and increasing our leisure time. The splitting of the atom, space travel, and developments in the field of electronics such as the laser and the silicon chip, promise improvements and adventures that are beyond the scope of most people's imagination. All these improvements have resulted from the investigation of biological and physical sciences.

However, there is less confidence about the improvement of the nonphysical aspects of our world. Despite all their marvelous gadgets, there is some doubt whether people are happier or more satisfied or whether their basic needs are being fulfilled more effectively today than they were a century ago. The fear of nuclear plant failures and the uncertainty about the safe disposal of nuclear waste is uppermost in the minds of people throughout the world. Our apparent inability to solve various social problems raises the spector of malnutrition, terrorism, and illiteracy. There is great concern that our children are not learning sufficiently to compete in our more technologically complex society. Standard scores indicate that high school children are less prepared for college today than were their parents and older siblings.

Scientific methods must be applied with greater vigor and imagination to the behavioral aspects of our culture. The development of the behavioral sciences and their application to education and other human affairs present some of our greatest challenges.

THE ROLE OF THEORY

At this stage in the discussion, a statement about theory is appropriate. To many people the term *theory* suggests an ivory tower, something unreal and of little practical value. On the contrary, a theory establishes a cause and effect relationship between variables with the purpose of explaining and predicting phenomena. Those who engage in pure research devote their energies to the formulation and reformulation of theories and may not be concerned with their practical applications. However, when a theory has been established, it may suggest many applications of practical value. John Dewey once said that there was nothing more practical than a good theory.

Theories about the relationship between the position of the earth and other moving celestial bodies were essential to the successful launching and return of manned space vehicles. Theories of the behavior of gases were essential to the development of refrigeration and air conditioning. Controlled atomic energy could not have been achieved without the establishment of theories about the nature of mass and energy and the structure of the atom. The real purpose of scientific methods is prediction, the discovery of certain theories or generalizations that anticipate future occurrences with maximum probability.

Piaget's theory of cognitive development is a good example of a theory that has been developed with little or no concern for application. Only one of Piaget's many books discussed education in any great detail (Piaget, 1970), and even this book does not deal with the specifics that most teachers need. However, innumerable books, chapters, and articles written by followers of Piaget have explicated the usefulness of his theory for teaching practices from preschool (e.g., Kamii, 1973; Lavatelli, 1973) to high school (e.g., Karplus, et al., 1977; Staver & Gabel, 1979), and even for teaching mentally retarded (e.g., Kahn, 1984, in press) and other handicapped children (e.g., Wolinsky, 1970). So although Piaget's aim was to understand the cognitive structures and functioning of children and adults, his theory has been embraced by educators and psychologists who have investigated ways in which his theory could be used to improve educational practice.

But what do we mean by the term *theory*? A theory is an attempt to develop a general explanation for some phenomenon. A theory defines nonobservable constructs that are inferred from observable facts and events and that are thought to have an effect on the phenomenon under study. A theory describes the relationship among key variables for purposes of explaining a current state or predicting future occurrences. A theory is primarily concerned with explanation and therefore focuses on determining cause-effect relationships.

THE HYPOTHESIS

Two important functions that hypotheses serve in scientific inquiry are the development of theory and the statement of parts of an existing theory in testable form. Snow (1973) describes six levels of theory, with the first level being hypothesis formation. At this initial level, the theory developer has a hunch based on past experience, observations, and/or information gained from others. A hypothesis is formulated in such a way that this hunch can be tested. Based upon the findings of the subsequent research, the hypothesis is supported or rejected and more hypotheses are formulated to continue the process of building a cohesive theory.

The more common use of hypotheses is to test whether an existing theory can be used to solve a problem. In everyday situations, those who confront problems often propose informal hypotheses that can be tested directly. For example, when a lamp fails to light when the switch is turned on, several hypotheses come to mind based upon our understanding of electricity and our past experiences with lamps:

1. The plug is not properly connected to the wall outlet.
2. The bulb is burned out.

3. The fuse is burned out or the circuit breaker has been tripped.
4. There has been a power failure in the neighborhood.

Each of these speculations can be tested directly by checking the plug connection, substituting a bulb known to be in working condition, inspecting the fuse or circuit breaker, or by noting whether or not other lights in the house or in neighbors' houses are on.

The Research Hypothesis

The *research* or *scientific hypothesis* is a formal affirmative statement predicting a single research outcome, a tentative explanation of the relationship between two or more variables. For the hypothesis to be testable, the variables must be operationally defined. That is, the researcher specifies what operations were conducted, or tests used, to measure each variable. Thus, the hypothesis focuses the investigation on a definite target and determines what observations, or measures, are to be used.

A number of years ago the hypothesis was formulated that there is a positive causal relationship between cigarette smoking and the incidence of coronary heart disease. This hypothesis proposed a tentative explanation that led to many studies comparing the incidence of heart disease among cigarette smokers and nonsmokers. As a result of these extensive studies, the medical profession now generally accepts that this relationship has been established.

In the behavioral sciences, the variables may be abstractions that cannot be observed. These variables must be defined operationally by describing some samples of actual behavior that are concrete enough to be observed directly. The relationship between these observable incidents may be deduced as consistent or inconsistent with the consequences of the hypothesis. Thus, the hypothesis may be judged to be probably true or probably false.

For example, one might propose the hypothesis that third-grade children taught the Chisanbop hand-calculating process would learn to perform the basic arithmetic processes more effectively (that is, score higher on a specified measure or test of arithmetic processing) than those using the conventional method. Children would be randomly assigned in two groups, one taught the Chisanbop system (experimental group) and the other using the conventional method (control group). The experiment would be carried on for a period of nine months. If the hypothesis were true, the experimental group's mean scores on a standardized arithmetic achievement test would be significantly higher than those of the control group.

The Null Hypothesis (H_0)

In the early stage of their study, researchers state an affirmative scientific or research hypothesis as a prediction of the outcome that they propose to test. Later, at the stage of the statistical analysis of the observed data, they restate the hypothesis in negative or null form. For example, the previous research hypothesis would be restated: There is *no significant difference* between the arithmetic achievement of students taught the Chisanbop system of hand calculation and those using the conventional method.

The null hypothesis relates to a statistical method of interpreting conclusions about population characteristics that are inferred from the variable relationships observed in samples. The null hypothesis asserts that observed differences or relationships merely result from chance errors inherent in the sampling process. If the researcher rejects the null hypothesis, he or she accepts the research hypothesis, concluding that the magnitude of the observed variable relationship is probably too great to attribute to sampling error.

The logic of the use of the null hypothesis, which may be confusing to students, is explained in greater detail in the discussions of sampling error and the central limit theorem in Chapter 8.

SAMPLING

The primary purpose of research is to discover principles that have universal application, but to study a whole population to arrive at generalizations would be impracticable, if not impossible. Some populations are so large that their characteristics cannot be measured; before the measurement could be completed, the populations would have changed.

Imagine the difficulty of conducting a reading experiment with all American fifth-grade children as subjects. The study of a population of this size would require the services of thousands of researchers, the expenditure of millions of dollars, and hundreds of thousands of class hours.

Fortunately, the process of sampling makes it possible to draw valid inferences or generalizations on the basis of careful observation of variables within a relatively small proportion of the population. A measured value based upon sample data is a *statistic*. A population value inferred from a statistic is a *parameter*.

A *population* is any group of individuals that have one or more characteristics in common that are of interest to the researcher. The population may be all the individuals of a particular type, or a more restricted part of that group. All public school teachers, all male secondary school teachers, all elementary school teachers, or all Chicago kindergarten teachers may be populations.

A *sample* is a small proportion of a population selected for observation and analysis. By observing the characteristics of the sample, one can make certain inferences about the characteristics of the population from which it is drawn. Contrary to some popular opinion, samples are not selected haphazardly; they are chosen in a systematically random way, so that chance or the operation of probability can be utilized.

RANDOMNESS

The concept of *randomness* has been basic to scientific observation and research. It is based on the assumption that, while individual events cannot be predicted with accuracy, aggregate events can. For instance, although it may not predict with great accuracy an individual's academic achievement, it will predict accurately the average academic performance of a group.

Randomization has two important applications in research:

1. Selecting a group of individuals for observation who are representative of the population about which the researcher wishes to generalize; or

2. Equating experimental and control groups in an experiment. Assigning individuals by random assignment is the best method of providing for their equivalence.

It is important to note that a random sample is not necessarily an identical representation of the population. Characteristics of successive random samples drawn from the same population may differ to some degree, but it is possible to estimate their variation from the population characteristics and from each other. The variation, known as *sampling error*, does not suggest that a mistake has been made in the sampling process. Rather, sampling error refers to the chance variations that occur in sampling; with randomization, these variations are predictable and taken into account in data analysis techniques.

The topic of sampling error is considered in greater detail in Chapter 8 in the discussion of the central limit theorem, the standard error of the mean, and the level of significance.

The Simple Random Sample

The individual observations or individuals are chosen in such a way that each has an equal chance of being selected, and each choice is independent of any other choice. If we wished to draw a sample of 50 individuals from a population of 600 students enrolled in a school, we could place the 600 names in a container and, blindfolded, draw one name at a time until the sample of 50 was selected. This procedure is cumbersome and is rarely used.

Random Numbers

A more convenient way of selecting a random sample, or assigning individuals to experimental and control groups so that they are equated, is by the use of a table of random numbers. Many such tables have been generated by computers producing a random sequence of digits. *The million random digits with 100,000 normal deviates* of the Rand Corporation (1965) and Fisher and Yates (1963) *Statistical tables for biological, agricultural and medical research* are frequently used. In addition, many packaged computer programs include the capability to produce a random numbers table.

When using a table, it is necessary to assign consecutive numbers to each member of the population from which the sample is to be selected. Then, entering the table at any page, row, or column, the researcher can select the sample from 001 to 999, three digits; and from 0001 to 9999, four digits. When a duplicated number or a number larger than the population size is encountered, it is skipped and the process continues until the desired sample size is selected.

As an illustration, let us assume that a sample of 30 is to be selected from a serially numbered population of 835. Using a portion of a table of random numbers reproduced here, 30 three-digit numbers are selected by reading from left to right. When using the table of random numbers to select a sample, one must number the population members serially.

TABLE 1–1   An Abbreviated Table of Random Numbers

50393	13330	92982	17442	63378	02050
09038	31974	22381	24289	72341	61530
82066	06997	44590	23445	72731	61407
91340	84979	39117	89344	46694	95596

The sample

503	426	197	161	590	~~913~~	444
~~931~~	337	422	530	~~234~~	408	669
333	802	381	820	457	497	
092	050	242	660	273	~~939~~	
~~982~~	090	~~897~~	699	~~161~~	117	
074	383	234	744	407	~~893~~	

In selecting this sample, eight numbers were deleted. Numbers 931, 982, 897, 913, 939, and 893 were deleted because they were larger than the population of 835 described. Numbers 234 and 161 were deleted because they duplicate previous selections.

Then, enter the table at any page, row, or column at random, and the sample can be selected by reading to the left, right, up, down, or diagonally. For populations up to 99 in number, two digits are selected; from 001 to 999, three digits; and from 0001 to 9999, four digits.

These 30 numbered members of the population comprise the sample. If this group were to be divided into two equated groups of 15 each, the first 15 could compose one group and the second 15 the other. There are many varieties of random assignment, such as assigning the odd numbers to one group (1, 3, 5, 7, . . .) and the even numbers (2, 4, 6, 8, . . .) to the other. It is apparent that in order to select a random sample, one must not consciously select any particular individual or observation. The size of the sample may or may not be significantly related to its adequacy. A large sample, carelessly selected, may be biased and inaccurate, whereas a smaller one, carefully selected, may be relatively unbiased and accurate enough to make satisfactory inference possible. However, a well-selected large sample will be more representative of the population than a well-selected smaller sample. This is explained in greater detail in the discussions of sampling error and the central limit theorem in Chapter 8.

In addition to caution in the sampling process, definition of the population about which inferences are to be made is extremely important. When the now defunct *Literary Digest* drew its sample for the purpose of predicting the results of the 1936 presidential election, subjects were chosen from the pages of telephone directories and from automobile registration lists. The prediction of Alfred Landon's victory over Franklin D. Roosevelt proved to be wrong, and a postelection analysis revealed that the population for which the prediction was made was not the same population sampled. Large numbers of eligible voters did not own automobiles and were not telephone subscribers, and consequently were not included in the sample. In fact, the resulting sample was systematically biased to overrepresent the wealthy and underrepresent the poor and unemployed.

The Systematic Sample

If a population can be accurately listed or is finite, a type of systematic selection will provide what approximates a random sample. A *systematic sample* consists of the selection of each *n*th term from a list. For example, if a sample of 200 were to be selected from a telephone directory with 200,000 listings, one would select the first name by selecting a randomly selected name from a randomly selected page. Then every thousandth name would be selected until the sample of 200 names was complete. If the last page were reached before the desired number had been selected, the count would continue from the first page of the directory. Systematic samples of automobile owners could be selected in similar fashion from a state licensing bureau list or file, or a sample of eighth-grade students from a school attendance roll.

The Stratified Random Sample

At times it is advisable to subdivide the population into smaller homogeneous groups to get more accurate representation. This method results in the *stratified random sample.* For example, in an income study of wage earners in a community, a true sample would approximate the same relative number from each socioeconomic level of the whole community. If, in the community, the proportion were 15 percent professional workers, 10 percent managers, 20 percent skilled workers, and 55 percent unskilled workers, the sample should include approximately the same proportions in order to be considered representative. Within each subgroup a random selection should be used. This process gives the researcher a more representative sample than one selected from the entire community, which might be unduly weighted by a preponderance of unskilled workers.

In addition to, or instead of, socioeconomic status, such characteristics as age, sex, extent of formal education, racial origin, religious or political affiliation, or rural-urban residence might provide a basis for choosing a stratified sample. The characteristics of the entire population, together with the purposes of the study, must be carefully considered before a stratified sample is decided upon.

The Area or Cluster Sample

The *area* or *cluster sample* is a variation of the simple random sample that is particularly appropriate when the population of interest is infinite, when a list of the members of the population does not exist, or when the geographic distribution of the individuals is widely scattered. Suppose, for the purpose of a survey, we wanted to select a sample of all public school elementary teachers in the United States. A simple random sample would be impracticable.

From the 50 states a random sample of 20 could be selected. From these 20 states, all counties could be listed and a random sample of eighty counties selected. From the 80 counties, all the school districts could be listed and a random sample of 30 school districts selected. It would not be difficult to compile a list of all elementary teachers from the 30 school districts and to select a random sample of 500 teachers. This successive random sampling of states, counties, school districts, and finally, of individuals would involve a relatively efficient and inexpensive method of selecting a sample of individuals.

This method of sampling is likely to introduce an element of sample bias because of the unequal size of some of the subsets selected. Only when a simple random sample would be impracticable is this method recommended.

Nonprobability Samples

Nonprobability samples are those that use whatever subjects are available, rather than following a specific subject selection process. Some nonprobability sampling procedures may produce samples that do not accurately reflect the characteristics of a population of interest. Such samples may lead to unwarranted generalizations and should not be used if random selection is practicable.

Educational researchers, because of administrative limitations in randomly selecting and assigning individuals to experimental and control groups, often use available classes as samples. The status of groups may be equated by such statistical means as the analysis of covariance (discussed in Chapter 8). In certain types of descriptive studies, the use of available samples may restrict generalizations to similar populations. For example, when a psychology professor uses students from Introduction to Psychology classes as subjects, the professor may safely generalize only to other similar groups of psychology students.

A sample made up of those who volunteer to participate in a study may represent a biased sample. Volunteers are not representative of a total population, for volunteering results in a selection of individuals who are different and who really represent a population of volunteers. In a sense, those who respond to a mailed questionnaire are volunteers and may not reflect the characteristics of all who were on the mailing list. It may be desirable to send another copy of the instrument to nonrespondents with an appeal for their participation.

Sample Size

There is usually a trade-off between the desirability of a large sample and the feasibility of a small one. The ideal sample is large enough to serve as an adequate representation of the population about which the researcher wishes to generalize and small enough to be selected economically—in terms of subject availability, expense in both time and money, and complexity of data analysis. There is no fixed number or percentage of subjects that determines the size of an adequate sample. It may depend upon the nature of the population of interest or the data to be gathered and analyzed. A national opinion poll randomly selects a sample of about 1500 subjects as a reflection of the opinions of a population of more than 150 million United States citizens of voting age, with an error factor from 2 to 3 percent.

Before the second decade of the twentieth century, statisticians believed that samples should be relatively large so that the normal probability table could be used to estimate sampling error, explained by the central limit theorem. (See Chapter 8 for a discussion of sampling error and student's distribution.) The work of William Sealy Gosset in 1915, in which he developed data on the probability distribution of small sample means (students' t distribution), led to the effective use of small samples. Gosset's contribution made feasible research studies that necessarily had to be limited to a small number of subjects. Small-sample research has made a significant contribution to statistical analysis of research data, particularly in experimental studies.

It is often stated that samples of 30 or more are to be considered large samples and those with fewer than 30, small samples. It is approximately at this sample size of 30 that the magnitude of students' t critical values for small samples approach the z critical values of the normal probability table for large samples. (See Chapter 8 for a discussion of z and t critical values.)

More important than size is the care with which the sample is selected. The ideal method is random selection, letting chance or the laws of probability determine which members of the population are to be selected. When random sampling is employed, whether the sample is large or small, the errors of sampling may be estimated, giving research-ers an idea of the confidence that they may place in their findings.

In summary, several practical observations about sample size are listed:

1. The larger the sample, the smaller the magnitude of sampling error.
2. Survey-type studies probably should have larger samples than needed in experimental studies.
3. When sample groups are to be subdivided into smaller groups to be compared, the researcher initially should select large enough samples so that the subgroups are of adequate size for his or her purpose.
4. In mailed questionnaire studies, because the percentage of responses may be as low as 20 to 30 percent, a larger initial sample mailing is indicated.
5. Subject availability and cost factors are legitimate considerations in determining appropriate sample size.

WHAT IS RESEARCH?

How is research related to scientific method? The terms *research* and *scientific method* are sometimes used synonymously in educational discussions. Although it is true that the terms have some common elements of meaning, a distinction is helpful.

For the purposes of this discussion, *research* is considered to be the more formal, systematic, and intensive process of carrying on a scientific method of analysis. Scientific method in problem solving may be an informal application of problem identification, hypothesis formulation, observation, analysis, and conclusion. You could reach a conclusion why your car wouldn't start or why a fire occurred in an unoccupied house by employing a scientific method, but the processes involved probably would not be as structured as those of research. Research is a more systematic activity that is directed toward discovery and the development of an organized body of knowledge. *Research may be defined as the systematic and objective analysis and recording of controlled observations that may lead to the development of generalizations, principles, or theories, resulting in prediction and possibly ultimate control of events.*

Because definitions of this sort are rather abstract, a summary of some of the characteristics of research may help to clarify its spirit and meaning.

1.   Research is directed toward the solution of a problem. The ultimate goal is to discover cause-and-effect relationships between variables, though researchers often have to settle for the useful discovery of a systematic relationship because the evidence for a cause-and-effect relationship is insufficient.

2.   Research emphasizes the development of generalizations, principles, or theories that will be helpful in predicting future occurrences. Research usually goes beyond the specific objects, groups, or situations investigated and infers characteristics of a target population from the sample observed. Research is more than information retrieval, the simple gathering of information. Although many school research departments gather and tabulate statistical information that may be useful in decision making, these activities are not properly termed research.

3.   Research is based upon observable experience or empirical evidence. Certain interesting questions do not lend themselves to research procedures because they cannot be observed. Research rejects revelation and dogma as methods of establishing knowledge and accepts only what can be verified by observation.

4.   Research demands accurate observation and description. Researchers use quantitative measuring devices, the most precise form of description. When this is not possible or appropriate, they use qualitative or nonquantitative descriptions of their observations. They select or devise valid data-gathering procedures and, when feasible, employ mechanical, electronic, or psychometric devices to refine observation, description, and analysis of data.

5. Research involves gathering new data from primary or firsthand sources or using existing data for a new purpose. Teachers frequently assign a so-called research project that involves writing a paper dealing with the life of a prominent person. The students are expected to read a number of encyclopedias, books, or periodical references and to synthesize the information in a written report. This is not research, for the data are not new. Merely reorganizing or restating what is already known and has already been written, valuable as it may be as a learning experience, is not research. It adds nothing to what is known.

6. Although research activity may at times be somewhat random and unsystematic, it is more often characterized by carefully designed procedures that apply rigorous analysis. Although trial and error are often involved, research is rarely a blind, shotgun investigation or an experiment just to see what happens.

7. Research requires expertise. The researcher knows what is already known about the problem and how others have investigated it. He or she has searched the related literature carefully and is also thoroughly grounded in the terminology, concepts, and technical skills necessary to understand and analyze the data gathered.

8. Research strives to be objective and logical, applying every possible test to validate the procedures employed, the data collected, and the conclusions reached. The researcher attempts to eliminate personal bias. There is no attempt to persuade or to prove an emotionally held conviction. The emphasis is on testing rather than on proving the hypothesis. Although absolute objectivity is as elusive as pure righteousness, the researcher tries to suppress bias and emotion in his or her analysis.

9. Research involves the quest for answers to unsolved problems. Pushing back the frontiers of ignorance is its goal, and originality is frequently the quality of a good research project. However, previous important studies are deliberately repeated, using identical or similar procedures, with different subjects, different settings, and at a different time. This process is *replication,* a fusion of the words *repetition* and *duplication.* Replication is always desirable to confirm or to raise questions about the conclusions of a previous study.

10. Research is characterized by patient and unhurried activity. It is rarely spectacular, and researchers must expect disappointment and discouragement as they pursue the answers to difficult questions.

11. Research is carefully recorded and reported. Each important term is defined, limiting factors are recognized, procedures are de-

scribed in detail, references are carefully documented, results are objectively recorded, and conclusions are presented with scholarly caution and restraint. The written report and accompanying data are made available to the scrutiny of associates or other scholars. Any competent scholar will have the information necessary to analyze, evaluate, and even replicate the study.

12.   Research sometimes requires courage. The history of science reveals that many important discoveries were made in spite of the opposition of political and religious authorities. The Polish scientist Copernicus (1473–1543) was condemned by church authorities when he announced his conclusion concerning the nature of the solar system. His theory, in direct conflict with the older Ptolemaic theory, held that the sun, not the earth, was the center of the solar system. Copernicus angered supporters of prevailing religious dogma, who viewed his theory as a denial of the story of creation as described in the book of *Genesis.* Modern researchers in such fields as genetics, sexual behavior, and even business practices have aroused violent criticism from those whose personal convictions, experiences, or observations were in conflict with some of the research conclusions.

The rigorous standards of scientific research are apparent from an examination of these characteristics. The research worker should be a scholarly, imaginative person of the highest integrity, who is willing to spend long hours painstakingly seeking truth. However, it must be recognized that researchers are human beings. The ideals that have been listed are probably never completely realized. Like righteousness, they are goals to strive for and are not all achieved by every researcher.

Many people have a superficial concept of research, picturing research workers as strange introverted individuals who, shunning the company of their fellows, find refuge in their laboratory. There, surrounded by test tubes, retorts, beakers, and other gadgets, they carry on their mysterious activities. In reality the picture is quite different. Research is not all mysterious, and it is carried on by thousands of quite normal individuals, more often in teams than alone, very often in the factory, the school, or the community, as well as in the laboratory. Its importance is attested to by the tremendous amounts of time, manpower, and money spent on research by industry, universities, government agencies, and the professions. The key to the cultural development of the Western world has been research, the reduction of areas of ignorance by discovering new truths, which in turn lead to better predictions, better ways of doing things, and new and better products. We recognize the fruits of research: better consumer products, better ways of preventing and treating disease, better ways of understanding the behavior of individuals and groups, and a better understanding of the world in which we live. In the field of education, we identify research with a better understanding of the individual and a better understanding of the teaching-learning process and the conditions under which it is most successfully carried on.

PURPOSES OF RESEARCH

Fundamental or Basic Research

To this point we have described research in its more formal aspects. Research has drawn its pattern and spirit from the physical sciences and has represented a rigorous, structured type of analysis. We have presented the goal of research as the development of theories by the discovery of broad generalizations or principles. We have employed careful sampling procedures in order to extend the findings beyond the group or situation studied. So far, our discussion has shown little concern for the application of the findings to actual problems in areas considered to be the concern of people other than the investigator. This methodology is the approach of *basic* or *fundamental research.*

Fundamental research is usually carried on in a laboratory situation, often with animals as subjects. This type of research has been primarily the activity of psychologists rather than educators.

Applied Research

Applied research has most of the characteristics of fundamental research, including the use of sampling techniques and the subsequent inferences about the target population. However, its purpose is improving a product or a process—testing theoretical concepts in actual problem situations. Most educational research is applied research, for it attempts to develop generalizations about teaching-learning processes and instructional materials.

Fundamental research in the behavioral sciences may be concerned with the development and testing of theories of behavior. Educational research is concerned with the development and testing of theories of how students behave in an educational setting.

Action Research

Since the late 1930s the fields of social psychology and education have shown great interest in what has been called *action research.* In education this movement has had as its goal the involvement of both research specialist and classroom teacher in the study and application of research to educational problems in a particular classroom setting.

Action research is focused on immediate application, not on the development of theory or on general application. It has placed its emphasis on a problem here and now in a local setting. Its findings are to be evaluated in terms of local applicability, not universal validity. Its purpose is to improve school practices and, at the same time, to improve those who try to improve the practices: to combine the research processes, habits of thinking, ability to work harmoniously with others, and professional spirit.

If most classroom teachers are to be involved in research activity, it will probably be in the area of action research. Modest studies may be made for the purpose of trying to improve local classroom practices. It is not likely that many teachers will have the time, resources, or technical background to engage in the more formal aspects of research activity. Fundamental research must continue to make its essential contribution to behavioral theory, and applied research to the improvement of educational practices. These activities, however, will be primarily the function of research specialists, many of them subsidized by universities, private and government agencies, professional associations, and philanthropic foundations.

Many observers have deprecated action research as nothing more than the application of common sense or good management. But whether or not it is worthy of the term *research*, it does apply scientific thinking and methods to real life problems and represents a great improvement over teachers' subjective judgments and decisions based upon folklore and limited personal experiences.

In concluding this discussion, it is important to realize that research may be carried on at various levels of complexity. Respectable research studies may be the simple descriptive fact-finding variety that lead to useful generalizations. Actually, many of the early studies in the behavioral sciences were useful in providing needed generalizations about the behavior or characteristics of individuals and groups. Subsequent experimental studies of a more complex nature needed this groundwork information to suggest hypotheses for more precise analysis. For example, descriptive studies of the intellectually gifted, carried on since the early 1920s by the late Lewis M. Terman and his associates, have provided useful generalizations about the characteristics of this segment of the school population. Although these studies did not explain the factors underlying giftedness, they did provide many hypotheses to be investigated by more sophisticated experimental methods.

ASSESSMENT, EVALUATION, AND DESCRIPTIVE RESEARCH

The term *descriptive research* has often been used incorrectly to describe three types of investigation that are basically different. Perhaps their superficial similarities have obscured their differences. Each of them employs the process of disciplined inquiry through the gathering and analysis of empirical data and each attempts to develop knowledge. To be done competently, each requires the expertise of the careful and systematic investigator. A brief explanation may serve to put each one in proper perspective.

Assessment is a fact-finding activity that describes conditions that exist at a particular time. No hypotheses are proposed or tested, no variable relationships are examined, and no recommendations for action are suggested.

The national census is a massive assessment type of investigation conducted by the Bureau of the Census, a division of the United States Department of Commerce. Every 10 years an enumeration of the population is conducted, with data classified by nationality, citizenship, age, sex, race, marital status, educational level, regional and community residence, employment, economic status, births, deaths, and other characteristics. These data provide a valuable basis for social analysis and government action.

In education, assessment may be concerned with the determination of progress that students have made toward educational goals. The *National Assessment of Educational Progress* (NAEP), originally known as the Committee on Assessment of the Progress of Education, has been financed by the National Center for Educational Statistics. Since 1969 a nationwide testing program has been conducted in such fields as science, mathematics, literature, reading, and social studies, in four age groupings, in various geographical areas of the country, in communities of various sizes, and in particular states, and has reported interesting evidence of the degree to which learning goals have or have not been realized.

Evaluation is concerned with the application of its findings and implies some judgment of the effectiveness, social utility, or desirability of a product, process, or program in terms of carefully defined and agreed-upon objectives or values. It may involve recommendations for action. It is not concerned with generalizations that may be extended to other settings. In education, it may seek answers to such questions as: How well is the science program developing the competencies that have been agreed upon by the faculty curriculum committee? Should the program in vocational agriculture education be dropped? Are the library facilities adequate? Should the reading textbook series currently in use be retained?

Descriptive research, unlike assessment and evaluation, is concerned with hypothesis formulation and testing, the analysis of the relationships between nonmanipulated variables, and the development of generalizations. Unlike the experimental method, in which variables are deliberately arranged and manipulated through the intervention of the researcher, in descriptive research variables that exist or have already occurred are selected and observed. This process is described as *ex post facto, explanatory observational,* or *causal-comparative research* in Chapter 4. Both descriptive and experimental methods employ careful sampling procedures so that generalizations may be extended to other individuals, groups, times, or settings.

TYPES OF EDUCATIONAL RESEARCH

Any attempt to classify types of educational research poses a difficult problem. The fact that practically every textbook suggests a different system of classification provides convincing evidence that there is no generally accepted scheme.

To systematize a method of presentation, however, some pattern is desirable. At the risk of seeming arbitrary, and with a recognition of the danger of oversimplification, we suggest a framework that might clarify understanding of basic principles of research methodology. It should be noted that the system of classification is not important in itself but only has value in making the analysis of research processes more comprehensible.

Actually, *all* research involves the elements of observation, description, and the analysis of what happens under certain circumstances. A rather simple three-point analysis may be used to classify educational research. Practically all studies fall under one, or a combination, of these types.

1. *Historical research* describes *what was.* The process involves investigating, recording, analyzing, and interpreting the events of the past for the purpose of discovering generalizations that are helpful in understanding the past and the present, and, to a limited extent, in anticipating the future.

2. *Descriptive research* describes *what is,* describing, recording, analyzing, and interpreting conditions that exist. It involves some type

of comparison or contrast and attempts to discover relationships between existing nonmanipulated variables.

3. *Experimental research* describes *what will be* when certain variables are carefully controlled or manipulated. The focus is on variable relationships. As defined here, deliberate manipulation is always a part of the experimental method.

A complete chapter is devoted to each of these types of research, to techniques of data-gathering, to areas of application, and to methods of analysis.

SUMMARY

Human beings' desire to know about their world has led them from primitive superstition to modern scientific knowledge. From mysticism, dogma, and the limitations of unsystematic observation based upon personal experience, they have examined the process of thinking itself to develop the method of deductive-inductive thinking, which has become the foundation of scientific method. Although first applied as a method of the physical sciences, the process of scientific inquiry has also become the prevailing method of the behavioral sciences.

There is no single scientific method, for scientists carry on their investigations in a number of ways. However, accuracy of observation and the qualities of imagination, creativity, objectivity, and patience are some of the common ingredients of all scientific methods.

The hypothesis is an essential research device that gives a focus to the investigation and permits researchers to reach probability conclusions. After researchers formulate an affirmative research hypothesis at the outset of their project, they restate the hypothesis in negative or null form for the purposes of statistical analysis of their observations. This procedure facilitates inferring population characteristics from observed variable relationships as they relate to the error inherent in the sampling process.

Sampling, a deliberate rather than haphazard method of selecting subjects for observation, enables the scientist to infer conclusions about a population of interest from the observed characteristics of a relatively small number of cases. Simple random, systematic, stratified random, area or cluster, and available (nonprobability) samples have been described. Methods of determining the size of an appropriate sample are suggested and the sources of sample bias are considered.

Research has been defined as *the systematic and objective analysis and recording of controlled observations that may lead to the develop-*

ment of generalizations, principles, or theories, resulting in prediction and possibly ultimate control of events. The characteristics of research that may help to clarify its spirit and meaning have been presented.

Fundamental or *basic* research is the formal and systematic process of deductive-inductive analysis, leading to the development of theories. *Applied* research adapts the theories, developed through fundamental research, to the solution of problems. *Action* research, which may fail to attain the rigorous qualities of fundamental and applied research, attempts to apply the spirit of scientific method to the solution of problems in a particular setting, without any assumptions about the general application of findings beyond the situation studied.

In this chapter we have established assessment, evaluation, and descriptive research as three distinct types of investigation, and we have classified research as historical, descriptive, or experimental.

Remember that research is essentially an intellectual and creative activity. The mastery of techniques and processes does not confer research competence, though these skills may help the creative problem-solver to reach his or her objectives more efficiently.

EXERCISES

1. Construct two syllogisms:
    a. one that is sound
    b. one that is faulty. Indicate the nature of the fallacy.
2. Illustrate the application of Dewey's steps in problem solving. Choose one of the problems listed, or one of your own:
    a. brown patches on your lawn
    b. your car won't start when you leave for home
    c. getting an economical buy on canned peaches
    d. most of the members of your class failed an examination
3. Give an example of:
    a. a pure research problem
    b. an applied research problem
    c. an action research problem
4. To what extent have religious institutions resisted the claims of science?
5. Is there necessarily a conflict between the disciplines of the sciences and the humanities?
6. Explain why you agree or disagree with the following statements:
    a. Excessive effort is spent on the development of theories, because they don't usually work in real situations.
    b. Science is more properly thought of as a method of problem solving than as a field of knowledge.

  c. Applied research is more important than pure research in contributing to human welfare.

7. How would you select a sample of 40 college students for a morale study from a freshman class of 320?

8. From a metropolitan school district staff directory, you wish to select a sample of 300 teachers from a listing of 3800. Discuss several ways that the sample could be selected, considering the issues that may be involved.

9. What are the distinctive characteristics of descriptive research as contrasted with:
  a. assessment
  b. evaluation
  c. experimental research

10. How is the term *research* sometimes misused in classroom assignments and television interviews?

REFERENCES

DEWEY, J. (1938). *Logic: The theory of inquiry.* New York: Holt, Rinehart & Winston.

FISHER, R. A. & YATES, F. (1963). *Statistical tables for biological, agricultural, and medical research.* Edinburgh: Oliver & Boyd.

KAHN, J. V. (1984). Cognitive training and its relationship to the language of profoundly retarded children. In J. M. Berg (Ed.), *Perspectives and progress in mental retardation.* Baltimore: University Park Press.

KAHN, J. V. (in press). Uses of scales of psychological development with mentally retarded populations. In I. C. Uzgiris & J. McV. Hunt (Eds.), *Research with scales of psychological development in infancy.* Champaign, IL: University of Illinois Press.

KAMII, C. (1973). Piaget's interactionism and the process of teaching young children. In M. Schwebel & J. Raph (Eds.), *Piaget in the classroom.* New York: Basic Books.

KARPLUS, R., LAWSON, A. E., WOLMAN, W., APPEL, M., BERNOFF, R., HOWE, A., RUSCH, J. J., & SULLIVAN, F. (1977). *Science teaching and the development of reasoning.* Berkeley: Lawrence Hall of Science, University of California.

LAVATELLI, C. S. (1973). *Teacher's guide: Early childhood curriculum.* New York: American Science and Engineering Co.

MEES, C. E. K. (1934). Scientific thought and social reconstruction. *American Scientist, 22,* 13–14.

PIAGET, J. (1970). *Science of education and the psychology of the child.* New York: Viking Press.

Rand Corporation (1965). *A million random digits with 100,000 normal deviates.* New York: Free Press.

SNOW, R. E. (1973). Theory construction for research on teaching. In R. M. W. Travers (Ed.), *Second handbook of research on teaching.* Chicago: Rand McNally.

STAVER, J. R. & GABEL, D. L. (1979). The development and construct validation of a group-administered test of formal thought. *Journal of Research in Science Teaching, 16,* 535–544.

WOLINSKY, G. F. (1970). Piaget's theory of perception: Insights for educational practices with children who have perceptual difficulties. In I. J. Athey, & D. O. Rubadeau (Eds.), *Educational implications of Piaget's theory.* Waltham, MA: Ginn-Blaisdell.

ADDITIONAL READINGS

BARZUN, J. (1964). *Science: The glorious entertainment.* New York: Harper & Row.

CONANT, J. B. (1951). *Science and common sense.* New Haven: Yale University Press.

CONANT, J. B. (1964). *Two modes of thought.* New York: Simon & Schuster.

DEWEY, J. (1933). *How we think.* Boston: Raytheon Education Co.

EBEL, R. (1967). Some limitations of basic research in education. *Phi Delta Kappan, 49,* 81–84.

FEIGL, H., & BROADBECK, M. (1953). *Readings in the philosophy of science.* New York: Appleton-Century-Crofts.

FRANK, G. (1961). *The validation of scientific theories.* New York: Collier Books.

HAYS, W. L. (1967). *Quantification in psychology.* Monterey, CA: Brooks/Cole Publishing Co.

HELMSTADTER, G. C. (1970). *Research concepts in human behavior.* New York: Appleton-Century-Crofts.

JONES, W. T. (1965). *The sciences and the humanities: Conflict and reconciliation.* Berkeley: University of California Press.

KAPLAN, A. (1964). *The conduct of inquiry.* San Francisco: Chandler Publishing Co.

KUHN, T. S. (1970). *The structure of scientific revolutions* (2nd ed.). Chicago: University of Chicago Press.

REAGAN, M. D. (1967). Basic and applied research: A meaningful distinction? *Science, 155,* 1383–1386.

SKINNER, B. F. (1948). *Walden Two.* New York: Macmillan Co.

SLAVIN, R. E. (1978). Basic vs. applied research: A response. *Educational Researcher, 7,* 15–17.

SNOW, C. P. (1959). *Two cultures and the scientific revolution.* New York: Cambridge University Press.

Chapter 2

Selecting a Problem
and Preparing
a Research Proposal

One of the most difficult phases of the graduate research project is the choice of a suitable problem. Beginners are likely to select a problem that is much too broad in scope. This may be due to their lack of understanding of the nature of research and systematic problem-solving activity. It may also be due to their enthusiastic but naive desire to solve an important problem quickly and immediately.

Those who are more experienced know that research is often tedious, painfully slow, and rarely spectacular. They realize that the search for truth and the solution of important problems take a great deal of time and energy and the intensive application of logical thinking. Research makes its contribution to human welfare by countless small additions to knowledge. The researcher has some of the characteristics of the ant, which brings its single grain of sand to the anthill.

Before considering the ways in which problems may be identified, we should discuss a few of the characteristics of research and the activities of the researcher. Research is more often a team endeavor than an individual activity. Researchers working in groups attack problems in different ways, pooling their knowledge and ideas and sharing the results of their efforts. Highly publicized discoveries usually result from the cumulative efforts of many, working as teams over long periods of time. They are rarely the product of a single individual working in isolation.

Great discoveries rarely happen by accident. When they do, the researcher is usually well-grounded and possesses the ability, known as *serendipity,* to recognize the significance of these fortunate occurrences. He or she is imaginative enough to seize the opportunity presented and to carry it through to a fruitful conclusion. Pasteur observed that chance favors the prepared mind.

Researchers are specialists rather than generalists. They employ the principle of the rifle rather than the shotgun, analyzing limited aspects of broad problems. Critics have complained that much social research consists of learning more and more about less and less until the researcher knows everything about nothing. This is a clever statement but an exaggeration. The opposite statement, equally clever and exaggerated, characterizes much ineffective problem solving: learning less and less about more and more until one knows nothing about everything.

There is a danger, however, that research activity may focus upon such fragmentary aspects of a problem that it has little relevance to the formulation of a general theory. An analysis of the relationship among a few isolated factors in a complex situation may seem attractive as a research project, but it will make little or no contribution to a body of knowledge. Research is more than compiling, counting, and tabulating data. It involves deducing the consequences of hypotheses through careful observation and the application of rigorous logic.

It is sometimes important to discover that a generalization is probably *not* true. Beginning researchers frequently associate this type of conclusion with a sense of personal failure, for they become emotionally committed to their hypotheses. Research, however, is a process of *testing* rather than *proving,* and it implies an objectivity that lets the data lead where they will.

THE ACADEMIC RESEARCH PROBLEM

Academic research projects have been subjected to much criticism, both by the academic community and by the general public. The academic research project is usually a requirement in partial fulfillment of the requirements of a graduate course or for an advanced degree. The initial motivation may not be the desire to engage in research but the practical need of meeting a requirement. Unfortunately, few such studies make a significant contribution to the development or refinement of knowledge or to the improvement of practice. The lack of time, financial resources, experience, and expertise of the researcher, and the academic hazard of departing from a relatively safe, short-range project are, understandably, hindrances to significant contributions. But these projects are often justified on the grounds that once students develop some research competency they will use their "know-how" to seek solutions to basic problems and will make a contribution to the body of knowledge upon which sound practices are based. Too often this expectation is not realized, for too few students carry on further studies.

Few graduate students in education are full-time students; consequently they are often victims of the competing demands of teaching, supervising student activities, attending meetings, and participating in administrative activity. Many are not on campus while they are writing their thesis or dissertation, and they miss the continuing intellectual stimulation of the university faculty, discussions with fellow graduate students, the ready availability of library resources, and the opportunity of the full-time student to absorb the scholarly atmosphere of the university community. Thus, most graduate students tend to select narrow, practical problems that are closely related to their school experience but are frequently low-level investigations, with little relevance to theory.

Perhaps more significant master's degree or doctoral studies could be carried on under the direction of an advisor or major professor who is devoting his or her own energies to research on a significant problem. The efforts of degree candidates thus could be directed toward certain restricted phases of the major problem, making possible long-term longitudinal studies. Such studies as those by the late Lewis M. Terman at Stanford University of gifted children, followed over 50 years, represent the cumulative attack that is likely to yield more significant results than the uncoordinated investigations of candidates whose efforts lack this unifying direction and continuity.

Levels of Research Projects

In the light of the varied types and purposes of students' projects, choice of a problem will depend upon the level at which the research is done. A problem appropriate for a beginner in a first course in research is different from that selected for the more rigorous requirements of the master's thesis or the doctoral dissertation. The first topic will necessarily be a modest one which can be carried on by an inexperienced researcher in a limited period of time. The emphasis will be placed upon the learning process of the beginning researcher rather than on his or her actual contribution to education. This statement does not imply that the product is unimportant. It merely recognizes that, because of the limitations of the first research project, the emphasis is on learning *how*, with the hope that subsequent investigations will progressively yield more significant contributions to the advancement of knowledge.

Some students choose a first problem that can be expanded later into a more comprehensive treatment at the level of the master's thesis or the doctoral dissertation. The first study thus serves as an exploratory process.

Sources of Problems

The choice of a suitable problem is always difficult. Few beginners possess real problem awareness, and even the more experienced researcher hesitates at this step. It is a serious responsibility to commit oneself to a problem that will inevitably require much time and energy and that is so academically significant.

What are the most likely sources to which one may go for a suitable research problem, or from which one may develop a sense of problem awareness?

Many of the problems confronted in the classroom, the school, or the community lend themselves to investigation, and they are perhaps more appropriate for the beginning researcher than are problems more remote from his own teaching experience. What organizational or management procedures are employed? How is learning material presented? To what extent does one method yield more effective results than another? How do teachers feel about these procedures? How do pupils and parents feel about them? What out-of-school activities and influences seem to affect students and the teaching-learning process?

Teachers will discover "acres of diamonds" in their own back yards, and an inquisitive and imaginative mind may discover in one of these problem areas an interesting and worthwhile research project.

Technological changes and curricular developments are constantly bringing forth new problems and new opportunities for research. Perhaps more than ever before, educational innovations are being advocated in classroom organization, in teaching materials and procedures, and in the application of technical devices and equipment. Such innovations as computer-assisted instruction, teaching by television, programmed instruction, modified alphabets, new subject matter concepts and approaches, flexible scheduling, and team teaching need to be carefully evaluated through the research process.

The graduate academic experience should stimulate the questioning attitude toward prevailing practices and effectively promote problem awareness. Classroom lectures, class discussions, seminar reports, and out-of-class exchanges of ideas with fellow students and professors will suggest many stimulating problems to be solved. Students who are fortunate enough to have graduate assistantships have a special opportunity to profit from the stimulation of close professional relationships with faculty members and fellow assistants.

Reading assignments in textbooks, special assignments, research reports, and term papers will suggest additional areas of needed research. Research articles often suggest techniques and procedures for the attack on other problems. A critical evaluation may reveal faults or defects that made published findings inconclusive or misleading. Many research articles suggest problems for further investigation that may prove fruitful.

Consultation with the course instructor, advisor, or major professor is helpful. Although the student should not expect research problems to be assigned, consultation with the more experienced faculty member is desirable. Most students feel insecure as they approach the choice of a research problem. They wonder if the problem they may have in mind is significant enough, feasible, and reasonably free of unknown hazards. To expect the beginner to arrive at the advisor's office with a completely acceptable problem is quite unrealistic. One of the most important functions of the research advisor is to help students clarify their thinking, achieve a sense of focus, and develop a manageable problem from one that may be too vague and complex.

The following list may suggest some problem areas from which research problems may be defined.

1. Programmed instruction; scrambled texts; teaching machines; computer-assisted instruction
2. Television instruction; closed circuit TV
3. Modified alphabets: Unifon, Initial Teaching Alphabet
4. Flexible scheduling
5. Team teaching
6. Evaluation of learning; reporting to parents
7. Student regulation/control
8. Learning styles
9. Evaluation of learning: practices and philosophies
10. Homework policies and practices
11. Field trips
12. School buildings and facilities: lighting; space; safety
13. Extracurricular programs
14. Student out-of-school activities: employment; recreation; cultural activity; reading; television viewing
15. Teacher out-of-school activities: employment; political activity; recreation
16. The open classroom
17. Linguistics
18. New approaches to biology/chemistry/physics
19. Language laboratories: foreign languages; reading
20. Multiple textbooks
21. Independent study programs
22. Advanced placement program
23. Audiovisual programs
24. Sociometry
25. Health services
26. Guidance-counseling programs
27. Teacher morale: annoyances and satisfactions
28. Teacher welfare: salaries; merit rating; retirement; tenure
29. Educational organizations: local, state, and national; NEA; AFT
30. Inner city schools; the culturally deprived; Head Start; Upward Bound; tutoring
31. Preservice education of teachers: student teaching

32. Teacher attitudes on a variety of issues, e.g., mainstreaming
33. In-service programs
34. Racial integration: student; teacher
35. Parochial/private school problems; tax credits
36. Follow-up of graduates; early school leavers
37. Religion and education: released time programs; dismissed time; shared time
38. Nonschool-sponsored social organizations or clubs
39. School district reorganization
40. Community pressures on the school: academic freedom; controversial issues
41. Legal liability of teachers
42. Cadet teaching; teacher recruitment
43. Teaching internship
44. Sex education
45. Ability grouping: acceleration; retardation/promotion
46. Special education: speech therapy; clinical services; social services
47. Problems in higher education: selection; prediction of success; graduate programs
48. Work-study programs
49. Attribution of success and failure
50. Comparison of the effectiveness of two teaching methods/procedures
51. Self-image analysis
52. Vocational objectives of students
53. History of an institution, program, or organization
54. Factors associated with the selection of teaching/nursing/social work as a career
55. Case studies
56. Socioeconomic status and academic achievement
57. Perceptions of administrative leadership
58. The effect of stress on academic achievement
59. Minimal competency tests for promotion and/or graduation
60. Merit pay for teachers

For those students who are not teachers, some of the problem areas listed may be appropriate in social agency, hospital, or industrial situations.

Evaluating the Problem

Before the proposed research problem can be considered appropriate, several searching questions should be raised. Only when those questions are answered in the affirmative can the problem be considered a good one.

1. Is this the type of problem that can be effectively solved through the process of research? Can relevant data be gathered to test the theory or find the answer to the question under consideration?

2. Is the problem significant? Is an important principle involved? Would the solution make any difference as far as educational theory or practice is concerned? If not, there are undoubtedly more significant problems waiting to be investigated.

3. Is the problem a new one? Is the answer already available? Ignorance of prior studies may lead a student to spend time needlessly on a problem already investigated by some other worker. However, although novelty or originality is an important consideration, the fact that a problem has been investigated in the past does not mean that it is no longer worthy of study. There are times when it is appropriate to replicate (repeat) a study to verify its conclusions or to extend the validity of its findings to a different situation or population.

4. Is research on the problem feasible? After a research project has been evaluated, there remains the problem of suitability for a particular researcher. The student should ask: Although the problem may be a good one, is it a good problem for me? Will I be able to carry it through to a successful conclusion? Some of the questions the student should consider are the following:

    a. Am I competent to plan and carry out a study of this type? Do I know enough about this field to understand its significant aspects and to interpret my findings? Am I skillful enough to develop, administer, and interpret the necessary data-gathering devices and procedures? Am I well grounded in the necessary knowledge of research design and statistical procedures?

    b. Are pertinent data accessible? Are valid and reliable data-gathering devices and procedures available? Will school authorities permit me to contact the students, conduct necessary experiments or administer necessary tests, interview teachers, or have access to important cumulative records? Will I be able to get the sponsorship necessary to open doors that otherwise would be closed to me?

c. Will I have the necessary financial resources to carry on this study? What will be the expense involved in data-gathering equipment, printing, test materials, travel, and clerical help? If the project is an expensive one, what is the possibility of getting a grant from a philanthropic foundation or from such governmental agencies as the National Institute of Education?

d. Will I have enough time to complete the project? Will there be time to devise the procedures, select the data-gathering devices, gather and analyze the data, and complete the research report? Since most academic programs impose time limitations, certain worthwhile projects of a longitudinal type are precluded.

e. Will I have the courage and determination to pursue the study in spite of the difficulties and social hazards that may be involved? Will I be willing to work aggressively when data are difficult to gather and when others are reluctant to cooperate? Sex education, racial integration, and other controversial problem areas, however, may not be appropriate for a beginning research project.

THE RESEARCH PROPOSAL

The preparation of a research proposal is an important step in the research process. Many institutions require that a proposal be submitted before any project is approved. This provides a basis for the evaluation of the project and gives the advisor a basis for assistance during the period of his or her direction. It also provides a systematic plan of procedure for the researcher to follow.

The proposal is comparable to the blueprint which the architect prepares before the bids are let and building commences. The initial draft proposal is subject to modification in the light of the analysis by the student and his or her project advisor. Because good research must be carefully planned and systematically carried out, procedures that are improvised from step to step will not suffice. A worthwhile research project is likely to result only from a well-designed proposal.

The seven-part proposal format presented here should not be considered the only satisfactory sequence. Many institutions suggest other formats for the research proposal.

Part 1: The statement of the problem. This is usually a declarative statement but may be in question form. This attempt to focus on a stated goal gives direction to the research process. It must be limited enough in scope to make a definite conclusion possible. The major statement may be followed by minor statements. The problem areas that previously have been listed in this chapter are not statements of problems. They are merely broad areas of concern from which problems may be selected.

A problem suggests a specific answer or conclusion. Usually a controversy or a difference of opinion exists. A cause-and-effect relationship may be suggested upon the basis of theory or previous research findings. Personal observation and experience may be the basis of a problem. Some examples of problem statements are as follows: (1) Children who have had kindergarten experience might demonstrate greater academic achievement in the first grade than those who have not had this experience. (2) Participation in high school competitive athletics may be detrimental to academic achievement. (3) Racial segregation may have a damaging effect upon the self-image of minority group children. (4) Knowledge of participation in an experiment may have a stimulating effect upon the reading achievement of participants. These problem statements involve more than information gathering. They suggest answers or conclusions and provide a focus for research activity.

Part 2: The significance of the problem. It is important that the researcher point out how the solution to the problem or the answer to the question can influence educational theory or practice. Careful formulation and presentation of the implications or possible applications of knowledge helps to give the project an urgency, justifying its worth.

Failure to include this step in the proposal may well leave the researcher with a problem without significance—a search for data of little ultimate value. Many of the tabulating or "social bookkeeping" research problems should be abandoned if they do not pass the critical test of significance. Perhaps university library shelves would not groan with the weight of so many unread and forgotten dissertations if this criterion of significance had been rigorously applied. With so many gaps in educational theory, and so many areas of education practice in need of analysis, there is little justification for the expenditure of research effort on trivial or superficial investigations.

Part 3: Definitions, assumptions, limitations, and delimitations. It is important to define all unusual terms that could be misinterpreted. These definitions help to establish the frame of reference with which the researcher approaches the problem. The variables to be considered should be defined in operational terms. Such expressions as academic achievement and intelligence are useful concepts, but they cannot be used as criteria unless they are defined as observable samples of behavior. Academic grades assigned by teachers or scores on standardized achievement tests are operational definitions of achievement. A score on a standardized intelligence test is an operational definition of intelligence.

Assumptions are statements of what the researcher believes to be facts but cannot verify. A researcher may state the assumption that the participant observers in the classroom, after a period of three days, will establish rapport with the students and will not have a reactive effect on the behavior to be observed.

Limitations are those conditions beyond the control of the researcher that may place restrictions on the conclusions of the study and their application to other situations. Administrative policies that preclude using more than one class in an experiment, a data-gathering instrument that has not been validated, or the inability to randomly select and assign subjects to experimental and control groups are examples of limitations.

Delimitations are the boundaries of the study. A study of attitudes toward racial minorities may be concerned only with middle class, fifth-grade pupils, and conclusions are not to be extended beyond this population sampled.

Part 4: Review of related literature. A summary of the writings of recognized authorities and of previous research provides evidence that the researcher is familiar with what is already known and what is still unknown and untested. Since effective research is based upon past knowledge, this step helps to eliminate the duplication of what has been done and provides useful hypotheses and helpful suggestions for significant investigation. Citing studies that show substantial agreement and those that seem to present conflicting conclusions helps to sharpen and define understanding of existing knowledge in the problem area, provides a background for the research project, and makes the reader aware of the status of the issue. Parading a long list of annotated studies relating to the problem is ineffective and inappropriate. Only those studies that are plainly relevant, competently executed, and clearly reported should be included.

In searching related literature, the researcher should note certain important elements:

1. Reports of studies of closely related problems that have been investigated
2. Design of the study, including procedures employed and data-gathering instruments used
3. Populations that were sampled and sampling methods employed

4. Variables that were defined
5. Extraneous variables that could have affected the findings
6. Faults that could have been avoided
7. Recommendations for further research

Capitalizing on the reviews of expert researchers can be fruitful in providing helpful ideas and suggestions. Although review articles that summarize related studies are useful, they do not provide a satisfactory substitute for an independent search. Even though the review of related literature is presented as step number 4 in the finished research proposal, the search for related literature is one of the first steps in the research process. It is a valuable guide to defining the problem, recognizing its significance, suggesting promising data-gathering devices, appropriate study design, and sources of data.

Part 5: The hypothesis. It is appropriate here to formulate a major hypothesis and possibly several minor hypotheses. This approach further clarifies the nature of the problem and the logic underlying the investigation, and gives direction to the data-gathering process. A good hypothesis has several basic characteristics:

1. It should be reasonable.
2. It should be consistent with known facts or theories.
3. It should be stated in such a way that it can be tested and found to be probably true or probably false.
4. It should be stated in the simplest possible terms.

The research hypothesis is a tentative answer to a question. It is an educated guess or hunch, generally based upon prior research and/or theory, to be subjected to the process of verification or disconfirmation. The gathering of data and the logical analysis of data relationships provide a method of confirming or disconfirming the hypothesis by deducing its consequences.

It is important that the hypothesis be formulated before data are gathered. Suppose that the researcher gathers some data and, on the basis of these, notes something that looks like the basis for an alternative hypothesis. Since any particular set of observations may display an extreme distribution, using such observations to test the hypothesis would possibly lead to an unwarranted conclusion.

The formulation of the hypothesis in advance of the data-gathering process is necessary for an unbiased investigation. It is not inappropriate to formulate additional hypotheses after data are collected, but they should be tested on the basis of new data, not on the old data that suggested them.

Part 6: Methods. This part of the research proposal usually consists of two parts: *subjects* and *procedures*. The *subjects* section details the population from which the researcher plans to select the sample. Variables that are frequently included, depending on the type of project proposed, include: chronological age, grade level, socioeconomic status, sex, race, IQ (if other than average), mental age (if significantly different from chronological age), academic achievement level, and other pertinent attributes of the targeted population. The number of subjects desired from the population and how they will be selected are also indicated in this section. The reader should be able to understand exactly from where and how the subjects are to be selected.

The *procedures* section outlines the research plan. It describes in detail what will be done, how it will be done, what data will be needed, what data-gathering devices will be used (see Chapter 6), and the method of analyzing the data. The information given in this section should be specific and detailed enough to demonstrate to the reader exactly what is planned. No details should be left open to question.

Part 7: Time schedule. Although this step may not be required by the study advisor, a time schedule should be prepared so that the researcher may budget his or her time and energy effectively. Dividing the project into manageable parts and assigning dates for their completion helps to systematize the study and minimize the natural tendency to procrastinate.

Some phases of the project cannot be started until other phases have been completed. Such parts of the final research report as the review of related literature can be completed and typed while waiting for the data-gathering process. If the project is complicated, a flow chart or time-task chart may be useful in describing the sequence of events. Since academic research projects usually involve critical time limitations and definite deadlines for filing the complete report, the planning of procedures with definite date goals is most important. From time to time the major professor or advisor may request a progress report. This device also serves as a stimulus, helping the researcher to move systematically toward the goal of a completed project.

ETHICS IN HUMAN EXPERIMENTATION

In planning a research project involving human subjects, it is important to consider the ethical guidelines designed to protect your subjects. In particular, medical and psychological experimentation using human subjects involves some element of risk, however minor, and raises questions about the ethics of the process. Any set of rules or guidelines that attempts to define ethical limits for human experimentation raises controversy among members of the scientific community and other segments of society. Too rigid controls may limit the effectiveness of research, possibly denying society the answers to many important questions. On the other hand, without some restraints, experimental practices could cause serious injury and infringe upon human rights.

These issues go beyond courtesy or etiquette and concern the appropriate treatment of persons in a free society. Some of these questions have been dealt with by scientists and philosophers, by enactments of legislative bodies, by codes of ethics and professional organizations, or by guidelines established by educational institutions.

In 1974, the Congress of the United States established The National Commission for the Protection of Human Subjects of Biomedical and Behavioral Research to formulate guidelines for the research activities of the National Institute of Health and the National Institute of Mental Health.

The Commission's 4-year, monthly deliberations, supplemented by discussions held at the Smithsonian Institution's Belmont Conference Center, resulted in the publication of the *Belmont report: Ethical principles and guidelines for the protection of human subjects of research* (1979).

Universities have established human experiment review committees to advise academic investigators about appropriate procedures and to approve those studies that conform to their ethical guidelines. Most funding agencies, private and governmental, require such a review prior to awarding of grants. The university may have ad hoc committees concerned with a particular study or standing committees that deal with all experimental activities involving the institution or division. In cases where there are serious risks that must be weighed against the potential benefits to society, reviews by both ad hoc and institution-wide committees may be deemed necessary. Some faculty researchers have complained that review committees have unduly restricted their experimental activities. It is possible in some cases that particular members of the committee did not have the technical background to make sound judgments outside their own fields of competence. Others have felt that, because the committee assignment demanded so much of their time, they could not contribute their best effort. However, because it is the primary function of the human experiment review committee to maintain the ethical standards of the institution and to supervise the ethical guidelines of the funding agencies, it serves a useful and necessary purpose.

In 1953, the American Psychological Association issued its first code of ethics for psychologists. In 1963, the code was revised and its preamble contained the following statement:

> The psychologist believes in the dignity and worth of the individual human being. He is committed to increasing man's knowledge of himself and others. While pursuing this endeavor he protects the welfare of any persons who may seek his services, or any subject, human or animal, that may be the object of his study. He does not use his professional position or relationship, nor does he knowingly permit his own services to be used by others, for purposes inconsistent with these values. While demanding for himself freedom of inquiry and communication, he accepts the responsibility this freedom confers; for competence where he claims it, for objectivity in the report of his findings, and for the consideration of the best interests of his colleagues and of society. (American Psychological Association, 1963, p. 2)

In 1970, the Board of Directors appointed an Ad Hoc Committee on Ethical Standards in Psychological Research to bring the 1963 code up to date in light of changes in the science, in the profession, and in the broader social context in which psychologists practice. The first draft of the committee report was circulated among 18,000 members of the association. About 5,000 responded with suggestions. In addition, journal editors, staff members of research review committees, directors of research organizations, writers on research ethics, and leaders in such special fields as hypnosis were interviewed. These contributions were supplemented by discussions at regional and national meetings of the association. Psychology departments of universities, hospitals, clinics, and government agencies, as well as anthropologists, economists, sociologists, lawyers, philosophers, and psychiatrists were consulted.

As a result of these conversations and correspondence with professionals from all scholarly disciplines, a final draft was adopted and published in 1973. In 1978, A Committee for the Protection of Human Subjects in Psychological Research was established and charged with making annual reviews and recommendations regarding the official APA position. These annual reviews led to a revision which went through a similar process of consultation as the 1973 edition. A final draft which incorporated various suggestions was adopted and published in 1982.

Ten principles were formulated that deal with the experimenter's responsibilities toward participants. In the published report, *Ethical Principles in the Conduct of Research with Human Participants* (American Psychological Association, 1982), each principle is stated with discussion of issues, problems, and recommendations for appropriate action. The meticulous care with which this code was developed attests to the concern of this professional organization for ethical practices in psychological research. Readers who are interested in a more complete discussion on ethics in human experimentation are urged to read this report.

The following discussion, while not a summary of the American Psychological Association (APA) code of ethics, is consistent with the APA code. The guidelines discussed here are not ethical absolutes. Rather, they characterize writing in the field of ethics and a number of professional codes that the authors have examined. The guidelines deal with the following areas of concern: informed consent; invasion of privacy; confidentiality; protection from stress, harm, or danger; and knowledge of outcome.

Informed consent. Recruitment of volunteers for an experiment should always involve the subject's complete understanding of the procedures employed, the risks involved, and the demands that may be made upon participants. Whenever possible, subjects should also be informed of the purpose of the research. When subjects are minors or mentally incapacitated due to age, illness, or disability, the informed consent of parents, guardians, or responsible agents must be secured. This freedom to participate or to decline to participate is basic, and it includes the freedom to withdraw from an experiment at any time without penalty. Coercion to participate or to remain as a participant must not be applied and any exploitation of participants is an unethical practice.

The following are examples of experiment recruitment practices that raise ethical questions:

1. Subjects who are inmates of penal institutions volunteer to participate because of a need for money or in anticipation of more favorable treatment or recommendation of earlier parole.
2. Medical students who need money are recruited for experiments by offers of financial reward.
3. Participants who do not have the mental capacity to give rational consent—the mentally ill, the mentally retarded, or those with reduced capacity—are recruited in institutions.
4. Members of a college class are required to participate in an experiment in order to meet a course requirement.

Invasion of privacy. Ordinarily it is justifiable to observe and record behavior that is essentially public, behavior that others normally would be in a position to observe. It is an invasion of privacy to observe and record intimate behavior that the subject has reason to believe is private. Concealed observers, cameras, microphones, or the use of private correspondence without the subject's knowledge and permission are invasions of privacy. If these practices are to be employed, the researcher should explain the reasons and secure permission.

This statement is not to suggest that intimate behavior cannot be observed ethically. The sexual behavior studies of Doctors Masters and Johnson are based upon observation and recording of the most intimate acts, but subjects volunteer to participate with full knowledge of the purposes and procedures employed. The motivation is based upon confidence in the integrity of the researchers and the importance of their scientific contributions to human welfare.

Confidentiality.   The ethical researcher holds all information that he or she may gather about the subject in strict confidence, disguising the participant's identity in all records and reports. No one should be in a position to threaten the subject's anonymity nor should any information be released without his or her permission.

Protection from physical and mental stress, harm, or danger.   In using treatments that may have a temporary or permanent effect on the subjects, the researcher must take all precautions to protect their well-being. Treatments are administered under the direction of competent professional practitioners in clinical or research facilities where effective and thorough precautions and safeguards may be assured.

Knowledge of outcome.   The participant has a right to receive an explanation for the reasons for the experimental procedures and the results of the investigation. The researcher may explain the results and their significance orally, in writing, or by informing participants of the issue of the journal in which the report is published.

Ethical researchers not only observe these ethical guidelines but take complete responsibility for the actions of their coexperimenters, colleagues, assistants, technical personnel, secretaries, and clerks involved in the project, constantly monitoring their research activities. Researchers have obligations to their subjects, their professional colleagues, and the public. They do not discard unfavorable data that would modify the interpretation of their investigation. They make their data available to their professional peers so that they may verify the accuracy of the results. They honor promises made to subjects as a consideration for their participation in a study. They give appropriate credit to those who have aided them in their investigations, participated in the data analysis, or contributed to the preparation of the research report. They place scientific objectivity above personal advantage and recognize their obligation to society for the advancement of knowledge.

Some researchers have been known to justify deception, coercion, invasion of privacy, breach of confidentiality, or risks to subjects in the name of science, but one might suspect that the prestige, ambition, or ego of the experimenter was the primary motivation.

USING THE LIBRARY

The student should become thoroughly acquainted with the university library, the location of its varied facilities, and the services it provides. In addition to the traditional card catalog, many university libraries have computerized their holdings and have placed terminals in various locations for ease of finding books and periodicals.

Sometimes a student learns of a reference that is not available in the local library. Most libraries belong to one of three major shared cataloging systems: Online Computer Library Center (OCLC) with the holdings of over 3000 libraries; Research Library Network; and, in the Pacific Northwest, the Washington Library Network. The list of books and periodicals available, and the libraries holding these materials, can be quickly accessed on a time-sharing computer system available in most libraries. The student's library requests the books or a photocopy of the article, which is then loaned to the student by his or her library.

FINDING RELATED LITERATURE

Students often waste time searching for references in an unsystematic way. The search for references is an ever-expanding process, for each reference may lead to a new list of sources. Researchers may consider these sources as basic:

1. *The Education Index*
2. *Resources in Education*
3. *Current Index to Journals in Education*
4. *Index to Doctoral Dissertations* and *Dissertation Abstracts International*
5. Other specialized indexes or abstracts indicated by the area of investigation (e.g., *Psychological Abstracts*)

Appendix I lists indexes and abstracts that the student or researcher may use to find articles and books on his or her topic. Many of these data bases, including Educational Research Information Centers (ERIC), *Exceptional Child Education Resources, Psychological Abstracts*, and dozens of others can be accessed directly through one of the computer services available to libraries. Almost all college and university libraries, and many public libraries, offer this service. The investigator, with the help of a librarian, uses key words to let the computer system know which materials are desired. For instance, if a researcher is reviewing the literature that has used Piagetian theory with mentally retarded persons, she or he might use the key words Piaget *with* mental retardation, mentally retarded, and retardation. The computer then searches all the titles and abstracts for those containing both Piaget and one of the other key words. The investigator can then have the titles or titles and abstracts printed either "online" or, less expensively, overnight at the computer services facilities. Considering the time that is saved by using a computer search facility, the cost is minimal.

Microfiche

The development of microfiche has been one of the most significant contributions to library services by providing economy and convenience of storing and distribution of scholarly materials.

A microfiche is a sheet of film that contains micro-images of printed materials. Filmed at a reduction of 1 to 24 or higher, nearly one hundred $8\frac{1}{2}'' \times 11''$ pages of copy can be reproduced on one $4'' \times 6''$ film card. Microfiche readers that magnify the micro-images to original or larger copy size are available at libraries. Some microfiche readers provide up to 40× magnification on screens as large as $15'' \times 21''$.

There are many document reproduction services that supply microfiche to libraries upon subscription or upon special order.

The Educational Resources Information Center (ERIC) has prepared for the National Institute of Education a directory of nearly 600 libraries that possess extensive collections or receive regular periodic shipments of ERIC microfiche collections. These libraries receive approximately 17,000 microfiche per year. Other document reproduction sources that provide microfiche to libraries or individuals are described later in this chapter.

Super- and Ultra-Microfiche

Recent developments in the field of micro-printing will transform the process of storage, retrieval, and distribution of published materials in libraries of the future. A super-microfiche has been developed that contains up to 1000 pages of printed material on a single $4'' \times 6''$ transparent card, the equivalent of two or more books. An even more spectacular development is the ultra-microfiche that contains up to 3200 microdots on a single card. When projected, each dot contains the equivalent of several pages. Thus, seven to ten volumes could be contained on a single $4'' \times 6''$ transparent card. Reader printers make hard copy printouts ($8\frac{1}{2}'' \times 11''$ reproductions) of any page in a few seconds.

NOTE TAKING

One of the most important research activities of the graduate student is note taking—putting materials in a form that can easily be recalled and used in the future. Notes will result from speeches and lectures, class discussions, conversation, from solitary meditation, and from reading reference materials. In preparing term papers and research reports the notes that result from reading will be most significant. Without a careful, systematic method of note taking, much of what is read is quickly forgotten.

Reading-reference notes have been classified under four principal categories:

1. *Quotation.* The exact words of an author are reproduced, enclosed in quotation marks. It is essential to copy each statement accurately, and to indicate the exact page reference so that the quotations may be properly referenced in the written report.
2. *Paraphrase.* The reader restates the author's thoughts in his or her own words.
3. *Summary.* The reader states in condensed form the contents of the article.
4. *Evaluation.* The reader records his or her own reaction, indicating agreement or disagreement, or interpreting the point of view of the writer.

A single note card may include several of these types when it seems appropriate.

A SUGGESTED METHOD FOR TAKING NOTES

1. Skim the reference source before taking any notes. A bird's-eye view is essential before one can decide what material to record and use. Selecting the most significant material is a skill to be cultivated.
2. Use 4″ × 6″ index cards. They are easily sorted by subject headings and are large enough to include a reasonable amount of material. Some students prefer 5″ × 8″ cards, which are less convenient to carry but provide more space for notes.
3. File each note card under a definite topic or heading. Place the subject heading at the top of the card for convenient filing. A complete bibliographic citation should be placed at the bottom of the note card. If a book has been used, the call number should be indicated to facilitate library location in the future.
4. Include only one topic on a card. This makes organization of notes flexible. If the notes are lengthy, use consecutively numbered cards, and slip a rubber band around them before filing.
5. Be sure that notes are complete and clearly understandable, for they are not likely to be used for some time after they have been taken.

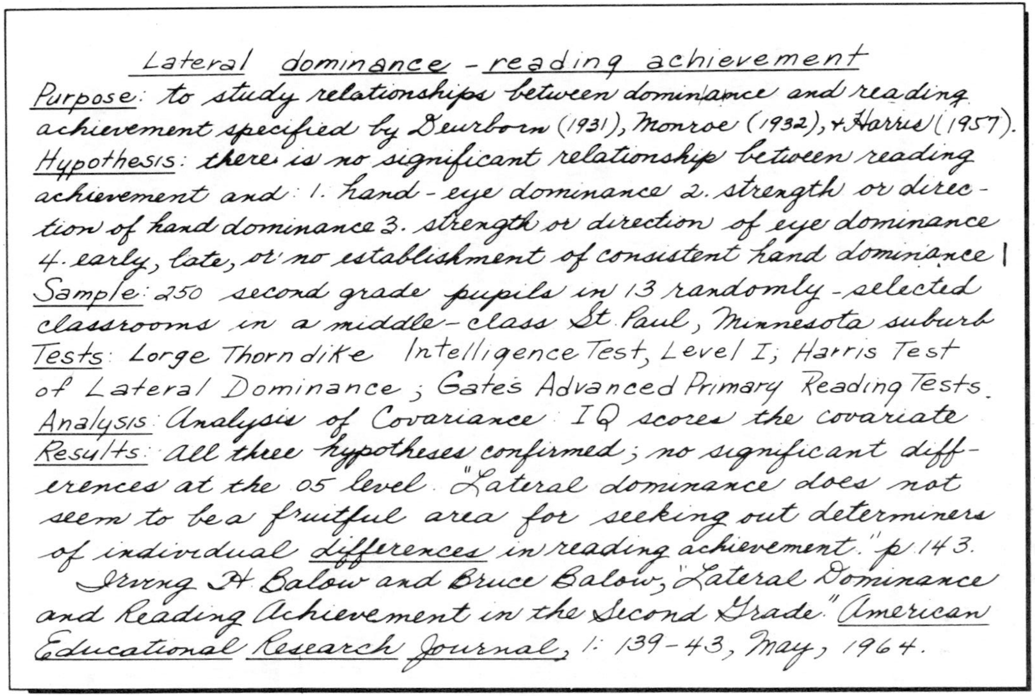

Lateral dominance - reading achievement

Purpose: to study relationships between dominance and reading achievement specified by Deurborn (1931), Monroe (1932), + Harris (1957).

Hypothesis: there is no significant relationship between reading achievement and: 1. hand-eye dominance 2. strength or direction of hand dominance 3. strength or direction of eye dominance 4. early, late, or no establishment of consistent hand dominance

Sample: 250 second grade pupils in 13 randomly-selected classrooms in a middle-class St. Paul, Minnesota suburb

Tests: Lorge Thorndike Intelligence Test, Level I; Harris Test of Lateral Dominance; Gates Advanced Primary Reading Tests.

Analysis: Analysis of Covariance IQ scores the covariate

Results: All three hypotheses confirmed; no significant differences at the .05 level. "Lateral dominance does not seem to be a fruitful area for seeking out determiners of individual differences in reading achievement." p. 143.

Irving H. Balow and Bruce Balow, "Lateral Dominance and Reading Achievement in the Second Grade." American Educational Research Journal, 1: 139-43, May, 1964.

FIGURE 2–1 Note card (4″ × 6″).

6. Distinguish clearly between a summary, a direct quotation of the author, a reference to the author's source, and an evaluative statement.

7. Do not plan to recopy or type your notes. It wastes time and increases possibility of error and confusion. Copy your notes carefully the first time.

8. Keep a supply of note cards with you at all times, so that you can jot down ideas that come to you while waiting, riding the bus, or listening to a lecture or discussion.

9. Be careful not to lose your notes. As soon as they are copied, file them in a card index box. If you must carry them with you, use the $4'' \times 6''$ or $5'' \times 8''$ accordion file folder, and be sure that your name and address is clearly printed on it.

10. Keep a permanent file of your notes. You may find the same notes useful in a number of courses or in writing a number of reports.

When taking notes, consider the advisability of making photostatic copies of book and journal pages so that they can be examined more efficiently at home. Many book and journal materials are reproduced on microfiche cards that may include as many as 1000 pages on one $4'' \times 6''$ card. The rapid trend toward microfilming and microfiching professional literature will continue as the constantly increasing volume of published materials burdens limited shelf space. Coin-operated microfilm and microfiche printers are found in most university libraries. Reproduction is not expensive and the quality of the copy is excellent. It is much more convenient to take notes from an $8\frac{1}{2}'' \times 11''$ print copy than from film projected on a screen.

References and Bibliography

In preparing a journal report, paper, or research proposal the author is expected to include a list of the references that have been cited in the text. Sometimes it is preferable to include additional materials that were used by the author but not actually cited in the paper. In this case the author would provide a bibliography which includes all the relevant references, cited or not.

The most convenient way to assemble and organize references or a bibliography is by the use of bibliography cards. The card includes the names of the authors, the facts of publication, and the annotation (see Chapter 10 for examples using the American Psychological Association system). Placing the information on cards makes it easy to assemble the authors' names in the alphabetical order in which they are listed in the bibliography of the report.

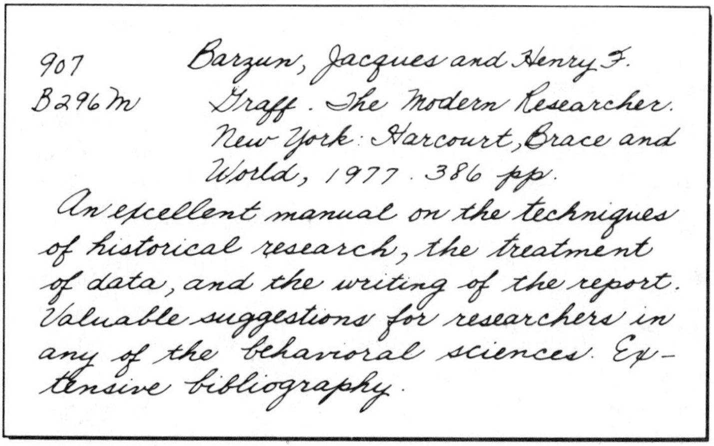

907
B296m

Barzun, Jacques and Henry F. Graff. *The Modern Researcher.* New York: Harcourt, Brace and World, 1977. 386 pp. An excellent manual on the techniques of historical research, the treatment of data, and the writing of the report. Valuable suggestions for researchers in any of the behavioral sciences. Extensive bibliography.

FIGURE 2-2 Bibliography card.

THE FIRST RESEARCH PROJECT

Experience has indicated that one way to understand the methodology and processes of research is to engage in research. Such a project may be very modest in nature and necessarily limited by time, the experience of the student, and many other factors associated with the graduate student's other obligations. However, the methodology may be learned by actively engaging in the research process under the careful supervision of the instructor in the beginning course in research. Respectable research projects have been undertaken and reported on within a semester's time, even within an 8-week summer session. Although most of these studies have been of the descriptive-survey type, some simple historical and experimental studies have also been completed. The emphasis must necessarily be placed on the process rather than on the product or its contribution to the improvement of educational practice. A study chosen for this first project, however, may not be of great enough significance to serve as an appropriate thesis problem.

The full-scale project may be either an individual or a group enterprise. Groups of three to five graduate students can profitably work together on the planning of the study. Data-gathering devices may be chosen or constructed through joint enterprise. Data may be gathered within the university graduate class, or in the classrooms, schools, or communities in which the group's members teach. However, it is recommended that the next steps—organization and analysis of data and the writing of the final report—be an individual project. There is always the danger in a group project of "letting George do it," and incidentally letting George get all the benefit from the experience.

This recommended combination of group effort in the initial stages and individual effort in the later stages represents a compromise that seems effective and enables students to carry through a study in a limited amount of time with reasonable opportunity for personal growth. For some of those who will write a thesis in partial fulfillment of degree requirements, this first project may serve as preparation. For others, it may initiate a study capable of subsequent expansion into a thesis or dissertation.

Many research-course instructors believe that a more practical requirement would be the preparation of a carefully designed research proposal rather than a limited-scope study. There is much to be said for this point of view because the beginning research student is inexperienced, the time is short, and there is a real danger of conveying a superficial concept of sound research.

The following topics were selected by inexperienced student researchers who were carrying on a project or writing a proposal in partial fulfillment of the requirements of a beginning course in educational research. Most of the topics were short, action-type descriptive studies, not based upon random selection and random assignment of subjects or observations. Notice that the wording of the titles did not imply generalization of the conclusions to a wider population. The primary purpose was a learning exercise, not a contribution to a field of knowledge.

TOPICS USED BY STUDENTS
IN A BEGINNING GRADUATE COURSE
IN EDUCATIONAL RESEARCH

1. The Attitudes of a Group of University Seniors toward Coeducational Dormitories
2. The Reading Skill Development of a Deaf First-grade Child
3. The Status of Latin in Indiana High Schools
4. Discipline Problems at Washington High School as Viewed by a Group of Seniors
5. A Study of the Effectiveness of Chisanbop Calculation with a Group of Third-grade Pupils
6. The Status of Music in the Western Yearly Meeting of the Society of Friends
7. The Rehabilitation of a Group of Heroin Addicts in a Federally Funded Drug Treatment Center
8. The Social Development of a 6-year-old Autistic Child
9. The Effect of Trial Promotion on the Academic Achievement of a Group of Underachievers
10. The Effects of Parent Visitation upon the Reading Performance of a Group of Fourth-grade Students

11. The Predictive Value of Entrance Examinations at the Methodist School of Nursing
12. The Interests of a 3-year-old Boy
13. Student Participation in the Activity Program at Lawrence Central High School
14. A Comparison of Regular Classroom and Learning Disabled Children's Expressive Language Skills
15. The Effect of Verbal Mediation upon the Mathematical Achievement of Learning Disabled Students
16. The Effect of Teacher Education on Attitudes toward Mainstreaming
17. Effect of Verbalization on Performance and On-Task Behavior of Reading Disabled Children
18. Prevalence of Behavior Problems of Hearing Siblings of Deaf Children
19. The Influence of Kindergarten Experience on the Subsequent Reading Achievement of a Group of Third-grade Pupils
20. The Views of Selected Baptist Laymen, Ministers, and National Church Leaders Concerning Issues Relating to the Tradition of Separation of Church and State
21. The Attitudes and Behavior of Freshmen and Seniors Regarding Classroom Dishonesty at Sheridan High School
22. The Attitudes of a Group of Florida School Superintendents toward Mandated Minimum Competency Testing
23. Authority Images of a Selected Group of Inner City Children
24. The Achievement of Twins, Both Identical and Fraternal, in the Lebanon, Indiana Metropolitan School District
25. A Follow-up Study of Nonpromoted Students at School #86
26. A History of the Indiana Boy's School, Plainfield, Indiana
27. A Comparative Analysis of the Self-Concepts of a Group of Gifted and Slow-learning Children
28. The Attitudes of a Group of High School Seniors toward Nuclear Protest Movements
29. The Educational Backgrounds of 129 American Celebrities Listed in the 1966 Current Biography Yearbook
30. The Attitudes of a Group of Graduate Students toward Mandated Smoking Restrictions in Public Facilities
31. The Influence of Entering Age upon the Subsequent Achievement at First-, Second-, and Third-grade Levels in Washington Township
32. The Attitudes of a Selected Group of Black and White Parents toward Busing to Achieve Racial Integration

33. A Study of Socioeconomic Status in the Butler-Tarkington Area, a Racially Integrated Community
34. A Follow-up Study of the 1970 Graduates of Grace Lutheran School
35. The Effect of Title IX, Prohibiting Sex Discrimination in Public Schools, upon the Athletic Budgets of Illinois Public Colleges and Universities

For experienced researchers, projects would necessarily be more theory-oriented, with conclusions generalized beyond the specific group observed. At this more advanced level a careful process of randomization would be desirable, if not necessary, and the research design would be much more rigorous. The details of some of the more sophisticated procedures are partially explained in subsequent chapters of this text and in other relevant sources, particularly discussion of experimental and descriptive research processes, the selection or construction of data-gathering devices, and the statistical analysis of data.

SUBMITTING A RESEARCH PROPOSAL TO A FUNDING AGENCY

Seasoned researchers may plan to submit research proposals to foundations or government agencies for financial support. The beginning researcher may not feel the need for suggestions, but it may be helpful to understand the detailed type of information that a foundation or agency would expect to receive before committing its funds.

The following is a list of suggestions for those who seek financial support:

1. Write the proposal very carefully. A carelessly written proposal suggests to the evaluators that the research project would be carelessly done. It is also useful to follow the format recommended by the agency in writing the proposal.
2. Pay attention to stated goals and priorities of the foundation or agency. It is important to point out how your study would be relevant to these goals.
3. State your problem in such a way that the proposal evaluators, who are capable and experienced in judging research proposals but know nothing about your project, will be able to judge its worth and the likelihood of its contributing to a significant area of knowledge.
4. Indicate how your study will add to or refine present knowledge.
5. State your hypothesis or hypotheses in both conceptual and operational terms and in both substantive and null form.

6. Indicate that you are completely familiar with the field of investigation and are aware of all recent studies in the problem area.
7. Indicate how you propose to test your hypotheses, describing your research design and the data-gathering instruments or procedures that you will use, indicating their known validity and reliability.
8. Describe your sampling procedures, indicating how you will randomly select and randomly assign your subjects or observations.
9. Indicate the extraneous variables that must be recognized and explain how you propose to minimize their influence.
10. Explain the statistical procedures that you will employ, indicating any computer application that you will use.
11. Prepare a budget proposal estimating the funds required for
    a. wages, including any fringe benefits
    b. purchase or rental of special equipment or supplies
    c. travel expenses
    d. clerical expenses
    e. additional overhead expenses that may be involved
    f. publication costs
12. Provide some tangible evidence of your competence by listing
    a. research projects that you have carried on or actively participated in
    b. your scholarly journal articles, including abstracts of your studies
    c. your academic training and other qualifications

SUMMARY

Academic research projects are usually required in partial fulfillment of the requirements of a course or a degree program. The motivation is not always a genuine desire to engage in research. In addition, limitations of time, money, and experience usually preclude the consideration of problems that could make significant contributions to educational theory and practice.

The choice of a suitable problem is one of the most difficult tasks facing the beginning researcher. Students tend to define problems that are too broad in scope or that deal with too fragmentary aspects of the problem. Consultation with the course instructor or advisor is particularly helpful in identifying a problem that is manageable and significant enough to justify the time and effort that will be required.

Problems are found in the teachers' daily classroom, school, and community experiences. Technological and social changes call for research evidence to chart new courses in educational practice. Graduate academic experience helps to promote problem awareness through classroom activities, the reading of research studies, and interaction with instructors, advisors, and fellow students.

A good research problem has the qualities of significance, originality, and feasibility. The researcher should evaluate a proposed problem in the light of his or her competence, the availability of data, the financial demands of the project, the limitations of time, and the possible difficulties and social hazards involved.

A research proposal is required by many institutions and serves as a useful basis for the evaluation of a project as well as a guide for the researcher. The proposal contains a clear and concise statement of the problem; the hypothesis or hypotheses involved; a recognition of the significance of the problem; definitions of important terms; assumptions, delimitations, and limitations; a review of related literature; an analysis of proposed research procedures; a reference list; and a time schedule. Some advisors request a progress report from time to time to evaluate the progress of the investigation.

One way to learn about research is to conduct a study in connection with the beginning research course. Another way is to write a research proposal which may involve all the steps in the research process except the gathering and analysis of data and the formulation of conclusions. Either of these exercises gives a focus to the discussion about research and may help in developing some competence and the research point of view. It may even encourage some teachers to conduct modest studies in their own schools during or after the completion of their graduate programs.

EXERCISES

1. The following research topics are faulty or are completely inappropriate. Revise each one, if possible, so that it describes a feasible project or proposal for this course.
   a. The Attitudes of Teachers toward Merit Rating
   b. How to Teach Poetry Most Effectively
   c. The Best Way to Teach Spelling
   d. The Evils of Alcohol
   e. Does Ability Grouping Meet the Needs of Students?
   f. The Adequacy of Law Enforcement
   g. The Hazards of Smoking
   h. Why the Discussion Method is Better than the Lecture Method
   i. The Fallacy of Evolution
2. State a hypothesis, first in scientific or research form, and then in null or statistical form.

3. Define the following terms in operational form:
   a. intelligence
   b. creativity
   c. coordination
   d. authorization
   e. memory
4. In a research study, is a hypothesis to be tested always preferable to a question to be remembered? Why or why not?
5. What are some of the more effective ways to find a suitable research problem?

REFERENCES

American Psychological Association (1963). *Ethical standards of psychologists.* Washington, D.C.: APA.

American Psychological Association (1973). *Ethical principles in the conduct of research with human participants.* Washington, D.C.: APA.

American Psychological Association (1982). *Ethical principles in the conduct of research with human participants.* Washington, D.C.: APA.

Belmont report: *Ethical principles and guidelines for the protection of human subjects of research.* (1979). Washington, D.C.: Smithsonian Institution, Superintendent of Documents, U.S. Government Printing Office.

ADDITIONAL READINGS

A bibliography of publications about the educational resources information center. (1978). Washington, D.C.: National Institute of Education.

DIENER, E. & CRANDALL, R. (1978). *Ethics in social and behavioral research.* Chicago: University of Chicago Press.

ENNIS, R. (1964). Operational definitions. *American Educational Research Journal, 1,* 183–201.

Funding opportunities of the national institute of education. (1979). Washington, D.C.: National Institute of Education.

GAGE, N. L. *Handbook of research on teaching.* (1963). Chicago: Rand McNally & Co.

Grants for research on law and government in education. (1979). Washington, D.C.: National Institute of Education.

Guide to federal funding in career education, education and work, and vocational education. (1978). Washington, D.C.: National Institute of Education.

How to use ERIC. (1979). Washington, D.C.: National Institute of Education.

HOWE, H. (1980). Two views of the new Department of Education and its first secretary: I. *Phi Delta Kappan, 61,* 446–447.

National Institute of Education: Summary of the reorganization plan (1978). Washington, D.C.: National Institute of Education.

Review of research in education. (Annual; 1973–date). Itasca, IL: F. E. Peacock, Publishers.

Submitting documents to ERIC. (1979). Washington, D.C.: National Institute of Education.

TRAVERS, R. M. W. (Ed.). (1973). *Handbook of research on teaching* (2nd ed.). Chicago: Rand McNally & Co.

WARD, A. W. ET AL. (1975). Evaluation of published research in education. *American Educational Research Journal, 12,* 109–128.

WESTBURY, I. & BELLACK, A. A. (Eds.). (1971). *Research into classroom procedures.* New York: Teachers College Press.

WYNN, RICHARD. (1980). Two views of the new Department of Education and its first secretary: II. *Phi Delta Kappan, 61,* 447–448.

ZIGLER, E. (1977). Twenty years of mental retardation research. *Mental Retardation, 15,* 51–53.

Chapter 3

Historical Research

Historical research differs markedly from the sort of research conducted by most scientists, including behavioral and social scientists. In fact, it is so different from other types of research that it almost does not belong as a topic in this book. It is included because many areas of concern to education can best be studied in this way, because the quantity and quality of research on the history of education has increased greatly in the past two decades (e.g., Best, 1983; Warren, 1978), and because a review of the research literature which is done prior to other types of research is, in effect, a historical study.

History is a meaningful record of human achievement. It is not merely a list of chronological events but a truthful integrated account of the relationships between persons, events, times, and places. We use history to understand the past and to try to understand the present in light of past events and developments. We also use it to prevent "reinventing the wheel" every few years. Historical analysis may be directed toward an individual, an idea, a movement, or an institution. However, none of these objects of historical observation can be considered in isolation. People cannot be subjected to historical investigation without some consideration of their interaction with the ideas, movements, and/or institutions of their times. The focus merely determines the points of emphasis toward which historians direct their attention.

Table 3–1 illustrates several historical interrelationships that have been taken from the history of education. For example, no matter whether the historian chooses for study the Jesuit Society, religious teaching orders, the Counter-Reformation, or Ignatius of Loyola, each of the other elements appears as a prominent influence or result and as an indispensable part of the account. The interrelationship of this institution, movement, and man would make the study of one in isolation from the others meaningless, if not impossible.

Those who wish to engage in historical research should read the works of historians regarding the methods and approaches to conducting historical studies in education (e.g., Best, 1983; Billington, 1975; Gottschalk, 1950; Hockett, 1948; Warren, 1978).

TABLE 3–1   Some Examples of the Historical Interrelationship between Men, Movements, and Institutions

		INSTITUTIONS	
MEN	MOVEMENTS	General Type	Name
Ignatius of Loyola	Counter-Reformation	Religious Teaching Order	Society of Jesus, 1534 (Jesuit Society)
Benjamin Franklin	Scientific Movement Education for Life	Academy	Philadelphia Academy, 1751
Daniel Coit Gilman G. Stanley Hall Wm. Rainey Harper	Graduate Study and Research	University Graduate School	Johns Hopkins University, 1876 Clark University, 1887 University of Chicago, 1892
John Dewey	Experimentalism Progressive Education	Experimental School	University of Chicago Elementary School, 1896
W. E. B. Dubois Walter White	Racial Integration in the Public Schools	Persuasion Organization	National Assn. for the Advancement of Colored People, 1909
B. R. Buckingham	Scientific Research in Education	Research Periodical, Research Organization	Journal of Ed. Research, 1920 American Educational Research Assn., 1931

THE HISTORY OF AMERICAN EDUCATION

Historical studies deal with almost every aspect of American education. Such investigations have pointed out the important contributions of both educators and statesmen. They have examined the growth and development of colleges and universities, elementary and secondary schools, educational organizations and associations, the rise and decline of educational movements, the introduction of new teaching methods, and the issues that have persistently confronted American education.

An understanding of the history of education is important to professional workers in this field. It helps them to understand the *how* and *why* of educational movements that have appeared and, in some cases, continue to prevail in the schools. It helps them to evaluate not only lasting contributions but also the fads and "bandwagon" schemes that have appeared on the educational scene only to be discarded.

An examination of many developments of the past seems to confirm the observation that little in education is really new. Practices hailed as innovative are often old ideas that have previously been tried and replaced by something else. Innovators should examine the reasons why such practices were discarded and consider whether their own proposals are likely to prove more successful. Several studies, briefly described, illustrate the historical background of some contemporary educational movements and issues.

Organized programs of individualized instruction introduced in a number of school systems in the 1960s seem to be similar in many respects to those introduced in a number of schools in the 1890s and in the first quarter of the twentieth century. First introduced at Pueblo, Colorado, and known as the Pueblo Plan, later modified and known as the Winnetka and Dalton Plans, these programs do seem to have common elements. Dispensing with group class activity in academic courses, students were given units of work to complete at their own rate before proceeding to more advanced units. Individual progress based upon mastery of subject matter units was the criterion for promotion or completion of a course. Search (1901) advocated this plan, and his influence upon Carleton Washburn in the elementary schools of Winnetka, Illinois, and Helen Parkhurst in the secondary schools at Dalton, Massachusetts, is generally recognized. Whether the Pueblo, Winnetka, or Dalton plans were fads or sound programs, the fact remains that they disappeared from the schools before reappearing in the 1960s.

The place of religion in public education is an issue that concerns many people. In the period following World War II, in a series of Supreme Court decisions, religious instruction and religious exercises within public schools have been declared unconstitutional and in violation of the First Amendment of the United States Constitution. In 1963, in the case of *Abington School District* v. *Schempp*, the Court held that a Pennsylvania law requiring daily Bible reading was in violation of the First Amendment. Much resentment and criticism of the Supreme Court followed this decision, and several efforts have been made to introduce amendments to the Constitution to permit religious exercises in the public schools.

The Bible reading issue was also a bitter one more than 100 years ago. The Philadelphia Bible Riots of 1840 (Lannie & Diethorn, 1968) resulted in the deaths of about 45 soldiers and civilians, serious injury to about 140, and property damage to homes and churches valued at nearly $500,000. Nativist/foreign-born, and Catholic/Protestant conflicts produced the tense atmosphere, but the Bible reading issue precipitated the riots. It is apparent that Bible reading is not an issue of recent origin and that an understanding of previous conflicts places the issue in clearer perspective.

The contributions of Thomas Jefferson, Benjamin Franklin, Calvin

Stowe, Catherine Beecher, Horace Mann, Maria Montessori, Henry Barnard, Ella Flagg Young, William Holmes McGuffey, Daniel Coit Gilman, John Dewey, and many other eminent educators have been carefully examined in many studies, and their impact on American education has been noted.

Thursfield (1945) studied Henry Barnard's *American Journal of Education*, published in 31 massive volumes between 1855 and 1881. He points out the *Journal's* vital contribution to the development of American education. Through its comprehensive treatment of all aspects of education it provided a readily available medium for the presentation and exchange of ideas of many of the great educators of the period. It has been stated that almost every educational reform adopted in the last half of the nineteenth century was largely due to the influence of the *Journal*. Among its contributors were Henry Barnard, Horace Mann, Bronson Alcott, Daniel Coit Gilman, William T. Harris, Calvin Stowe, and Herbert Spencer, in addition to many prominent foreign contributors.

Cremin (1961) examined the reason for the rise and decline of the Progressive Education movement, including the major changes in philosophy and practices that transformed American education and the forces that brought the movement to a halt in the 1950s. Although some historians differ with his conclusions, Cremin's analysis is the definitive history of Progressive Education in America.

These historical studies are examples of but a few of the thousands of books, monographs, and periodical articles that depict the story of American education. In addition to examining these works, students are urged to consult the *History of Education Quarterly*, in which scholarly book reviews and critical analyses of contemporary historical research are presented.

HISTORY AND SCIENCE

Opinions differ as to whether or not the activities of the historian can be considered scientific or whether there is such a thing as historical research.

Those who take the negative position may point out the following limitations:

1. Although the purpose of science is prediction, the historian cannot usually generalize on the basis of past events. Because past events were often unplanned or did not develop as planned, because there were so many uncontrolled factors, and because the influence of one or a few individuals was so crucial, the same pattern of factors is not repeated.

2. The historian must depend upon the reported observations of others, often witnesses of doubtful competence and sometimes of doubtful objectivity.

3. The historian is much like a person trying to complete a complicated jigsaw puzzle with many of the parts missing. On the basis of what is often incomplete evidence, the historian must fill in the gaps by inferring what has happened and why it happened.

4. History does not operate in a closed system such as may be created in the physical science laboratory. The historian cannot control the conditions of observation nor manipulate the significant variables.

Those who contend that historical investigation may have the characteristics of scientific research activity present these arguments:

1. The historian delimits a problem, formulates hypotheses or raises questions to be answered, gathers and analyzes primary data, tests the hypotheses as consistent or inconsistent with the evidence, and formulates generalizations or conclusions.

2. Although the historian may not have witnessed an event or gathered data directly, he or she may have the testimony of a number of witnesses who have observed the event from different vantage points. It is possible that subsequent events have provided additional information not available to contemporary observers. The historian rigorously subjects the evidence to critical analysis in order to establish its authenticity, truthfulness, and accuracy.

3. In reaching conclusions, the historian employs principles of probability similar to those used by physical scientists.

4. Although it is true that the historian cannot control the variables directly, this limitation also characterizes most behavioral research, particularly nonlaboratory investigations in sociology, social psychology, and economics.

5. The observations of historians may be described in *qualitative* or *quantitative* terms depending upon the subject matter. The absence of quantitative measurement in some historical studies, however, does not preclude the application of scientific methodology, for the application of both quantitative and qualitative description can be appropriately employed in scientific investigations.

Historical Generalization

There is some difference of opinion, even among historians, as to whether or not historical investigations can establish generalizations. Most historians would agree that some generalizations are possible, but they disagree on the validity of applying them to different times and places. Gottschalk (1963) states the case of the comparative historian in this way:

> Sooner or later one or more investigators of a period or area begin to suspect some kind of nexus within the matter of their historical investigation. Though such "hunches," "insights," "guesses," "hypotheses"— whatever you may call them—may be rejected out of hand by some of them, the bolder or rasher among them venture to examine the possibility of objective reality of such a nexus, and then it is likely to become a subject of debate, and perhaps of eventual refinement to the point of wide recognition in the learned world. The process is not very different from the way analytical scholars in other fields proceed—Darwin, for example, or Freud. If this process serves no other purpose, it at least may furnish propositions upon which to focus future investigations and debates. . . .
>
> But do not these historical syntheses, no matter what their author's intention, invariably have a wider applicability than to any single set of data from which they rose? If Weber was right, isn't it implicit in this concept of the Protestant ethic that where a certain kind of religious attitude prevails, there the spirit of capitalism will, or at least may, flourish? . . . If Mahan was right, couldn't victory in war (at least before the invention of the airplane) be regarded as dependent on maritime control? If Turner was right, won't his frontier thesis apply to some extent to all societies that have frontiers to conquer in the future, as well as it has applied to American society in the past? (pp. 121–122)[1]

Finley (1963) comments on generalization:

> Ultimately the question at issue is the nature of the historian's function. Is it only to recapture the individual concrete events of a past age, as in a mirror, so that the progress of history is merely one of rediscovering lost data and of building bigger and better reflectors? If so, then the chronicle is the only correct form for his work. But if it is to understand—however one chooses to define the word—then it is to generalize, for every explanation is, or implies, one or more generalizations. (p. 34)

Aydelotte (1963) states the argument for generalization:

> Certainly the impossibility of final proof of any historical generalization must be at once conceded. Our knowledge of the past is both too limited and too extensive. Only a minute fraction of what has happened has been recorded, and only too often the points on which we need most information are those on which our sources are most inadequate. On the other hand, the fragmentary and incomplete information we do have about the past is too abundant to prevent our coming to terms with it; its sheer bulk prevents its being easily manipulated, or even easily assimilated, for historical purposes. Further, historians deal with complex problems, and the pattern of the events they study, even supposing it to exist, seems too intricate to

[1] From "Categories of Historical Generalization" in *Generalization in the Writing of History*, Louis Gottschalk, ed. (Chicago: University of Chicago Press, 1963), 121–22. Used with permission of the publisher.

be easily grasped. Doubtless, finality of knowledge is impossible in all areas of study. We have learned through works of popularization how far this holds true even for the natural sciences, and, as Crane Brinton says, the historian no longer needs to feel that "the uncertainties and inaccuracies of his investigation leave him in a position of hopeless inferiority before the glorious certainties of physical science." (pp. 156–157)

The foregoing quotations are presented in support of the position that the activities of the historian are not different from those of the scientist. Historical research as it is defined in this chapter includes delimiting a problem, formulating hypotheses or generalizations to be tested or questions to be answered, gathering and analyzing data, and arriving at probability-type conclusions or at generalizations based upon deductive-inductive reasoning.

THE HISTORICAL HYPOTHESIS

Nevins (1962) illustrates the use of hypotheses in the historical research of Edward Channing in answering the question, "Why did the Confederacy collapse in April 1865?" Channing formulated four hypotheses and tested each one in light of evidence gathered from letters, diaries, and official records of the army and the government of the Confederacy. He hypothesized that the Confederacy collapsed because of

1. The military defeat of the Confederate army
2. The dearth of military supplies
3. The starving condition of the Confederate soldiers and the civilians
4. The disintegration of the will to continue the war

Channing produced evidence that seemed to refute the first three hypotheses. More than 200,000 well-equipped soldiers were under arms at the time of the surrender, the effective production of powder and arms provided sufficient military supplies to continue the war, and enough food was available to sustain fighting men and civilians.

Channing concluded that hypothesis 4, *the disintegration of the will to continue the war,* was substantiated by the excessive number of desertions of enlisted men and officers. Confederate military officials testified that they had intercepted many letters from home urging the soldiers to desert. Although the hypothesis sustained was not specific enough to be particularly helpful, the rejection of the first three did claim to dispose of some commonly held explanations. This example illustrates a historical study in which hypotheses were explicitly stated.

Hypotheses in Educational Historical Research

Hypotheses may be formulated in historical investigations of education. Several examples are listed.

1. The educational innovations of the 1950s and 1960s were based upon practices that previously have been tried and discarded.
2. Christian countries whose educational systems required religious instruction have had lower church attendance rates than those countries in which religious instruction was not provided in the schools.
3. The observation of European school systems by American educators during the nineteenth century had an important effect upon American educational practices.
4. The monitorial system had no significant effect upon American education.

Although hypotheses are not always *explicitly* stated in historical investigations, they are usually implied. The historian gathers evidence and carefully evaluates its trustworthiness. If the evidence is compatible with the consequences of the hypothesis, it is confirmed. If the evidence is not compatible, or negative, the hypothesis is not confirmed. It is through such synthesis that historical generalizations are established.

The activities of the historian, when education is his or her field of inquiry, are no different from those employed in any other field. The sources of evidence may be concerned with schools, educational practices and policies, movements, or individuals, but the historical processes are the same.

Difficulties Encountered in Historical Research

The problems involved in the process of historical research make it a somewhat difficult task. A major difficulty is delimiting the problem so that a satisfactory analysis is possible. Too often, beginners state a problem much too broadly; the experienced historian realizes that historical research must involve a penetrating analysis of a limited problem rather than a superficial examination of a broad area. The weapon of research is the target pistol, not the shotgun.

Since historians may not have lived during the time they are studying and may be removed from the events they investigate, they must often depend upon inference and logical analysis, using the recorded experience of others rather than direct observation. To ensure that their information is as trustworthy as possible, they must rely on primary, or first-hand, accounts. Finding appropriate primary sources of data requires imagination, hard work, and resourcefulness.

Historians must also keep in mind the context in which the events being studied occurred and were recorded. It is necessary to keep the biases and beliefs of those who recorded the events in mind, as well as the social and political climate in which they wrote.

SOURCES OF DATA

Historical data are usually classified into two main categories:

1. Primary sources are eyewitness accounts. They are reported by an actual observer or participant in an event.
2. Secondary sources are accounts of an event that were not actually witnessed by the reporter. The reporter may have talked with an actual observer or read an account by an observer, but his or her testimony is not that of an actual participant or observer. Secondary sources may sometimes be used, but because of the distortion in passing on information, the historian uses them only when primary data are not available.

Primary Sources of Data

Documents.   Documents are the records kept and written by actual participants in, or witnesses of, an event. These sources are produced for the purpose of transmitting information to be used in the future. Documents classified as primary sources are constitutions, charters, laws, court decisions, official minutes or records, autobiographies, letters, diaries, genealogies, census information, contracts, deeds, wills, permits, licenses, affidavits, depositions, declarations, proclamations, certificates, lists, handbills, bills, receipts, newspaper and magazine accounts, advertisements, maps, diagrams, books, pamphlets, catalogs, films, pictures, paintings, inscriptions, recordings, transcriptions, and research reports.

Remains or relics.   Remains or relics are objects associated with a person, group, or period. Fossils, skeletons, tools, weapons, food, utensils, clothing, buildings, furniture, pictures, paintings, coins, and art objects are examples of those relics and remains that were not deliberately intended for use in transmitting information or as records. However, these sources may provide clear evidence about the past. The contents of an ancient burial place, for instance, may reveal a great deal of information about the way of life of a people—their food, clothing, tools, weapons, art, religious beliefs, means of livelihood, and customs. Similarly, the contents of an institution for the mentally ill or mentally retarded can reveal a good deal of information about the way the clients were treated, including the quality of food, the opportunity for work and recreational activities, and whether abuses regularly occurred.

Oral testimony.   Oral testimony is the spoken account of a witness of, or participant in, an event. This evidence is obtained in a personal interview and may be recorded or transcribed as the witness relates his or her experiences.

Primary Sources of Educational Data

Many of the old materials mentioned in the preceding section provide primary evidence that may be useful specifically in studying the history of education. A number are listed here.

Official records and other documentary materials.   Included in this category are records and reports of legislative bodies and state departments of public instruction, city superintendents, principals, presidents, deans, department heads, educational committees, minutes of school boards and boards of trustees, surveys, charters, deeds, wills, professional and lay periodicals, school newspapers, annuals, bulletins, catalogs, courses of study, curriculum guides, athletic game records, programs (for graduation, dramatic, musical, and athletic events), licenses, certificates, textbooks, examinations, report cards, pictures, drawings, maps, letters, diaries, autobiographies, teacher and pupil personnel files, samples of student work, and recordings.

Oral testimony.   Included here are interviews with administrators, teachers and other school employees, students and relatives, school patrons or lay citizens, and members of governing bodies.

Relics.   Included in this category are buildings, furniture, teaching materials, equipment, murals, decorative pictures, textbooks, examinations, and samples of student work.

Secondary Sources of Data

Secondary sources are the reports of a person who relates the testimony of an actual witness of, or participant in, an event. The writer of the secondary source was not on the scene of the event, but merely reports what the person who *was* there said or wrote. Secondary sources of data are usually of limited worth for research purposes because of the errors that may result when information is passed on from one person to another. Most history textbooks and encyclopedias are examples of secondary sources, for they are often several times removed from the original, first-hand account of events.

Some types of material may be secondary sources for some purposes and primary sources for another. For example, a high school textbook in American history is ordinarily a secondary source. But if one were making a study of the changing emphasis on nationalism in high school American history textbooks, the book would be a primary document or source of data.

HISTORICAL CRITICISM

It has been noted that the historian does not often use the method of direct observation. Past events cannot be repeated at will. Because the historian must get much of the data from the reports of those who witnessed or participated in these events, the data must be carefully analyzed to sift the true from the false, irrelevant, or misleading.

Trustworthy, usable data in historical research are known as *historical evidence*. That body of validated information can be accepted as a trustworthy and proper basis for the testing and interpretation of a hypothesis. Historical evidence is derived from historical data by the process of criticism, which is of two types: *external* and *internal*.

External Criticism

External criticism establishes the authenticity or genuineness of data. Is the relic or document a true one rather than a forgery, a counterfeit, or a hoax? Various tests of genuineness may be employed.

Establishing the age or authorship of documents may require intricate tests of signature, handwriting, script, type, spelling, language usage, documentation, knowledge available at the time, and consistency with what is known. It may involve physical and chemical tests of ink, paint, paper, parchment, cloth, stone, metals, or wood. Are these elements consistent with known facts about the person, the knowledge available, and the technology of the period in which the remain or the document originated?

Internal Criticism

After the authenticity of historical documents or relics has been established, there is still the problem of evaluating their accuracy or worth. Although they may be genuine, do they reveal a true picture? What of the writers or creators? Were they competent, honest, unbiased, and actually acquainted with the facts, or were they too antagonistic or too sympathetic to give a true picture? Did they have any motives for distorting the account? Were they subject to pressure, fear, or vanity? How long after the event did they make a record of their testimony, and were they able to remember accurately what happened? Were they in agreement with other competent witnesses?

These questions are often difficult to answer, but the historian must be sure that the data are authentic and accurate. Only then may he or she introduce them as historical evidence, worthy of serious consideration.

The following examples describe ways in which evidence is tested for authenticity. The first is an example of historical criticism of a scholarly type, carried on by scientists and biblical scholars, in which historic documents were proven to be genuine.

The Dead Sea Scrolls. One of the most interesting and significant historical discoveries of the past century was the finding of the Dead Sea Scrolls. This collection of ancient manuscripts was discovered in 1947 by a group of Bedouins of the Ta'amere tribe. Five leather scrolls were found, sealed in tall earthenware jars in the Qumran caves near Aim Feshkha, on the northwest shore of the Dead Sea (Davies, 1956).[2]

The Bedouins took the scrolls to Metropolitan Mar Athanesius Yeshue Samuel, of St. Mark's monastery in Jerusalem, who purchased them after discovering that they were written in ancient Hebrew. A consultation with biblical scholars confirmed the fact that they were very old and possibly valuable. They were later purchased by Professor Sukenik, an archaeologist of Hebrew University at Jerusalem, who began to translate them. He also had portions of the scrolls photographed to send to other biblical scholars for evaluation. Upon examining some of the photographs, Dr. William F. Albright of Johns Hopkins University pronounced them "the greatest manuscript discovery of modern times."

A systematic search of the Wadi Qumran area caves in 1952 yielded other leather scrolls, many manuscript fragments, and two additional scrolls of copper that were so completely oxidized that they could not be unrolled without being destroyed. By 1956, scientists at the University of Manchester, England, had devised a method of passing a spindle through the scrolls, spraying them with aircraft glue, baking them, and then sawing them across their rolled-up length to yield strips which could be photographed.

The origin, the age, and the historic value of the scrolls have been questioned. By careful and systematic external and internal criticism, however, certain facts have been established and are quite generally accepted by biblical scholars and scientists.

The scrolls are very old, probably dating back to the first century

---

[2] From *The Meaning of the Dead Sea Scrolls* (New York: New American Library of World Literature, 1956), 9. Used with permission of the publisher.

A.D. They are written in ancient Hebrew and probably originated in a pre-Christian monastery of one of the Jewish sects. The writings contain two versions (one complete and one incomplete) of the Book of Isaiah, a commentary or *Midrash* on the Book of Habakkuk, a set of rules of the ancient Jewish monastery, a collection of about twenty psalms similar to those of the Old Testament, and several scrolls of apocalyptic writings, similar to the Book of Revelation.

The contents of the copper scrolls and other fragments have now been translated. It is possible that more scrolls and writings may be discovered in the area, and it is likely that these ancient documents may throw new light on the Bible and the origins of Christianity.

It is interesting to note how these documents were authenticated, dated, and evaluated by:

1. Paleography, an analysis of the Hebrew alphabet forms used. These written characters were similar to those observed in other documents known to have been written in the first century.

2. A radiocarbon test of the age of the linen scroll covering conducted by the Institute of Nuclear Research at the University of Chicago. All organic matter contains radiocarbon 14, which is introduced by the interaction of cosmic rays from outer space with the nitrogen in the earth's atmosphere. The radioactivity constantly introduced throughout the life of the specimen ceases at death and disintegrates at a constant known rate. At the time of death, all organic matter yields 15.3 disintegrations per minute per gram of carbon content. The number of disintegrations is reduced by one-half after 5568 years, plus or minus 30 years. By measuring disintegrations by using a Geiger-type counter, it is possible to estimate the age of specimens within reasonable limits of accuracy. Through use of this technique, the date of the scrolls was estimated at A.D. 33, plus or minus 200 years.

3. Careful examination of the pottery form in which the scrolls were sealed. These jars, precisely shaped to fit the manuscripts, were the type commonly used during the first century.

4. Examination of coins found in the caves with the scrolls. These dated Roman coins provided convincing evidence of the age of the scrolls.

5. Translation of the scrolls. When translated, the scrolls compared to other writings, both biblical and nonbiblical, of known antiquity.

Although external criticism has now produced convincing evidence of the genuineness and age of the Dead Sea Scrolls, internal criticism of their validity and relevance will be pursued by biblical scholars for many years to come and may provide many new hypotheses concerning biblical writings and the early history of Christianity and the pre-Christian Jewish sects.

Modern approaches to historical research have applied advanced technology, emphasizing the usefulness of both qualitative and quantitative data. As we have seen in this example, researchers employed the radiocarbon 14 test to verify the authenticity of the scrolls. The next example illustrates the use of the computer in archaeological and historical research.

Stonehenge (Hanging Stones). For centuries historians and archaeologists have debated the origin and purpose of Stonehenge, a curious arrangement of stones and archways, each weighing more than 40 tons, located on the Salisbury Plain about 90 miles southwest of London. From the beginning of recorded history, writers have speculated about the stones. Their construction and arrangement have been attributed to many tribes and national groups who invaded or inhabited England. Modern radiocarbon dating of a deer antler found in the stone fill seems to date their erection at about 1900 to 1600 B.C. Their purpose has been explained in many legends—a city of the dead, a place of human sacrifice, a temple of the sun, a pagan cathedral, and a Druid ceremonial place.

More recently some scientists and historians have suggested that Stonehenge was a type of astronomical computer calendar used by early Britons who were apparently sophisticated enough to compute the position of the sun and the moon at their various stages. Using an IBM 704 computer, Gerald S. Hawkins, an astronomer at the Smithsonian Astrophysical Observatory at Cambridge, Massachusetts, entered into the computer 240 stone alignments, translated into celestial declinations. Accomplishing in less than a minute a task that would have required more than 4 months of human calculator activity, the computer compared the alignments with the precise sun/moon extreme positions as of 1500 B.C. and indicated that they matched with amazing accuracy.

Hawkins suggests that the stone arrangements may have been created for several possible reasons: They made a calendar that would be useful for planting crops; they helped to create and maintain priestly power, by enabling the priest to call out the people to see the rise and setting of the midsummer sun and moon over the heel stone and midwinter sunset through the great trilithon; or possibly they served as an intellectual exercise. Hawkins concludes:

> In any case, for whatever reasons those Stonehenge builders built as they did, their final completed creation was a marvel. As intricately aligned as an interlocking series of astronomical instruments (which indeed it was)

and yet architecturally perfectly simple, in function subtle and elaborate, in appearance stark, imposing, awesome, Stonehenge was a thing of surpassing ingenuity of design, variety of usefulness and grandeur—in concept and construction an eighth wonder of the world. (Hawkins and White, 1966, pp. 117–118)

This interesting historical-archaeological controversy illustrates the use of sophisticated computer technology to test a hypothesis.

WRITING THE HISTORICAL REPORT

No less challenging than research itself is the writing of the report, which calls for creativity in addition to the qualities of imagination and resourcefulness already illustrated. It is an extremely difficult task to take often seemingly disparate pieces of information and synthesize them into a meaningful whole. Research reports should be written in a dignified and objective style. However, the historian is permitted a little more freedom in reporting. Hockett suggests that "the historian is not condemned to a bald, plain, unattractive style" and that "for the sake of relieving the monotony of statement after statement of bare facts, it is permissible, now and then, to indulge in a bit of color." He concludes, however, by warning that "above all, embellishments must never become a first aim, or be allowed to hide or distort the truth" (Hockett, 1948, p. 139).

An evaluation of graduate students' historical-research projects generally reveals one or more of the following faults:

1. Problem too broadly stated
2. Tendency to use easy-to-find secondary sources of data rather than sufficient primary sources, which are harder to locate but usually more trustworthy
3. Inadequate historical criticism of data because of failure to establish authenticity of sources and trustworthiness of data. For example, there is often a tendency to accept the truth of a statement if several observers agree. It is possible that one may have influenced the other or that all were influenced by the same inaccurate source of information.
4. Poor logical analysis resulting from:
    a. Oversimplification—failure to recognize the fact that causes of events are more often multiple and complex than single and simple
    b. Overgeneralization on the basis of insufficient evidence, and false reasoning by analogy, basing conclusions upon superficial similarities of situations

c. Failure to interpret words and expressions in the light of their accepted meaning in an earlier period
d. Failure to distinguish between significant facts in a situation and those that are irrelevant or unimportant
e. Failure to consider the documents in the context of their time, i.e., the existing beliefs, biases, etc.

5. Expression of personal bias, as revealed by statements lifted out of context for purposes of persuasion, assuming too generous or un-critical an attitude toward a person or idea (or being too unfriendly or critical), excessive admiration for the past (sometimes known as the "old oaken bucket" delusion), or an equally unrealistic admiration for the new or contemporary, assuming that all change represents progress

6. Poor reporting in a style that is dull and colorless, too flowery or flippant, too persuasive or of the "soap-box" type, or improper in usage

It is apparent that historical research is difficult and demanding. The gathering of historical evidence requires long hours of careful examination of such documents as court records, records of legislative bodies, letters, diaries, official minutes of organizations, or other primary sources of data. Historical research may involve traveling to distant places to examine the necessary documents or relics. In fact, any significant historical study would make demands that few students have the time, financial resources, patience, or expertise to meet. For these reasons, good historical studies are not often attempted for the purpose of meeting academic degree requirements.

SUMMARY

History, the meaningful record of human achievement, helps us to understand the present and, to some extent, to predict the future. Historical research is the application of scientific method to the description and analysis of past events.

Historians ordinarily draw their data from the observations and experience of others. Because they are not likely to have been at the scene of the event, they must use logical inferences to supplement what is probably an incomplete account.

Primary sources may be "unconscious" testimony, not intended to be left as a record—relics or remains such as bones, fossils, clothing, food, utensils, weapons, coins, and art objects are useful. Conscious testimony, in the form of records or documents, is another primary source of information—examples are constitutions, laws, court decisions, official minutes, autobiographies, letters, contracts, wills, certificates, newspaper and magazine accounts, films, recordings, and research reports.

Historical criticism is the evaluation of primary data. External criticism is concerned with the authenticity or genuineness of remains or documents, and internal criticism is concerned with the trustworthiness or veracity of materials. The accounts of the Dead Sea Scrolls and Stonehenge illustrate the processes of historical criticism.

The historical research studies of graduate students often reveal serious limitations. Frequently encountered are such faults as stating the problem too broadly, inadequate primary sources of data, unskillful historical criticism, poor logical analysis of data, personal bias, and ineffective reporting.

EXERCISES

1. Write a proposal for a historical study in a local setting. You may select a community, school, church, religious or ethnic group, or individual.
   State an appropriate title, present your hypothesis, indicate the primary sources of data that you would search, and tell how you would evaluate the authenticity and validity of your data.
2. Select a thesis of the historical type from the university library and analyze it in terms of
   a. hypothesis proposed or questions raised
   b. primary and secondary sources of data used
   c. external and internal criticism employed
   d. logical analysis of data relationships
   e. soundness of conclusions
   f. documentation

REFERENCES

Abington School District v. *Schempp*, 374 U.S. 203 (1963).
AYDELOTTE, W. O. (1963). Notes on the problem of historical generalization. In L. Gottschalk (Ed.), *Generalization in the writing of history*. Chicago: University of Chicago Press.
BEST, J. H. (Ed.). (1983). *Historical inquiry in education: A research agenda*. Washington D.C.: American Educational Research Association.
BILLINGTON, R. A. (1975). *Allan Nevins on history*. New York: Charles Scribner's Sons.
CREMIN, L. (1961). *The transformation of the school: Progressivism in American education*. New York: Alfred A. Knopf.
DAVIES, A. P. (1956). *The meaning of the Dead Sea Scrolls*. New York: New American Library of World Literature.
FINLEY, M. I. (1963). Generalizations in ancient history. In L. Gottschalk (Ed.), *Generalization in the writing of history*. Chicago: University of Chicago Press.
GOTTSCHALK, L. R. (1950). *Understanding history*. New York: Alfred A. Knopf.
GOTTSCHALK, L. R. (1963). Categories of historical generalizations. In L. Gottschalk (Ed.), *Generalization in the writing of history*. Chicago: University of Chicago Press.

HAWKINS, G. S. & WHITE, J. B. (1965). *Stonehenge decoded.* Garden City, NY: Doubleday & Co.

HOCKETT, H. C. (1948). *Introduction to research in American history.* New York: Macmillan Co.

LANNIE, V. L. & DIETHORN, B. C. (1968). For the honor and glory of God: The Philadelphia Bible riots of 1840. *History of Education Quarterly, 8,* 44–106.

NEVINS, A. (1962). *The gateway to history* (Rev. ed.). Boston: Raytheon Education Co.

SEARCH, P. W. (1901). *An ideal school: Looking forward.* New York: Appleton-Century-Crofts.

THURSFIELD, R. E. (1945). *Henry Barnard's American Journal of Education.* Baltimore: Johns Hopkins University Press.

WARREN, D. R. (Ed.). (1978). *History, education, and public policy: Recovering the American past.* Berkeley: McCutchan.

ADDITIONAL READINGS

BARZUN, J. & GRAFF, H. F. (1977). *The modern researcher* (2nd ed.). New York: Harcourt Brace Jovanovich.

BRICKMAN, W. W. (1949). *Guide to research in educational history.* New York: New York University Bookstore.

CARR, H. (1962). *What is history?* New York: Alfred A. Knopf.

EDGERTON, H. E. (1960). Stonehenge: New light on an old riddle. *National Geographic. 117,* 846–866.

GARRAGHAN, G. J. (1946). *A guide to historical method.* New York: Fordham University Press.

GOTTSCHALK, L. R., (Ed.). (1963). *Generalization in the writing of history. Report of the Committee of Historical Analysis of Social Science Research Council.* Chicago: University of Chicago Press.

HOCKETT, H. C. (1955). *The critical method in historical research and writing.* New York: Macmillan Co.

KLEIN, A. (Ed.). (1955). *Grand deception.* Philadelphia: J. B. Lippincott Co.

MOEHLMAN, A., ET AL., (1969). *A guide to computer assisted historical research in American education.* Austin: The Center for the History of Education, University of Texas.

NORDIN, V. D. & TURNER, W. L. (1980). More than segregation academies: The growing Protestant fundamentalist schools. *Phi Delta Kappan, 61,* 391–394.

PETERSON, C. S. (1946). *America's Rune stone.* New York: Hobson Book Press.

STEBBINS, C. L. (1960). *Here I shall finish my voyage: The death site of Father Jacques Marquette.* Orema, MI: Solle's Press.

ZIRKEL, P. A. (1979). *A digest of Supreme Court decisions affecting education.* Bloomington, IN: Phi Delta Kappa.

Chapter 4

Assessment, Evaluation, and Descriptive Research

A descriptive study describes and interprets what *is*. It is concerned with conditions or relationships that exist, opinions that are held, processes that are going on, effects that are evident, or trends that are developing. It is primarily concerned with the present, although it often considers past events and influences as they relate to current conditions.

The term *descriptive study* conceals an important distinction, for not all descriptive studies fall into the category of research. In Chapter 1 the similarities and differences between assessment, evaluation, and research were briefly discussed. We will restate those similarities and differences in this discussion of descriptive studies.

Assessment describes the status of a phenomenon at a particular time. It describes without value judgment a situation that prevails; it attempts no explanation of underlying reasons and makes no recommendations for action. It may deal with prevailing opinion, knowledge, practices, or conditions. As it is ordinarily used in education, assessment describes the progress students have made toward educational goals at a particular time. For example, in the National Assessment of Education Progress program, the data are gathered by a testing program and a sampling procedure in such a way that no individual is tested over the entire test battery. It is not designed to determine the effectiveness of a particular process or program but merely to estimate the degree of achievement of a large number of individuals who have been exposed to a great variety of educational and environmental influences. It does not provide recommendations, but there may be some implied judgment on the satisfactoriness of the situation or the fulfillment of society's expectations.

Evaluation adds the ingredient of value judgment of the social utility, desirability, or effectiveness of a process, product, or program, and it sometimes includes a recommendation for some course of action. School surveys are usually evaluation studies; educational products and programs are examined to determine their effectiveness in meeting accepted objectives, often with recommendations for constructive action.

Descriptive research, sometimes known as nonexperimental or correlational research, deals with the relationships between variables, the testing of hypotheses, and the development of generalizations, principles, or theories that have universal validity. It is concerned with functional relationships. The expectation is that if variable A is systematically associated with variable B, prediction of future phenomena may be possible and the results may suggest additional or competing hypotheses to test.

In carrying on a descriptive research project, in contrast to an experiment, the researcher does not manipulate the variable or arrange for events to happen. In fact, the events that are observed and described would have happened even though there had been no observation or analysis. Descriptive research involves events that have already taken place and may be related to a present condition.

The method of descriptive research is particularly appropriate in the behavioral sciences because many of the types of behavior that interest the researcher cannot be arranged in a realistic setting. Introducing significant variables may be harmful or threatening to human subjects. Ethical considerations often preclude exposing human subjects to harmful manipulation. For example, it would be unthinkable to prescribe cigarette smoking to human subjects for the purpose of studying its possible relationship to throat or lung cancer or to deliberately arrange auto accidents, except when manikins are used, in order to evaluate the effectiveness of seat belts or restraints in preventing serious injury.

Although many experimental studies of human behavior can be appropriately carried on both in the laboratory and in the field, the prevailing research method of the behavioral sciences is descriptive. Under the conditions that naturally occur in the home, the classroom, the recreational center, the office, or the factory, human behavior can be systematically examined and analyzed.

The many similarities between these types of descriptive studies may have tended to cloud the distinctions between them. They are all characterized by disciplined inquiry, which requires expertise, objectivity, and careful execution. They all develop knowledge, adding to what is already known. They use similar techniques of observation, description, and analysis. The differences between them lie in the motivation of the investigator, the treatment of the data, the nature of the conclusions, and the use of the findings. Studies that illustrate these types of descriptive analysis are presented in this chapter.

ASSESSMENT STUDIES

The Survey

The survey method gathers data from a relatively large number of cases at a particular time. It is not concerned with characteristics of individuals *as* individuals. It is concerned with the generalized statistics that result when data are abstracted from a number of individual cases. It is essentially cross-sectional.

Ninety-four percent of American homes have at least one television set. About three out of five students who enter the American secondary school remain to graduate. Fifty-six percent of adult Americans voted in the 1972 presidential election. The average American consumes about 103 pounds of refined sugar annually. The ratio of female births to male births in the United States in 1974 was 946 to 1000. The population of Illinois, according to the 1980 census, was 11,426,518. Data like these result from many types of surveys. Each statement pictures a prevailing condition at a particular time.

In analyzing political, social, or economic conditions, one of the first steps is to get the facts about the situation—or a picture of conditions that prevail or that are developing. These data may be gathered from surveys of the entire population. Others are inferred from a study of a sample group, carefully selected from the total population. And at times, the survey may describe a limited population which is the only group under consideration.

The survey is an important type of study. It must not be confused with the mere clerical routine of gathering and tabulating figures. It involves a clearly defined problem and definite objectives. It requires expert and imaginative planning, careful analysis and interpretation of the data gathered, and logical and skillful reporting of the findings.

Social Surveys

In the late 1930s a significant social survey was directed by the Swedish sociologist Gunnar Myrdal and sponsored by the Carnegie Foundation. Myrdal and his staff of researchers made a comprehensive analysis of the social, political, and economic life of black persons in the United States, yielding a great mass of data on race relations in America (Myrdal, 1944).

The late Alfred Kinsey (1948) of Indiana University made a comprehensive survey of the sexual behavior of the human male, based on data gathered from more than 12,000 cases. His second study (Kinsey, 1953) of the behavior of the human female followed later. Although these studies have raised considerable controversy, they represent a scientific approach to the study of an important social problem and have many implications for jurists, legislators, social workers, and educators.

Witty (1967) has studied the television viewing habits of school children, and has published annual reports on his investigations. These studies were conducted in the Chicago area and indicate the amount of time devoted to viewing and the program preferences of elementary and secondary students, their parents, and their teachers. Witty attempted to relate television viewing to intelligence, reading habits, academic achievement, and other factors.

Shaw and McKay (1942) conducted a study of juvenile delinquency in Chicago yielding significant data on the nature and extent of delinquency in large urban communities.

The National Safety Council conducts surveys on the nature, extent, and causes of automobile accidents in all parts of the United States. State high school athletic associations conduct surveys on the nature and extent of athletic injuries in member schools.

Public Opinion Surveys

In our culture, where so many opinions on controversial subjects are expressed by well-organized special interest groups, it is important to find out what the people think. Without a means of polling public opinion, the views of only the highly organized minorities are effectively presented through the printed page, radio, and television.

How do people feel about legalized abortion, the foreign aid program, busing to achieve racial integration in the public schools, or the adequacy of the public schools? What candidate do they intend to vote for in the next election? Such questions can be partially answered by means of the public opinion survey. Many research agencies carry on these surveys and report their findings in magazines and in syndicated articles in daily newspapers.

Since it would be impracticable or even impossible to get an expression of opinion from every person, sampling techniques are employed in such a way that the resulting opinions of a limited number of people can be used to infer the reactions of the entire population.

The names Gallup, Roper, and Harris are familiar to newspaper readers in connection with public opinion surveys. These surveys of opinion are frequently analyzed and reported by such classifications as age groups, sex, educational level, occupation, income level, political affiliation, or area of residence. Researchers are aware of the existence of many publics, or segments of the public, who may hold conflicting points of view. This further analysis of opinion by subgroups adds meaning to the analysis of public opinion in general.

Those who conduct opinion polls have developed more sophisticated methods of determining public attitudes through more precise sampling procedures and by profiting from errors that plagued early efforts. In prediction of voter behavior several well-known polls have proved to be poor estimators of election results.

In 1936, a prominent poll with a sample of over 2 million voters predicted the election of Alfred Landon over President Roosevelt by

nearly 15 percentage points. The primary reason for this failure in prediction was the poll's sampling procedure. The sample was taken from
telephone directories and automobile registration lists which did not
adequately represent poor persons, who in this election voted in unprec-
edented numbers. Gallup, on the other hand, correctly predicted that
Roosevelt would win, using a new procedure, *quota sampling*, in which
various components of the population are included in the sample in the
same proportion that they are represented in the population. However,
there are problems with this procedure, which resulted in Gallup and
others being wrong in 1948 (Babbie, 1973).

In the 1948 election campaign most polls predicted the election of
Thomas E. Dewey over President Truman. This time the pollsters were
wrong, perhaps partly because of the sampling procedure and partly
because the polls were taken too far before the election despite a trend
toward Truman throughout the campaign. Had the survey been made
just prior to election day, a more accurate prediction might have resulted. In addition, most survey researchers (including pollsters) use
probability sampling today instead of quota sampling. This results in all
members of a given population having the same probability of being
chosen for the sample. In the 1968 election the predictions of both Gallup and Harris polls were less than 2 percentage points away from
Richard Nixon's actual percent of the vote with samples of only about
2000 voters. This accuracy was possible due to the use of probability
sampling (Babbie, 1973).

In addition to the limitations suggested, there is a hazard of careless
responses, given in an offhand way, that are sometimes at variance with
the more serious opinions that are expressed as actual decisions.

Since 1969 the Gallup organization has conducted an annual nationwide opinion poll of public attitudes toward education. Using a stratified cluster sample of 1500 or more individuals over 18 years of age, the
data have been gathered by personal interviews from seven geographic
areas and four size-of-community categories. The responses were analyzed by age, sex, race, occupation, income level, political affiliation, and
level of education. A wide range of problem areas has been considered:
In the 1975 poll such problem areas confronting education were the use
of drugs and alcohol; programs on drugs or alcohol; behavior standards
in the schools; policies on suspension from school; work required of
students, including amount of homework; requirements for graduation
from high school; federal aid to public schools; the nongraded school
program; open education; alternative schools; job training; right of
teachers to strike; textbook censorship; and the role of the school principal as part of management (Elam, 1979). The 1982 poll indicated the
public's clear support for education. Education was ranked first among
12 funding categories considered in the survey—above health care, wel-

fare, and military defense—with 55 percent selecting public education as one of their first three choices (*Nation at Risk*, 1983, p. 17).

National Assessment of Educational Progress

The National Assessment of Educational Progress was the first nationwide, comprehensive survey of educational achievement to be conducted in the United States. Originally financed by the Carnegie Foundation and the Fund for the Advancement of Education, with a supporting grant from the U.S. Office of Education, the Committee on Assessing the Progress of Education (CAPE) began its first survey in the spring of 1969. It gathered achievement test data by a sampling process such that no one individual was tested over the whole test battery or spent more than 40 minutes in the process. Achievement was assessed every 3 years in four age groups (9, 13, 17, and young adults between 26 and 35), in four geographical areas (Northeast, Southeast, Central, and West), for four types of communities (large city, urban fringe, rural, and small city), and for several socioeconomic levels and ethnic groups.

Achievement has been assessed in art, reading, writing, social studies, science, mathematics, literature, citizenship, and music. Comparisons between individuals, schools, or school systems have never been made.

The agency now conducting the assessment is the National Assessment of Educational Progress (NAEP), financed by the National Center for Educational Statistics, a division of the Department of Education. Periodic reports are provided for educators, interested lay adults, and for the general public through press releases to periodicals.

International Assessment

The International Association for the Evaluation of Educational Achievement, with headquarters in Stockholm, Sweden, has been carrying on an assessment program in a number of countries since 1964. The first study, *The International Study of Achievement in Mathematics* (Torsten, 1967), compared achievement in twelve countries: Austria, Belgium, England, Finland, France, West Germany, Israel, Japan, the Netherlands, Scotland, Sweden, and the United States. Short answer and multiple choice tests were administered to 13-year-olds and to students in their last year of the upper secondary schools, prior to university entrance. More than 132,000 pupils and 5000 schools were involved in the survey. Japanese students excelled above all others, regardless of their socioeconomic status, and United States students ranked near the bottom.

Although the purpose of assessment is not to compare school systems, the data lead observers to make such comparisons. Critics of the first assessment pointed out the inappropriateness of comparing 17-year-olds in the United States, where more than 75 percent are enrolled in secondary schools, with 17-year-olds in other countries in which those enrolled in upper secondary schools comprise a small, highly selected population.

More recent assessments reveal that, although 10 percent of the top United States students surpassed similar groups in all other countries in reading, in science they occupied seventh place (Hechinger & Hechinger, 1974).

Other assessments have been carried out and the number of participating countries has been increased to twenty-two.

Activity Analysis

The analysis of the activities or processes that an individual is called upon to perform is important, both in industry and in various types of social agencies. This process of analysis is appropriate in any field of work and at all levels of responsibility. It is useful in the industrial plant, where needed skills and competencies of thousands of jobs are carefully studied, jobs ranging in complexity from unskilled laborer to plant manager.

In school systems the roles of the superintendent, the principal, the teacher, and the custodian have been carefully analyzed to discover what these individuals do and need to be able to do. The Commonwealth Teacher Training Study (Charters and Waples, 1929) described and analyzed the activities of several thousand teachers, and searched previous studies for opinions of writers on additional activities in which classroom teachers should engage. A more recent study (Morris, Crowson, Porter-Gehrig, and Hurwitz, 1984) described and analyzed the activities of school principals. This study is described in some detail later in this chapter as an example of ethnographic research.

This type of analysis may yield valuable information that would prove useful in establishing

1. The requirements for a particular job or position
2. A program for the preparation or training of individuals for various jobs or positions
3. An in-service program for improvement in job competence or for upgrading of individuals already employed
4. Equitable wage or salary schedules for various jobs or positions.

Trend Studies

The trend study is an interesting application of the descriptive method. In essence it is based upon a longitudinal consideration of recorded data, indicating what has been happening in the past, what the present situation reveals, and on the basis of these data, what is likely to happen in the future. For example, if the population in an area shows consistent growth over a period of time, one might predict that by a certain date in the future the population will reach a given level. These assumptions are based upon the likelihood that the factors producing the change or growth will continue to exert their influence in the future. The trend study points to conclusions reached by the combined methods of historical and descriptive analysis, and is illustrated by *Problems and Outlook of Small Private Liberal Arts Colleges: Report to the Congress of the United States by the Comptroller General* (1978). In response to a questionnaire sent to 332 institutions, 283 furnished data on facility construction, loan repayments, enrollment, the effectiveness of methods used to attract more students, financial aid provided, and the general financial health of their institutions.

Based upon past and present experience, such influences as the growth of the community college, the effect of inflation on operating costs, tuition, living expenses and fees, and the decline in the number of college-age students were projected for the years 1978 to 1985 and their impact upon the financial stability of the small liberal arts college assessed.

The following trend study topics would also be appropriate:

1. The Growing Participation of Women in Intercollegiate Sports Programs
2. Trends in the Methods of Financial Support of Public Education
3. The Growth of Black Student Enrollment in Graduate Study Programs
4. The Minimum Competency Requirement Movement in American Secondary Education

EVALUATION STUDIES

School Surveys

What has traditionally been called a school survey is usually an assessment and evaluation study. Its purpose is to gather detailed information to be used as a basis for judging the effectiveness of the instructional facilities, curriculum, teaching and supervisory personnel, and financial resources in terms of best practices and standards in education. For example, professional and regional accrediting agencies send visitation teams to gather data on the characteristics of the institution seeking accreditation. Usually, following a self-evaluation by the school staff, the visiting educators evaluate the institution's characteristics on the basis of agency guidelines.

Many city, township, and county school systems have been studied by this method for the purpose of determining status and adequacy. These survey-evaluations are sometimes carried on by an agency of a university in the area. Frequently a large part of the data is gathered by local educators, with the university staff providing direction and advisory services.

ASSESSMENT AND EVALUATION IN PROBLEM SOLVING

In solving a problem or charting a course of action, several sorts of information may be needed. These data may be gathered through the processes of assessment and evaluation methods.

The first type of information is based upon *present conditions.* Where are we now? From what point do we start? These data may be gathered by a systematic description and analysis of all the important aspects of the present situation.

The second type of information involves *what we may want.* In what direction may we go? What conditions are desirable or are considered to represent best practice? This clarification of objectives or goals may come from a study of what we think we want, possibly resulting from a study of conditions existing elsewhere, or of what experts consider to be adequate or desirable.

The third type of information is concerned with *how to get there.* This analysis may involve finding out about the experience of others who have been involved in similar situations. It may involve the opinions of experts, who presumably know best how to reach the goal.

Some studies emphasize only one of these aspects of problem solving. Others may deal with two, or even three, of the elements. Although a study does not necessarily embrace all the steps necessary for the solution of a problem it may make a valuable contribution by clarifying only one of the necessary steps—from description of present status to the charting of the path to the goal.

Assessment and evaluation methods may supply some or all of the needed information. An example will illustrate how they can be used to help solve an educational problem.

Washington Township has a school building problem. Its present educational facilities seem inadequate, and if present developments continue, conditions may be much worse in the future. The patrons and educational leaders in the community know that a problem exists, but they realize that this vague awareness does not provide a sound basis for action. Three steps are necessary to provide such a basis.

The first step involves a systematic analysis of present conditions. How many school-age children are there in the township? How many children are of preschool age? Where do they live? How many classrooms now exist? How adequate are they? What is the average class size? How are these present buildings located in relation to residential housing? How adequate are the facilities for food, library, health, and recreational services? What is the present annual budget? How is it related to the tax rate and the ability of the community to provide adequate educational facilities?

The second step projects goals for the future. What will the school population be in 5, 10, or 20 years? Where will the children live? How many buildings and classrooms will be needed? What provisions should be made for special school services, for libraries, cafeterias, gymnasiums, and play areas to take care of expected educational demands?

Step three considers how to reach those goals which have been established by the analysis of step two. Among the questions to be answered are the following: Should existing facilities be expanded or new buildings constructed? If new buildings are needed, what kind should be provided? Should schools be designed for grades 1 through 8, or should 6-year elementary schools and separate 2- or 3-year junior high schools be provided? How will the money be raised? When and how much should the tax rate be increased? When should the construction program get underway?

Many of the answers to the questions raised in step three will be arrived at by analysis of practices of other townships, the expressed opinions of school patrons and local educational leaders, and the opinions of experts in the areas of school buildings, school organization, community planning, and public finance. Of course, this analysis of school building needs is but one phase of the larger educational problem of providing an adequate educational program for tomorrow's children. There remain problems of curriculum, pupil transportation, and school personnel. These problems can also be attacked by using similar methods of assessment and evaluation.

THE FOLLOW-UP STUDY

The follow-up study investigates individuals who have left an institution after having completed a program, a treatment, or a course of study. The study is concerned with what has happened to them, and what has been the impact upon them of the institution and its program. By examining their status or seeking their opinions, one may get some idea of the adequacy or inadequacy of the institution's program. Which courses, experiences, or treatments proved to be of value? Which proved to be ineffective or of limited value? Studies of this type enable an institution to evaluate various aspects of its program in light of actual results.

Dillon's (1949) study of early school leavers has yielded information that may lead to the improvement of the curriculum, guidance services, administrative procedures, and thus the holding power of the American secondary school.

Project Talent (U.S. Office of Education, 1965) was an educational survey conducted by the University of Pittsburgh with support from the Cooperative Research Program of the U.S. Office of Education, the National Institutes of Health, the National Science Foundation, and the Department of Defense. The survey consisted of the administration of a 2-day battery of aptitude, ability, and achievement tests, and inventories of the background characteristics of 440,000 students enrolled in 1353 secondary schools in all parts of the United States. Five basic purposes of the survey were stated:

1. To obtain an inventory of the capacities and potentialities of American youth
2. To establish a set of standards for educational and psychological measurement
3. To provide a comprehensive counseling guide indicating patterns of career success
4. To provide information on how youth choose their life work
5. To provide better understanding of the educational experiences which prepare students for their life work.

In addition to the testing program, questionnaire follow-up studies have been conducted, and are planned at regular intervals, to relate the information gathered to patterns of aptitude and ability required by various types of occupations. The vast amount of data stored in the data bank, now available in the computer files, will make significant educational research possible and may provide a basis for possible changes in the educational patterns of American secondary schools.

Project Talent, described as an example of an educational survey, also provides an illustration of a follow-up study. One phase of the longitudinal study reported by Combs and Cooley (1968), involved the follow-up of the ninth grade group who failed to complete the high school program. This group, which represented a random sample of the ninth grade secondary school population, provided an estimate of the characteristics of the dropout population, compared with those of a random sample of students who graduated but did not enter a junior college or 4-year institution of higher learning. These two samples were compared on a number of characteristics, such as academic achievement, participation in extracurricular activities, work experiences, hobbies, contacts with school counselors, and self-reported personal qualities.

The students who graduated scored significantly higher on most of the characteristics, except self-reported qualities of leadership and impulsiveness. One unusual finding indicated that the dropouts earned as much as those who had finished high school and had been earning it longer. It was pointed out, however, that the economic advantages of finishing high school could not be adequately evaluated until later in life.

Project Talent, funded by the National Institute of Education, maintained contact with the original students and has completed the eleventh-year follow-up survey. Many of the students expressed dissatisfaction with their schooling and regretted that they had not gone on to college or vocational school and that they had married too early. More than half still live within 30 miles of their high schools, a surprising observation in a society that is believed to be extremely mobile. The more mobile half were the high academic achievers. Eighty percent of the men, but only 65 percent of the women, expressed satisfaction with their jobs in meeting their long-range goals.

DESCRIPTIVE RESEARCH

The examples discussed up to this point in the chapter have been designated as assessment studies and evaluation studies. Descriptive research studies have characteristics that distinguish them from the type previously described and from those described in the next chapter.

1. They involve hypothesis formulation and testing.
2. They use the logical methods of inductive-deductive reasoning to arrive at generalizations.
3. They often employ methods of randomization so that error may be estimated when inferring population characteristics from observations of samples.
4. The variables and procedures are described as accurately and completely as possible so that the study can be replicated by other researchers.
5. They are nonexperimental, for they deal with the relationships between nonmanipulated variables in a natural rather than artificial setting. Since the events or conditions have already occurred or exist, the researcher selects the relevant variables for an analysis of their relationships.

Document or Content Analysis

Documents are an important source of data in many areas of investigation, and the methods of analysis are similar to those used by historians. The analysis is concerned with the explanation of the status of some phenomenon at a particular time or its development over a period of time. The activity may be classified as descriptive research, for problem identification, hypothesis formulation, sampling, and systematic observation of variable relationships may lead to generalizations. It serves a useful purpose in adding knowledge to fields of inquiry and in explaining certain social events. Its application to educational research is suggested in some of the studies listed as examples.

In documentary analysis, the following may be used as sources of data: records, reports, printed forms, letters, autobiographies, diaries, compositions, themes or other academic work, books, periodicals, bulletins or catalogues, syllabi, court decisions, pictures, films, and cartoons.

When using documentary sources, one must bear in mind that data appearing in print are not necessarily trustworthy. Documents used in descriptive research must be subjected to the same careful types of criticism employed by the historian. Not only is the authenticity of the document important, but the validity of its contents is crucial. It is the researcher's obligation to establish the trustworthiness of all data that he or she draws from documentary sources.

The following purposes may be served through documentary analysis (examples of actual studies are given as illustrations):

1. To describe prevailing practices or conditions.

   Entrance Requirements of Ohio Colleges as Revealed by an Analysis of College Bulletins
   Criteria for Primary Pupil Evaluation Used on Marion County Report Cards

2. To discover the relative importance of, or interest in, certain topics or problems.

   Public Information on Education as Measured by Newspaper Coverage in Three Indianapolis Daily Newspapers during the Month of December, 1958
   Statistical Concepts Presented in College Textbooks in Educational Research Published since 1940

3. To discover the level of difficulty of presentation in textbooks or in other publications.

   The Vocabulary Level of Intermediate Science Textbooks
   Abstract Concepts Found in First Grade Readers

4. To evaluate bias, prejudice, or propaganda in textbook presentation.

The Soviet Union as Presented in High School History Textbooks
The Free Enterprise System as Pictured in High School Social Problems Textbooks
Racial and Religious Stereotypes in Junior High School Literature Textbooks

5. To analyze types of errors in students' work.

   Typing Errors of First Semester Typing Students at Shortridge High School
   Errors in English Usage Found in Letters of Application for Admission to the University of Wisconsin

6. To analyze the use of symbols representing persons, political parties or institutions, countries, or points of view.

   Great Britain as a Symbol, as Represented in New York City Newspaper Cartoons in the Decade, 1930–1940
   The New Dealer as Depicted in the American Press from 1932 to 1942

7. To identify the literary style, concepts, or beliefs of a writer.

   Shakespeare's Use of the Metaphor
   Alexander Campbell's Concept of the Trinity, as Revealed in His Sermons
   John Dewey's Interpretation of Education as Growth

8. To explain the possible causal factors related to some outcome, action, or event.

   The Effect of Media Coverage upon the Outcome of the 1976 Presidential Election
   The Influence of Newspaper Editorials upon the Action of the State Assembly on Sales Tax Legislation

Content or document analysis should serve a useful purpose in yielding information that is helpful in evaluating or explaining social or educational practices. Since there are so many significant areas to be investigated, setting up studies for the pure joy of counting and tabulating has little justification. "The Uses of Shall and Will in the Spectator Papers," or "The Use of Too, Meaning Also, in the Works of Keats" would seem to add little useful knowledge to the field of literature.

The Case Study

The case study is a way of organizing social data for the purpose of viewing social reality. It examines a social unit as a whole. The unit may be a person, a family, a social group, a social institution, or a community.

The purpose is to understand the life cycle or an important part of the life cycle of the unit. The case study probes deeply and analyzes interactions between the factors that explain present status or that influence change or growth. It is a longitudinal approach, showing development over a period of time.

The element of typicalness, rather than uniqueness, is the focus of attention, for an emphasis upon uniqueness would preclude scientific abstraction and generalization of findings.

Data may be gathered by a wide variety of methods, including

1. Observation by the researcher or his or her informants of physical characteristics, social qualities, or behavior
2. Interviews with the subject(s), relatives, friends, teachers, counselors, and others
3. Questionnaires, opinionnaires, psychological tests and inventories
4. Recorded data from newspapers, schools, courts, clinics, government agencies, or other sources.

A single case study emphasizes analysis in depth. Though it may be fruitful in developing hypotheses to be tested, it is not directed toward broad generalizations. One cannot generalize from a number (N) of 1. To the extent that a single case may represent an atypical situation, the observation is sound. But if the objective analysis of an adequate sample of cases leads researchers to consistent observations of significant variable relationships, hypotheses may be confirmed, leading to valid generalizations.

The individual case study has been a time-honored procedure in the field of medicine and medical research. Sigmund Freud was a pioneer in using case study methods in the field of psychiatry. In an effort to treat his psychoneurotic patients, he began to discover consistent patterns of experience. Under his careful probing, patients recalled long-forgotten, traumatic incidents in their childhood and youth. Freud hypothesized that these incidents probably explained their neurotic behavior (Strachey, 1964).

His famous case history of Sergei Petrov, "the Wolf Man," published in 1918 under the title *From the History of an Infantile Neurosis,* is one of the classic examples of Freud's use of the case study. He believed that these case studies confirmed his hypothesis, leading to psychoanalysis as a method of treatment. He also used them to demonstrate how theoretical models could be used to provide concrete examples.

Case studies are not confined to the study of individuals and their behavioral characteristics. Case studies have been made of all types of communities, from hamlet to great metropolis, and of all types of individuals—alcoholics, drug addicts, juvenile delinquents, migratory workers, sharecroppers, industrial workers, members of professions, executives, army wives, trailer court residents, members of social classes, Quakers, Amish, members of other religious sects and denominations, black Americans, American Indians, Chinese-Americans, Hispanics, and many other social and ethnic groups. Such institutions as colleges, churches, corrective institutions, welfare agencies, fraternal organizations, and business groups have been studied as cases. These studies have been conducted for the purpose of understanding the culture and the development of variable relationships.

For example, a community study is a thorough observation and analysis of a group of people living together in a particular geographic location in a corporate way. The study deals with such elements of community life as location, appearance, prevailing economic activity, climate and natural resources, historical development, mode of life, social structure, goals or life values and patterns, the individuals or power groups that exert the dominant influence, and the impact of the outside world. It also evaluates the social institutions that meet the basic human needs of health, protection, making a living, education, religious expression, and recreation.

The early community studies made by Lynd and Lynd are well known. The first, *Middletown* (1929), and the second, *Middletown in Transition* (1937), described the way of life in Muncie, Indiana, a typical midwestern, average-size city, tracing its development from the gas boom of the 1890s through World War I, the prosperity of the twenties, and the depression of the thirties. West (1945) described the nature of a very small community in the Ozark region in *Plainville, USA*. Sherman and Henry (1933) studied the way of life in five "hollow" communities, hidden in the Blue Ridge Mountains, in *Hollow Folk*.

Some community studies have singled out particular aspects for special investigation. Drake and Cayton (1945) described life in the black section of Chicago in *Black Metropolis*. Hollingshead (1949) portrayed the life of adolescents in a small Illinois community in *Elmtown's Youth*. Warner and Lunt (1941) developed a hypothesis of social class structure in a New England community in their study of Newburyport, Massachusetts, in *Social Life in a Modern Community*. Lucas (1970) compared the way of life in three Canadian communities in *Minetown, Milltown, Railtown: Life in Canadian Communities of Single Industry*.

Although the case study is a useful method of organizing research observations, certain precautions should be considered:

1. The method may look deceptively simple. To use it effectively, the researcher must be thoroughly familiar with existing theoretical knowledge of the field of inquiry, and skillful in isolating the significant variables from many that are irrelevant. There is a tendency to

select variables because of their spectacular nature rather than for their crucial significance.

2. Subjective bias is a constant threat to objective data-gathering and analysis. The danger of selecting variable relationships based upon preconceived convictions and the apparent consistency of a too limited sample of observations may lead the researcher to an unwarranted feeling of certainty about the validity of his or her conclusions.

3. Effects may be wrongly attributed to factors that are merely associated rather than cause-and-effect related. While the case study process is susceptible to this *post hoc* fallacy, it is a hazard associated with other types of nonexperimental studies.

Ethnographic Studies

Ethnography, sometimes known as cultural anthropology, is a method of field study observation that became popular in the latter part of the nineteenth century. It has continued to show significant development, suggesting promising techniques for the study of behavior in an educational situation. In its early application, it consisted of participant observation, conversation, and the use of informants to study the cultural characteristics of primitive people: African, South Sea Island, and American Indian tribes. These groups were small in number, geographically and culturally isolated, with little specialization in social function, and with simple economies and technology. Such cultural features as language, marriage and family life, child-rearing practices, religious beliefs and practices, social relations and rules of conduct, political institutions, and methods of production were analyzed.

The data gathered consisted of observation of patterns of action, verbal and nonverbal interaction between members of the tribe as well as between the subjects and the researcher and his or her informants, and the examination of whatever records or artifacts were available.

Many early studies were subsequently criticized on the grounds that the anthropologist spent too little time among the people of the tribe to get more than a superficial view, didn't learn the native language and had to depend too much on the reports of poorly trained informants, and relied too much on his or her own cultural perspective, reaching ethnocentric, judgmental conclusions that resulted in stereotyped theories of the development of the primitive society.

Later investigators realized that studies of this type would be invalid unless the observer

1. Lived for a much more extensive period of time among the tribe and became an integrated member of the social group

2. Learned the native language, enabling him or her to develop the sensitivity to think, feel, and interpret observations in terms of the tribe's concepts, feelings, and values, while at the same time supplementing his or her own objective judgment in interpreting observations

3. Trained his or her informants to systematically record field data in their own language and cultural perspective.

This refinement of participant observation resulted in more objective and valid observation and analysis. Some studies were directed toward the examination of the total way of life of a group. Other studies singled out a particular phase of the culture for intensive analysis, taking into account those elements that were relevant to the problem.

In her study *Coming of Age in Samoa,* Mead (1928) observed the development of 53 adolescent girls in a permissive Samoan society. She concluded that there were no differences in the physical processes of adolescent growth between Samoan and American girls: The differences were differences in response. The difficulties of this period of development, a troublesome feature of American life, do not occur in Samoa. She attributed the difference to Samoa's more homogeneous culture, a single set of religious and moral beliefs, and a wider kinship network that conferred authority and affection. The difficulties of American girls were attributed to cultural restraints, not nature.

Many of the time-honored techniques of the ethnographic study involving integration into the group and using participant observation are being applied to psychology and education, as well as anthropology and sociology. An excellent example of this methodology applied to an educational issue is a recent study of school principals. Morris, Crowson, Porter-Gehrie, and Hurwitz (1984) were interested in determining exactly what principals actually do and how much time is spent on those activities. Their procedure was to have each principal observed for up to 12 full work days. The observers followed the principal wherever he or she went. The authors "were interested in whom the principal interacted with and by what means (verbal face to face, written word, telephone, etc.). We wanted to know which party initiated each interchange, whether it was planned or spontaneous, how long it lasted, and where it took place. Most important, we wanted to follow the changing subject matters of these conversations, not only to see what topics consumed the principal's time but also to trace the rhythm of the principal's working hours" (Morris, et al., 1984, p. v).[1] One of the conclusions of this study was that principals usually spend less than half their work day in their offices, that they have a good deal of discretion in their decision-making, and that the principal's behavior "affects four distinct 'constituencies'":

[1] Used with the permission of the authors and of Charles E. Merrill Publishing Co.

teachers and students, parents and others in the community, superiors, and the principal him or her self (Morris, et al., 1984, p. v).

The ethnographic study is a qualitative approach, employing few, if any, quantitative data-gathering instruments. Using the methods of participant observation, the researcher observes, listens to, and converses with the subjects in as free and natural an atmosphere as possible. The assumption is that the most important behavior of individuals in groups is a dynamic process of complex interactions and consists of more than a set of facts, statistics, or even discrete incidents. The strength of this kind of study lies in the observation of natural behavior in a real-life setting, free from the constraints of more conventional research procedures.

Another assumption is that human behavior is influenced by the setting in which it occurs. The researcher must understand that setting and the nature of the social structure; its traditions, values, and norms of behavior. It is important to observe and interpret as an outside observer but also to observe and interpret in terms of the subjects—how they view the situation, how they interpret their own thoughts, words, and activities, as well as those of others in the group. The researcher gets inside the minds of the subjects, while at the same time interpreting the behavior from his or her own perspective.

The relationship of researchers to their subjects is based upon trust and confidence. Researchers do not allow themselves to be aligned with either the authority figures or the subjects. A position of neutrality is essential to objective participant observation.

Unlike conventional deductive quantitative research, participant observers begin without preconceptions and hypotheses. Using inductive logic, they build their hypotheses as they are suggested by observations. They periodically reevaluate them on the basis of new observations, modifying them when they appear to be inconsistent with the evidence. They look for negative evidence to challenge their temporary hypotheses. In a sense, this type of research has the characteristics of a series of consecutive studies. Unlike the conventional research study, the interpretation is not deferred to the conclusion but is a constant ongoing process of testing tentative hypotheses against additional observations in a real situation.

Ethnographic methods of research have been used to investigate such problems as:

1. Student Leadership Roles in an Urban, Racially Integrated High School
2. Pupil-Teacher Relationships in a Suburban Junior High School
3. Social Relationships in a Class of Emotionally Disturbed Children
4. Changes in Attitudes and Behavior in a Drug Abuse Rehabilitation Center

5. The Social Class Structure of a Florida, Cuban-American Community

EX POST FACTO OR EXPLANATORY OBSERVATIONAL STUDIES

Descriptive research seeks to find answers to questions through the analysis of variable relationships. What factors seem to be associated with certain occurrences, outcomes, conditions, or types of behavior? Because it is often impracticable to arrange occurrences, an analysis of past events may be the only feasible way to study causation. This type of study is usually referred to as *ex post facto* or *causal-comparative research.*

For example, one would not arrange automobile accidents in order to study their causes. The automobile industry, police departments, safety commissions, and insurance companies study the conditions associated with the accidents that have occurred. Such factors as mechanical faults or failures, excessive speed, driving under the influence of alcohol, and others have been identified as causal.

However, while studies of past events may be the only practicable way to investigate certain problems, the researcher needs to be aware of the problems inherent in this type of research. The researcher must be cognizant of the fact that the information used in *ex post facto* studies may be incomplete. That is, the researcher may not have sufficient information about all of the events and variables that were occurring at the time being studied. This lack of control or even of knowledge regarding what variables were controlled makes causal statements based upon this type of research very difficult to make.

Seat belt research has had an important influence upon auto-safety equipment. Federal legislation requires that all new cars sold after January 1, 1968, be equipped with lap and shoulder belts. A Detroit news story cites research evidence that supports the effectiveness of safety belts (*U.S. News and World Report*, 1968, p. 12).[2]

> Now that U.S. autos are being equipped with a maze of belts and harnesses for drivers and passengers, this question is being asked by many car buyers: Are they really useful, or are they more trouble than they are worth?
>
> The answer, from the best available evidence, seems to be: The new harnesses can be an important factor in reducing injuries and death from accidents.
>
> The widest research done to date on this subject was a Swedish survey of 28,780 accidents, showing how the use or non-use of shoulder harnesses

[2] Reprinted from *U.S. News and World Report* issue of Jan. 29, 1968. Copyright, 1968, U.S. News & World Report, Inc.

affected the drivers and passengers. Main results of the survey were made public late in 1967. The survey by the manufacturers of Volvo autos also showed this: Use of a combined shoulder-lap belt reduced skull damage by 69 percent for drivers and 88 percent for passengers. Facial injuries dropped by 73 percent for drivers and 83 percent for passengers.

The U.S. auto industry has accepted the Federal Government edict that it provide the belts and harnesses—a total of 16 straps in each new auto. Now being worked on are plans to make them less unsightly and less awkward to use.

But dealers are finding a number of buyers unenthusiastic about all the belts. Some dealers asked if they could remove the belts at the request of the customers. The answer from manufacturers: No. The dealer, it was explained, might be breaking the law if he did so.

Some industry officials have also raised the question of whether the belts themselves can cause injury in case of accident. So far there has been no broad study in the United States to back this theory. The Swedish survey, however, did show this: In the 28,780 accidents studied, safety belts caused 34 injuries to drivers, 25 to front seat passengers. Most were minor injuries.

Figures below show results of 28,780 traffic accidents in Sweden. In these accidents 98 percent of the cars were equipped with lap and shoulder belts. But only 25 percent of the drivers and 30 percent of the front seat passengers were using the belts. This is what happened:

	KILLED	SEVERELY INJURED	SLIGHTLY INJURED
Drivers			
Among 6,870 using belts	2	51	175
Among 21,910 not using belts	37	263	835
Front Seat Passengers			
Among 2,699 using belts	1	22	109
Among 6,032 not using belts	12	160	439

Although these statistics may appear to present convincing evidence in favor of the use of lap and shoulder belts in reducing fatalities and serious injuries, one might speculate that motorists who are prudent enough to wear them are likely to be more careful drivers and therefore have fewer and less serious accidents than those who do not.

Studies of juvenile delinquency may compare the social and educational backgrounds of delinquents and nondelinquents. What factors, if any, were common to the nondelinquent group? Any factors common to one group, but not to the other, might serve as a possible explanation of the underlying causes of delinquency.

Some efforts have been made to associate good or poor teaching with the type of educational institution in which the teachers prepared. Those studies have proved inconclusive, possibly for a number of reasons. In addition to the difficulty of finding valid and satisfactory criteria of good and poor teaching, many factors other than type of college attended seem to be significant. Such variables as quality of scholarship, socioeconomic status, personality qualities, types of nonschool experiences, attitudes toward the teaching profession, and a host of others have possible relevancy.

Sesame Street studies. Minton (1975) studied the effect of viewing the children's television program, "Sesame Street," on the reading readiness of kindergarten children. Of three sample groups, a 1968, a 1969, and a 1970 group, only the 1970 group had viewed the program.[3]

Reading Readiness and "Sesame Street"

SAMPLE GROUP	N	WHITE	BLACK	SPANISH-SPEAKING
1968	482	431	51	18
1969	495	434	61	9
1970	524	436	88	25

Scores on the Metropolitan Reading Readiness Test battery, consisting of six subtests (word meaning, listening, matching, alphabet letter recognition, numbers, and copying text) were used to measure readiness. Using pretest-posttest design, the mean gain scores of the 1970 group were compared with those of the 1968 and 1969 groups.

No significant differences at the 0.05 level were observed in total scores. On only one of the subtests, letter recognition, was a significant difference observed, favoring the 1970 group. In a classification by socioeconomic status, advantaged children watched more and scored higher than disadvantaged children. The hypothesis that viewing "Sesame Street" would help to close the gap between advantaged and disadvantaged children was not supported; rather, the gap was widened.

Anderson and Levin (1976) studied the effect of age on the viewing attention of small children to a 57-minute taped "Sesame Street" program, consisting of 41 bits, each ranging in length from 10 to 453 seconds. Six groups of five boys and five girls, ages 12, 18, 24, 30, 36, 42, and 48 months were observed by video tape recordings. In a viewing room, in the presence of parents, toys were provided as alternatives to viewing. The following observations were reported:

1. Length of attention increased with age. The younger children appeared to be more interested in the toys and interacting with their mothers.

---

[3] From "Impact of Sesame Street on Reading Readiness" by J. M. Minton, *Sociology of Education*, 1975, *48*, 141–51. Reprinted by permission.

2. Length of attention decreased as bit length increased.
3. Attention to animals increased to 24 months but dropped thereafter.
4. Children showed more interest in the presence of women, lively music, puppets, peculiar voices, rhyming, repetition, and motion.
5. Children showed less interest in the presence of adult men, animals, inactivity, and still drawings.

REPLICATION AND SECONDARY ANALYSIS

Replication, a combination of the terms *repeat* and *duplicate*, has been described as an important method of challenging or verifying the conclusions of a previous study. Using different subjects at a different time and in a different setting, arriving at conclusions that are consistent with those of the previous study would strengthen its conclusions and justify more confidence in its validity. Replication is essential to the development and verification of new generalizations and theories.

Another useful procedure, known as *secondary analysis*, consists of reanalyzing the data gathered by a previous investigator, and may involve different hypotheses, different experimental designs, or different methods of statistical analysis. The subjects are the same and the data are the same. The difference is that of alternative methods of analysis.

Secondary analysis has a number of advantages that commend its use:

1. The new investigator may bring an objectivity, a fresh point of view, to the investigation and may think of better questions to be raised or hypotheses to be tested. For example, the viewpoint of a psychologist rather than that of a sociologist (or vice versa) may find greater meaning in the data already available.
2. Secondary analysis may bring greater expertise to the area of investigation and greater skill in experimental design and statistical analysis.
3. The reanalysis would involve less expense in both time and money. Because the data are already available, a more modest appropriation of funds would be possible. It would not be necessary to intrude upon the time of subjects (teachers and students) whose primary activities had been diverted in the original investigation.
4. Secondary analysis may provide useful experience for students of research methodology by enabling them to use real data, rather than simulated or inferior data, for the purposes of the exercise.

Secondary analysis has played an important part in educational research. No investigation has been subjected to as great a degree of secondary analysis as the *Equality of Educational Opportunity* study, described next.

Equality of Educational Opportunity study.   In 1964, the Congress of the United States passed the Civil Rights Act, which directed the United States Commissioner of Education to carry out a study of "the lack of educational opportunity by reason of race, color, religion or national origin in public educational institutions at all levels in the United States, its territories and possessions, and the District of Columbia."

This authorization assumed that educational opportunity for members of minority groups was unequal to that available for white students. This study was one of the largest of its type ever conducted. The report of its findings, commonly known as the Coleman Report, was titled *Equality of Educational Opportunity* (Coleman, et al., 1966).

The nationwide investigation selected, by a two-stage probability sample, 640,000 public school pupils in grades 1, 3, 6, 9, and 12, and 60,000 teachers in more than 4,000 schools. Data were also gathered from parents, school principals, school district superintendents, and prominent community members. In addition, case studies of individual cities were conducted by educators, lawyers, and sociologists. For comparative purposes the data were organized by geographic location as northern, northern metropolitan, southern and southwestern, southern metropolitan, and midwestern and western. Individuals were classified as white, black, Asian, Indian, Mexican-American, and Puerto Rican.

As much as possible, data-gathering instruments were checked for validity and reliability. Methods of data analysis included multiple correlation and factorial analysis of variance and covariance.

Although it would not be feasible to present a detailed account of the findings of the study, a few of the major conclusions are included:

1. The report rejected the assumption that the educational opportunities provided for minority children were unequal. There seemed to be little difference in almost all school facilities that would relate to equality of opportunity. In some areas, minority schools seemed to be more adequate than predominantly white schools.

2. Family background, rather than the characteristics of the school, appeared to be the major influence on school achievement. It was apparent that, over the years, the school experience did little to narrow the initial achievement gap.

3. The socioeconomic composition of the student body was more highly related to achievement than any school factor.

4. The achievement level in rank order was white, Asian-American, American Indian, Mexican-American, Puerto Rican, and black. While white students scored significantly higher than any other

group, Asian-Americans excelled in nonverbal and mathematics achievement.

5. Inequalities of educational opportunity were more closely related to regional differences, rather than to differences between predominantly black and white schools. Schools in the North, Midwest, and West seemed to have better facilities than those in the South and Southwest.

6. Social class differences within all groups appeared to be more significant than the differences between ethnic groups.

The Coleman Report has been subjected to criticism both by experienced researchers and by members of special interest groups. The findings were unacceptable to some, who pointed out flaws in the gathering of data and their interpretation. Others found procedural defects in sampling and statistical analysis of the data.

Of 900,000 pupils solicited, only about 640,000, or about two-thirds of the invited sample, were tested. Twenty-one metropolitan school districts refused to participate in the study, including such large cities as Boston, Chicago, Indianapolis, and Los Angeles. In addition, twenty-three other school districts, who participated to a limited degree, refused to test their pupils. The provision for an equal number of white and nonwhite participants in the sample introduced a possible element of invalidity in the statistical analysis of the data.

The questionnaires were criticized for their lack of what has been termed a "qualitative bite," the effort to get beneath the surface for more meaningful responses. There was also a high degree of nonresponse to the questionnaires, particularly on some items of an emotional or controversial nature. For example, one-third of the principals failed to answer questions on the racial composition of their faculties.

Some critics believed that the report did not make a highly significant contribution to education, but most agreed that it did stimulate interest in further research concerning the relationship of the family, the school, and the community.

The fact that no previous study has generated so much controversy is not surprising considering the complexity of the problems involved and the sensitive nature of the issues. For example, both advocates and opponents of school busing viewed the data in the light of their own established positions.

A number of studies using secondary analysis were authorized by various government agencies, special commissions, and philanthropic foundations. Using the Coleman Report data, various aspects of the problem were examined more closely, using different statistical procedures and raising different questions. Some confined their investigations to data relating to a single geographic area while others considered a wider range of data analysis. Helpful resumes of several of these studies are included in the publication, *On Equality of Educational Opportunity,* edited by Mosteller and Moynihan (1972).

Meta-Analysis. A relatively recent innovation that allows a researcher to systematically and statistically combine the findings of several previous studies is known as *meta-analysis, research synthesis,* or *research integration.* There are a number of quantitative techniques, ranging from fairly simple to quite complex, by which the data from previously published studies can be combined. Glass (1978) and his colleagues (Glass, Smith, and Barton, 1979), have developed and described some of these techniques. Walberg and his colleagues have conducted a number of studies using these techniques. See the special issue of *Evaluation in Education,* 1980, Vol. 4, pp. 1–142, edited by Walberg and Haertel, for a selection of these and other research integration efforts.

THE *POST HOC* FALLACY

One of the most serious dangers of *ex post facto* research is the *post hoc* fallacy, the conclusion that because two factors go together one must be the cause and the other the effect. Because there seems to be a high relationship between the number of years of education completed and earned income, many educators have argued that staying in school will add *x* number of dollars of income over a period of time for each additional year of education completed. Although there may be such a relationship, it is also likely that some of the factors that influence young people to seek additional education are more important than the educational level completed. Such factors as socioeconomic status, persistence, desire, willingness to postpone immediate gratification, and intelligence level are undoubtedly significant factors in vocational success. Staying in school may be a symptom rather than the cause.

Some critics of cigarette-cancer research have advanced a similar argument. The case that they propose follows this line of reason: Let us suppose that certain individuals with a type of glandular imbalance have a tendency toward cancer. The imbalance induces a certain amount of nervous tension. Because excessive cigarette smoking is a type of nervous tension release, these individuals tend to be heavy smokers. The cancer could result from the glandular imbalance rather than from the smoking, which is only a symptom. This error of confusing symptoms or merely associated factors with cause could lead researchers to deduce a false cause-and-effect relationship.

This illustration is not presented to discredit this type of cancer research. Substantial evidence does suggest a significant relationship.

Laboratory experiments have supported a causal relationship between the coal-tar products that are distilled from cigarette combustion and malignant growth in animals. The association explanation, however, is one that should always be examined carefully.

Ex post facto research is widely and appropriately used, particularly in the behavioral sciences. In education, because it is impossible, impracticable, or unthinkable to manipulate such variables as aptitude, intelligence, personality traits, cultural deprivation, teacher competence, and some variables that might present an unacceptable threat to human beings, this method will continue to be used.

However, its limitations should be recognized:

1. The independent variables cannot be manipulated.
2. Subjects cannot be randomly assigned to treatment groups.
3. Causes are often multiple rather than single.

For these reasons scientists are reluctant to use the expression *cause and effect* in nonexperimental studies in which the variables have not been carefully manipulated. They prefer to observe that when variable A appears, variable B is consistently associated, possibly for reasons not completely understood or explained.

Since there is a danger of confusing symptoms with causes, *ex post facto* research should test not just one hypothesis but other logical alternate or competing hypotheses as well. Properly employed and cautiously interpreted, it will continue to provide a useful methodology for the development of knowledge.

Students who have completed a course in research methods should be sensitive to the operation of extraneous variables that threaten the validity of conclusions. Glass (1968) cautions educators of the need for critical analysis of reported research. He cites a number of interesting examples of carelessly conducted studies that resulted in completely false conclusions. Unfortunately, these conclusions were accepted by gullible readers and widely reported in popular periodicals and some educational psychology textbooks.

The authors trust that the experience of the introductory course in educational research will help students and educators to read research reports more carefully and to apply more rigorous standards of judgment.

SUMMARY

The term *descriptive studies* has been used to classify a number of different types of activity. This chapter points out the distinctions between three major categories: assessment, evaluation, and descriptive research.

Assessment describes the status of a phenomenon at a particular time *without* value judgment, explanation of reasons or underlying causes, or recommendations for action.

Evaluation adds to the description of status the element of value judgment, in terms of effectiveness, desirability, or social utility, and may suggest a course of action. No generalizations are extended beyond the situation evaluated.

Descriptive research is concerned with the analysis of the relationships between nonmanipulated variables and the development of generalizations, extending its conclusions beyond the sample observed.

Assessment types of studies described are surveys, public opinion polls, the *National Assessment of Educational Progress,* the *International Assessment of Educational Achievement,* activity analysis, and trend studies.

Evaluation studies included are school surveys and follow-up studies. The application of evaluation findings to social problem solving is discussed.

Descriptive research studies include document or content analysis, case studies, community studies, ethnographic studies, and *ex post facto* or explanatory observational studies. These methods have been described and examples provided. The hazards of the *post hoc* fallacy have been emphasized.

EXERCISES

1. Why is it sometimes difficult to distinguish between an assessment study, an evaluation study, and a descriptive research project? Illustrate with an example.

2. Public opinion polls base their conclusions on a sample of approximately 1500 respondents. Is this an adequate sample for a nationwide survey?

3. In a 1974 study, the West Virginia State Department of Education reported that counties with the highest per-pupil expenditure were the counties with the highest level of academic achievement, and that this "shows for the first time the clearest possible relationship between student achievement and the amount of money invested in the public schools." Can you suggest several competing hypotheses that might account for high academic achievement?

4. What is the difference between a study and a research project?

5. In what ways does conducting longitudinal studies run the risk of the violation of confidentiality of personal information?

6. How can a study of money and investment trends help you provide for your future financial security?

7. Draw up a proposal for a follow-up study of your high school graduating class of 5 years ago. Indicate what information you believe would be helpful in improving the curriculum of the school.

8. Of what value are the findings of the annual Gallup poll of public attitudes toward education?

9. How could the survey type of study be helpful in arriving at solutions to the crime problem in large cities?

REFERENCES

AHMANN, J. S. (1979). Differential changes in levels of achievement for students in three age groups. *Educational Studies, 10,* 35–45.

AHMANN, J., CRANE, R., SEARLS, D. & LARSON, R. (1975). Science achievement: The trend is down. *Science Teacher, 42*(7), 23–25.

ANDERSON, D. B. & LEVIN, S. B. (1976). Young children's attention to Sesame Street. *Child Development, 47,* 806–811.

BABBIE, E. R. (1973). *Survey Research Methods.* Belmont, CA: Wadsworth.

BRANSCOMBE, A. (1975). Checklist on consumer mathematics. *American Education, 11,* 21–24.

CHARTERS, W. W. & WAPLES, D. (1929). *The Commonwealth teacher training study.* Chicago: University of Chicago Press.

COLEMAN, J. S., CAMPBELL, E. Q., HOBSON, C. J., MCPORTLAND, J., MOOD, A. M., WEINFELD, F. D., & YORK, R. L. (1966). *Equality of educational opportunity.* Washington, D.C.: U.S. Government Printing Office.

COMBS, J. & COOLEY, W. W. (1968). Dropouts: In high school and after school. *American Educational Research Journal, 5,* 343–363.

DILLON, H. J. (1949). *Early school leavers.* New York: National Child Labor Committee.

DRAKE, S. C. & CAYTON, H. R. (1945). *Black metropolis.* New York: Harcourt, Brace, and World.

ELAM, S. M. (1979). *A decade of Gallup polls of attitudes toward education: 1969–1978.* Bloomington, IN: Phi Delta Kappa.

GLASS, G. V. (1968). Educational Piltdown men. *Phi Delta Kappan, 50,* 148–151.

GLASS, G. V. (1978). Integrating findings: The meta-analysis of research. In L. Shulman (Ed.), *Review of research in education, 5,* 351–379.

GLASS, G. V., SMITH, M. L. & BARTON, M. (1979). *Methods of integrative analysis.* Annual report on grant NIE-G-78-0148. Boulder, Colorado: University of Colorado.

HECHINGER, F. M. & HECHINGER, G. (1974). Are schools better in other countries? *American Education, 10,* 6–8.

HOLLINGSHEAD, A. B. (1949). *Elmtown's youth.* New York: John Wiley.

HUSEN, T. (Ed.) (1967). *International study of achievement in mathematics.* New York: John Wiley.

KINSEY, A. C., POMEROY, W. B., & MARTIN, C. E. (1948). *Sexual behavior in the human male.* Philadelphia: W. B. Saunders.

KINSEY, A. C., POMEROY, W. B., MARTIN, C. E., & GEBHARD, P. H. (1953). *Sexual behavior in the human female.* Philadelphia: W. B. Saunders.

LUCAS, R. A. (1970). *Minetown, milltown, railtown: Life in Canadian communities of single industry.* Toronto: University of Toronto Press.

LYND, R. S. & LYND, H. M. (1929). *Middletown.* New York: Harcourt, Brace.

LYND, R. S. & LYND, H. M. (1937). *Middletown in transition.* New York: Harcourt, Brace, and World.

MEAD, M. (1931). *The changing culture of an Indian tribe.* New York: William Morrow.

MEAD, M. (1928). *Coming of age in Samoa.* New York: William Morrow.

MINTON, J. M. (1975). Impact of Sesame Street on reading readiness. *Sociology of Education, 48,* 141–151.

MORRIS, V. C., CROWSON, R., PORTER-GEHRIE, C. & HURWITZ, E. (1984). *Principals in action.* Columbus, OH: Charles Merrill.

MOSTELLER, F. & MOYNIHAN, D. P. (Eds.). (1972). *On equality of educational opportunity.* New York: Random House.

MYRDAL, G. (1944). *An American dilemma.* New York: Harper and Row.

Nation at risk (1983). Washington, D.C.: National Commission on Excellence in Education, U.S. Department of Education.

NEILL, G. (1976). Writing skills drop: 20% can't cope, studies show. *Phi Delta Kappan, 57,* 355–356.

Problems and outlook of small private liberal arts colleges: Report to the Congress of the United States by the Comptroller General. (1978). Washington, D.C.: United States General Accounting Office.

Progress towards the goals of project talent. (1965). Washington, D.C.: U.S. Office of Education.

SHAW, C. R. & McKAY, H. D. (1942). *Juvenile delinquency in urban areas.* Chicago: University of Chicago Press.

SHERMAN, M. & HENRY, T. R. (1933). *Hollow folk.* New York: Thomas Y. Crowell.

TORSTEN, H. (Ed.). (1967). *International study of achievement in mathematics.* New York: John Wiley.

U.S. News and World Report. (1968, Jan. 29), p. 12.

U.S. OFFICE OF EDUCATION. (1965). *Progress toward the goal of Project Talent.* Washington, D.C.: Government Printing Office.

VANDERMYN, G. (1974). Assessing students: political I.Q. *American Education, 10,* 21–25.

WARNER, W. L. & LUNT, P. S. (1941). *Social life in a modern community, Vol. 1.* New Haven, CT: Yale University Press.

WEST, J. (1945). *Plainville, U.S.A.* New York: Columbia University Press.

WITTY, P. (1967). Children of the T.V. era. *Elementary English, 64,* 528–535.

ADDITIONAL READINGS

ANDERSON, C. (1967). The international comparative study of achievement in mathematics. *Comparative Education Review, 11,* 182–196.

BACKSTROM, H. & HURSH, D. (1963). *Survey research.* Evanston, IL: Northwestern University Press.

BURSTEIN, L. (1978). Secondary analysis: An important resource for educational research and evaluation. *Educational Researcher, 7,* 9–12.

CHALL, J. (1967). *Learning to read: The great debate.* New York: McGraw-Hill Book Co.

COLEMAN, J. S. (1975). International assessment for evaluation of schools. *Review of Educational Research, 45,* 355–386.

COLEMAN, J. S. (1975). Racial segregation in the schools: New research with new policy implications. *Phi Delta Kappan, 57,* 75–77.

COLEMAN, J. S. (1975). Social research and advocacy: A response to Young and Bress. *Phi Delta Kappan, 57,* 66–69.

COMBS, J. & COOLEY, W. W. (1968). Dropouts: In high school and after school. *American Educational Research Journal, 5,* 343–363.

COOLEY, W. W. (1978). Explanatory Observational Studies. *Educational Researcher, 7,* 9–15.

COOLEY, W. & LOHNES, P. R. (1976). *Evaluation research in education.* New York: Irvington Publishers.

COPPERMAN, P. (1979). The achievement decline of the 1970s. *Phi Delta Kappan, 60,* 736–739.

ENNIS, H. (1973). On causality. *Educational Researcher, 2,* 4–16.

FLANNIGAN, J. C. (1964). *The American high school student.* Pittsburgh: Project Talent Office.

GLASS, G. V. & WORTHEN, B. R. (1971). Educational evaluation and research: Similarities and differences. *Curriculum Theory Network, 3,* 149–165.

HARRIS, D. B. (1963). *Children's drawings as measures of intellectual maturity.* New York: Harcourt, Brace, & World.

HENDERSON, K. B. & GOERTWITZ, J. E. (1950). *How to conduct a follow-up study.* Illinois Secondary School Curriculum Program Bulletin No. 11, Springfield, IL: Superintendent of Public Instruction.

HESS, R. D. & TORNEY, J. V. (1967). *The development of political attitudes in children.* Chicago: Aldine Publishing Co.

HIRSCHI, T. & SELVIN, H. C. (1967). *Delinquency research: An appraisal of analytical methods.* New York: Free Press.

HYMAN, H. H. (1955). *Survey design and analysis.* Beverly Hills, CA: Glencoe Press.

International Association for the Evaluation of Educational Achievement (1974). Bibliography of publications, 1962–1974. *Comparative Education Review, 18,* 327–329.

JACKSON, G. (1975). Reanalysis of Coleman's recent trend in school integration. *Educational Researcher, 4,* 21–25.

LESSER, S. (1974). *Children learn lessons from Sesame Street.* New York: Random House.

OVERHOLT, G. E. & STALLINGS, E. W. (1977). Ethnographic and experimental hypotheses in educational research. *Educational Researcher, 6,* 12–14.

PIAGET, J. (1971). *Biology and knowledge.* Chicago: University of Chicago Press.

POLSKY, R. M. (1974). *Getting to Sesame Street.* New York: Praeger.

POPHAM, W. J. (1975). *Educational evaluation.* Englewood Cliffs, NJ: Prentice-Hall.

RAPH, J. B., GOLDBERG, M. L., & PASSOW, A. H. (1966). *Bright underachievers: Studies of scholastic underachievement among intellectually superior high school students.* New York: Teachers College Press.

ROGERS, J. M. (1972). A summary of literature on Sesame Street. *Journal of Special Education, 6,* 270–272.

RYANS, D. G. (1966). *Characteristics of teachers: Their description, comparison, and appraisal.* Washington, D.C.: American Council on Education.

ST. JOHN, N. (1975). *School desegregation: Outcomes for children.* New York: John Wiley.

SCOTT, W. R. (1965). Field methods in the study of organizations, in J. G. March (Ed.), *Handbook of organizations.* Chicago: Rand McNally.

STAKE, R. E. (1978). The case method in social inquiry. *Educational Researcher, 7,* 5–8.

WILSON, S. (1977). The use of ethnographic techniques in educational research. *Review of Educational Research, 47,* 245–265.

WORTHEN, B. R. & SANDERS, J. R. (1973). *Educational evaluation: Theory and practice.* Worthington, OH: Charles A. Jones.

Chapter 5

Experimental
and
Quasi-Experimental
Research

Experimental research provides a systematic and logical method for answering the question, "If this is done under carefully controlled conditions, what will happen?" Experimenters manipulate certain stimuli, treatments, or environmental conditions and observe how the condition or behavior of the subject is affected or changed. Their manipulation is deliberate and systematic. They must be aware of other factors that could influence the outcome and remove or control them so that they can establish a logical association between manipulated factors and observed effects.

Experimentation provides a method of hypothesis testing. After experimenters define a problem, they propose a tentative answer, or hypothesis. They test the hypothesis and confirm or disconfirm it in the light of the controlled variable relationship that they have observed. It is important to note that the confirmation or rejection of the hypothesis is stated in terms of probability rather than certainty.

Experimentation is the classic method of the science laboratory, where elements manipulated and effects observed can be controlled. It is the most sophisticated, exacting, and powerful method for discovering and developing an organized body of knowledge.

Although the experimental method finds its greatest utility in the laboratory, it has been effectively applied within nonlaboratory settings such as the classroom, where significant factors or variables can be controlled to some degree. The immediate purpose of experimentation is to predict events in the experimental setting. The ultimate purpose is to generalize the variable relationships so that they may be applied outside the laboratory to a wider population of interest.

EARLY EXPERIMENTATION

The earliest assumptions of experimental research were based upon what was known as the *law of the single variable*. John Stuart Mill defined this principle. He stated five rules or canons that he believed would include all types of logical procedure required to establish order among controlled events.

One of his canons, known as the *method of difference*, states:

If an instance in which the phenomenon under investigation occurs, and an instance in which it does not occur have every circumstance in common save one, that one occurring only in the former, the circumstance in which alone the two instances differ is the effect, or the cause, or an indispensable part of the cause of the phenomenon. (Mill, 1873, p. 222)

In simpler language, if two situations are alike in every respect, and one element is added to one but not the other, any difference that develops is the effect of the added element; or, if two situations are alike in every respect, and one element is removed from one but not from the other, any difference that develops may be attributed to the subtracted element.

The law of the single variable provided the basis for much early laboratory experimentation. In 1962, Robert Boyle, an Irish physicist, used this method in arriving at a principle upon which he formulated his law of gases: When temperature is held constant, the volume of an ideal gas is inversely proportional to the pressure exerted upon it. In other words, when pressure is raised, volume decreases; when pressure is lowered, volume increases. In Boyle's Law, *pressure* is the single variable.

$$\frac{V_1}{V_2} = \frac{P_2}{P_1}$$

A little more than a century later, Jacques A. C. Charles, a French physicist, discovered a companion principle, now known as Charles' Law. He observed that when the pressure was held constant, the volume of an ideal gas was directly proportional to the temperature. When temperature is raised, volume increases; when temperature is lowered, volume decreases. In Charles' Law, *temperature* is the single variable.

$$\frac{V_1}{V_2} = \frac{T_1}{T_2}$$

Although the concept of the single variable proved useful in some areas of the physical sciences, it failed to provide a sound approach to experimentation in the behavioral sciences. Despite its appealing simplicity and apparent logic, it did not provide an adequate method for studying complex problems. It assumed a highly artificial and restricted relationship between single variables. Rarely, if ever, are human events the result of single causes. They are usually the result of the interaction of many variables, and an attempt to limit variables so that one can be isolated and observed proves impossible.

The contributions of R. A. Fisher, first applied in agricultural experimentation, have provided a much more effective way of conducting realistic experimentation in the behavioral sciences. His concept of achieving pre-experimental equating of conditions through random selection of subjects and random assignment of treatments, and his concepts of analysis of variance and analysis of covariance, made possible the study of complex interactions through factorial designs, in which the influence of more than one independent variable upon more than one dependent variable could be observed. Current uses of this type of design will be discussed more fully later in this chapter.

EXPERIMENTAL AND CONTROL GROUPS

An experiment involves the comparison of the effects of a particular treatment with that of a different treatment or of no treatment. In a simple conventional experiment, reference is usually made to an *experimental group* and to a *control group*.

These groups are equated as nearly as possible. The experimental group is exposed to the influence of the factor under consideration; the control group is not. Observations are then made to determine what difference appears or what change or modification occurs in the experimental as contrasted with the control group.

Sometimes it is also necessary to control for the effect of actually participating in an experiment. Medical researchers have long recognized that patients who receive any medication, regardless of its real efficacy, tend to feel better or perform more effectively. In medical experiments, a harmless or inert substitute is administered to the control group to offset the psychological effect of medication. These substitutes, or *placebos*, are indistinguishable from the real medication under investigation, and neither experimental nor control subjects know whether they are receiving the medication or the placebo. The effectiveness of the true medication is the difference between the effect of the medication and that of the placebo.

What seems to be a similar psychological effect was recognized in a series of experiments at the Hawthorne Plant of the Western Electric Company and originally published in 1933 (Mayo, 1960). The studies concerned the relationships between certain working conditions and worker output efficiency. Illumination was one of these manipulated experimental variables. The researchers found that as light intensity was increased, worker output increased. After a certain peak was apparently reached, it was decided to see what effect the reduction of intensity of illumination would have. To the surprise of the researchers, as intensity was decreased by stages, output continued to increase. The researchers concluded that the attention given the workers and their awareness of participation in our experiment apparently were important motivating factors. From these studies the term *Hawthorne Effect* was introduced into the psychological literature.

It has been commonly believed that this reactive effect of knowledge of participation in an experiment, the Hawthorne Effect, is similar to the medical placebo effect. Researchers have frequently devised non-medical placebos to counteract this potential effect. One such device, used in connection with experiments involving the comparison of traditional teaching materials with new experimental materials, is to reprint the traditional, or control materials and label both these and the new, experimental materials: "Experimental Method."

A group receiving a placebo is usually known as a placebo control group to distinguish it from the more common control group that receives nothing additional as a result of the study.

Even when the subjects of a study are unlikely to know or care that they are participants in an experiment, it may be necessary to utilize a placebo control group. Research with severely and profoundly retarded children may result in increased time spent with the experimental group children over the control group children unless a placebo is introduced. An example is a study in which Kahn (1978) investigated the effect of a cognitive training program. Rather than have the usual control group, this study made sure that the nonexperimental group children received as much individual instruction as the experimental group children, albeit in areas other than the experimental treatment. Thus, this study used a placebo control group in order to assure that group differences were a result of the training procedure rather than additional attention.

Experiments are not always characterized by a treatment-nontreatment comparison. Varying types, amounts, or degrees of the experimental factor may be applied to a number of groups. For example, an experiment to test the effectiveness of a particular medication in reducing body temperature might involve administering a massive dosage to one group, a normal dosage to a second, and a minimal dosage to a third. Because all the groups receive medication, there is no control group in the limited sense of the term, but control of the experimental factors and observation of their effects are essential elements.

VARIABLES

Independent and Dependent Variables

Variables are the conditions or characteristics that the experimenter manipulates, controls, or observes. The *independent* variables are the conditions or characteristics that the experimenter manipulates or controls in his or her attempt to ascertain their relationship to observed phenomena. The *dependent* variables are the conditions or characteristics that appear, disappear, or change as the experimenter introduces, removes, or changes independent variables.

In educational research an independent variable may be a particular teaching method, a type of teaching material, a reward, or a period of exposure to a particular condition, or an attribute such as sex or level of intelligence. The dependent variable may be a test score, the number of errors, or measured speed in performing a task. Thus, the dependent variables are the measured changes in pupil performance attributable to the influence of the independent variables.

There are two types of independent variables: *treatment* and *organismic or attribute* variables. Treatment variables are those factors that the experimenter manipulates and to which he or she assigns subjects. Attribute variables are those characteristics that cannot be altered by the experimenter. Such independent variables as age, sex, race, and intelligence level have already been determined, but the experimenter can decide to include them or remove them as variables to be studied. The question of whether 8-year-old girls show greater reading achievement than 8-year-old boys is an example of the use of an organismic variable, sex. The teaching procedure is the same for both groups so there is no treatment independent variable.

Confounding Variables

Confounding variables are those aspects of a study or sample that might influence the dependent variable (outcome measure) and whose effect may be confused with the effects of the independent variable. Confounding variables are of two types: intervening and extraneous variables.

Intervening variables. In many types of behavioral research the relationship between the independent and dependent variables is not a simple one of stimulus to response. Certain variables which cannot be controlled or measured directly may have an important effect upon the outcome. These modifying variables intervene between the cause and the effect.

In a classroom language experiment a researcher is interested in determining the effect of immediate reinforcement upon learning the parts of speech. He or she suspects that certain factors or variables may influence the relationship, even though they cannot be observed directly. Anxiety, fatigue, and motivation, for example, may be *intervening* variables and are difficult to define in operational terms. These intervening variables cannot be ignored, however, and must be controlled as much as is feasible through the use of appropriate designs.

Extraneous variables. *Extraneous* variables are those uncontrolled variables (i.e., variables not manipulated by the experimenter) that *may* have a significant influence upon the results of a study. Many research conclusions are questionable because of the influence of these extraneous variables.

In a widely publicized study, the effectiveness of three methods of social studies teaching was compared. Intact classes were used, and the researchers were unable to randomize or control such variables as teacher competence or enthusiasm, or the age, socioeconomic level, or academic ability of the student subjects. The criterion of effectiveness was achievement, measured by scores on standardized tests. It would seem clear that the many extraneous variables precluded valid conclusions about the relative effectiveness of the independent variables, which were teaching methods. It should be noted that in order for an extraneous variable to confound the results of a study, it must be correlated strongly enough with both the independent and dependent variables that its influence can be mistaken for that of the independent variable.

Although it is impossible to eliminate all extraneous variables, particularly in classroom research, sound experimental design enables the researcher to largely neutralize their influence.

CONTROLLING EXTRANEOUS VARIABLES

Variables that are of interest to the researcher can be controlled by building them into the study as independent variables. For instance, a researcher comparing two different reading programs may wish to control for the potentially confounding extraneous variable sex by making it an independent attribute variable and, thereby, investigating the effect of sex on the two different reading programs.

Variables that are not of direct interest to the researcher may be removed or their influence minimized by several methods, which are discussed in the following sections.

Removing the variable. Variables may be controlled by eliminating them completely. Observer distraction may be removed by separating the observer from both experimental and control groups by a one-way glass partition. Some variables between subjects may be eliminated by selecting cases with uniform characteristics. Using only female subjects removes sex as a variable but thereby reduces the generalization from the study to only females.

Randomization. Randomization involves pure chance selection and assignment of subjects to experimental and control groups for a limited supply of available subjects. Random selection was discussed in Chapter 1. Here we are referring to random assignment, the method by which everyone already selected for the sample has an equal chance of being assigned to the various treatment conditions (e.g., experimental and control).

If two groups are involved, randomization could be achieved by tossing a coin, assigning a subject to one group if heads appeared, to the other if the toss were tails. When more than two groups are involved, dice or a table of random numbers could be used.

Randomization provides the most effective method of eliminating systematic bias and of minimizing the effect of extraneous variables. The principle is based upon the assumption that through random assignment, differences between groups result only from the operation of probability or chance. These differences are known as *sampling error* or *error variance,* and their magnitude can be established by the researcher.

In an experiment, differences in the dependent variables that may be attributed to the effect of the independent variables are known as *experimental variance.* The significance of an experiment may be tested by comparing experimental variance with error variance. If at the conclusion of the experiment the differences between experimental and control groups are too great to attribute to error variance, it may be assumed that these differences are attributable to experimental variance. This process is described in detail in Chapter 8.

Matching cases. When randomization is not feasible (e.g., there are too few subjects), selecting pairs or sets of individuals with identical or nearly identical characteristics and assigning one of them to the experimental group and the other to the control group provides another method of control. This method is limited by the difficulty of matching on more than one variable. It is also likely that some individuals will be excluded from the experiment if a matching subject is not available. Matching is not considered satisfactory unless the members of the pairs or sets are then randomly assigned to the treatment groups, a method known as matched randomization.

Balancing cases, or group matching. Balancing cases consists of assigning subjects to experimental and control groups in such a way that the means and the variances of the groups are as nearly equal as possible. Because identical balancing of groups is impossible, the researcher must decide how much departure from equality can be tolerated without loss of satisfactory control. This method also presents a similar difficulty noted in the matching method; namely, the difficulty of equating groups on the basis of more than one characteristic or variable.

Analysis of covariance. This method permits the experimenter to eliminate initial differences on several variables between the experimental and control groups by statistical methods. The use of pretest mean scores as covariants is considered preferable to the conventional matching of groups. Analysis of covariance is a rather complicated statistical procedure, beyond the scope of this elementary treatment. For a complete discussion, readers may wish to consult Glass and Hopkins (1984), Hays (1981), Kerlinger (1973), Kirk (1972), or Winer (1971).

OPERATIONAL DEFINITIONS OF VARIABLES

Such variables as giftedness, academic achievement, and creativity are conceptualizations that are defined in dictionary terms. But because they cannot be observed directly, they are vague and ambiguous and provide a poor basis for identifying variables. Much more precise and unambiguous definitions of variables can be stated in operational form, which stipulates the operation by which they can be observed and measured. Giftedness could be operationally defined as a score two or more standard deviations above the mean on the *Wechsler Adult Intelligence Scale,* academic achievement as a score on the 1973 edition of the *Stanford Achievement Test,* or creativity as a score on the *Torrance Tests of Creative Thinking.* When an operational definition is used, there is no doubt about what the researcher means.

To be useful, however, operational definitions must be based upon a theory that is generally recognized as valid. Operational terms do not necessarily prove to be useful in describing variables, for they could conceivably be based upon irrelevant behavior. Defining degree of self-esteem in terms of the number of times an individual smiles per minute would not be a useful or realistic definition, even though such behavior could easily be observed and recorded.

EXPERIMENTAL VALIDITY

To make a significant contribution to the development of knowledge, an experiment must be valid. Campbell and Stanley (1966) described two types of experimental validity, *internal validity* and *external validity.* Cook and Campbell (1979) further divided experimental validity, adding two other types, *statistical validity* and *construct validity.* For purposes of this introductory treatment of the issue, we will confine our discussion to the two types of experimental validity described by Campbell and Stanley.

Internal validity.   An experiment has internal validity to the extent that the factors that have been manipulated (independent variables) actually have a genuine effect on the observed consequences (dependent variables) in the experimental setting.

External validity. The researcher would achieve little of practical value if these observed variable relationships were valid only in the experimental setting and only for those participating. External validity is the extent to which the variable relationships can be generalized to other settings, other treatment variables, other measurement variables, and other populations.

Experimental validity is an ideal to aspire to, for it is unlikely that it can ever be completely achieved. Internal validity is very difficult to achieve in the nonlaboratory setting of the behavioral experiment where there are so many extraneous variables to attempt to control. When experimental controls are tightened to achieve internal validity, the more artificial, less realistic situation may prevail, reducing the external validity or generalizability of the experiment. Some compromise is inevitable so that a reasonable balance may be established between control and generalizability—between internal and external validity.

Threats to Internal Experimental Validity

In educational experiments, or in any behavioral experiments, a number of extraneous variables are present in the situation or are generated by the experimental design and procedures. These variables influence the results of the experiment in ways that are difficult to evaluate. In a sense, they introduce rival hypotheses that could account for experimental change not attributable to the experimental variables under consideration. Although these extraneous variables usually cannot be completely eliminated, many of them can be identified. It is important that behavioral researchers anticipate them and take all possible precautions to minimize their influence through sound experiment design and execution.

A number of factors jeopardize the power of the experimenter to evaluate the effects of independent variables unambiguously. Campbell and Stanley (1966) have discussed these factors in their excellent definitive treatment. They include the following:

Maturation. Subjects change in many ways over a period of time, and these changes may be confused with the effect of the independent variables under consideration. Between initial and subsequent observations subjects may become tired, bored, wiser, or influenced by the incidental learnings or experiences that they encounter through normal maturation.

History. Specific external events occurring between the first and second measurements and beyond the control of the researcher may have a stimulating or disturbing effect upon the performance of subjects. The effect of a fire drill, the emotional tirade of a teacher, a pep session, the anxiety produced by a pending examination, or a catastrophic event in the community may significantly affect the test performance of a group of students.

In some experiments these external events might have a similar effect upon both experimental and control subjects, but because they are specific events, they may affect one group but not the other. The effect of these uncontrolled external events is one of the hazards inherent in experiments carried on outside the laboratory. In laboratory experiments these extraneous variables can be controlled more effectively.

Testing.   The process of pretesting at the beginning of an experiment may produce a change in subjects. Pretesting may produce a practice effect that may make subjects more proficient in subsequent test performance. Testing presents a threat to internal validity that is common to pretest-posttest experiments.

Unstable instrumentation.   Unreliable instruments or techniques used to describe and measure aspects of behavior are threats to the validity of an experiment. If tests used as instruments of observation are not accurate or consistent, a serious element of error is introduced. If human observers are used to describe behavior changes in subjects, changes in observers or in their standards due to fatigue, increased insight or skill, or changes in criteria of judgment over a period of time are likely to introduce error.

Statistical regression.   Statistical regression, also known as *regression to the mean,* is a phenomenon that sometimes operates when subjects are selected on the basis of extremely high or extremely low pretest scores and when the measurement device is not totally reliable, which is common. Subjects who score very high, near the ceiling, on a pretest, will most likely score lower (nearer the mean) on a subsequent testing. Subjects who score very low, near the floor, on a pretest will most likely score higher (nearer the mean) on a subsequent testing. The reader should be aware that this phenomenon only occurs when subjects are selected as a group because of their extreme scores and that the regression we are referring to is for the group as a whole, not all individuals. Posttest scores for individuals may go in the opposite direction expected by this phenomenon for the group.

Selection bias.   Selection bias is represented by the nonequivalence of experimental and control groups, and its most effective deterrent is the random assignment of subjects to treatments. Selection bias is likely when, upon invitation, volunteers are used as members of an experimental group. Although they may appear to be equated to the nonvolunteers, their characteristics of higher motivation may introduce a bias that would invalidate reasonable comparison. Selection bias may be introduced when intact classes are used as experimental and control groups: Because of scheduling arrangements, an English class meeting during the fourth period may consist of particularly able students who are scheduled at that period because they are also enrolled in an advanced mathematics class.

Interaction of selection and maturation. This type of threat to the internal validity of a study is not the same as selection bias. The interaction of selection and maturation may occur wherever the subjects can select which treatment (e.g., which instructional method) they will receive. Even though the groups may be equivalent on the pretest and other cognitive measures, the reasons why some people choose one treatment over another may be related to the outcome measure (dependent variable). Thus, if more motivated students chose method A for learning calculus over method B because A is harder and requires greater academic motivation, that differential motivation might be confused for the effects of the experimental variable.

Experimental mortality. Mortality, or loss of subjects, particularly likely in a long-term experiment, introduces a potentially confounding element. Even though experimental and control groups are randomly assigned, the survivors might represent groups that are quite different from the unbiased groups that began the experiment. Those who survive a period of experimentation are likely to be healthier, more able, or more highly motivated than those who are absent frequently or who drop out of school and do not remain for the duration of the experiment. The major concern here is whether the groups experienced different loss rates or reasons for dropouts that might confound the results.

Experimenter bias. This is a type of bias introduced when the researcher has some previous knowledge about the subjects involved in an experiment. This knowledge of subject status may cause the researcher to convey some clue that affects the subject's reaction or may affect the objectivity of his or her judgment.

In medical research it is common practice to conceal from the subject the knowledge of who is receiving the placebo and who the experimental medication. This is known as a *blind*. Having someone other than the experimenter administer the treatments and record which subjects are receiving the medication and which the placebo provides an additional safeguard. This practice, known as a *double blind*, helps to minimize contamination.

Beginners in educational research have been known to contaminate a study by classifying student performance when they know the nature of the variable to be correlated with that performance. In a simple *ex post facto* study a student proposed to determine the relationship between academic achievement and citizenship grades in her class. Since she proposed to assign the citizenship grades herself, it would seem apparent that an element of contamination would result. Her knowledge of the student's previous academic achievement would tend to precondition her judgment in assigning citizenship grades.

In educational studies of this type, researchers would minimize contamination if outside observers rated the subjects without any knowledge of their academic status.

Threats to External Experimental Validity

Laboratory research has the virtue of permitting the experimenter to carefully avoid threats to internal validity. However, the artificial nature of such a setting greatly reduces the generalizability of the findings from such research. Since educational researchers are primarily concerned with the practical uses of their findings, they frequently conduct their studies in real classroom situations. While these real life settings present opportunities for greater generalization, they do not automatically result in externally valid research. Campbell and Stanley (1966) also discussed the factors that may lead to reduced generalizability of research to other settings, persons, variables, and measurement instruments. The factors they discussed include the following:

Interference of prior treatment. In some types of experiments the effect of one treatment may carry over to subsequent treatments. In an educational experiment, learning produced by the first treatment is not completely erased and its influence may accrue to the advantage of the second treatment. This is one of the major limitations of the single-group, equated-materials experimental design in which the same subjects serve as members of both control and experimental groups.

The artificiality of the experimental setting. In an effort to control extraneous variables the researcher imposes careful controls which may introduce a sterile or artificial atmosphere that is not at all like the real-life situation about which generalizations are desired. The reactive effect of the experimental process is a constant threat.

Interaction effect of testing. The use of a pretest at the beginning of a study may sensitize individuals by making them more aware of concealed purposes of the researcher and may serve as a stimulus to change. This is a different potential problem than that of testing, discussed earlier as a threat to internal validity.

Interaction of selection and treatment. Researchers are rarely, if ever, able to randomly select samples from the wide population of interest or randomly assign to groups; consequently, generalization from samples to populations is hazardous. Samples used in most classroom experiments are usually composed of intact groups, not randomly selected individuals. They are based upon an accepted invitation to participate. Some school officials agree to participate; others refuse. One cannot assume that samples taken from cooperating schools are necessarily representative of the target population. Such schools are usually characterized by faculties that have high morale, less insecurity, greater willingness to try a new approach, and a greater desire to improve their performance.

The extent of treatment verification. Due to the potential threat of experimenter bias, most researchers have research assistants, or others who are not directly involved in the formulation of the research hypotheses, deliver the treatment. This leads to a potential threat to external validity. Was the treatment administered as intended and described by the researcher? The researcher must have a verification procedure (e.g., direct observation, videotape) to make sure that the treatment was properly administered.

After reading about these threats to experimental validity, the beginner is probably ready to conclude that behavioral research is too hazardous to attempt. Particularly outside of the laboratory, ideal experimental conditions and controls are never likely to prevail. However, an understanding of these threats is important so that the researcher can make every effort to remove or minimize their influence. If one were to wait for a research setting free from all threats, no research would ever be carried on. Knowing the limitations and doing the best that he or she can under the circumstances, the researcher may conduct experiments, reach valid conclusions, provide answers to important questions, and solve significant problems.

EXPERIMENTAL DESIGN

Experimental design is the blueprint of the procedures that enable the researcher to test hypotheses by reaching valid conclusions about relationships between independent and dependent variables. Selection of a particular design is based upon the purposes of the experiment, the type of variables to be manipulated, and the conditions or limiting factors under which it is conducted. The design deals with such practical problems as how subjects are to be assigned to experimental and control groups, the way variables are to be manipulated and controlled, the way extraneous variables are to be controlled, how observations are to be made, and the type of statistical analysis to be employed in interpreting data relationships.

The adequacy of experimental designs is judged by the degree to which they eliminate or minimize threats to experimental validity. Three categories are presented here:

1. *Pre-experimental design*—the least effective, for it provides either no control group or no way of equating the groups that are used.
2. *True experimental design*—employs randomization to provide for control of the equivalence of groups and exposure to treatment.
3. *Quasi-experimental design*—provides a less satisfactory degree of control, used only when randomization is not feasible.

A complete discussion of experimental design would be too lengthy and complex for this introductory treatment. Therefore, only a relatively few designs will be described. Readers may wish to refer to Campbell and Stanley's (1966) and Cook and Campbell's (1979) excellent treatments of the subject, in which many more designs are described.

In discussing experimental designs, we have followed Campbell and Stanley's symbol system.

R   random assignment of subjects to groups or treatments
X   exposure of a group to an experimental (treatment) variable
C   exposure of a group to the control or placebo condition
O   observation or test administered

Pre-Experimental Designs

The *least adequate* of designs is characterized by: (1) the lack of a control group, or (2) a failure to provide for the equivalence of a control group.

The one-shot case study

$$X \quad O$$

Carefully studied results of a treatment are compared with a general expectation of what would have happened if the treatment had not been applied. This design provides the weakest basis for generalization.

Mr. Jones used a 25-minute film on racial integration in his junior high school history class. In a test administered after the showing of the film, the mean score was 86 (a high score indicated a favorable attitude toward acceptance of all racial groups). Mr. Jones believes that the mean score was higher than it would have been had the film not been viewed and, as he recalls, higher than the mean score of a test that he had administered to a similar class several years before. He concludes that the film has been effective in reducing racial prejudice.

However, Mr. Jones has come to this conclusion on the basis of inadequate data. The reader has no way of knowing if a change has occurred due to the lack of a pretest, or if a similar group who had not seen the film (a control group) would have scored differently than the group viewing the film. This design is the poorest available and should not be used.

The one-group, pretest-posttest design

$$O_1 \quad X \quad O_2$$

$$O_1 = \text{pretest} \qquad O_2 = \text{posttest}$$

This design provides some improvement over the first, for the effects of the treatment are judged by the difference between the pretest and the posttest scores. No comparison with a control group is provided.

In the same setting, Mr. Jones administered a pretest before showing the film and a posttest after the viewing. He computed the mean difference between the pretest and the posttest scores and found that the mean had increased from 52 to 80, a mean gain of 28 score points. He also apparently detected some temporary improvement in attitude toward racial integration. He concludes that there has been a significant improvement in attitude as a result of viewing the film. But what about the sensitizing effect of the pretest items that may have made the students aware of issues that they had not even thought of before? What would the gain have been if the pretest and the posttest had been administered to another class that had not viewed the film? Threats to the internal validity that are not controlled include history, maturation, testing, etc. External validity is also poor.

The static-group comparison design

$$X \quad O$$

$$C \quad O$$

This design compares the status of a group that has received an experimental treatment with one that has not. There is no provision for establishing the equivalence of the experimental and control groups, a very serious limitation.

A beginning researcher administered the 25-minute racial integration film to a group of elementary teachers in one school. He then administered the attitude scale and computed the mean score. At another elementary school he administered the attitude scale to teachers who had not viewed the film. A comparison of mean scores shows that the teachers who had viewed the film had a higher mean score than those who had not. He concluded that the film was an effective device in reducing racial prejudice.

What evidence did he have that the initial attitudes of groups were equivalent? Without some evidence of equivalence of the control and experimental groups, attributing the difference to the experimental variable is unwarranted.

True Experimental Designs

In a true experiment the equivalence of the experimental and control groups is provided by random assignment of subjects to experimental and control treatments. Although it is difficult to arrange a true experimental design, particularly in school classroom research, it is the strongest type of design and should be used whenever possible. Three experimental designs are discussed in the following sections.

The posttest-only, equivalent-groups design

$$R \quad X \quad O_1$$
$$R \quad C \quad O_2$$

This design is one of the most effective in minimizing the threats to experimental validity. It differs from the static group comparison design in that experimental and control groups are equated by random assignment. At the conclusion of the experimental period the difference between the mean test scores of the experimental and control groups are subjected to a test of statistical significance, a t test, or an analysis of variance. The assumption is that the means of randomly assigned experimental and control groups from the same population will differ only to the extent that random sample means from the same population will differ as a result of sampling error. If the difference between the means is too great to attribute to sampling error, the difference may be attributed to the treatment variable effect.

Using a table of random numbers, the researcher selects 80 students from a school population of 450 sophomores. The 80 students are randomly assigned to experimental and control treatments, using 40 as the experimental group and 40 as the control group. The experimental group is taught the concepts of congruence of triangles by an experimental procedure method X, and the control group is taught the same set of concepts by the usual method, method C. All factors of time of day, treatment length in time, and other factors are equated. At the end of a 3-week period the experimental and control groups are administered a test, and the difference between mean scores is subjected to a test of statistical significance. The difference between mean scores is found to favor the experimental group, but not by an amount that is statistically significant. The researcher rightly concludes that the superiority of the X group could well have been the result of sampling error and that there was no evidence of the superiority of the X method.

The pretest-posttest equivalent-groups design

$$R \quad O_1 \quad X \quad O_2 \qquad X \text{ gain} = O_2 - O_1 \qquad O_1 \quad O_3 \text{—pretests}$$

$$R \quad O_3 \quad C \quad O_4 \qquad C \text{ gain} = O_4 - O_3 \qquad O_2 \quad O_4 \text{—posttests}$$

This design is similar to the previously described design, except that pretests are administered before the application of the experimental and control treatments and posttests at the end of the treatment period. Gain scores may be compared and subjected to a test of the significance of the difference between means. Pretest scores can also be used in analysis of covariance to statistically control for any differences between the groups at the beginning of the study. This is a strong design, but there may be a possibility of the influence of the effect of testing and the interaction with the experimental variable.

Watanabe, Hare, and Lomax (1984) have reported on a study that included a pretest-posttest equivalent groups design. This study compared a procedure for teaching eighth-grade students to be better able to predict the content of newspaper stories from their headlines than a control group of eighth-grade students. A pilot study, reported in their article, indicated that even good middle-school readers have difficulty predicting the content of news stories from the headlines, but that college students have no trouble with this task. Because the eighth-graders they surveyed reported reading primarily comics, movie, and sport sections (which might explain their poor prediction of content from headlines) and because most teachers would prefer that their students read more of the newspaper, the authors felt that it would be useful to determine if a training program could teach eighth-graders how to better understand headlines.

Watanabe et al. randomly assigned 46 eighth-graders to either headline reading instruction (experimental group) or regular reading instruction (control group). All 46 students were asked to read 20 headlines and predict story content prior to, and after, a 3-week period of instruction. The authors scored each attempt to predict story content on a scale of 0 to 4, with 0 indicating that the student's response explained nothing and 4 indicating an "on-target potential prediction" (pp. 439–440). Thus each student could receive a score from 0 to 80 on each of the testings.

At the end of the 3 weeks of instruction, the authors compared the two groups using analysis of covariance (ANCOVA) and found that the experimental group was better able to predict story content from headlines after training than the control group. ANCOVA was used because even with random assignment the groups were not exactly equal. ANCOVA permitted the authors to statistically control for differences on the pretest so that posttest differences would not be due to initial differences prior to training.

The Solomon four-group design

$$R \quad O_1 \quad X \quad O_2$$
$$R \quad O_3 \quad C \quad O_4$$
$$R \qquad\;\; X \quad O_5$$
$$R \qquad\;\; C \quad O_6$$

In this design:

1. Subjects are randomly assigned to four groups.
2. Two groups receive the experimental treatment (X).
3. One experimental group receives a pretest (O_1).
4. Two groups (control) do not receive treatment (C).
5. One control group receives a pretest (O_3).
6. All four groups receive posttests $(O_2\ O_4\ O_5\ O_6)$.

The design is really a combination of the two group designs previously described, the posttest only and the pretest-posttest. It is possible to evaluate the effects of testing, history, and maturation. Analysis of variance is used to compare the four posttest scores, analysis of covariance to compare gains in O_2 and O_4.

Because this design provides for two simultaneous experiments, the advantages of a replication are incorporated. A major difficulty is finding enough subjects to assign randomly to four equivalent groups.

Quasi-Experimental Designs

These designs provide control of when and to whom the measurement is applied, but *because random assignment to experimental and control treatments has not been applied,* the equivalence of the groups is not assured. Of the many quasi-experimental designs, only five are described. See Cook and Campbell (1979) for a comprehensive review of quasi-experimental designs.

The pretest-posttest nonequivalent-groups design

$$O_1 \quad X \quad O_2 \qquad O_1 \quad O_3 = \text{pretests}$$

$$O_3 \quad C \quad O_4 \qquad O_2 \quad O_4 = \text{posttests}$$

This design is often used in classroom experiments when experimental and control groups are such naturally assembled groups as intact classes, which may be similar. The difference between the mean of the O_1 and O_2 scores and the difference between the mean of the O_3 and O_4 scores (mean gain scores) are tested for statistical significance. Analysis of covariance may also be used. Because this design may be the only feasible one, the comparison is justifiable, but the results should be interpreted cautiously.

Two first-grade classes in a school were selected for an experiment. One group was taught by the initial teaching alphabet approach to reading, and the other was taught by the traditional alphabet approach. Prior to the introduction of the two reading methods and again at the end of the school year, both groups were administered a standardized reading test, and the mean scores of the two groups were compared. The i/t/a group showed a significant superiority in test scores over the conventional alphabet group. However, without some evidence of the equivalence of the groups in intelligence, maturity, readiness, and other factors at the beginning of the experimental period, conclusions should be cautiously interpreted.

The Follow Through Planned Variation Study.

An interesting example of the pretest-posttest nonequivalent groups design was the *Follow Through Planned Variation Study* (Abt Associates, 1977), conceived in the late 1960s and initiated and funded by the United States Office of Education. The purpose of the program was to implement and evaluate a variety of compensatory programs, extending the services of Project Head Start for disadvantaged children into the primary grades. Head Start was a large scale enterprise, including many innovative instructional models and involving the expenditure of more than a half billion dollars. The program extended over a period of more than 9 years, with more than 79,000 first-, second-, and third-grade children participating. Of the twenty different instructional models and 170 projects, 17 models and 70 projects were selected for evaluation. Approximately 2 percent of the total number of children were included in the evaluation.

Participation by school districts was voluntary, with each district selecting the particular model that it wished to implement and helping to choose the groups that were to be used as controls. Treatments were not randomly assigned nor control groups randomly selected.

The unit of analysis was pupil mean gain for groups K–3 and 1–3 growth scores, statistically compared by instructional model and by project, using variants of linear regression and analysis of covariance. Outcome measures were derived from gain scores on the following measuring instruments:

1. *The Metropolitan Achievement Test Battery* covering such basic skills as reading comprehension, spelling, word usage and analysis, and mathematical computation, concepts, and problem solving.
2. *The Raven's Coloured Matrices Test,* a nonverbal test of problem-solving ability, requiring the manipulation of geometric patterns, essentially a measure of intelligence rather than a measure of learning outcomes.
3. *The Coopersmith Self-Image Inventory,* a measure of self-esteem, but questioned on the grounds that it required a maturity of judgment beyond the competence of primary age children.
4. *The Intellectual Achievement Responsibility Scale* which attempts to assess the child's experience of success or failure, indicating the degree to which the child attributes success to internal or external causes. This instrument was also judged to require insights beyond the maturity level of small children.

There have been many analyses and evaluations of the program by official and independent agencies funded by the United States Office of Education and by private philanthropic foundations. Among the evaluating agencies were the Office of Education; Abt Associates, Inc.; The Stanford Research Institute; The Huron Institute; and The Center for Research and Curriculum Evaluation of the University of Illinois.

It is unlikely that any large scale study has been scrutinized so extensively concerning research design, procedures employed, and interpretation of the data. There have been critiques of the evaluations and critiques of the critiques, with sharp disagreement on most aspects of the study (Anderson, St. Pierre, Propere, and Stebbins, 1978; House, Glass, McLean, and Walker, 1978; Wisler, Burns, and Iwamoto, 1978).

However, the consensus is that the findings were disappointing, because most of the experimental effects were negligible. Only a few of the treatment effects produced as much as a one quarter standard deviation change. (This concept is discussed in Chapter 7.) Of those that met this criterion, two instructional models with at least one positive effect were structured approaches. Three models with at least one negative effect were unstructured approaches. Few of either cognitive, structured approaches or child-centered, non-structured approaches yielded significant effects.

Much of the disagreement centered around the reasons why the study was ineffective. Several explanations have been suggested.

1. The research was deficient in design, implementation, statistical analysis, and interpretation. Because experimental treatments were not randomly selected and control groups were not randomly assigned, mismatching resulted and comparisons were really made between different populations.

2. There was great intersite difference in effectiveness within a given instructional model. Most of the within-model differences were greater than the between-models difference. There may have been serious deficiencies in the competence of those who implemented the innovative procedures or in the actual method implemented, even though the teachers and their teacher aides were specially trained and their activities monitored by the project sponsors.

3. The measuring instruments may have been incompatible with the goals of the project because of inadequate identification and definition of appropriate outcome variables. The more effective instruments seemed to focus on basic skills or traditional educational goals rather than on goals ordinarily associated with nonstructured approaches to education. Some measured intellectual status rather than achievable learning goals. Others appeared to require a maturity of response too complex for primary age children.

Not all reactions to the study were negative. Hodges, a member of the Follow Through Task Force, lists a number of reasons for viewing the program as significant and worthwhile. "Just because Follow Through has not proved to be an easy, workable, inexpensive solution for all the educational problems of poor children does not mean it should be dismissed as just another failure in compensatory education" (Hodges, 1978, p. 191).

In behavioral research, the random selection and assignment of subjects to experimental and control groups may be impracticable. Because of administrative difficulties in arranging school experiments, it may be necessary to use the same group as both the experimental and control group. These designs have two apparently attractive features. They can be carried on with one intact group without a noticeable reorganization of the classroom schedule. The changes in procedures and testing can be concealed within ordinary classroom routines. Artificiality can be minimized, for the procedures can be introduced without the subjects' awareness of participation in an experiment.

The time-series design. At periodic intervals, observations (measurement) are applied to an individual (N of 1 study) or group of individuals. An experimental variable (X) is introduced and its effect may be judged by the change or gain in the measurement immediately following its introduction.

In the time-series experimental design, a measured change or gain after the introduction of the experimental variable in observation 5 would serve as an indication of the influence of the treatment. This design is particularly sensitive to the failure to control the extraneous variable, history, for it is possible that some distracting, simultaneous event at the time of testing would provide a rival hypothesis for the change.

$$O_1 \quad O_2 \quad O_3 \quad O_4 \quad X \quad O_5 \quad O_6 \quad O_7 \quad O_8$$

The diagram showing just one X and several Os does not necessarily represent the relative number of sessions for each. For instance, in studies with just one subject it is common for the first series of observations (known as the baseline) to be of shorter duration than the treatment. In addition, in this type of study, data is still collected during the treatment period and graphed to show rate of change, if any.

Another common aspect of N of 1 studies is a multiple baseline design. In this design, more than one dependent variable is observed even though the treatment is only directed at changing one of them. Because many interventions may have multiple effects, this design permits the experimenter to test for such ancillary changes. For example, a researcher who is using positive reinforcement to increase the performance of a child in arithmetic skills may use a multiple baseline to see if the child's disruptive behavior is reduced as academic performance increases. It is also important with this type of study to do a follow-up some months after the treatment to determine the long term effects.

The equivalent time-samples design. Instead of having equivalent samples of persons, it may be necessary to use one group as the experimental and control group. In this design, the experimental condition (X_1) is present between some observations and not (X_0) between others. This may be diagrammed as shown below, although the number of observations and interventions vary and the alternation of the experimental condition with the control condition would normally be random rather than systematic as shown here.

$$O_1 \quad X_1 \quad O_2 \quad X_0 \quad O_3 \quad X_1 \quad O_4 \quad X_0 \quad O_5$$

A study by Hall et al. (1973) illustrates a version of the equivalent time-samples design. Five subjects, identified as the most violently aggressive, were selected from a group of 46 retarded boys living in an institution dormitory. Their ages ranged from 12 to 16 (mean, 13.8); their IQs from 40 to 62 (mean, 50). Each subject was observed for 10 weeks in 10 randomly selected 3-minute periods, during which time acts of aggressive behavior were recorded. Acts were classified as motor aggressive (throwing objects, kicking, fighting, scratching) and nonmotor aggressive (verbal abuse, screaming or shouting, insubordination).

The observations were scheduled in four periods:

1. Observation (baseline)   session 1
2. On-reinforcement   sessions 2, 3, 4, 5
3. Off-reinforcement   sessions 6, 7
4. On-reinforcement   sessions 8, 9, 10

Positive reinforcement as a reward for nonaggressive behavior consisted of candy, praise, or trips to the canteen. Negative reinforcement following aggressive acts consisted of ostracizing from group activities, taking away a favorite toy, or reprimanding verbally. Two observers were employed, one observing motor aggressive acts, the other, nonmotor aggressive acts.

The researchers concluded that reinforcement affected the amount of aggressive output. Motor aggressive behavior was reduced more effectively than nonmotor aggressive behavior (see Figure 5–1). To assess the permanence of behavior change after the conclusion of the experiment, a phase-out period of 89 days of observation was scheduled. The only reinforcement used was the posting of stars for nonaggressive behavior. Observations during the phase-out period indicated much more acceptable dormitory behavior.

Designs of this type have a number of limitations. Although they may minimize the effect of history, it is possible that they may increase the influence of maturation, unstable instrumentation, testing, and experimental mortality.

The equivalent materials, pretest, posttest design

$$O_1 \quad X_{MA} \quad O_2 \quad O_3 \quad X_{MB} \quad O_4$$

X_{MA} = teaching method A X_{MB} = teaching method B
O_1 and O_3 are pretests O_2 and O_4 are posttests

Another experimental design, using the same group or class for both experimental and control groups, involves two or more cycles. The class may be used as a control group in the first cycle and as an experi-

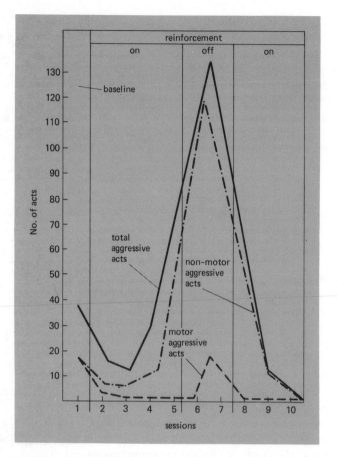

FIGURE 5–1   Number of motor aggressive, nonmotor aggressive, and total aggressive acts during on-reinforcement and off-reinforcement experimental conditions.

mental group in the second. The order of exposure to experimental and control can be reversed—experimental first and control following.

Essential to this design is the selection of learning materials that are different but as nearly equal as possible in interest to the students and in difficulty of comprehension. An example may help to clarify the procedure.

Ms. Smith hypothesized that the students in her class who were used to background music while doing their homework would learn to spell more efficiently in the classroom if music were provided. Because she was unable to arrange a parallel group experiment, she decided to use her class as both an experimental and a control group.

To equate the words to be learned, she randomly selected two sets of 100 words from an appropriate graded word list. For cycle I, the control cycle, she pretested the class on word list A. Then for 20 minutes each day the students studied the words, using drill and the usual spelling rules. At the end of 2 weeks she retested the class and computed the mean gain score in correct spelling.

For cycle II, the experimental cycle, she pretested the class on word list B. Then for 20 minutes each day, with soft, continuous music in the background (the independent variable), the students studied their word list, using the same drill and spelling rules. At the end of the second 2-week period she retested the class and computed the mean gain score in correct spelling.

The mean gain score for the experimental cycle was significantly greater than the mean gain score for the control cycle. She concluded that the introduction of the experimental variable had indeed improved the effectiveness of the learning experience.

The apparent simplicity and logic of this design is somewhat misleading, and when examined in light of the threats to experimental validity, the design's weaknesses become apparent.

1. It is often difficult to select equated materials to be learned. For types of learning other than spelling, finding learning materials that are equally interesting, difficult, and unfamiliar would be a serious problem.

2. As the students enter the second cycle, they are older and more mature.

3. Outside events (history) would be more likely to affect the experience in one cycle than in the other.

4. There would be an influence of prior treatment carrying over from the first cycle to the second.

5. The effects of testing would be more likely to have a greater impact on the measurement of gain in the second cycle.

6. Mortality, or loss of subjects from the experiment, would be more likely in an experimental design spread over a longer period of time.

7. When the experimenter's judgment was a factor in evaluation, contamination, the experimenter's knowledge of subject performance in the first cycle, could possibly influence evaluation of performance in the second.

Some of the limitations of the equivalent-materials, single-group, pretest-posttest design can be partially minimized by a series of replications in which the order of exposure to experimental and control treatments is reversed. This process, known as *rotation,* is illustrated by this pattern in a four-cycle experiment.

I	II	III	IV
O_1 X O_2	O_3 C O_4	O_5 C O_6	O_7 X O_8

O_1 O_3 O_5 O_7 = pretests O_2 O_4 O_6 O_8 = posttests

If the experimental treatment yielded significantly greater gains regardless of the order of exposure, its effectiveness could be accepted with greater confidence. However, it is apparent that this design is not likely to equate materials, subjects, or experimental conditions.

All single-group experimental designs are sensitive to the influences of many of the threats to validity previously mentioned in this chapter: history, maturation, unstable instrumentation, testing, and experimental mortality. Replication of the studies, using different units as subjects, is an effective way to improve their validity. However, single-group experiments may be performed when randomly equated group designs cannot be arranged.

Counterbalanced designs.   These are designs in which experimental control derives from having all the subjects receive all the treatment conditions. The subjects are placed into, in the case of this example, four groups. Each of the groups then receives all four treatments, but in different orders. This may be diagrammed as follows:

Replication	O_1 X_1	O_2 X_2	O_3 X_3	O_4 X_4	O_5
1	Group A	B	C	D	
2	Group B	D	A	C	
3	Group C	A	D	B	
4	Group D	C	B	A	

In the first sequence following a pretest (O_1), group A receives treatment 1, group B receives treatment 2, group C receives treatment 3, and group D receives treatment 4. After a second test (O_2), each group then receives a second treatment, and so on. Thus each group receives all treatments, and each treatment is first, second, third, or fourth in the order received by one of the groups.

This design has excellent internal validity because history, maturation, regression, selection, and mortality are all generally well controlled. The major limitation is that an order effect could wipe out any potential differences among the treatments. Four randomly assigned groups would therefore be preferable. Thus, this design should be used when random assignment is not possible and when it is expected that the different treatments will not interfere too much with each other.

Factorial Designs

When more than one independent variable is included in a study, whether a true experiment or a quasi-experiment, a factorial design is necessary. Because most real world outcomes are the result of a number of factors acting in combination, most significant experimentation involves the analysis of the interaction of a number of variable relationships. By using factorial designs, researchers can determine, for example, if the treatment interacts significantly with sex or age. That is, the experimenter can determine if one treatment is more effective with boys and another with girls, or if older girls do better on the treatment than younger girls, whereas older and younger boys do equally well on the treatment.

The simplest case of a factorial design would be to have two independent variables with two conditions of each, known as a 2 × 2 factorial design. This design would be used if a researcher decided to compare a new (experimental) method of teaching reading to reading-disabled children with a commonly used (control) method, and also wanted to determine if boys and girls would do differently on the two methods. Such a design would look like Figure 5–2.

With this design we have four *cells*, each of which represents a subgroup (for example, experimental females, control males, and so

Treatment

	Experimental	Control
Females	**CELL 1**	**CELL 2**
Males	**CELL 3**	**CELL 4**

FIGURE 5–2 Factorial design.

forth). This design will permit the researcher to determine if there is a significant overall effect, known as *main effect*, for treatment and/or sex. It also permits the determination whether these two variables interact significantly, such that boys do best in the experimental condition and girls do best in the control condition. If this were the case, the subjects in Cell 2 would have a higher average score than those in Cell 1, and the subjects in Cell 3 would outperform those in Cell 4.

In a recent study, Nucci and Nucci (1982) examined the responses of children to the social transgressions (such as spitting on the ground) of their peers. They observed boys and girls between 7 and 10 and between 11 and 14 years of age and coded their observations of the responses into one of eight categories. They found an interaction effect of sex by age for just one of the categories. This interaction effect could be graphically represented as in Figure 5–3. We see that the two lines actually cross, thus clearly indicating that "With increased age the girls provided greater frequencies of ridicule responses to [social transgres-

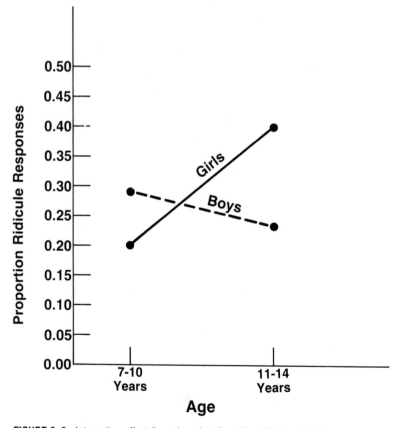

FIGURE 5–3 Interaction effect (based on data from Nucci & Nucci, 1982).

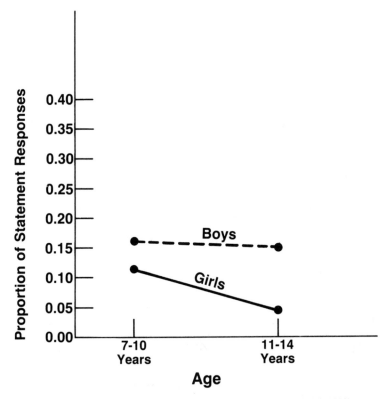

FIGURE 5–4 No interaction effect (based on data from Nucci & Nucci, 1982).

sions] while the boys responded with approximately the same frequencies as at the younger age" (Nucci & Nucci, 1982, p. 1341). Figure 5–4 shows an example of another type of response, stating the rule being violated, for which Nucci and Nucci found no interaction effect. Here we see two relatively parallel lines.

Of course, factorial designs can have more than two independent variables and more than two conditions of each variable. A study might have three treatment conditions (e.g., three methods of reading instruction), the two sexes, three age groups, and three intelligence levels (gifted, average, and mildly retarded) as the independent variables. This would be a $3 \times 2 \times 3 \times 3$ design and would have a total of 54 subgroups or cells. Such designs are too complex for this elementary treatment. We mention such a complex design only to make the reader aware that these designs exist and that they are frequently appropriate and necessary. Advanced students may wish to refer to such sources as Glass and Hopkins (1984), Kirk (1982), and Winer (1971) for more detailed information.

This discussion, which has examined the many limitations of the experimental method in behavioral research, may convey a sense of futility. As is true in many other areas of significant human endeavor, researchers do not work under ideal conditions. They must do the best they can under existing circumstances. They will find, however, that in spite of its limitations, the well-designed and well-executed experiment provides a legitimate method for testing hypotheses and making probability decisions about the relationships between variables.

Some variables cannot be manipulated. The ethical problems that would be raised if some others were manipulated indicates a place for such nonexperimental methods as *ex post facto* research. The researcher starts with the observation of dependent variables and goes back to the observation of independent variables that have previously occurred under uncontrolled conditions. Such studies are *not* experiments, for the researcher has had no control over the events; they occurred before he or she began the investigation. The description of cigarette-smoking cancer research in Chapter 4 is an example of *ex post facto* research.

SUMMARY

The experimental method provides a logical, systematic way to answer the question, "If this is done under carefully controlled conditions, what will happen?" To provide a precise answer, experimenters manipulate certain influences, or variables, and observe how the condition or behavior of the subject is affected or changed. Experimenters control or isolate the variables in such a way that they can be reasonably sure that the effects they observe can be attributed to the variables they have manipulated, rather than to some other uncontrolled influences. In testing hypotheses or evaluating tentative answers to questions, experimenters make decisions based upon probability rather than certainty. Experimentation, the classic method of the laboratory, is the most powerful method for discovering and developing a body of knowledge about the prediction and control of events. The experimental method has been used with some success in the school classroom, where, to some degree, variables can be controlled.

The early applications of experimental method, based upon John Stuart Mill's law of the single variable, have been replaced by the more effective applications of factorial designs made possible by the contributions of R. A. Fisher. His concept of equating groups by random selection of subjects and random assignment of treatments, and his development of the analysis of variance and the analysis of covariance, have made possible the study of complex multivariate relationships that are basic to the understanding of human behavior.

Experimenters must understand and deal with threats to the internal validity of the experiment so that the variable relationships they observe can be interpreted without ambiguity. They must also understand and deal with threats to the external validity of the experiment so that their findings can be extended beyond their experimental subjects and generalized to a wider population of interest.

Experimental design provides a plan or blueprint for experimentation. Three pre-experimental, three true experimental, and five quasi-experimental designs have been presented, and their appropriate use, advantages, and disadvantages have been briefly discussed.

Experimentation is a sophisticated technique for problem solving and may not be an appropriate activity for the beginning researcher. It has been suggested that teachers may make their most effective contribution to educational research by identifying important problems that they encounter in their classrooms and working cooperatively with research specialists in the conduct and interpretation of classroom experiments.

EXERCISES

1. Why is it more difficult to control extraneous variables in a classroom experiment than in a pharmaceutical laboratory experiment?
2. What significant element distinguishes a quasi-experiment from a true experiment?
3. Why is an *ex post facto* study not an experiment?
4. A researcher, in proposing a research project, defines the dependent variable as achievement in mathematics. What difficulty does this definition present? How would you improve it?
5. How could a double blind be applied in an educational experiment?
6. Under what circumstances could an independent variable in one study be a dependent variable in another study?
7. Why is randomization the best method for dealing with extraneous variables?
8. How could a high degree of experimental mortality seriously affect the validity of an experiment?
9. Read the report of an experiment in an educational research journal.
   a. Was the problem clearly stated?
   b. Were the variables defined in operational terms?
   c. Was the hypothesis clearly stated?
   d. Were the delimitations stated?
   e. Was the design clearly described?
   f. Were extraneous variables recognized? What provisions were made to control them?
   g. Were the population and the sampling method described?
   h. Were appropriate methods used to analyze the data?

i. Were the conclusions clearly presented?
j. Were the conclusions substantiated by the evidence presented?

REFERENCES

Abt Associates (1977). *Education as experimentation: A planned variation model.* Cambridge, MA: Abt Associates. Also issued as *The follow through planned variation experiment series.* Washington, D.C.: U.S. Office of Education, 1978.

ANDERSON, R. B., ST. PIERRE, R. G., PROPER, E. C. & STEBBINS, L. B. (1978). Pardon us, but what was the question again?: A response to the critique of the follow through evaluation. *Harvard Educational Review, 48,* 161–170.

CAMPBELL, D. T. & STANLEY, J. C. (1960). *Experimental and quasi-experimental designs for research.* Chicago: Rand McNally.

COOK, T. D. & CAMPBELL, D. T. (1971). The design and analysis of quasi-experiments for field settings. Chicago: Rand McNally.

GLASS, G. V. & HOPKINS, K. D. (1984). *Statistical methods in education and psychology* (2nd ed.). Englewood Cliffs, NJ: Prentice-Hall.

HALL, H. V., PRICE, A. B., SHINEDLING, M., PEIZER, S. B., & MASSEY, R. H. (1973). Control of aggressive behavior in a group of retardates using positive and negative reinforcement. *Training School Bulletin, 70,* 179–186.

HAYS, W. L. (1981). *Statistics* (3rd ed.) New York: Holt, Rinehart, and Winston.

HODGES, W. L. (1978). The worth of the follow through experience. *Harvard Educational Review, 48,* 186–192.

HOUSE, E. L., GLASS, G. V., MCLEAN, L. D., & WALKER, D. F. (1978). No simple answer: Critique of the follow through evaluation. *Harvard Educational Review, 48,* 128–160.

KAHN, J. V. (1978). Acceleration of object permanence with severely and profoundly retarded children. *The Association for Severely Handicapped Review, 3,* 15–22.

KERLINGER, F. N. (1973). *Foundations of behavioral research* (2nd ed.). New York: Holt, Rinehart, and Winston.

KIRK, R. (1982). *Experimental design: Procedures for the behavioral sciences.* Belmont, CA: Brooks/Cole.

MAYO, E. (1960). *The human problems of an industrial civilization.* New York: Viking Press.

MILL, J. S. (1873). *A system of logic.* New York: Harper and Row.

NUCCI, L. P. & NUCCI, M. S. (1982). Children's responses to moral and social conventional transgressions in free-play settings. *Child Development, 53,* 1337–1342.

WATANABE, P., HARE, V. C., & LOMAX, R. G. (1984). Predicting news story content from headlines: An instructional study. *Journal of Reading, 27,* 436–442.

WINER, B. J. (1971). *Statistical principles in experimental design.* New York: McGraw-Hill.

WISLER, C. E., BURNS, G. P., & IWAMOTO, D. (1978). Follow through redux: A response to the critique by House, Glass, McLean, and Walker. *Harvard Educational Review, 48,* 177–185.

Chapter 6

Methods and Tools
of Research

To carry out any of the types of research investigation described in the preceding chapters, data must be gathered with which to test the hypothesis. Many different methods and procedures have been developed to aid in the acquisition of data. These tools employ distinctive ways of describing and quantifying the data. Each is particularly appropriate for certain sources of data, yielding information of the kind and in the form that can be most effectively used.

Many writers have argued the superiority of the interview over the questionnaire, or the use of the psychological test over the interview. The late Arvil S. Barr, University of Wisconsin teacher and researcher, resolved discussions of this sort by asking, "Which is better, a hammer or a handsaw?" Like the tools in the carpenter's chest, each is appropriate in a given situation.

Some researchers become preoccupied with one method of inquiry and neglect the potential of others. Examining the publications of some authors shows that many studies use the same method applied to many different problems, possibly indicating that the authors have become attached to one particular method and choose problems that are appropriate to its use.

There is probably too much dependence upon single methods of inquiry. Because each data-gathering procedure or device has its own particular weakness or bias, there is merit in using multiple methods, supplementing one with others to counteract bias and generate more adequate data. Students of research should familiarize themselves with each of these research tools and attempt to develop skill in their use and sensitivity to their effectiveness in specific situations.

RELIABILITY AND VALIDITY OF RESEARCH TOOLS

Reliability and *validity* are essential to the effectiveness of any data-gathering procedure. These terms are defined here in the most general way. A more detailed discussion is presented later in the chapter.

Reliability is the degree of consistency that the instrument or procedure demonstrates: Whatever it is measuring, it does so consistently. *Validity* is that quality of a data-gathering instrument or procedure that enables it to measure what it is supposed to measure. Reliability is a necessary but not sufficient condition for validity. That is, a test must be reliable for it to be valid, but a test can be reliable and still not be valid.

It is feasible through a variety of statistical treatments to quantitatively assess the reliability and validity of psychological tests and inventories. It is more difficult to determine these qualities for some other data-gathering instruments or procedures, such as observation, interview, or the use of the questionnaire, in which responses are more qualitative and yield data that are not always readily quantifiable. One should attempt to improve the reliability and validity of the procedures, but precise determination of the degree to which they are achieved is often elusive, particularly in the case of validity.

A brief consideration of the problems of validity and reliability follows the discussion of each type of data-gathering procedure.

QUANTITATIVE STUDIES

Quantification has been defined as a numerical method of describing observations of materials or characteristics. When a defined portion of the material or characteristic is used as a standard for measuring any sample, a valid and precise method of data description is provided. Scientists distinguish among four levels of measurement, listed and described in the following.

A nominal scale. A nominal scale is the least precise method of quantification. A nominal scale describes differences between things by assigning them to categories—such as professors, associate professors, assistant professors, instructors, or lecturers—and to subsets such as males or females (see Table 6–1).

Nominal data are counted data. Each individual can be a member of only one set, and all other members of the set have the same defined characteristic. Such categories as nationality, gender, socioeconomic sta-

TABLE 6–1 Academic Rank of Members of the Instructional Staff of Southland College

	MALE	FEMALE	TOTAL
Professors	20	4	24
Associate professors	34	22	56
Assistant professors	44	30	74
Instructors	26	14	40
Lecturers	17	5	22
Totals	141	75	216

tus, race, occupation, or religious affiliation provide other examples. Nominal scales are nonorderable, but in some situations this simple enumeration or counting is the only feasible method of quantification and may provide an acceptable basis for statistical analysis.

An ordinal scale.   Sometimes it is possible to indicate not only that things differ but that they differ in amount or degree. Ordinal scales permit the ranking of items or individuals from highest to lowest. The criterion for highest to lowest ordering is expressed as relative position or rank in a group: 1st, 2nd, 3rd, 4th, 5th, . . . , nth. Ordinal measures have no absolute values, and the real differences between adjacent ranks may not be equal. Ranking spaces them equally, though they may not actually be equally spaced. The following example illustrates this limitation:

SUBJECT	HEIGHT IN INCHES	DIFFERENCE IN INCHES	RANK
Jones	76		1st
Smith	68	8	2nd
Brown	66	2	3rd
Porter	59	7	4th
Taylor	58	1	5th

An interval scale.   An arbitrary scale based on equal units of measurements indicates how much of a given characteristic is present. The difference in amount of the characteristic possessed by persons with scores of 90 and 91 is assumed to be equivalent to that between persons with scores of 60 and 61.

The interval scale represents a decided advantage over nominal and ordinal scales because it indicates the relative amount of a trait or characteristic. Its primary limitation is the lack of a true zero. It does not have the capacity to measure the complete absence of the trait, and a measure of 90 does not mean that a person has twice as much of the trait as someone with a score of 45. Psychological tests and inventories are interval scales and have this limitation although they can be added, subtracted, multiplied, and divided.

A ratio scale.   A ratio scale has the equal interval properties of an interval scale but has two additional features:

1. The ratio scale has a true zero. It is possible to indicate the complete absence of a property. For example, the zero point on a centimeter scale indicates the complete absence of length or height.
2. The numerals of the ratio scale have the qualities of real numbers and can be added, subtracted, multiplied, and divided and ex-

pressed in ratio relationships. For example, 5 grams is one-half of 10 grams; 15 grams is three times 5 grams; and on a laboratory weighing scale, two 1-gram weights will balance a 2-gram weight. One of the advantages enjoyed by practitioners in the physical sciences is the ability to describe variables in ratio scale form. The behavioral sciences are generally limited to describing variables in interval scale form, a less precise type of measurement.

Proceeding from the nominal scale (the least precise type) to ratio scale (the most precise), increasingly relevant information is provided. If the nature of the variables permits, the scale that provides the most precise description should be used.

In behavioral research, many of the qualities or variables of interest are abstractions and cannot be observed directly. It is necessary to define them in terms of observable acts, from which the existence and amount of the variables are inferred. This operational definition tells what the researcher must do to measure the variable. For example, intelligence is an abstract quality that cannot be observed directly. Intelligence may be defined operationally as scores achieved on a particular intelligence test.

Operational definitions have limited meaning. Their interpretation is somewhat subjective, which may lead experts to disagree about their validity. The fact that numerical data are generated does not insure valid observation and description, for ambiguities and inconsistencies are often represented quantitatively.

Some behavioral scientists feel that excessive emphasis on quantification may result in the measurement of fragmentary qualities not relevant to real behavior. The temptation to imitate the descriptive measures of the physical scientist has led some behavioral researchers to focus their attention on trivial, easy-to-measure elements of behavior, resulting in pretentious studies of little value.

The limitations that have been mentioned are not intended to minimize the significance of quantitative methods. Progress is being made in developing more valid operational definitions and better observation techniques. The quantitative approach is not only useful but may be considered indispensable in most types of research. It has played an essential role in the history and development of science as it progressed from pure philosophical speculation to modern empirical, verifiable observation.

QUALITATIVE STUDIES

Qualitative studies are those in which the description of observations is not ordinarily expressed in quantitative terms. It is not that numerical measures are never used but that other means of description are emphasized. For example, in the ethnographic studies described in Chapter 4, when the researcher gathers data by participant observation, interviews, and the examination of documentary materials, little measurement may be involved. However, observations may be classified into discrete categories, yielding nominal level data.

Piaget, a scientist who had a distinguished research career of more than 50 years, came to the conclusion that a nonquantitative search for explanations would be fruitful in the study of human development. His qualitative approach, known as *genetic epistemology*, has suggested another method of observing behavior and the nature of human growth and development. He built his logic of operations upon what he observed when children of different age levels were confronted with tasks that required reasoning for their solution.

In some types of investigation, events and characteristics may appropriately be described qualitatively. Topics such as these may serve as examples:

The Effect of Diplomatic Failure upon a Presidential Election

Types of Political Leaders and Their Influence upon Social Unrest

The Terrorist as an Agent of Social Change

The Extended Tribal Family and Its Influence upon Child-Rearing Practices

The Influence of Tribal Religious Beliefs upon Attitudes toward Death and Dying

The Influence of the Socioeconomic Status of a Group of High School Students in the Selection of Career Goals

The Influence of the Home on Pupil-Teacher Relationships

To conclude this discussion on quantitative and qualitative studies, several observations may be appropriate. It may be unwise to try to draw a hard-and-fast distinction between qualitative and quantitative studies. The difference is not absolute; it is one of emphasis. One emphasis should not be considered superior to the other. The appropriate approach would depend upon the nature of the variables under consideration and the objectives of the researcher.

Traditionally, educational research has emphasized the quantitative approach. A substantial number of researchers feel that qualitative studies have, for too long, remained outside the mainstream of educational research. Some investigations could be strengthened by supplementing one approach with the other.

PSYCHOLOGICAL TESTS AND INVENTORIES

As data-gathering devices, psychological tests are among the most useful tools of educational research, for they provide the data for most experimental and descriptive studies in education. Because here we are able to examine only limited aspects of the nature of psychological testing, students of educational research should consult other volumes for a more complete discussion (such as Anastasia, 1982; Cronbach, 1970).

A psychological test is an instrument designed to describe and measure a sample of certain aspects of human behavior. Tests may be used to compare the behavior of two or more persons at a particular time or of one or more persons at different times. Psychological tests yield objective and standardized descriptions of behavior, quantified by numerical scores. Under ideal conditions, achievement or aptitude tests measure the best performance of which individuals are capable. Under ideal conditions, inventories attempt to measure typical behavior. Tests and inventories are used to describe status (or a prevailing condition at a particular time), to measure changes in status produced by modifying factors, or to predict future behavior on the basis of present performance.

In the simple experiment on reading headlines described in the chapter on experimental research (Chapter 5), test scores were used to equate the experimental and control groups, to describe relative skill at this task prior to the application of the teaching methods, to measure student gains resulting from the application of the experimental and control teaching methods, and to evaluate the relative effectiveness of teaching methods. This example of classroom experimentation illustrates how experimental data may be gathered through the administration of tests.

In descriptive research studies, tests are frequently used to describe prevailing conditions at a particular time. How does a student compare with those of his or her own age or grade in school achievement? How does a particular group compare with groups in other schools or cities?

In school surveys for the past several decades, achievement tests have been used extensively in the appraisal of instruction. Because tests yield quantitative descriptions or measure, they make possible more precise analysis than can be achieved through subjective judgment alone.

There are many ways of classifying psychological tests. One distinction is made between *performance tests* and *paper-and-pencil tests*. Performance tests, usually administered individually, require that the subjects manipulate objects or mechanical apparatus while their actions are observed and recorded by the examiner. Paper-and-pencil tests, usually administered in groups, require the subjects to mark their response on a prepared sheet.

Two other classes of tests are *power* versus *timed* or *speed* tests. Power tests have no time limit, and the subjects attempt progressively more difficult tasks until they are unable to continue successfully. Timed or speed tests usually involve the element of power, but in addition, they limit the time the subjects have to complete certain tasks.

Another distinction is that made between *nonstandardized,*

teacher-made tests and *standardized* tests. The test that the classroom teacher constructs is likely to be less expertly designed than that of the professional, although it is based upon the best logic and skill that the teacher can command and is usually "tailor-made" for a particular group of pupils.

Which type of test is used depends on the test's intended purpose. The standardized test is designed for general use. The items and the total scores have been carefully analyzed, and validity and reliability have been established by careful statistical controls. Norms have been established based upon the performance of many subjects of various ages living in many different types of communities and geographic areas. Not only has the content of the test been standardized, but the administration and scoring have been set in one pattern so that those subsequently taking the tests will take them under like conditions. As far as possible, the interpretation has also been standardized.

Although it would be inaccurate to claim that all standardized tests meet optimum standards of excellence, the test authors have attempted to make them as sound as possible in the light of the best that is known by experts in test construction, administration, and interpretation.

Nonstandardized or teacher-made tests are designed for use with a specific group of persons. Reliability and validity are not usually established. However, more practical information may be derived from a teacher-made test than from a standardized one because the test is given to the group for whom it was designed and is interpreted by the teacher/ test-maker.

Psychological tests may also be classified in terms of their purpose—that is, what types of psychological traits they describe and measure.

Achievement Tests

Achievement tests attempt to measure what an individual has learned—his or her present level of performance. Most tests used in schools are achievement tests. They are particularly helpful in determining individual or group status in academic learning. Achievement test scores are used in placing, advancing, or retaining students at particular grade levels. They are used in diagnosing strengths and weaknesses and as a basis for awarding prizes, scholarships, or degrees.

Frequently achievement test scores are used in evaluating the influences of courses of study, teachers, teaching methods, and other factors considered to be significant in educational practice. In using tests for evaluative purposes, it is important not to generalize beyond the specific elements measured. For example, to identify effective teaching exclusively with the limited products measured by the ordinary achievement test would be to define effective teaching too narrowly. It is essential that researchers recognize that the elements of a situation under appraisal need to be evaluated on the basis of a number of criteria, not merely on a few limited aspects.

Aptitude Tests

Aptitude tests attempt to predict the degree of achievement that may be expected from individuals in a particular activity. To the extent that they measure past learning, they are similar to achievement tests. To the extent that they measure nondeliberate or unplanned learning, they are different. Aptitude tests attempt to predict an individual's capacity to acquire improved performance with additional training.

Actually, capacity (or aptitude) cannot be measured directly. Aptitude can only be inferred on the basis of present performance, particularly in areas where there has been no deliberate attempt to teach the behaviors to be predicted.

Intelligence is a good example of a trait that cannot be measured directly. An individual's intelligence quotient (IQ) is generally derived from comparing his or her current knowledge with a group of persons of equal chronological age who were administered the test by the author or the author's employees. If a person scores relatively high, average, or low, we assume that it is a measure of how effectively a person has profited from both formal and informal opportunities for learning. To the extent that others have had similar opportunities, we predict an individual's ability for future learning. This is a matter of inference rather than of direct measurement. Because it has proved useful in predicting future achievement, particularly in academic pursuits, we consider this concept of intelligence measurement a valid application.

Aptitude tests have been designed to predict improved performance with further training in many areas. These inferred measurements have been applied to mechanical and manipulative skills, musical and artistic pursuits, and many professional areas involving many types of predicted ability.

In music, for example, ability to remember and discriminate between differences in pitch, rhythm pattern, intensity, and timbre seems to be closely related to future levels of development in musicianship. Present proficiency in these tasks provides a fair predictive index of an individual's ability to profit from advanced instruction, particularly when the individual has had little formal training in music prior to the test.

Aptitude tests may be used to divide students into relatively homogeneous groups for instructional purposes, identify students for scholarship grants, screen individuals for particular educational programs, or help guide individuals into areas where they are most likely to succeed.

Aptitude tests, particularly those that deal with academic aptitude, that are used for purposes of placement and classification have become highly controversial, and their use has been prohibited in many communities. The fact that some individuals with culturally different backgrounds do not score well on these tests has led to charges of discrimination against members of minority groups. The case has been made that most of these tests do not accurately predict academic achievement because their contents are culturally biased. Efforts are being made to develop culture-free tests that eliminate this undesirable quality. However, it is extremely difficult to eliminate culture totally and develop one test that is equally fair for all.

Interest Inventories

Interest inventories attempt to yield a measure of the types of activities that an individual has a tendency to like and to choose. One kind of instrument has compared the subject's pattern of interest to the interest patterns of successful practitioners in a number of vocational fields. A distinctive pattern has been discovered to be characteristic of each field. The assumption is that an individual is happiest and most successful working in a field most like his or her own measured profile of interest.

Another inventory is based on the correlation between a number of activities from the areas of school, recreation, and work. These related activities have been identified by careful analysis with mechanical, computational, scientific, persuasive, artistic, literary, musical, social service, and clerical areas of interest. By sorting the subject's stated likes and dislikes into various interest areas, a percentile score for each area is obtained. It is then assumed that the subject will find his or her area of greatest interest where the percentile scores are relatively high.

Interest blanks or inventories are examples of self-report instruments in which individuals note their own likes and dislikes. These self-report instruments are really standardized interviews in which the subjects, through introspection, indicate feelings that may be interpreted in terms of what is known about interest patterns.

Personality Inventories

Personality scales are usually self-report instruments. The individual checks responses to certain questions or statements. These instruments yield scores which are assumed or have been shown to measure certain personality traits or tendencies.

Because of individuals' inability or unwillingness to report their own reactions accurately or objectively, these instruments may be of limited value. Part of this limitation may be due to the inadequate theories of personality upon which some of these inventories have been based. At best, they provide data that are useful in suggesting the need for further analysis. Some have reasonable empirical validity with particular groups of individuals but prove to be invalid when applied to others. For example, one personality inventory has proven valuable in yielding scores that correlate highly with the diagnoses of psychiatrists in clinical situations. But when applied to college students, its diagnostic value has proved disappointing.

The development of instruments of personality description and measurement is relatively recent, and it is likely that continued research in this important area will yield better theories of personality and better instruments for describing and measuring its various aspects.

The Mooney Problems Check List (1941) is an inventory to be used by students in reporting their own problems of adjustment. The subjects are asked to indicate on the checklist the things that trouble them. From a list of these items, classified into different categories, a picture of the students' problems, from their own viewpoint, is drawn. Although the most useful interpretation may result from an item analysis of personal problems, the device does yield a quantitative score which may indicate the degree of difficulty that students feel they are experiencing in their adjustment. This instrument has been used as a research device to identify and describe the nature of the problems facing individuals and groups of individuals in a school.

The tendency to withhold embarrassing responses and to express those that are socially acceptable, emotional involvement of individuals with their own problems, lack of insight—all these limit the effectiveness of personal and social-adjustment scales. Some psychologists believe that the projective type of instrument offers greater promise, for these devices attempt to disguise their purpose so completely that the subject does not know how to appear in the best light.

Projective Devices

A projective instrument enables subjects to project their internal feelings, attitudes, needs, values, or wishes to an external object. Thus the subjects may unconsciously reveal themselves as they react to the external object. The use of projective devices is particularly helpful in counteracting the tendency of subjects to try to appear in their best light, to respond as they believe they should.

Projection may be accomplished through a number of techniques:

1. *Association.* The respondent is asked to indicate what he or she sees, feels, or thinks when presented with a picture, cartoon, ink blot, word, or phrase. The Thematic Apperception Test, the Rorschach Ink Blot Test, and various word-association tests are familiar examples.

2. *Completion.* The respondent is asked to complete an incomplete sentence or task. A sentence-completion instrument may include such items as:

> My greatest ambition is
> My greatest fear is
> I most enjoy
> I dream a great deal about •
> I get very angry when
> If I could do anything I wanted it would be to

3. *Role-playing.* Subjects are asked to improvise or act out a situation in which they have been assigned various roles. The researcher may observe such traits as hostility, frustration, dominance, sympathy, insecurity, prejudice—or the absence of such traits.

4. *Creative or constructive.* Permitting subjects to model clay, finger paint, play with dolls, play with toys, or draw or write imaginative stories about assigned situations may be revealing. The choice of color, form, words, the sense of orderliness, evidence of tensions, and other reactions may provide opportunities to infer deep-seated feelings.

QUALITIES OF A GOOD TEST OR INVENTORY

Reliability

A test is *reliable* to the extent that it measures whatever it is measuring consistently. In tests that have a high coefficient of reliability, errors of measurement have been reduced to a minimum. Reliable tests are stable in whatever they measure and yield comparable scores upon repeated administration. An unreliable test is comparable to a stretchable rubber yardstick that yields different measurements each time it is applied.

The reliability or stability of a test is usually expressed as a correlation coefficient. There are a number of types of reliability:

1. Stability over time (test-retest). The scores on a test will be highly correlated with scores on a second administration of the test to the same subjects at a later date if the test has good test-retest reliability.

2. Stability over item samples (equivalent or parallel forms). Some tests have two or more forms that may be used interchangeably. In these cases, the scores on a test will be highly correlated with scores on an alternative form of the test (for example, scores on form A will be highly correlated with scores on form B) if the test has this type of reliability.

3. Stability of items (internal consistency). Scores on certain test items will be highly correlated with scores on other test items. There are two methods of measuring for internal consistency.
   a. Split halves. This can be accomplished in two different ways. Scores on the odd-numbered items can be correlated with the scores on the even-numbered items. Second, on some but not most tests, the scores on the first half of the test can be correlated with scores on the second half of the test. Because the correlations that would result from the above splits would be for only half a test, and because generally the longer a test is, the more internal consistency it has, the correlation coefficient is modified using the Spearman-Brown formula explained in Chapter 7.
   b. Kuder-Richardson formula. This formula is a mathematical test that results in the average correlation of all possible split half correlations (Cronbach, 1951).
4. Stability over scorers (inter-scorer reliability). Certain types of tests, in particular projective tests, leave a good deal to the judgment of the person scoring the test. Scorer reliability can be determined by having two persons independently score the same set of test papers and then calculating a correlation between their scores, determined by the scores.
5. Standard error of measurement. This statistic permits the interpretation of individual scores obtained on a test. Because tests are not perfectly reliable, we know that the score an individual receives on a given test is not necessarily a *true* measure of his or her trait. The standard error of measurement tells us how much we can expect an *obtained* score to differ from the individual's *true* score.

The reliability of a test may be raised by increasing the number of items of equal quality to the other items. Carefully designed directions for the administration of the test with no variation from group to group, providing an atmosphere free from distractions and one that minimizes boredom and fatigue, will also improve the reliability of the testing instrument.

Validity

In general, a test is valid if it measures what it claims to measure. Validity can also be thought of as utility. For the tester's particular purpose, is the test useful? There are several types of validity, and different types of tests and uses of tests need different types of validity. *Content validity* refers to the degree to which the test actually measures, or is specifically related to, the traits for which it was designed. It shows how adequately the test samples the universe of knowledge and skills that a student is expected to master. Content validity is based upon careful examination of course textbooks, syllabi, objectives, and the judgments of subject matter specialists. The criterion of content validity is often assessed by a panel of experts in the field who judge its adequacy, but there is no numerical way to express it. Content validity is particularly important for achievement tests but not very important for aptitude tests.

Construct validity is the degree to which scores on a test can be accounted for by the explanatory constructs of a sound theory. If one were to study such a construct as dominance, one would hypothesize that people who have this characteristic will perform differently from those who do not. Theories can be built describing how dominant people behave in a distinctive way. If this is done, dominant people can be identified by observation of their behavior, rating or classifying them in terms of the theory. A device could then be designed to have construct validity to the degree that instrument scores are systematically related to the judgments made by observation of behavior identified by the theory as dominant. Intelligence tests also require adequate construct validity. Because different tests are based on different theories, each test should be shown to measure what the appropriate theory defines as intelligence. Construct validity is particularly important for personality and aptitude tests.

Criterion-related validity is a broad term that actually refers to two different types of validity with different time frames.

1. *Predictive validity* refers to the usefulness of a test in predicting some future performance, such as the usefulness of the high school Scholastic Aptitude Test in predicting college grade-point averages. If a test is designed to pick out good candidates for appointment as shop foremen, and test scores show a high positive correlation with later actual success on the job, the test has a high degree of predictive validity, whatever factors it actually measures. It predicts well. It serves a useful purpose.

    But before a test can be evaluated on the basis of predictive validity, success on the job must be accurately described and measured. The criteria of the production of the department, the judgment of supervisors, or measures of employee morale might serve as evidence. Because these criteria might not be entirely satisfactory, however, predictive validity is not easy to assess. It is often difficult to discover whether the faults of prediction lie in the test, in the criteria of success, or both.

2. *Concurrent validity* refers to the usefulness of a test in closely relating to other measures, such as present academic grades, teacher ratings, or scores on another test of known validity.

    Tests are often validated by comparing their results with a test of known validity. A well-known scale of personal adjustment, the

Minnesota Multiphasic Personality Inventory, required sorting nearly 500 cards into three categories, *yes, no,* and *cannot say.* The equipment was expensive, and it could not be easily administered to large groups at the same time. A paper-and-pencil form was devised, using the simple process of checking responses to printed items on a form. This form could be administered to a large group at one time and then scored by machine, all with little expense. The results were so similar to the more time-consuming, expensive card-sorting process, that the latter has been largely replaced. This is the process of establishing *concurrent validity;* in this case, by comparing an expensive individual device with an easy-to-administer group instrument.

In like manner, performance tests have been validated against paper-and-pencil tests, and short tests against longer tests. Through this process, more convenient and more appropriate tests can be devised to accomplish the measurement of behavior more effectively.

Criterion-related validity is expressed as the coefficient of correlation between test scores and some measure of future performance, or between test scores and scores on another test or measure of known validity. The subject of correlation is explained in detail in Chapter 7.

A test may be reliable even though it is not valid. However, in order for a test to be valid, it must also be reliable. That is, a test can consistently measure (reliability) nothing of interest (be invalid), but if a test measures what it is designed to measure (validity), it must do so consistently (reliably).

Economy

Tests that can be given in a short period of time are likely to gain the cooperation of the subject and to conserve the time of all those involved in test administration. The matter of expense of administering a test is often a significant factor if the testing program is being operated on a limited budget.

Ease of administration, scoring, and interpretation is an important factor in selecting a test, particularly when expert personnel or an adequate budget are not available. Many good tests are easily and effectively administered, scored, and interpreted by the classroom teacher, who may not be an expert.

Interest

Tests that are interesting and enjoyable help to gain the cooperation of the subject. Those that are dull or seem silly may discourage or antagonize the subject. Under these unfavorable conditions, the test is not likely to yield useful results.

In selecting a test, it is important to recognize that a good test does not necessarily possess all the desirable qualities for all subjects on all levels of performance. Within a certain range of age, maturity, or ability, a test may be suitable. For other individuals outside that range, the test may be quite unsatisfactory and a more appropriate one needed.

The selection should be made after careful examination of the standardizing data contained in the test manual and extensive analysis of published evaluations of the instrument. Research workers should select the most appropriate standardized tests available. Detailed reports of their usefulness and limitations are usually supplied in the manual furnished by the publisher. The considered judgments of outside experts are also available. Buros (1978) *Mental Measurements Yearbook*, the best single reference on psychological tests, contains many critical evaluations of published tests, each contributed by an expert in the field of psychological measurement. Usually, several different evaluations are included for each test. Because the reports are not duplicated from one volume to another, it is advisable to consult *Tests in Print* (Mitchell, 1983) or previous *Yearbooks* for additional reports not included in the current volume. In addition to the reviews and evaluations, the names of test publishers, prices, forms, and appropriate uses are included. Readers are also urged to consult the listings and reviews of newly published psychological tests in the *Journal of Educational Measurement*.

When psychological tests are used in educational research, one should remember that standardized test scores are only approximate measures of the traits under consideration. This limitation is inevitable and may be ascribed to a number of possible factors:

1. The choice of an inappropriate test for the specific purpose in mind
2. Errors inherent in any psychological test—no test is completely valid or reliable
3. Errors that result from poor test conditions, inexpert or careless administration or scoring of the test, or faulty tabulation of test scores
4. Inexpert interpretation of test results.

OBSERVATION

From the earliest history of scientific activity, observation has been the prevailing method of inquiry. Observation of natural phenomena, aided by systematic classification and measurement, led to the development of theories and laws of nature's forces. Observation continues to characterize all research: experimental, descriptive, and historical. The use of the technique of participant observation in ethnological research has been described in Chapter 4.

Observation is very useful in behavioral research. Observational studies typically are experiments that use very few subjects, sometimes only one subject, but they intensively observe the subject(s) prior to, during, and after the intervention. The study by Hall et al. (1973), which attempted to reduce aggressive behavior of five mentally retarded boys (described in Chapter 5), is an example of experimental research that requires careful observation.

As a data-gathering device, direct observation may make an important contribution to descriptive research. Certain types of information can best be obtained through direct examination by the researcher. When the information concerns aspects of material objects or specimens, the process is relatively simple, and may consist of classifying, measuring, or counting. But when the process involves the study of a human subject in action, it is much more complex.

One may study the characteristics of a school building by observing and recording such aspects as materials of construction, number of rooms for various purposes, size of rooms, amount of furniture and equipment, presence or absence of certain facilities, and other relevant aspects. Adequacy could then be determined by comparing these facilities with reasonable standards previously determined by expert judgment and research.

In university athletic departments or professional football organizations, observation has been used effectively to scout the performance of opposing football teams. Careful observation and recording of the skills and procedures of both team and individual players are made, and defenses and offenses are planned to cope with them. What formations or patterns of attack or defense are employed? Who carries the ball? Who does the passing, and where and with what hand does he pass? Who are the likely receivers, and how do they pivot and cut?

During a game a coaching assistant may sit high in the stands, relaying strategic observations by phone to the coach on the bench. At the same time, every minute of play is being recorded on film for careful study by the coaching staff and players. Who missed his tackle when that play went through for 20 yards? Who missed his block when play number two lost 6 yards? Careful study of these films provides valuable data on weaknesses to be corrected before the following game. Through the use of binoculars, the phone, the motion picture camera, and the video tape recorder, observations can be carefully made and recorded.

Although this example may seem inappropriate in a discussion of observation as a research technique, improving the performance of a football team is not altogether different from analyzing learning behavior in a classroom. The difference is one of degree of complexity. The objectives of the football team are more concretely identifiable than are the more complex purposes of the classroom. Yet some of the procedures of observation so effective in football coaching may also be systematically employed in studying classroom performance. In some schools, teachers make short periodic classroom or playground observations of pupil behavior, which are filed in the cumulative folder. These recorded observations, known as *anecdotal reports,* may provide useful data for research studies.

Laboratory experimentation seeks to describe action or behavior that will take place under carefully arranged and controlled conditions. But many important aspects of human behavior cannot be observed under the contrived conditions of the laboratory. Descriptive research seeks to describe behavior under less rigid controls and more natural conditions. The behavior of children in a classroom situation cannot be effectively analyzed by observing their behavior in a laboratory. It is necessary to observe what they actually do in a real classroom.

This does not suggest that observation is haphazard or unplanned. On the contrary, observation as a research technique must always be systematic, directed by a specific purpose, carefully focused, and thoroughly recorded. Like other research procedures, it must be subject to the usual checks for accuracy, validity, and reliability.

The observer must know just what to look for. He or she must be able to distinguish between the significant and insignificant aspects of the situation. Of course, objectivity is essential, and careful and accurate methods of measuring and recording must be employed.

Because human behavior is complex, and many important traits and characteristics are difficult or impossible to observe directly, they must be carefully defined in precise operational form. Perhaps a subject's interest can be operationally defined by the number of times a student volunteers to participate in discussion by raising his or her hand within a time sample period. Lack of concentration during a study period can be operationally defined by the number of times the student looks around, talks to another student, fiddles with a book, pen, or paper, or engages in other distracting acts within a time sample period. These examples of operational definitions may be unsatisfactory, but they do illustrate the kinds of behavior that can be directly observed.

Behaviors that might mean different things to different observers must also be carefully defined. Acting-out behavior may mean very disruptive acts such as fighting or, at the other extreme, any behavior for which the child did not first obtain permission, such as sharpening a pencil. In defining which behaviors meet the meaning of acting out, the researcher would need first to determine the class rules to avoid labeling permissible behavior as "acting out."

Instruments such as the stopwatch, mechanical counter, camera, audiometer, audio and video tape recorders, and other devices make possible observations that are more precise than mere sense observations.

Systematic observations of human behavior in natural settings are to some degree an intrusion into the dynamics of the situation. This intervention may produce confounding effects that cannot be ignored. It is widely believed that individuals do not behave naturally when they know that they are being observed. The situation may become too artificial, too unnatural, to provide for a valid series of observations.

Concealing the observer has been used to minimize this reactive effect. Cameras and one-way screens were used by Gesell (1948) to make unobtrusive observations of infant behavior. One-way glass and concealed microphones and video tape recorders have been used in observing the behavior of children in natural group activities so that the observers could see and hear without being seen and heard.

Some authorities believe that the presence of an outside observer in the classroom over a period of time will be taken for granted, viewed as a part of the natural setting, and have little effect on the behavior observed. Others feel that introducing observers as active participants in the activities of the group will minimize the reactive effect more efficiently.

Should the participant observers make their purposes known to the members of the group observed? Some feel that concealing the intentions of the participant observers raises ethical questions of invasion of privacy and establishes a false, hypocritical, interpersonal relationship with the individuals in the group. Do the ends of science justify the means of deception? In a society that increasingly questions the ethics of science, this issue must be confronted.

Validity and Reliability of Observation

For the researcher's observations to achieve a satisfactory degree of validity, the truly significant incidents of behavior must be identified. Supplementing the knowledge and skill of the researcher, the judgment of experts in the field may help in selecting a limited number of observable incidents whose relationship to the qualities of interest is based upon sound, established theories.

The reactive effect of the intrusion of the observer as a threat to the validity of the process has been mentioned. When researchers are sole observers, they unconsciously tend to see what they expect to see and to overlook those incidents that do not fit their theory. Their own values, feelings, and attitudes, based upon past experience, may distort their observations. It may be desirable to engage several others who are well prepared as observers, restricting the researchers' role to that of interpreter of the observations. Independent observers should be prepared by participation in

1. The development of the procedures for observing and recording observations
2. The try-out or dry run phase of the procedure
3. The critique of the results of the try-out phase.

If more than one observer is necessary (as is usually the case), reliability among the observers should be demonstrated. This is done by having each participant observe with at least one other participant for a period of time and compare their recorded observations. Percent of agreement among observers should be quite high if the behaviors to be observed are well defined and the observers well trained.

Randomly selected time samples of frequently occurring incidents may help to yield more representative samples of behavior. A *time-on-task* study, described in a previous chapter, involved randomly selected 5-second observations of each student per class period for 9 weeks. Some types of behavior would require longer time periods for each observation, perhaps at different times of the day. This method of selecting observation periods would enhance both reliability and validity of observation.

Recording Observations

If it does not distract or create a barrier between observer and those observed, simultaneous recording of observations is recommended. This practice minimizes the errors that result from faulty memory. There are other occasions when recording would more appropriately be done after observation. The recording of observations should be done as soon as possible, while the details are still fresh in the mind of the observer. But many authorities agree that objectivity is more likely when the interpretation of the meaning of the behavior described is deferred until a later time, for simultaneous recording and interpretation often interfere with objectivity.

Systematizing Data Collection

To aid in the recording of information gained through observation, a number of devices have been extensively used. Check lists, rating scales, score cards, and scaled specimens provide systematic means of summarizing or quantifying data collected by observation or examination.

Check List

The check list, the simplest of the devices, is a prepared list of items. The presence or absence of the item may be indicated by checking *yes* or *no*, or the type or number of items may be indicated by inserting the appropriate word or number. This simple "laundry-list" type of device systematizes and facilitates the recording of observations and helps to ensure the consideration of the important aspects of the object or act observed. Readers are familiar with checklists prepared to help buyers purchase a used car, choose a home site, or buy an insurance policy, which indicate characteristics or features that one should bear in mind before making a decision.

Appendix G illustrates a check list for the evaluation of a research report.

Rating Scale

The rating scale involves qualitative description of a limited number of aspects of a thing or of traits of a person. The classifications may be set up in five to seven categories in such terms as

superior	above average	average	fair	inferior
excellent	good	average	below average	poor
always	frequently	occasionally	rarely	never

Another procedure establishes positions in terms of behavioral or situational descriptions. These statements may be much more specific and enable the judge to identify more clearly the characteristic to be rated. Instead of deciding whether the individual's leadership qualities are superior or above average, it may be easier to decide between "Always exerts a strong influence on his associates," and "Sometimes is able to move others to action."

One of the problems of constructing a rating scale is conveying to the rater exactly which quality one wishes evaluated. It is likely that a brief behavioral statement is more objective than an adjective that may have no universal meaning in the abstract. For this to be considered an effective method in observational research, the traits and categories must be very carefully defined in observable (behavioral) terms.

Rating scales have several limitations. In addition to the difficulty of clearly defining the trait or characteristic to be evaluated, the halo effect causes raters to carry qualitative judgment from one aspect to another. Thus there is a tendency to rate a person who has a pleasing personality high on other traits such as intelligence or professional interest. This halo effect is likely to appear when the rater is asked to rate many factors, on a number of which he has no evidence for judgment.

This suggests the advisability of keeping at a minimum the number of characteristics to be rated.

Another limitation of rating is the raters' tendency to be too generous. A number of studies have verified the tendency to rate 60 to 80 percent of an unselected group above average in all traits. Rating scales should carry the suggestion that raters omit the rating of characteristics that they have had no opportunity to observe.

Score Card

The score card, similar in some respects to both the checklist and the rating scale, usually provides for the appraisal of a relatively large number of aspects. In addition, the presence of each characteristic or aspect, or the rating assigned to each, has a predetermined point value. Thus the score-card rating may yield a total weighted score that can be used in the evaluation of the object observed. Score cards are frequently used in evaluating communities, building sites, schools, or textbooks. Accrediting agencies sometimes use the score card in arriving at an overall evaluation of a school.

Score cards have been designed to help estimate the socioeconomic status of a family. Such aspects as type of neighborhood, home ownership, number of rooms, ownership of a piano, number of books in the library, number and type of periodicals subscribed to, presence of a telephone, occupations of parents, and organizational membership of the adults are all considered significant and have appropriate point values assigned.

The limitations of the score care are similar to those of the rating scale. In addition to the difficulty of choosing, identifying, and quantifying the significant aspects of the factor to be observed, there is the suspicion that the whole of a thing may be greater than the sum of its parts.

Colleges and universities are frequently evaluated in terms of such elements as size of endowment, proportion of faculty members holding the earned doctoral degree, pupil-teacher ratio, and number of volumes in the library. Although these aspects are important, the effectiveness of an institution may not be accurately appraised by their summation, for certain important intangibles do not lend themselves to score-card ratings.

The Scaled Specimen

The scale specimen, although not frequently encountered in behavioral research, provides a method for evaluating certain observed levels of performance or measures of a quality in question. Testing a solution for acidity in a chemistry laboratory involves a pH test. A drop of color indicator is introduced into a sample of the solution. The resulting color of the solution is matched with the color of one of a set of display vials, indicating the percentage of acidity in the solution.

One of the early scaled specimens developed in the field of education was the handwriting scale developed by Thorndike. From a large sample of handwriting exhibits taken at different ages and grade levels, norms were established. The handwriting to be evaluated was then matched with the exhibit sample, yielding a measure of handwriting quality.

The Goodenough-Harris Drawing Test (Harris, 1963) provides a 71-point scale with examples for comparing various details of a child's drawing of a man, a woman, or a self-portrait. Each point is scored + or 0, indicating the presence or absence of a part of body detail in the figure drawn. The total of + scores is equated with separate age norms, established for boys and girls. The scale is based on the assumption that as individuals mature intellectually, they perceive greater detail in the human figure that they reveal in their drawings. Variations of the test include *Draw a Man, Draw a Woman,* and *Draw Yourself.* Studies have reported correlations as high as +.60 to +.72 with the Stanford-Binet Intelligence Scale.

Characteristics of Good Observation

Observation, as a research data-gathering process, demands rigorous adherence to the spirit of scientific inquiry. The following standards should characterize observers and their observations:

Observation is carefully planned, systematic, and perceptive. Observers know what they are looking for and what is irrelevant in a situation. They are not distracted by the dramatic or the spectacular.

Observers are aware of the wholeness of what is observed. Although they are alert to significant details, they know that the whole is often greater than the sum of its parts.

Observers are objective. They recognize their likely biases, and they strive to eliminate their influence upon what they see and report.

Observers separate the facts from the interpretation of the facts. They observe the facts and make their interpretation at a later time.

Observations are checked and verified, whenever possible by repetition, or by comparison with those of other competent observers.

Observations are carefully and expertly recorded. Observers use appropriate instruments to systematize, quantify, and preserve the results of their observations.

INQUIRY FORMS: THE QUESTIONNAIRE

The general category of inquiry forms includes data-gathering instruments through which respondents answer questions or respond to statements in writing. A questionnaire is used when factual information is desired. When opinions rather than facts are desired, an *opinionnaire* or *attitude scale* is used.

Questionnaires administered personally to groups of individuals have a number of advantages. The person administering the instrument has an opportunity to establish rapport, explain the purpose of the study, and explain the meaning of items that may not be clear. The availability of a number of respondents in one place makes possible an economy of time and expense and provides a high proportion of usable responses. It is likely that a principal would get completely usable responses from teachers in the building, or a teacher from students in the classroom. However, individuals who have the desired information cannot always be contacted personally without the expenditure of a great deal of time and money in travel. It is in such situations that the mailed questionnaire may be useful. The mailed questionnaire is one of the most used and probably most criticized data-gathering device. It has been referred to as the lazy person's way of gaining information, although the careful preparation of a good questionnaire takes a great deal of time, ingenuity, and hard work. There is little doubt that the poorly constructed questionnaires that flood the mails have created a certain amount of contempt. This is particularly true when the accompanying letter pleads that the sender needs the information to complete the requirements for a graduate course, thesis, or dissertation. The recipient's reaction may be, "Why should I go to all this trouble to help this person get a degree?"

Filling out lengthy questionnaires takes a great deal of time and effort, a favor that few senders have any right to expect of strangers. The unfavorable reaction is intensified when the questionnaire is long, the subject trivial, the items vaguely worded, and the form poorly organized. The poor quality of so many mailed questionnaires helps to explain why so small a proportion is returned. As a result of low response rates, often less than 40 percent, the data obtained are often of limited validity. The information in the unreturned questionnaires might have changed the results of the investigation materially. The very fact of no response might imply certain types of reactions, reactions that can never be included in the summary of data.

Unless one is dealing with a group of respondents who have a genuine interest in the problem under investigation, know the sender, or have some common bond of loyalty to a sponsoring institution or organization, the rate of returns is frequently disappointing and provides a flimsy basis for generalization.

Although the foregoing discussion may seem to discredit the questionnaire as a respectable research technique, we have tried to consider the abuse or misuse of the device. Actually the questionnaire has unique advantages, and properly constructed and administered, it may serve as a most appropriate and useful data-gathering device in a research project.

The Closed Form

Questionnaires that call for short, check-mark responses are known as the *restricted* or *closed-form* type. Here you mark a *yes* or *no*, write a short response, or check an item from a list of suggested responses. The following example illustrates the closed-form item:

Why did you choose to do your graduate work at this university? Kindly indicate three reasons in order of importance, using the number 1 for the most important, 2 for the second most important, and 3 for the third most important.

RANK

(a) Convenience of transportation   _____
(b) Advice of a friend   _____
(c) Reputation of institution   _____
(d) Expense factor   _____
(e) Scholarship aid   _____
(f) Other _____   _____

(kindly indicate)

Even when using the closed form, it is well to provide for unanticipated response. Providing an "other" category permits respondents to indicate what might be their most important reason, one that the questionnaire builder had not anticipated. Note the instruction to rank choices in order of importance, which enables the tabulator to properly classify all responses.

For certain types of information the closed-form questionnaire is entirely satisfactory. It is easy to fill out, takes little time, keeps the respondent on the subject, is relatively objective, and is fairly easy to tabulate and analyze.

The Open Form

The *open-form* or *unrestricted* questionnaire calls for a free response in the respondent's own words. The following open-form item seeks the same type of information as did the closed-form item:

Why did you choose to do your graduate work at this university?

Note that no clues are given. The open form probably provides for greater depth of response. The respondents reveal their frame of reference and possibly the reasons for their responses. But because it requires greater effort on the part of the respondents, returns are often meager. The open-form item can sometimes be difficult to interpret, tabulate, and summarize in the research report.

Many questionnaires include both open- and closed-type items. Each type has its merits and limitations, and the questionnaire builder must decide which type is more likely to supply the information wanted.

Improving Questionnaire Items

Inexperienced questionnaire makers are likely to be naive about the clarity of their questions. One author of this book recalls a brilliant graduate student who submitted a questionnaire for his approval. She was somewhat irritated by his subsequent questions and suggestions, remarking that anyone with any degree of intelligence should know what she meant. At the advisor's suggestion, she duplicated some copies and personally administered the questionnaire to a graduate class in research.

She was swamped with questions of interpretation, many of which she could not answer clearly. There was considerable evidence of confusion about what she wanted to know. After she had collected the completed copies and had tried to tabulate the responses, she began to see the questionnaire's faults. Even her directions and explanation in class had failed to clarify the ambiguous intent of her questionnaire. Her second version was much improved.

Many beginning researchers are not really sure what they want to know. They use a shotgun approach, attempting to cover their field broadly in the hope that some of the responses will provide the answers for which they are groping. Unless researchers know exactly what they want, however, they are not likely to ask the right questions or to phrase them properly.

In addition to the problem of knowing what one wants, there is the difficulty of wording the questionnaire clearly. The limitations of words are particular hazards in the questionnaire. The same words mean different things to different people. After all, even questionnaire makers have their own interpretation, and the respondents may have many different interpretations. In the interview, as in conversation, we are able to clear up misunderstanding by restating our question, by inflection of the voice, by suggestions, and by a number of other devices. But the written question stands by itself, often ambiguous and misunderstood.

A simple example illustrates the influence of voice inflection alone. Consider the following question. Read it over, each time emphasizing the underlined word, noting how the change in inflection alters the meaning.

Were you there last night?
Were *you* there last night?
Were you *there* last night?
Were you there *last* night?
Were you there last *night*?

Questionnaire makers must depend on written language alone. Obviously they cannot be too careful in phrasing questions to insure their clarity of purpose. Although there are no certain ways of producing foolproof questions, certain principles can be employed to make questionnaire items more precise. A few are suggested here with the hope that students constructing questionnaires and opinionnaires will become critical of their first efforts and strive to make each item as clear as possible.

Define or qualify terms that could easily be misinterpreted.

What is the value of your house?

The meaning of the term *value* is not clear. It could imply several different meanings: the assessed value for tax purposes, what it would sell for on the present market, what you would be willing to sell it for, what it would cost to replace, or what you paid for it. These values may differ considerably. It is essential to frame questions specifically, such as, "What is the present market value of your house?"

As simple a term as *age* is often misunderstood. When is an individual twenty-one? Most people would say that a person is twenty-one from the day of the twenty-first birthday until the day of the twenty-second. But an insurance company considers a person twenty-one from age twenty and six months until age twenty-one and six months. Perhaps this question could be clarified by asking *age to nearest birthday* or *date of birth.*

Hundreds of words are ambiguous because of their many interpretations. One has only to think of such words and phrases as *curriculum, democracy, progressive education, cooperation,* and *integration*—and even such simple words as *how much* and *now.* To the question, "What work are you doing now?" the respondent might be tempted to answer, "Filling out your foolish questionnaire."

Be careful in using descriptive adjectives and adverbs that have no agreed-upon meaning. This fault is frequently found in rating scales as well as in questionnaires. *Frequently, occasionally,* and *rarely* do not have the same meanings to different persons (Hakel, 1968). One respondent's *occasionally* may be another's *rarely.* Perhaps a stated frequency—*times per week* or *times per month*—would make this classification more precise.

Beware of double negatives. Underline negatives for clarity.

Are you opposed to <u>not</u> requiring students to take showers after gym class?

Federal aid should <u>not</u> be granted to those states in which education is <u>not</u> equal regardless of race, creed, or color.

Be careful of inadequate alternatives.

Married?   Yes_____ No_____

Does this question refer to present or former marital status? How would the person answer who is widowed, separated, or divorced?

How late at night do you permit your children to watch television?

There may be no established family policy. If there is a policy, it may differ for children of different ages. It may be different for school nights or for Friday and Saturday nights, when watching a late movie may be permitted.

Avoid the double-barreled question.

Do you believe that gifted students should be placed in separate groups for instructional purposes and assigned to special schools?

One might agree on the advisability of separate groups for instructional purposes but be very much opposed to the assignment of gifted students to special schools. Two separate questions are needed.

Underline a word if you wish to indicate special emphasis.

A parent should <u>not</u> be told his child's IQ score.

Should all schools offer a <u>modern</u> foreign language?

When asking for ratings or comparisons, a point of reference is necessary.

How would you rate this student teacher's classroom teaching?
Superior_____ Average_____ Below average_____

With whom is the student teacher to be compared—an experienced teacher, other student teachers, former student teachers—or should the criterion be what a student teacher is expected to be able to do?

Avoid unwarranted assumptions.

Are you satisfied with the salary raise that you received last year?

A *no* answer might mean either that I did not get a raise or that I *did* get a raise but am not satisfied.

Do you feel that you benefited from the spankings that you received as a child?

A *no* response could mean either that the spankings did not help me, or that my parents did not administer corporal punishment. These unwarranted assumptions are nearly as bad as the classic, "Have you stopped beating your wife?"

Phrase questions so that they are appropriate for all respondents.

What is your monthly teaching salary?

Some teachers are paid on a nine-month basis, some on ten, some on eleven, and some on twelve. Three questions would be needed.

Your salary per month? _____
Number of months in school term? _____
Number of salary payments per year? _____

Design questions that will give a complete response.

Do you read the *Indianapolis Star*?   Yes_____ No_____

A *yes* or *no* answer would not reveal much information about the reading habits of the respondent. The question might be followed with an additional item, as in Figure 6–1.

Provide for the systematic quantification of responses. The type of question that asks respondents to check a number of items from a list is difficult to summarize, especially if not all respondents check the same

If your answer is *Yes*, kindly check *how often* and *what sections* of the *Star* you read.

Section	Always	Usually	Seldom	Never
National and inter-national news				
State and local news				
Editorial				
Sports				
Comic				
Society				
Financial				
Advertising				
Want ad				
Syndicated features				
Special features				
Other (specify)				

FIGURE 6–1   Sample questionnaire item.

number. One solution is to ask respondents to rank, in order of prefer-ence, a specific number of responses.

What are your favorite television programs? Rank in order of preference your first, second, third, fourth, and fifth choices.

The items can then be tabulated by inverse weightings.

1st choice   5 points
2nd choice   4 points
3rd choice   3 points
4th choice   2 points
5th choice   1 point

The relative popularity of the programs could be described for a group in terms of total weighted scores, the most popular having the largest total.

Consider the possibility of classifying the responses yourself, rather than having the respondent choose categories. If students were asked to classify their father's occupation in one of the following categories, the results might be quite unsatisfactory.

Unskilled labor _____
Skilled labor _____
Clerical work _____
Managerial work _____
Profession _____
Proprietorship _____

It is likely that by asking the children one or two short questions about their father's work, it could be classified more accurately.

1. At what place does your father work?
2. What kind of work does he do?

Very often, a researcher wants to gather information (facts) and attitudes (opinions). This allows later analyses that can determine if attitudes are related to personal characteristics such as age, sex, or race. Figure 6–2 is an example of just such a combination. This questionnaire/opinionnaire collects information about the individual and then asks for the opinion of the person regarding factors that contribute to teacher morale.

1. Male _____ Female _____
2. Age _____
3. Marital status: single _____ married _____ divorced/separated _____
4. Number of dependent children _____; their ages _____
5. Number of other dependents _____
6. Highest degree held _____
7. Years of teaching experience _____
8. Years of teaching at present school _____
9. Teaching level; primary _____ intermediate _____ upper grades _____ Jr. H.S. _____ Sr. H.S. _____; If secondary, your major teaching area _____
10. Enrollment of your school _____
11. Your average class size _____
12. Population of your community or school district _____
13. Your principal is: male _____ female _____

FIGURE 6–2 Teacher morale questionnaire–opinionnaire.

In the following questions kindly check the appropriate column:

a. *excellent* b. *good* c. *fair* d. *poor*	a	b	c	d
14. How does your salary schedule compare with those of similar school districts?				
15. How would you rate your principal on these traits? competence				
friendliness				
helpfulness				
ability to inspire				
16. How would you rate the consulting or advisory services that you receive? encourage creativity				
availability				
17. Provision made for teacher free time				
relaxation				
preparation				
lunch				
conferences				
18. How would you rate your faculty lounge?				
19. How would you rate your faculty professional library? books				
periodicals				
references				
20. How would you evaluate the adequacy of teaching materials and supplies? textbooks				
references				
AV aids				
supplies				
21. How would you evaluate the assignment of your nonteaching duties? (leave blank if item *does not apply*)				
reports				
meetings				
halls				
supervision of: { lunchroom				
playground				
study hall				
extra-class				
organizations				
22. How would you rate the compatibility of your faculty?				
23. How would you rate the parent support of your school?				
24. How would you rate your morale as a teacher?				

FIGURE 6–2 (Continued)

25. Kindly *rank in order of importance to you* at least *five* factors that you would consider most important in increasing your morale or satisfaction with your working conditions: Rank 1, most important, 2 next in importance, etc.

____ a. higher salary

____ b. smaller class size

____ c. more free time

____ d. more adequate faculty lounge

____ e. more compatible faculty

____ f. more adequate teaching materials

____ g. more effective principal

____ h. better consulting services

____ i. more effective faculty meetings

____ j. assistance of a teacher aide

____ k. more attractive classroom/building

____ l. fewer reports to make out

____m. fewer nonteaching duties

____ n. better provision for atypical students

____ o. more participation in policy making

____ p. fewer committee meetings

____ q. teaching in a higher socioeconomic area

____ r. teaching in a lower socioeconomic area

____ s. other (kindly specify)

On the back of this sheet kindly add any comments that you believe would more adequately express your feelings of satisfaction or dissatisfaction with teaching.

FIGURE 6–2   (Concluded)

CHARACTERISTICS OF A GOOD QUESTIONNAIRE

1. It deals with a significant topic, one the respondent will recognize as important enough to warrant spending his or her time on. The significance should be clearly and carefully stated on the questionnaire, or in the letter that accompanies it.

2. It seeks only that information which cannot be obtained from other sources such as school reports or census data.

3. It is as short as possible, and only long enough to get the essential data. Long questionnaires frequently find their way into the wastebasket.

4. It is attractive in appearance, neatly arranged, and clearly duplicated or printed.

5. Directions for a good questionnaire are clear and complete. Important terms are defined. Each question deals with a single idea and is

worded as simply and clearly as possible. The categories provide an opportunity for easy, accurate, and unambiguous responses.

6. The questions are objective, with no leading suggestions as to the responses desired. Leading questions are just as inappropriate on a questionnaire as they are in a court of law.

7. Questions are presented in good psychological order, proceeding from general to more specific responses. This order helps respondents to organize their own thinking so that their answers are logical and objective. It may be well to present questions that create a favorable attitude before proceeding to those that may be a bit delicate or intimate. If possible, annoying or embarrassing questions should be avoided.

8. It is easy to tabulate and interpret. It is advisable to preconstruct a tabulation sheet, anticipating how the data will be tabulated and interpreted, before the final form of the questionnaire is decided upon. This working backward from a visualization of the final analysis of data is an important step for avoiding ambiguity in questionnaire form. If computer tabulation is to be used, it is important to designate code numbers for all possible responses to permit easy transference to a computer program's format.

Preparing and Administering the Questionnaire

Get all the help you can in planning and constructing your questionnaire. Study other questionnaires, and submit your items for criticism to other members of your class or your faculty, especially those who have had experience in questionnaire construction.

In designing an inquiry form (questionnaire or opinionnaire), it is advisable to use a separate card or slip for each item. As the instrument is being developed, items can be refined, revised, or replaced by better items without recopying the entire instrument. This procedure also provides flexibility in arranging items in the most appropriate psychological order before the instrument is put into its final form.

Try out your questionnaire on a few friends and acquaintances. When you do this personally, you may find that a number of your items are ambiguous. What may seem perfectly clear to you may be confusing to a person who does not have the frame of reference that you have gained from living with and thinking about an idea over a long period. It is also a good idea to "pilot test" the instrument with a small group of persons similar to those who will be used in the study.

These dry runs will be well worth the time and effort. They may reveal defects that can be corrected before the final form is printed and committed to the mails. Once the instrument has been sent out, it is too late to remedy its defects.

Choose respondents carefully. It is important that questionnaires be sent only to those who possess the desired information and are likely to be sufficiently interested to respond conscientiously and objectively. A preliminary card, asking whether the individual would be willing to participate in the proposed study, is recommended by some research authorities. This is not only a courteous approach but a practical way of discovering those who will cooperate in furnishing the desired information.

In a study on questionnaire returns, See (1957) discovered that a better return was obtained when the original request was sent to the administrative head of an organization rather than directly to the person who had the desired information. It is likely that when a superior officer gives a staff member a questionnaire to fill out, there is an implied feeling of obligation.

Getting permission. If the questionnaire is to be used in a public school, it is essential that approval of the project be secured from the principal, who may then wish to secure approval from the superintendent of schools. Schools are understandably sensitive to public relations. One can imagine the unfavorable publicity that might result from certain types of studies made by individuals not officially designated to conduct the research.

School officials may also want to prevent the exploitation of teachers and pupils by amateur researchers, whose activities require an excessive amount of time and effort in activities not related to the purposes of the school.

If the desired information is delicate or intimate in nature, consider the possibility of providing for anonymous responses. The anonymous instrument is most likely to produce objective and honest responses. There are occasions, however, for purposes of classification or for a possible follow-up meeting, when it might be necessary to identify the respondents. If identification is needed, it is essential to convince the respondents that their responses will be held in strict confidence and that their answers will in no way jeopardize the status and security of their position.

Try to get the aid of sponsorship. Recipients are more likely to answer if a person, organization, or institution of prestige has endorsed the project. Of course, it is unethical to claim sponsorship unless it has been expressly given.

The cover letter. Be sure to include a courteous, carefully constructed cover letter to explain the purpose of the study. The letter should promise some sort of inducement to the respondent for compliance with the request. Commercial agencies furnish rewards in goods or money. In educational circles, a summary of questionnaire results is considered an appropriate reward, a promise that should be scrupulously honored after the study has been completed.

The cover letter should assure the respondent that delicate information will be held in strict confidence. And the matter of sponsorship might well be mentioned. Of course, a stamped, addressed return envelope should be included. To omit this would virtually guarantee that many of the questionnaires would go into the wastebasket. Some researchers suggest that two copies of the questionnaire be sent, one to be returned when completed and the other for the respondent's own file.

Follow-up procedures. Recipients are often slow to return completed questionnaires. To increase the number of returns, a vigorous follow-up procedure may be necessary. A courteous postcard reminding the recipient that the completed questionnaire has not been received may bring in some additional responses. This reminder will be effective with those who have just put off filling out the document or have forgotten to mail it. A further step in the follow-up process may involve a personal letter of reminder. In extreme cases a telegram, phone call, or personal visit may bring additional responses. In some cases it may be appropriate to send another copy of the questionnaire with the follow-up letter. However, the researcher must know who has already responded so as not to receive potential duplicates.

It is difficult to estimate, in the abstract, what percentage of questionnaire responses is to be considered adequate. The importance of the project, the quality of the questionnaire, the care used in selecting recipients, the time of year, and many other factors may be significant in determining the proportion of responses. In general, the smaller the percentage of responses, the smaller the degree of confidence one may place in the data collected. Of course, objectivity of reporting requires that the proportion of responses received should always be included in the research report. Babbie (1973) suggests that a response rate of 50 percent is adequate, 60 percent good, and 70 percent very good.

Validity and Reliability of Questionnaires

All too rarely do questionnaire designers deal consciously with the degree of validity or reliability of their instrument. Perhaps this is one reason why so many questionnaires are lacking in these qualities. It must be recognized, however, that questionnaires, unlike psychological tests and inventories, have a very limited purpose. They are often one-time data-gathering devices with a very short life, administered to a limited population. There are ways, however, to improve both validity and reliability of questionnaires.

Basic to the validity of a questionnaire is asking the right questions, phrased in the least ambiguous way. In other words, do the items sample a significant aspect of the purpose of the investigation?

The meaning of all terms must be clearly defined so that they have the same meaning to all respondents. Researchers need all the help they can get; suggestions from colleagues and experts in the field of inquiry may reveal ambiguities that can be removed or items that do not contribute to a questionnaire's purpose. The panel of experts may rate the instrument in terms of how effectively it samples significant aspects of its purpose, providing estimates of content validity.

It is possible to estimate the predictive validity of some types of questionnaires by follow-up observations of respondent behavior at the present time or at some time in the future. In some situations, overt behavior can be observed without invading the privacy of respondents. A correlation of questionnaire responses with voting data on a campus or community election may provide a basis for the computation of a coefficient of predictive validity.

Reliability of questionnaires may be inferred by a second administration of the instrument, comparing the responses with those of the first. Reliability may also be estimated by comparing responses of an alternate form with the original form.

INQUIRY FORMS: THE OPINIONNAIRE

An information form that attempts to measure the attitude or belief of an individual is known as an *opinionnaire,* or *attitude scale.* Because the terms *opinion* and *attitude* are not synonymous, clarification is necessary.

How people feel, or what they believe, is their attitude. But it is difficult, if not impossible, to describe and measure attitude. Researchers must depend upon what people *say* are their beliefs and feelings. This is the area of opinion. Through the use of questions, or by getting people's expressed reaction to statements, a sample of their opinions is obtained. From this statement of opinion, one may infer or estimate their attitude—what they *really* believe.

Inferring attitude from expressed opinion has many limitations. People may conceal their attitudes and express socially acceptable opinions. They may not really know how they feel about a social issue, never having given the idea serious consideration. People may be unaware of their attitude about a situation in the abstract; until confronted with a real situation, they may be unable to predict their reaction or behavior.

Even behavior itself is not always a true indication of attitude. When politicians kiss babies, their behavior may not be a true expression of affection toward infants. Social custom or the desire for social approval makes many overt expressions of behavior mere formalities, quite unrelated to people's inward feelings. Even though there is no sure method of describing and measuring attitude, the description and measurement of opinion may, in many instances, be closely related to people's real feelings or attitudes.

With these limitations in mind, psychologists and sociologists have explored an interesting area of research, basing their data upon people's expressed opinions. Several methods have been employed:

1. Asking people directly how they feel about a subject. This technique may employ a schedule or questionnaire of the open or closed form. It may employ the interview process, in which the respondents express their opinions orally.
2. Asking people to check in a list the statements with which they agree.
3. Asking people to indicate their degree of agreement or disagreement with a series of statements about a controversial subject.
4. Inferring their attitudes from reactions to projective devices, through which they may reveal attitudes unconsciously. (A *projective device* is a data-gathering instrument that conceals its purpose so that the subjects cannot guess how they should respond to appear in their best light. Thus their real characteristics are revealed.)

Three procedures for eliciting opinions and attitudes have been used extensively in opinion research, and they warrant a brief description.

Thurstone Technique

The first method of attitude assessment is known as the Thurstone Technique of Scaled Values (Thurstone & Chave, 1929). A number of statements, usually twenty or more, are gathered that express various points of view toward a group, institution, idea, or practice. They are then submitted to a panel of judges, each of whom arranges them in eleven groups ranging from one extreme to another in position. This sorting by each judge yields a composite position for each of the items. When there has been marked disagreement between the judges in assigning a position to an item, that item is discarded. For items that are retained, each is given its median scale value (see Chapter 7) between one and eleven as established by the panel.

The list of statements is then given to the subjects, who are asked to check the statements with which they agree. The median value of the statements that they check establishes their score, or quantifies their opinion.

Likert Method

The second method—the Likert Method of Summated Ratings—can be performed without a panel of judges and has yielded scores very similar to those obtained by the Thurstone method. The coefficient of correlation between the two scales was reported as high as +.92 in one study (Edwards & Kenney, 1946). Since the Likert-type scale takes much less time to construct, it offers an interesting possibility for the student of opinion research.

The first step in constructing a Likert-type scale is to collect a number of statements about a subject. The correctness of the statements is not important, as long as they express opinions held by a substantial number of people. It is important that they express definite favorableness or unfavorableness to a particular point of view and that the number of favorable and unfavorable statements is approximately equal.

After the statements have been gathered, a trial test should be administered to a number of subjects. Only those items that correlate with the total test should be retained. This testing for internal consistency will help to eliminate statements that are ambiguous or that are not of the same type as the rest of the scale.

The attitude or opinion scale may be analyzed in several ways. The simplest way to describe opinion is to indicate percentage responses for each individual statement. For this type of analysis by item, three responses—agree, undecided, and disagree—are preferable to the usual five. If a Likert-type scale is used, it may be possible to report percentage responses by combining the two outside categories: "strongly agree" and "agree"; "disagree" and "strongly disagree."

| strongly agree | undecided | disagree |
| agree | | strongly disagree |

For example, 70 percent of the male respondents agree with the statement, "Merit rating will tend to encourage conformity and discourage initiative."

The Likert scaling technique assigns a scale value to each of the five responses. Thus the instrument yields a total score for each respondent, and a discussion of each individual item, although possible, is not necessary. Starting with a particular point of view, all statements favoring the above position are scored:

SCALE VALUE

a.	strongly agree	5
b.	agree	4
c.	undecided	3
d.	disagree	2
e.	strongly disagree	1

For statements opposing this point of view, the items are scored in the opposite order:

SCALE VALUE

a.	strongly agree	1
b.	agree	2
c.	undecided	3
d.	disagree	4
e.	strongly disagree	5

The opinionnaire illustrated in Figure 6–3 attempts to measure Christian religious orthodoxy or conservatism. It is apparent that this type of instrument could be used to measure opinion in many controversial areas: racial integration, merit rating of teachers, universal military training, and many others. The test scores obtained on all the items would then measure the respondent's favorableness toward the given point of view.

Figure 6–4 illustrates an instrument that was used to seek the opinions of a group of classroom teachers toward merit rating.

If an opinionnaire consisted of 30 statements or items, the following score values would be revealing:

$30 \times 5 = 150$ Most favorable response possible
$30 \times 3 = 90$ A neutral attitude
$30 \times 1 = 30$ Most unfavorable attitude

The scores for any individual would fall between 30 and 150— above 90 if opinions tended to be favorable to the given point of view, and below 90 if opinions tended to be unfavorable.

It would be wise to conclude this discussion with a recognition of the limitations of this type of opinion measure. Obviously it is somewhat inexact and fails to measure opinion with the precision one would desire. There is no basis for belief that the five positions indicated on the scale are equally spaced. The interval between "strongly agree" and "agree" may not be equal to the interval between "agree" and "undecided." It is also unlikely that the statements are of equal value in "forness" or "against-ness." It is unlikely that the respondent can validly react to a short statement on a printed form in the absence of real-life qualifying situations. It is doubtful whether equal scores obtained by several individuals indicate equal favorableness toward the given position: Actually, different combinations of positions can yield equal score values without necessarily indicating equivalent positions of attitude or opinion. And even though the opinionnaire provides for anonymous re-

The following statements represent opinions, and your agreement or disagreement will be determined on the basis of your particular beliefs. Kindly check your position on the scale as the statement first impresses you. Indicate what you believe, rather than what you think you should believe.

     a. I strongly agree
     b. I agree
     c. I am undecided
     d. I disagree
     e. I strongly disagree

	a	b	c	d	e
1. Heaven does *not* exist as an actual place or location. ___					
2. God sometimes sets aside natural law, performing miracles. ___					
3. Jesus was born of a virgin, without a human father. ___					
4. Hell does *not* exist as an actual place or location. ___					
5. The inspiration that resulted in the writing of the Bible was no different from that of any other great religious literature. ___					
6. There is a final day of judgment for all who have lived on earth. ___					
7. The devil exists as an actual person. ___					
8. Prayer directly affects the lives of persons, whether or not they know that such prayer has been offered. ___					
9. There is another life after the end of organic life on earth. ___					
10. When on earth, Jesus possessed and used the power to restore the dead to life. ___					
11. God is a cosmic force, rather than an actual person. ___					
12. Prayer does *not* have the power to change such conditions as a drought. ___					
13. The creation of the world did *not* literally occur in the way described in the Old Testament. ___					
14. After Jesus was dead and buried, he actually rose from the dead, leaving an empty tomb. ___					
15. Everything in the Bible should be interpreted as literally true. ___					

FIGURE 6–3 A Likert-type opinionnaire.

sponse, there is a possibility that people may answer according to what they think they *should* feel rather than how they *do* feel.

Semantic Differential

The third method of attitude assessment was developed by Osgood, Suci, and Tannenbaum (1957). The semantic differential is similar to the Likert method in that the respondent indicates an attitude or opinion

MERIT RATING OPINIONNAIRE

Male _____ Female _____ Age _____
Teaching level: elementary _____ secondary _____
Marital status: single _____ married _____ divorced/separated _____
widowed _____
Years of teaching experience _____ years.

The following statements represent opinions, and your agreement or disagreement will be determined on the basis of your particular convictions. Kindly check your position on the scale as the statement first impresses you. Indicate what you believe, rather than what you think you should believe.

    a. I strongly agree
    b. I agree
    c. I am undecided
    d. I disagree
    e. I strongly disagree

	a	b	c	d	e
1. It is possible to determine what constitutes merit, or effective teaching. _____					
2. A valid and reliable instrument can be developed to measure varying degrees of teaching effectiveness. _____					
3. Additional remuneration will _not_ result in improved teaching. _____					
4. Merit rating destroys the morale of the teaching force by creating jealousy, suspicion, and distrust. _____					
5. Mutual confidence between teachers and administrators is impossible if administrators rate teachers for salary purposes. _____					
6. Merit salary schedules will attract more high-quality young people to the teaching profession.					
7. Merit salary schedules will hold quality teachers in the profession. _____					
8. Parents will object to having their children taught by nonmerit teachers. _____					
9. Merit rating can be as successful in teaching as it is in industry. _____					
10. The hidden purpose of merit rating is to hold down salaries paid to most teachers by paying only a few teachers well. _____					
11. There is no justification for paying poor teachers as well as good teachers are paid. _____					
12. Apple-polishers will profit more than superior teachers from merit rating. _____					
13. Merit rating will encourage conformity and discourage initiative. _____					
14. The way to make teaching attractive is to reward excellence in the classroom. _____					
15. Most administrators _do not_ know enough about teaching to rate their faculty members fairly.					
16. Salary schedules based on education and experience only encourage mediocre teaching. _____					

FIGURE 6–4 A Likert-type opinionnaire on merit rating.

The Average Retarded Child Is:

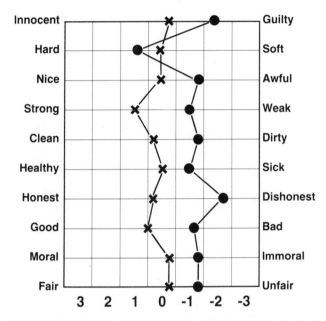

FIGURE 6–5 Semantic profiles for regular class and special class teachers. (Dots represent regular class teachers and Xs represent special class teachers.)

between two extreme choices. This method usually provides the individual with a seven-point scale with two adjectives at either end of the scale, such as good-bad, unhealthy-healthy, clean-dirty. The respondent is asked to rate a group, individual, or object on each of these bipolar scales.

One author of this book had a student who used the semantic differential method to compare the attitudes of regular teachers and special-education teachers toward mentally retarded, learning-disabled, and behavior-disordered children. The results of the semantic differential can be graphically displayed as profiles. Figure 6–5 shows a partial profile of the regular and special-education teachers when asked about mentally retarded children.

The semantic differential has limitations similar to those of the Thurstone and Likert approaches. In spite of these limitations, however, the process of opinion measurement has merit. Until more precise measures of attitude are developed, these techniques can serve a useful purpose in social research.

THE INTERVIEW

The interview is in a sense an oral questionnaire. Instead of writing the response, the subject or interviewee gives the needed information orally and face-to-face.

With a skillful interviewer, the interview is often superior to other data-gathering devices. One reason is that people are usually more willing to talk than to write. After the interviewer gains rapport or establishes a friendly, secure relationship with the subject, certain types of confidential information may be obtained that an individual might be reluctant to put in writing. (In order to establish sufficient rapport, however, it may be necessary to consider the sex, race, and possibly other characteristics of the interviewer in relation to the interviewee. For instance, a woman should probably interview rape victims, and a black person should interview other blacks regarding instances of discrimination that they have experienced.)

Another advantage of interviewing is that the interviewer can explain more explicitly the investigation's purpose and just what information he or she wants. If the subject misinterprets the question, the interviewer may follow it with a clarifying question. At the same time, he or she may evaluate the sincerity and insight of the interviewee. It is also possible to seek the same information in several ways at various stages of the interview, thus checking the truthfulness of the responses. And through the interview technique the researcher may stimulate the subject's insight into his or her own experiences, thereby exploring significant areas not anticipated in the original plan of investigation.

The interview is also particularly appropriate when dealing with young children. If one were to study what junior high school students like and dislike in teachers, some sort of written schedule would probably be satisfactory. But in order to conduct a similar study with first-grade pupils, the interview would be the only feasible method of getting responses. The interview is also well suited for illiterates and those with language difficulties.

Preparation for the interview is a critical step in the procedure. Interviewers must have a clear conception of just what information they need. They must clearly outline the best sequence of questions and stimulating comments that will systematically bring out the desired responses. A written outline, schedule, or checklist will provide a set plan for the interview, precluding the possibility that the interviewer will fail to get important and needed data.

An open-form question, in which the subject is encouraged to answer in his or her own words at some length, is likely to provide greater depth of response. In fact, this penetration exploits the advantage of the interview in getting beneath-the-surface reactions. However, distilling the essence of the reaction is difficult, and interviewer bias may be a hazard. The closed-form question (in the pattern of a multiple-choice response) is easier to record but may yield more superficial information.

Leading questions that unconsciously imply a specific answer should be avoided. The question, "Do you think that the United Nations has failed in its peace-keeping function?" illustrates the danger of eliciting agreement to an idea implanted in the question. It would be preferable to phrase it, "How effective do you feel the United Nations has been in its peace-keeping function?" This form is neutral and does not suggest a particular response. A question of this type would appropriately be followed by, "Could you explain how you reached this conclusion?"

The relationship between interviewer and subject requires an expertness and sensitivity that might well be called an art. The initial task of securing the confidence and cooperation of the subject is crucial. Talking in a friendly way about a topic of interest to the subject will often dispel hostility or suspicion, and before he or she realizes it, the subject is freely giving the desired information. As in the use of the questionnaire, the interviewer must be able to assure the subject that responses will be held in strict confidence. When interviews are not tape recorded, it is necessary for the interviewer to take written notes, either during the interview or immediately thereafter. The actual wording of the responses should be retained. It is advisable to make the interpretation later, separating this phase of analysis from the actual recording of responses.

Recording interviews on tape is preferred because they are convenient and inexpensive and obviate the necessity of writing during the interview, which may be distracting to both interviewer and subject. Interviews recorded on tape may be replayed as often as necessary for complete and objective analysis at a later time. In addition to the words, the tone of voice and emotional impact of the response are preserved by the tapes. It is unethical to record interviews without the knowledge and permission of the subject.

In order to obtain reliable and objective data, interviewers must be carefully trained. This training should include skills in developing rapport, asking probing questions, preparing for the interview, and a host of other details. The Institute for Social Research at the University of Michigan has published an excellent interview-training manual that includes a 90-minute audio cassette of a model interview and some exercises (Guenzel, Berkmans, & Cannell, 1983).

Validity and Reliability of the Interview

The key to effective interviewing is establishing rapport. This skill is somewhat intangible, including both a personality quality and a developed ability. Researchers have studied the relationship of interviewer status to the achievement of this confidence. Many studies have been conducted in which interviewers of different status have interviewed the same respondents. The responses were often significantly different both in how much the subject was willing to reveal and in the nature of the attitudes expressed.

Ethnic origin seems to be important. Interviewers of the same ethnic background as their subjects seem to be more successful in establishing rapport. When there is an ethnic difference, a certain amount of suspicion and even resentment may be encountered. The same relationship seems to prevail when the social status of the interviewer and respondent is different. Even the interviewer's clothing may have an inhibiting effect. Younger interviewers seem to be more successful than older, particularly when middle-aged respondents are involved. Women seem to have a slight advantage over men in getting candid responses, although depending on the topic (e.g., male impotence), male interviewers might be more successful. Of course, experience tends to improve interviewing skill.

Validity is greater when the interview is based upon a carefully designed structure, thus ensuring that the significant information is elicited. The critical judgment of experts in the field of inquiry is helpful in selecting the essential questions.

Reliability, or the consistency of response, may be evaluated by restating a question in slightly different form at a later time in the interview. Repeating the interview at another time may provide another estimate of the consistency of response. If more than one interviewer is used, the researcher must demonstrate reliability of technique and scoring among the interviewers. This can be done through observing the interviews and having more than one interviewer score each tape or transcript.

As a data-gathering technique, the interview has unique advantages. In areas where human motivation is revealed through actions, feelings, and attitudes, the interview can be most effective. In the hands of a skillful interviewer, a depth of response is possible that is quite unlikely to be achieved through any other means.

This technique is time-consuming, however, and one of the most difficult to employ successfully. The danger of interview bias is constant. Because the objectivity, sensitivity, and insight of the interviewer are crucial, this procedure is one that requires a level of expertness not ordinarily possessed by inexperienced researchers.

Q METHODOLOGY

Q methodology, devised by Stephenson (1953), is a technique for scaling objects or statements. It is a method of ranking attitudes or judgments (similar to the first step in the Thurstone technique) and is particularly effective when the number of items to be ranked is large. The procedure is known as a Q-sort, in which cards or slips bearing the statements or items are arranged in a series of numbered piles. Usually nine or eleven piles are established, representing relative positions on a standard scale. Some examples of simple polarized scales are illustrated.

most important	least important
most approve	least approve
most liberal	least liberal
most favorable	least favorable
most admired	least admired
most like me	least like me

The respondent is asked to place a specified number of items on each pile, usually on the basis of an approximately normal or symmetrical distribution. From 50 to 100 items should be used.

MOST LIKE ME					LEAST LIKE ME			
#	1	2	3	4	5	6	7	8	9
%	4	7	12	17	20	17	12	7	4

Self-concept Q-sort

Let us assume that a Q-sort has been designed to measure the before-and-after therapy status of a subject. A few examples of appropriate traits are presented to be placed on the scale.

afraid	ignored	discouraged
suspicious	admired	energetic
successful	disliked	loved
enthusiastic	cheerful	hated
friendly	happy	stupid

A change in position of items from before-therapy to after-therapy would indicate possible change or improvement in self-esteem. Computing the coefficient of correlation between the pile positions of items before and after therapy would provide a measure of change. If no change in item placement had occurred, the coefficient of correlation would be +1.00. If a completely opposite profile appeared, the coefficient would be −1.00. Although a perfect +1.00 or −1.00 coefficient is improbable, a high positive coefficient would indicate little change, whereas a high negative coefficient would indicate significant change.

Another type of Q-sort solicits the composite judgment of a selected panel of experts (in this case, professors of educational research). The criterion of judgment involves the relative importance of research concepts that should be included in the introductory course in educational research. One hundred slips, each listing a concept, were to be sorted into nine piles, ranging from most important to least important. A few of the concepts that were considered are listed:

hypothesis	historical method
probability	survey
dependent variable	null hypothesis
coefficient of correlation	preparing a questionnaire
sources of reference materials	deductive method
preparing the research report	descriptive method
randomization	sampling
post hoc fallacy	intervening variables
experimental method	independent variable
interviewing	Q-sorts
level of significance	standard deviation
the research proposal	nonparametric statistics
attitude studies	action research

The mean value of the positions assigned to each item indicates the composite judgment of the panel as to its relative importance.

Two applications of the Q-sort technique have been illustrated in our simplified discussion. The first attempted to measure change in the attitude of an individual toward himself or herself, the second the composite judgment of a group of individuals. Many types of analysis may be carried on in the area of attitudes by the use of Q methodology. Researchers contemplating the use of this technique should carefully consider the theoretical assumptions underlying the criteria and the items selected.

SOCIAL SCALING

Sociometry

Sociometry is a technique for describing the social relationships among individuals in a group. In an indirect way it attempts to describe attractions or repulsions between individuals by asking them to indicate whom they would choose or reject in various situations. Children in a school classroom may be asked to name in order of preference (usually two or three) the child or children that they would invite to a party, eat lunch with, sit next to, work on a class project with, or have as a close friend. Although some researchers object to the method, it is also common to ask the children to name the children, again in order of preference, that they would *least* like to invite to a party, eat lunch with, sit next to, and so forth.

There is an extensive body of sociometric research on classroom groups from kindergarten through college, fraternities and sororities, dormitory residents, camp groups, factory and office workers, military combat units, and entire communities. The United States Air Force has used sociometry to study the nature of leadership in various situations. For example, the following question was used in a study of air combat crews: "What member of the crew would you select, disregarding rank, as the most effective leader if your plane were forced down in a remote and primitive area? Name three, in order of your preference."

Scoring Sociometric Choices

One widely used procedure is to count the number of times an individual is chosen, disregarding the order of choice. This is the simplest method, and it is widely used. The objection has been raised that it is insensitive, for it does not distinguish between a first and third choice.

Another procedure is to score a first choice three points, a second choice two points, and a third choice one point. This plan's weakness is that it suggests that the difference between a third choice and no choice at all is identical to the differences between third, second, and first choices. This assumption is difficult to defend.

A third scoring procedure is based upon the concept of the normal curve standard score distribution. However, this method is more complex and seldom used.

Once obtained, the scores for each individual in the group can be related to such measures as intelligence or other traits that can be measured by tests, or to such categories as sex, race, nationality, religious affiliation, economic status, birth order, family size, grade-point average, teacher, employer, or other characteristics that may be of interest to the researcher.

The Sociogram

Sociometric choices may be represented graphically on a chart known as a *sociogram*. There are many versions of the sociogram pattern, and the reader is urged to consult specialized references on sociometry. A few observations will illustrate the nature of the sociogram.

In consulting a sociogram, boys may be represented by triangles and girls by circles. A choice may be represented by a single-pointed arrow, a mutual choice by an arrow pointing in opposite directions. Those chosen most often are referred to as *stars*, those not chosen by others as *isolates*. Small groups made up of individuals who choose one another are *cliques*.

Identifying numbers are placed within the symbols. Numbers of those chosen most often are placed nearest the center of the diagram, and numbers of those chosen less often are placed further outward. Those not chosen are, literally, on the outside (see Figure 6–6). Remember, however, that relationships among individuals in a group are changeable. Children's choices are most temporary, for stability tends to develop only with age.

Students of group relationships and classroom teachers may construct a number of sociograms over a period of time to measure changes that may have resulted from efforts to bring isolates into closer group relationships or to transform cliques into more general group membership. The effectiveness of socializing or status-building procedures can thus be measured by the changes revealed in the sociogram. Because sociometry is a peer rating rather than a rating by superiors, it adds another dimension to the understanding of members of a group.

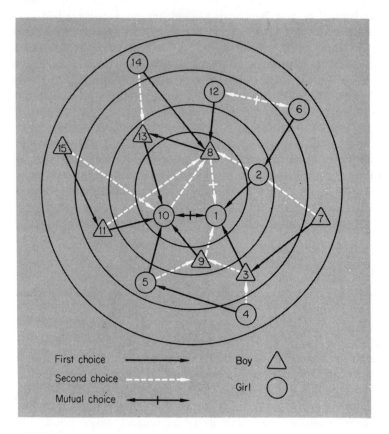

FIGURE 6–6 Sociogram showing first and second choices in a third grade class.

"Guess-who" Technique

A process of description closely related to sociometry is the "guess-who" technique. Developed by Hartshorne and May (1929), the process consists of descriptions of the various roles played by children in a group.

Children are asked to name the individuals who fit certain verbal descriptions.

This one is always happy.

This one is always picking on others.

This one is always worried.

This one never likes to do anything.

This one will always help you.

Items of this type yield interesting and significant peer judgments and are useful in the study of individual roles. Of course, the names of children chosen should not be revealed.

Social-distance Scale

Another approach to the description and measurement of social relationships is the social-distance scale, developed by Bogardus (1933). This device attempts to measure to what degree an individual or group of individuals is accepted or rejected by another individual or group.

Various scaled situations, with score values ranging from acceptance to rejection, are established. The individual checks his or her position by choosing one of the points on the scale. For example, in judging acceptance of different minority groups, the choices might range between these extremes:

Complete acceptance   I wouldn't object to having a member of this group become a member of my family by marriage.

Partial acceptance   I wouldn't mind sitting next to a member of this group on a bus.

Rejection   I don't think that members of this group should be admitted into our country.

When applied to an individual in a classroom situation, the choices might range between these extremes:

Complete acceptance   I'd like to have this student as my best friend.

Partial acceptance   I wouldn't mind sitting near this student.

Rejection   I wish this student weren't in my room.

Of course, in the real social-distance scale, illustrated by the sample items above, there would be a larger number of evenly spaced scaled positions (usually seven in number), giving a more precise measure of acceptance or rejection.

Devices of the type described here have many possibilities for the description and measurement of social relationships and, in this important area of social research, may yield interesting and useful data.

SIMPLE DATA ORGANIZATION

The following discussion is directed to the beginner and does not suggest appropriate procedures for the advanced researcher. Theses, dissertations, and advanced research projects usually involve sophisticated experimental designs and statistical analysis. The use of the computer has become standard procedure. Because it can effectively process complex variable relationships, it has made a significant contribution to research. Chapter 9 discusses computers and their uses for organizing and analyzing data.

When the results of an observation, interview, questionnaire, opinionnaire, or test are to be analyzed, problems of organization confront the researcher. The first problem is to designate appropriate logical and mutually exclusive categories for tabulation of the data. At times the hypothesis or question to be answered may suggest the type of organization. If the hypothesis involved the difference between the attitudes of men and women toward teacher merit rating, the categories *male* and *female* would be clearly indicated. In other instances the categories are not determined by the hypothesis, and other subdivisions of the group under investigation may be desirable. The researcher should keep these issues in mind when selecting, or designing, the data collection procedure. Proper attention given to this matter of organization early in the research process can save a great deal of time at the data analysis phase.

When the responses or characteristics of a group are analyzed, it is sometimes satisfactory to describe the group as a whole. In simple types of analysis, when the group is sufficiently homogeneous, no breakdown into subgroups is necessary. But in many situations the picture of the whole group is not clear. The heterogeneity of the group may yield data that have little meaning. One tends to get an unreal picture of a group of subjects that are actually very different from one another, and the differences are concealed by a description of a nonexistent or unreal average.

In such cases it may be helpful to divide the group into more homogeneous subgroups that have in common some distinctive characteristics that may be significant for the purpose of the analysis. Distinguishing between the response of men and women, between elementary and secondary teachers, or between gifted and average-learning children may reveal significant relationships.

For example, a new type of classroom organization may seem to have little impact on a group of students. But after dividing the group into two subgroups, the gifted and the average learners, some interesting relationships may become clear. The grouping may be effective for the bright students but most ineffective for the average learners.

Many studies employ the classification of data into dichotomous, or twofold, categories. When the categories are established on the basis of test scores, rankings, or some other quantitative measure, it may be advisable to compare those at the top with those at the bottom, omitting from the analysis those near the middle of the distribution. It is possible to compare the top third with the bottom third, or the top 25 percent with the bottom 25 percent. This eliminates those cases near the midpoint that tend to obscure the differences that may exist. Through elimination of the middle portion, sharper contrast is achieved, but the risk of the regression effect is increased.

Comparisons are not always dichotomous. At times it is desirable to divide a sample into more than two categories, depending on the nature of the variables that are to be considered.

Outside Criteria for Comparison

In addition to the comparisons that may be made between subgroups *within* the larger group, the group may be analyzed in terms of some *outside criteria*. Of course, it must be assumed that reasonably valid and reliable measuring devices are available for making such comparisons. These "measuring sticks" may consist of standardized tests, score cards, frequency counts, and physical as well as psychological measuring devices. Some of these outside criteria include the following:

1. *Prevailing conditions, practices, or performance of comparable units.* Comparison may be made with other communities, schools, and classes. Comparisons may be made with groups that represent best conditions or practices or typical or average status, or with equated groups that have been matched in terms of certain variables, leaving one variable or a limited number of variables for comparison.

2. *What experts believe to constitute best conditions or practices.* These experts may comprise a panel specially chosen for the pur-

pose. A group of practitioners in the field who are assumed to be most familiar with the characteristics under consideration, or the survey staff itself, may constitute the body of experts. The judgments of recognized authorities who publish their opinions are frequently selected as criteria.

3. *What a professional group, a commission, an accrediting agency, or another scholarly deliberative body establishes as appropriate standards.* These standards may be expressed as lists of objectives or may be quantitative measures of status for accreditation or approval. The American Medical Association's standards for accreditation of medical schools, the accreditation standards of the North Central Association of Secondary Schools and Colleges, or the standards of the National Commission on Teacher Education and Professional Standards for programs of teacher education are examples of evaluative criteria.

4. *Laws or rules that have been enacted or promulgated by a legislative or quasilegislative body.* Teacher certification regulations, school-building standards, or health and safety regulations provide appropriate criteria for comparison.

5. *Research evidence.* The factors to be analyzed may be examined in the light of principles confirmed by published scholarly research.

6. *Public opinion.* Although not always appropriate as a criterion of what should be, the opinions or views of "the man on the street" are sometimes appropriate as a basis for comparison.

Sorting and Tabulating Data

Tabulation is the process of transferring data from the data-gathering instruments to the tabular form in which they may be systematically examined. This process may be performed in a number of ways. In simple types of research, hand-tabulating procedures are usually employed. In more extensive investigations, a card-tabulating process may be used, possibly including machine methods.

Most simple research studies employ the method of hand-sorting and recording, with tabulations written on tabulation sheets. To save time and ensure greater accuracy, it is recommended that one person read the data while the other records them on the tabulation sheet. In constructing tally form sheets, it is important to provide enough space to record the tallies in each category.

The following discussion on hand tabulation emphasizes the importance of careful planning before the sorting and tabulation begin. Without careful planning, inexperienced researchers may waste effort when tabulating responses on a set of questionnaires filled out by a group of teachers. After completing the tabulation, they may decide to compare the responses of elementary teachers with secondary teachers. This would involve retabulating the responses of the questionnaire. It might then occur to them that it would be interesting to compare men's responses to women's. Another handling of the questionnaires would be necessary.

If they had decided upon their categories before tabulation, one handling of the questionnaires would have been sufficient. Sorting the questionnaires into two piles, one for elementary teachers and another for secondary teachers, then sorting each of these into separate piles for men and for women, would have yielded four stacks. Then, through the separate tabulation of each pile, one planned operation would have yielded the same amount of information as three unplanned operations.

Before tabulating questionnaires or opinionnaires, it is always important to decide upon the categories that are to be analyzed. If this decision is delayed, it may be necessary to retabulate the items a number of times, needlessly consuming a great deal of time and effort.

If the data-gathering device called for a larger number of responses, the system of presorting would be similar. It would be advisable, however, to set up a separate tabulation sheet for each of the categories, because a single sheet would become unwieldy.

Figure 6–7 illustrates how a three-item opinionnaire response could be tabulated for a question such as the following:

An honor system would eliminate cheating in examinations.

    I agree   ———

    I cannot say———

    I disagree   ———

Students may apply these procedures to classify and tabulate similar types of data. These data sheets are not ordinarily presented in the report, but they may suggest ways in which some of the data may be

	AGREE	*CANNOT SAY*	*DISAGREE*
Freshmen			
Sophomores			
Juniors			
Seniors			

FIGURE 6–7 Tabulation form providing for the analysis of 12 possible response categories based upon question 1 on an opinionnaire.

presented as tables or graphic figures. Relatively simple computer programs are available that can handle much of this sorting and tabulating if
the data are properly organized initially (see Chapter 9).

Tables and Figures

The process of tabulation which has just been described is the first
step in the construction of the tables for a research report. It is likely that
the beginning researcher thinks of tables purely as aids to understanding. Displaying data in rows and columns according to some logical plan
of classification may serve an even more important purpose in helping
researchers to see the similarities and relationships of their data in bold
relief.

A discussion of the construction and use of tables and figures is
presented in some detail in Chapter 10.

Percentage Comparisons

Presenting data by frequency counts has a number of limitations. If
the groups to be compared are unequal in size, the frequency count may
have little meaning. Converting to percentage responses enables the
researcher to compare subgroups of unequal size meaningfully. Trans-
lating frequency counts into percentages indicates the number-per-hun-
dred compared. The provision of a common base makes the comparison
clear.

Several limitations should be recognized in using percentage comparisons. Unless the number of frequencies is reasonably large, a percentage may be misleading and may seem to suggest an unwarranted
generalization. It may be appropriate to indicate that, of four physicians
interviewed, one believed that a particular medication would be harmful. To indicate that 25 percent of physicians interviewed believed that
the medication would be harmful creates an image of a larger sample of
physicians than was actually interviewed. It is essential that both frequency counts and percentage responses be included in the presentation and analysis of data.

In converting frequency counts to percentages, rounding to the
nearest percentage point is preferable. Because the type of data presented in educational research is not very precise, there is little value in
expressing percentages in decimal values. In other situations, however,
such as the drug industry, where ratio scales of measurement are often
used, it would be extremely important to carry a percentage reported to
four or five decimal places, particularly when a trace of an element
would be harmful if exceeded.

When using percentages in dichotomous comparisons, it is necessary to state the percentage in only one of the categories. If 65 percent of

the respondents are men, it is not necessary to indicate that 35 percent are women. Unnecessary duplication is evidence of poor reporting.

Crossbreaks

A *crossbreak* is a tabular way of presenting observations; it is a useful device for organizing and describing a data relationship. An example of an opinionnaire response is Figure 6–8. The topic presented on the opinionnaire was: "A legal abortion, during the first trimester, should be the right of any woman."

Ranking and Weighting Items

There are times when response categories are not mutually exclusive. Preferences for certain things or reasons for an act are usually explained in terms of a number of factors, rarely single ones. It would be unrealistic to expect respondents to indicate their favorite type of recreation or the single reason they decided to attend a particular university. In such instances it would be appropriate to ask the respondents to indicate two or three responses in order of importance or preference. This ranking of items makes possible a useful method of analysis. Items may be weighted in inverse order. For example, if three items are to be ranked, it is appropriate to assign weightings as follows:

1st choice	3 points
2nd choice	2 points
3rd choice	1 point

A composite judgment of the importance of the items could be determined by the weighted totals or averages for all the respondents.

Remember that when items are ranked in order, the differences between ranked items may not be equal. Ranking is not the most refined method of scaling.

	Agree	No Opinion	Disagree
Roman Catholic	8 (14)	10 (17)	40 (69)
Protestant	30 (61)	7 (14)	12 (24)
Jewish	25 (69)	9 (25)	2 (6)

Numbers are expressed frequencies of response
Numbers in parentheses are expressed as percentages

FIGURE 6–8 Crossbreak tabulation of attitudes regarding abortion.

LIMITATIONS AND SOURCES OF ERROR

A number of limitations and sources of error in the analysis and interpretation of data can jeopardize the success of an investigation. New researchers in particular need to be aware of these potential pitfalls. Some of these problems include:

1. Confusing statements with facts. A common fault is the acceptance of statements as facts. What individuals report may be a sincere expression of what they believe to be the facts in a case, but these statements are not necessarily true. Few people observe skillfully, and many forget quickly. It is the researcher's responsibility to verify all statements as completely as possible before they are accepted as facts.

2. Failure to recognize limitations. The very nature of research implies certain restrictions or limitations about the group or the situation described—its size, its representativeness, and its distinctive composition. Failure to recognize these limitations may lead to the formulation of generalizations that are not warranted by the data collected.

3. Careless or incompetent tabulation. When one is confronted with a mass of data, it is easy to make simple mechanical errors. Placing a tally in the wrong cell or incorrectly totaling a set of scores can easily invalidate carefully gathered data. Errors sometimes may be attributed to clerical helpers with limited ability and little interest in the research project.

4. Inappropriate statistical procedures. The application of the wrong statistical treatment may lead to invalid conclusions. This error may result from a lack of understanding of statistics or the limitations inherent in a particular application.

5. Computational errors. Because the statistical manipulation of data often involves large numbers and many separate operations, there are many opportunities for error. Readers may be familiar with the story of the engineer who, after witnessing the collapse of his bridge, remarked, "I must have misplaced a decimal point." There is no way to completely eliminate human fallibility, but the use of either calculators or computers will help to reduce error.

6. Faulty logic. This rather inclusive category embraces a number of errors in the thought processes of the researcher. Invalid assumptions, inappropriate analogies, inversion of cause and effect, confusion of a simple relationship with causation, failure to recognize that group phenomena may not be used indiscriminately to predict individual occurrences or behavior, failure to realize that the whole

may be greater than the sum of its parts, belief that frequency of appearance is always a measure of importance, and many other errors are limitations to accurate interpretation.

7. The researcher's unconscious bias. Although objectivity is the ideal of research, few individuals achieve it completely. There is great temptation to omit evidence unfavorable to the hypothesis and to overemphasize favorable data. Effective researchers are aware of their feelings and the likely areas of their bias and constantly endeavor to maintain the objectivity that is essential.

8. Lack of imagination. The quality of creative imagination distinguishes the true researcher from the compiler. Knowledge of the field of inquiry, skill in research procedures, experience, and skill in logical thinking are qualities that enable the adroit researcher to see relationships leading to possible generalizations that would escape the less skillful analyst. It is this ability to see all the implications in the data that produces significant discoveries.

SUMMARY

The researcher chooses the most appropriate instruments and procedures that provide for the collection and analysis of data upon which hypotheses may be tested. The data-gathering devices that have proven useful in educational research include psychological tests and inventories, questionnaires, opinionnaires, Q methodology, observation, checklists, rating scales, score cards, scaled specimens, document or content analyses, interviews, sociograms, "guess-who" techniques, and social-distance scales.

Some research investigations use but one of these devices. Others employ a number of them in combination. Students of educational research should make an effort to familiarize themselves with the strengths and limitations of these tools and should attempt to develop skill in constructing and using them effectively.

The analysis and interpretation of data represent the application of deductive and inductive logic to the research process. The data are often classified by division into subgroups and then analyzed and synthesized in such a way that hypotheses may be verified or rejected. The final result may be a new principle or generalization. Data are examined in terms of comparisons between the more homogeneous segments within the whole group and by comparison with some outside criteria.

The processes of classification, sorting, and tabulation of data are important parts of the research process. In extensive studies, mechanical and/or computer methods of sorting and tabulating are used to save time and effort and to minimize error. In smaller projects, hand-sorting and hand-tabulating processes are usually employed.

The researcher must guard against the limitations and sources of error inherent in the processes of analysis and interpretation of data.

EXERCISES

1. For what type of problem and under what circumstances would you find the following data-gathering techniques most appropriate:
   a. Likert scale
   b. Questionnaire
   c. Interview
   d. Observation
   e. Q-sort

2. Construct a short questionnaire that could be administered in class. The following topics are suggested:
   a. Leisure Interests and Activities
   b. Reasons for Selecting Teaching as a Profession
   c. Methods of Dealing with School Discipline
   d. Political Interests and Activities

3. Construct a Likert-type opinionnaire dealing with a controversial problem. One of the following topics may be appropriate:
   a. Teacher Affiliation with Professional Organizations
   b. Teacher Strikes and Sanctions
   c. Religious Activities in the School Program
   d. The Nongraded School

4. Construct a short rating scale to be used for the evaluation of the teaching performance of a probationary teacher.

5. To what extent is the administration of personal and social adjustment inventories an invasion of a student's privacy?

REFERENCES

ANASTASIA, A. (1982). *Psychological testing* (5th ed.). New York: Macmillan.

BABBIE, E. R. (1973). *Survey research methods*. Belmont, CA: Wadsworth.

BOGARDUS, E. S. (1933). A social distance scale. *Sociology and Social Research, 17*, 265–271.

BUROS, O. K. (Ed.). (1978). *Mental measurements yearbook* (8th ed.). Highland Park, NJ: Gryphon.

CRONBACH, L. J. (1951). Coefficient alpha and the internal structure of tests. *Psychometrika, 16*, 297–334.

CRONBACH, L. J. (1970). *Essentials of psychological testing*. New York: Harper and Row.

EDWARDS, A. L. & KENNEY, K. C. (1946). A comparison of the Thurstone and Likert techniques of attitude scale construction. *Journal of Applied Psychology, 30*, 72–83.

GESELL, A. (1948). *Studies in child development*. New York: Harper and Brothers.

GUENZEL, P. J., BERKMANS, T. R., & CANNELL, C. F. (1983). *General interviewing techniques: A self-instructional workbook for telephone and personal interviewer training*. Ann Arbor, MI: Institute of Social Research, University of Michigan.

HAKEL, M. (1968). How often is often? *American Psychologist, 23,* 533–534.

HALL, H. V., PRICE, A. B., SHINEDLING, M., PEIZER, S. B., & MASSEY, R. H. (1973). Control of aggressive behavior in a group of retardates, using positive and negative reinforcement. *Training School Bulletin, 70,* 179–186.

HARRIS, D. B. (1963). *Children's drawings as measures of intellectual maturity.* New York: Harcourt, Brace and World.

HARTSHORNE, H. & MAY, M. A. (1929). *Studies in deceit.* New York: Macmillan.

MITCHELL, J. V., JR. (Ed.) (1983). *Tests in print, III.* Lincoln: University of Nebraska Press.

MOONEY, R. L. (1941). *Problem checklist, high school form.* Columbus, OH: Bureau of Educational Research, Ohio State University.

OSGOOD, C. E., SUCI, G. J., & TANNENBAUM, P. H. (1957). *The measurement of meaning.* Urbana, IL: University of Illinois Press.

SEE, H. W. (1957). Send it to the President. *Phi Delta Kappan, 38,* 129–130.

STEPHENSON, W. (1953). *The study of behavior.* Chicago: University of Chicago Press.

THURSTONE, L. L. & CHAVE, E. J. (1929). *The measurement of attitudes.* Chicago: University of Chicago Press.

ADDITIONAL READINGS

ALEVIZOS, P. N., ET AL. (1978). Behavior observation instrument: A method of direct observation for program evaluation. *Journal of Applied Behavior Analysis, 11,* 243–257.

ALVERSON, L. G. (1978). Comparison of indirect measures for long duration behavior. *Journal of Applied Behavior Analysis, 11,* 530.

American Psychological Association Standards for Educational and Psychological Tests. (1974). Washington, DC: APA.

BONNEY, M. F. (1960). Sociometric methods. In *Encyclopedia of educational research.* New York: Macmillan.

CARTWRIGHT, C. A. & CARTWRIGHT, G. P. (1974). *Developing observation skills.* New York: McGraw-Hill.

EBEL, R. L. (1972). *Essentials of educational measurement.* Englewood Cliffs, NJ: Prentice-Hall.

FENLASON, A. (1952). *Essentials of Interviewing.* New York: Harper & Row.

GRONLUND, N. E. (1959). *Sociometry in the classroom.* New York: Harper & Brothers.

HERRIOTT, R. E. (1960). Survey research method. In *Encyclopedia of educational research.* New York: Macmillan.

HOPKINS, K. D. & STANLEY, J. C. (1972). *Educational and psychological measurement and evaluation* (5th ed.). Englewood Cliffs, NJ: Prentice-Hall.

HYMAN, H. H. (1975). *Survey design and analysis.* Beverly Hills, CA: Glencoe Press.

HYMAN, H. H., ET AL. (1954). *Interviewing in social research.* Chicago: University of Chicago Press.

KAHN, R. L. & CANNELL, C. F. (1957). *The dynamics of interviewing.* New York: John Wiley & Sons.

KERLINGER, F. N. (1973). *Foundations of behavioral research.* New York: Holt, Rinehart & Winston.

KISH, L. (1965). *Survey sampling.* New York: John Wiley & Sons.

MORENO, J. L. (1951). *Sociometry: Experimental method and the science of society.* New York: Beacon Press.

NUNNALY, J. C. (1972). *Educational measurement and evaluation.* New York: McGraw-Hill.

OPPENHEIM, A. N. (1966). *Questionnaire design and attitude measurement.* New York: Basic Books.

SUMMERS, G. F. (Ed.). (1970). *Attitude measurement.* Chicago: Rand McNally.

TORGERSON, W. S. (1958). *Theory and methods of scaling.* New York: John Wiley & Sons.

WEBB, E. J., CAMPBELL, D. T., SCHWARTZ, R. D. & SECHREST, L. (1966). *Unobtrusive measures: Nonreactive research in the social sciences.* Chicago: Rand McNally.

Chapter 7

Descriptive
Data Analysis

Because this textbook concentrates on educational research, the following discussion of statistical analysis is in no sense complete or exhaustive. Only some of the most simple and basic concepts are presented. Students whose mathematical experience includes high school algebra should be able to understand the logic and the computational processes involved and should be able to follow the examples without difficulty.

The purpose of this discussion is threefold:

1. To help the student, as a consumer, develop an understanding of statistical terminology and the concepts necessary to read with understanding some of the professional literature in educational research.
2. To help the student develop enough competence and know-how to carry on research studies using simple types of analysis.
3. To prepare the student for more advanced coursework in statistics.

The emphasis is upon intuitive understanding and practical application rather than on the derivation of mathematical formulas. Those who expect and need to develop real competence in educational research will have to take some of the following steps:

1. Take one or more courses in behavioral statistics and experimental design.
2. Study more specialized textbooks in statistics, particularly those dealing with statistical inference (e.g., Ferguson, 1981; Glass & Hopkins, 1984; Guilford & Fruchter, 1978; Kirk, 1982; Siegel, 1956; Winer, 1971).
3. Read research studies in professional journals extensively and critically.
4. Carry on research studies involving some serious use of statistical procedures.

WHAT IS STATISTICS?

Statistics is a body of mathematical techniques or processes for gathering, organizing, analyzing, and interpreting numerical data. Because research yields such quantitative data, statistics is a basic tool of measurement, evaluation, and research.

The word *statistics* is sometimes used to describe the numerical data that are gathered. Statistical data describe group behavior or group characteristics abstracted from a number of individual observations that are combined to make generalizations possible.

Everyone is familiar with such expressions as "the average family income," "the typical white-collar worker," or "the representative city." These are statistical concepts and, as group characteristics, may be expressed in measurement of age, size, or any other traits that can be described quantitatively. When we say that "the average fifth-grade boy is ten years old," we are generalizing about all fifth-grade boys, not any particular boy. Thus the statistical measurement is an abstraction that may be used in place of a great mass of individual measures.

The research worker who uses statistics is concerned with more than the manipulation of data. Statistical method serves the fundamental purposes of description and analysis, and its proper application involves answering the following questions:

1. What facts need to be gathered to provide the information necessary to answer the question or to test the hypothesis?
2. How are these observations to be selected, gathered, organized, and analyzed?
3. What assumptions underlie the statistical methodology to be employed?
4. What conclusions can be validly drawn from the analysis of the data?

Research consists of systematic observation and description of the characteristics or properties of objects or events for the purpose of discovering relationships between variables. The ultimate purpose is to develop generalizations that may be used to explain phenomena and to predict future occurrences. To conduct research, we must establish principles so that the observation and description have a commonly understood meaning. Measurement is the most precise and universally accepted process of description, assigning quantitative values to the properties of objects and events.

PARAMETRIC AND NONPARAMETRIC DATA

In the application of statistical treatments, two types of data are recognized.

1. *Parametric data.* Data of this type are measured data, and parametric statistical tests assume that the data are normally or nearly normally distributed. Parametric tests are applied to both interval- and ratio-scaled data.
2. *Nonparametric data.* Data of this type are either counted or ranked. Nonparametric tests, sometimes known as distribution-free tests, do not rest upon the more stringent assumption of normally distributed populations.

Table 7–1 presents a graphic summary of the levels of quantitative description and the types of statistical analysis appropriate for each level. These concepts will be developed later in the discussion.

However, the reader should be aware that many of the parametric statistics (*t* test, analysis of variance, and Pearson's *r* in particular) are still appropriate even when the assumption of normality is violated. This robustness has been demonstrated for the *t* test, analysis of variance, and

TABLE 7–1   Levels of Quantitative Description[1]

LEVEL	SCALE	PROCESS	DATA TREATMENT	SOME APPROPRIATE TESTS
4	Ratio	measured equal intervals true zero ratio relationship	parametric	*t* test analysis of variance analysis of covariance factor analysis Pearson's *r*
3	Interval	measured equal intervals no true zero		
2	Ordinal	ranked in order	nonparametric	Spearman's *rho* (ρ) Mann-Whitney Wilcoxon
1	Nominal	classified and counted		chi square median sign

[1] Refer to Chapter 6 for a discussion of the four levels of measurements.

analysis of covariance by a number of researchers including Glass, Peckham, and Sanders (1972), Lunney (1970), and Mandeville (1972). Thus, with ordinal data and even with dichotomous data (two choices such as Pass-Fail), these statistical procedures, which were designed for use with interval and ratio data, may be appropriate and useful. Pearson's *r*, which can also be used with any type of data, will be discussed later in this chapter.

DESCRIPTIVE AND INFERENTIAL ANALYSIS

Up until now we have not discussed the limits to which statistical analysis may be generalized. Two types of statistical application are relevant.

Descriptive analysis.   Descriptive statistical analysis limits generalization to the particular group of individuals observed. No conclusions are extended beyond this group, and any similarity to those outside the group cannot be assumed. The data describe one group and that group only. Much simple action research involves descriptive analysis and provides valuable information about the nature of a particular group of individuals.

Inferential analysis.   Inferential statistical analysis always involves the process of sampling and the selection of a small group that is assumed to be related to the population from which it is drawn. The small group is known as the *sample,* and the large group is the *population.* Drawing conclusions about populations based upon observations of samples is the purpose of inferential analysis.

A *statistic* is a measure based on observations of the characteristics of a sample. A statistic computed from a sample may be used to estimate a *parameter,* the corresponding value in the population from which the sample is selected. Statistics are usually represented by letters of our Roman alphabet such as X, S, and r. Parameters, on the other hand, are usually represented by letters of the Greek alphabet such as σ, and μ.

Before any assumptions can be made, it is essential that the individuals selected be chosen in such a way that the small group, or sample, approximates the larger group, or population. Within a margin of error, which is always present, and by the use of appropriate statistical techniques, this approximation can be assumed, making possible the estimation of population characteristics by an analysis of the characteristics of the sample.

It should be emphasized that when data are derived from a group without careful sampling procedures, the researcher should carefully state that findings apply only to the group observed and may not apply to or describe other individuals or groups. The statistical theory of sampling is complex and involves the estimation of error of inferred measurements, error that is inherent in estimating the relationship between a random sample and the population from which it is drawn. Inferential data analysis is presented in Chapter 8.

THE ORGANIZATION OF DATA

The list of test scores in a teacher's grade book provides an example of unorganized data. Because the usual method of listing is alphabetical, the scores are difficult to interpret without some other type of organization.

Alberts, James	60
Brown, John	78
Davis, Mary	90
Smith, Helen	70
Williams, Paul	88

The array. Arranging the same scores in descending order of magnitude produces what is known as an *array*.

90
88
78
70
60

The array provides a more convenient arrangement. The highest score (90), the lowest score (60), and the middle score (78) are easily

TABLE 7–2 Scores of 37 Students on a Semester Algebra Test

98	85	80	76	67
97	85	80	76	67
95	85	80	75	64
93	84	80	73	60
90	82	78	72	57
88	82	78	70	
87	82	78	70	
87	80	77	70	

Range = 98 − 57 = 41 + 1 = 42

TABLE 7–3　Scores on Algebra Test Grouped in Intervals of Five

SCORE INTERVAL	TALLIES	FREQUENCY (f)	INCLUDES
96–100	II	2	(96 97 98 99 100)
91–95	II	2	(91 92 93 94 95)
86–90	IIII	4	etc.
81–85	LHT II	7	
76–80	LHT LHT I	11	
71–75	III	3	
66–70	LHT	5	
61–65	I	1	
56–60	II	2	
		N = 37	

identified. Thus the range (the difference between the highest and lowest scores, plus one) can easily be determined.

Illustrated in Table 7–2 is an ungrouped data arrangement in array form.

Grouped Data Distributions

Data are often more clearly presented when scores are grouped and a frequency column is included. Data can be presented in frequency tables (see Table 7–3) with different class intervals, depending on the number and range of the scores.

A score interval with an odd number of units may be preferable because its midpoint is a whole number rather than a fraction. Because all scores are assumed to fall at the midpoint (for purposes of computing the mean) the computation is less complicated.

Even interval of four: 8　9　10　11 (midpoint 9.5)

Odd interval of five: 8　9　10　11　12 (midpoint 10)

There is no rule that rigidly determines the proper score interval, and intervals of ten are frequently used.

STATISTICAL MEASURES

Several basic types of statistical measures are appropriate in describing and analyzing data in a meaningful way.

Measures of central tendency or averages
Mean
Median
Mode
Measures of spread or dispersion
Range
Variance
Standard deviation
Measures of relative position
Percentile rank
Percentile score
Standard scores
Measures of relationship
Coefficient of correlation

Nonstatisticians use *averages* to describe the characteristics of groups in a general way. The climate of an area is often noted by average temperature or average amount of rainfall. We may describe students by grade-point averages or by average age. Socioeconomic status of groups is indicated by average income, and the return on an investment portfolio may be judged in terms of average income return. But to the statistician, the term *average* is unsatisfactory, for there are a number of types of averages, only one of which may be appropriate to use in describing given characteristics of a group. Of the many averages that may be used, three have been selected as most useful in educational research: the mean, the median, and the mode.

Measures of Central Tendency

The mean ($\overline{X}$). The mean of a distribution is commonly understood as the arithmetic average. The term *grade-point average*, familiar to students, is a mean value. It is computed by dividing the sum of all the scores by the number of scores. In formula form:

$$\overline{X} = \frac{\Sigma X}{N}$$

where $\overline{X}$ = mean
Σ = sum of
X = scores in a distribution
N = number of scores

EXAMPLE

$$X$$
$$6$$
$$5$$
$$4$$
$$3$$
$$2$$
$$\underline{1}$$

$\Sigma X = 21$
$N = 6$
$\bar{X} = 21/6 = 3.50$

The mean is probably the most useful of all statistical measures, for, in addition to the information that it provides, it is the base from which many other important measures are computed.

The median (Md).   The median is a point (not necessarily a score) in an array, above and below which one-half of the scores fall. It is a measure of position rather than of magnitude and is frequently found by inspection rather than by calculation. When there are an odd number of untied scores, the median is the middle score, as in the example below.

7
6   3 scores above
5
4—median
3
2   3 scores below
1

When there are an even number of untied scores, the median is the midpoint between the two middle scores, as in the example below.

6
5   3 scores above
4
  —median = 3.50
3
2   3 scores below
1

If the data includes tied scores at the median point, interpolation within the tied scores will be necessary. Each integer would be thought of as representing the interval from halfway between it and the next lower score to halfway between it and the next higher score. When ties occur at the midpoint of a set of scores, we portion out this interval into the number of tied scores and find the midpoint or median. Consider the following set of scores:

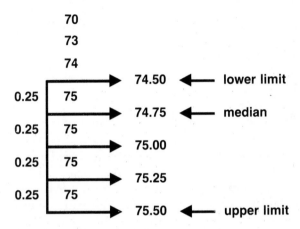

	70	
	73	
	74	
		74.50 ◄— **lower limit**
0.25	75	
		74.75 ◄— **median**
0.25	75	
		75.00
0.25	75	
		75.25
0.25	75	
		75.50 ◄— **upper limit**

FIGURE 7–1 Median calculation.

Because there are four scores tied, we divide the interval from 74.5 to 75.5 into four equal parts. Each of the scores is then considered to occupy 0.25 of the interval, and the median is calculated.

One purpose of the mean and the median is to represent the "typical" score; most of the time we are satisfied to use the mean for this purpose. However, when the distribution of scores is such that most scores are at one end and relatively few are at the other (known as a *skewed distribution*), the median is preferable because it is not influenced by extreme scores at either end of the distribution. In the following examples, the medians are identical. However, the mean of Group A is 4 and the mean of Group B is 10. The mean and median are both representative of Group A, but the median better represents the "typical" score of Group B.

GROUP A	GROUP B
7	50
6	6
5	5
4—Md	4—Md
3	3
2	2
1	0

Thus in skewed data distributions, the median is a more realistic measure of central tendency than the mean.

In a small school with five faculty members, the salaries are:

Teacher A $30,000
        B   16,000
        C   15,400 Md
        D   15,000
        E   <u>13,600</u>
            $90,000

$$\bar{X} = \frac{90,000}{5} = 18,000$$

The average salary of the group is represented with a different emphasis by the median salary ($15,400) than by the mean salary ($18,000), which is substantially higher than that of four of the five faculty members. Thus we see again that the median is less sensitive than the mean to extreme values at either end of a distribution.

The mode (Mo).

6
5
4⎤
 ⎥Mode
4⎦
3
2
1

The mode is the score that occurs most frequently in a distribution. It is located by inspection rather than by computation. In grouped data distributions, the mode is assumed to be the midscore of the interval in which the greatest frequency occurs.

For example, if the modal age of fifth-grade children is ten years, it follows that there are more ten-year-old fifth-graders than any other age. Or a menswear salesman might verify the fact that there are more sales of size 40 suits than of any other size; consequently, a larger number of size 40 suits are ordered and stocked, size 40 being the mode.

In some distributions there may be more than one mode. A two-mode distribution is bimodal, more than two, multimodal. If the number of auto accidents on the streets of a city were tabulated by hours of occurrence, it is likely that two modal periods would become apparent—

between 7 and 8 A.M. and between 5 and 6 P.M., the hours when traffic to and from stores and offices is heaviest and when drivers are in the greatest hurry. In a normal distribution of data there is one mode, and it falls at the midpoint, just as the mean and median do. In some unusual distributions, however, the mode may fall at some other point. When the mode or modes reveal such unusual behavior, they do not serve as measures of central tendency, but they do reveal useful information about the nature of the distribution.

Measures of Spread or Dispersion

Measures of central tendency describe location along an ordered scale. There are characteristics of data distributions that call for additional types of statistical analysis. The scores in Table 7–4 were made by a group of students on two different tests, one in reading and one in arithmetic.

The mean and the median are identical for both tests. It is apparent that averages do not fully describe the differences in achievement between students' scores on the two tests. To contrast their performance, it is necessary to use a measure of score spread or dispersion. The arithmetic test scores are homogenous, with little difference between adjacent scores. The reading test scores are decidedly heterogeneous, with performances ranging from superior to very poor.

TABLE 7–4   Sample Data

READING			ARITHMETIC	
Pupil	Score	Academic Grade	Score	Academic Grade
Arthur	95	A	76	C
Betty	90	A	78	C
John	85	B	77	C
Katherine	80	B	71	C
Charles	75	C	75	C
Larry	70	C	79	C
Donna	65	D	73	C
Edward	60	D	72	C
Mary	55	F	74	C

$$\Sigma X = 675 \qquad\qquad \Sigma X = 675$$
$$N = 9 \qquad\qquad N = 9$$
$$\bar{X} = \frac{675}{9} = 75 \qquad\qquad \bar{X} = \frac{675}{9} = 75$$
$$Md = 75 \qquad\qquad Md = 75$$

The range.   The range, the simplest measure of dispersion, is the difference between the highest and lowest scores plus one. For reading scores, the range is 41 (100 − 60 + 1). For arithmetic scores, the range is 5 (82 − 78 + 1).

The deviation from the mean (x).   A score expressed as its distance from the mean is called a *deviation score*. Its formula is:

$$x = (X - \bar{X})$$

If the score falls above the mean the deviation score is positive (+), if it falls below the mean the deviation score is negative (−).

Using the same example, compare two sets of scores:

READING			ARITHMETIC	
X	$(X\text{-}\bar{X})$		X	$(X\text{-}\bar{X})$
95	+20		76	+1
90	+15		78	+3
85	+10		77	+2
80	+ 5		71	−4
75	0		75	0
70	− 5		79	+4
65	−10		73	−2
60	−15		72	−3
55	−20		74	−1
$\Sigma X = 675$	$\Sigma x = 0$		$\Sigma X = 675$	$\Sigma x = 0$
$N = 9$			$N = 9$	
$\bar{X} = 75$			$\bar{X} = 75$	

It is interesting to note that the sum of the score deviations from the mean equals zero.

$$\Sigma(X - \bar{X}) = 0$$

$$\Sigma x = 0$$

In fact, we can give an alternative definition of the mean: The mean is that value in a distribution around which the sum of the deviation scores equals zero.

The variance (σ^2).   The sum of the squared deviations from the mean, divided by N, is known as the variance. We have noted that the sum of the deviations from the mean equals zero ($\Sigma x = 0$). From a mathematical point of view it would be impossible to find a mean value to describe these deviations (unless the signs were ignored). Squaring each deviation score yields a positive score. They can then be summed, divided by N, and the mean of the squared deviations computed. The variance formula is:

$$\sigma^2 = \frac{\Sigma(X - \bar{X})^2}{N} \text{ or } \frac{\Sigma x^2}{N}$$

$$x = (X - \bar{X})$$

Thus the variance is a value that describes how all of the scores in a distribution are dispersed or spread about the mean. This value is very useful in describing the characteristics of a distribution and will be employed in a number of very important statistical tests. However, since all of the deviations from the mean have been squared to find the variance, it is much too large to represent the spread of scores.

The standard deviation (σ).   The *standard deviation*, the square root of the variance, is most frequently used as a measure of spread or dispersion of scores in a distribution. The formula for standard deviation is:

$$\sigma = \sqrt{\frac{\Sigma(X - \bar{X})^2}{N}} \text{ or } \sqrt{\frac{\Sigma x^2}{N}}$$

In the following example using the reading scores from Table 7–4, the variance and the standard deviation are computed.

X	x	x^2
95	+20	+400
90	+15	+225
85	+10	+100
80	+ 5	+ 25
75	0	0
70	− 5	+ 25
65	−10	+100
60	−15	+225
55	−25	+400
		$\Sigma x^2 = 1500$

variance $\sigma^2 = 1500/9 = 166.67$

standard deviation $\sigma = \sqrt{1500/9} = \sqrt{166.67} = 12.91$

As can clearly be seen, a variance of 166.67 cannot represent, for most purposes, a spread of scores with a total range of only 41, but the standard deviation of 12.91 does make sense.

Although the deviation approach provides a clear example of the meaning of variance and standard deviation, in actual practice the deviation method can be awkward to use in computing the variances or standard deviations for a large number of scores. A less complicated method, which results in the same answer, uses the raw scores instead of the deviation scores. The number values tend to be large, but the use of a calculator facilitates the computation.

$$\text{variance } \sigma^2 = \frac{N\Sigma X^2 - (\Sigma X)^2}{N^2}$$

$$\text{standard deviation } \sigma = \sqrt{\frac{N\Sigma X^2 - (\Sigma X)^2}{N^2}}$$

The following example demonstrates the process of computation, using the raw score method:

X	X^2
95	9025
90	8100
85	7225
80	6400
75	5625
70	4900
65	4225
60	3600
55	3025
$\Sigma X = 675$	$\Sigma X^2 = 52,125$
$N = 9$	

$$\sigma^2 = \frac{9\,(52,125) - (675)^2}{9(9)} = \frac{469,125 - 455,625}{81}$$

$$\sigma^2 = \frac{13,500}{81} = 166.67$$

$$\sigma = \sqrt{166.67} = 12.91$$

The standard deviation is a very useful device for comparing characteristics that may be quite different or may be expressed in different units of measurement. The discussion that follows shows that when the normality of distributions can be assumed, it is possible to compare the proverbial apples and oranges. The standard deviation is independent of the magnitude of the mean and provides a common unit of measurement. To use a rather farfetched example, imagine a man whose height is one standard deviation below the mean and whose weight is one standard deviation above the mean. Because we assume that there is a normal relationship between height and weight (or that both characteristics are normally distributed), we have a picture of a short, overweight individual. His height, expressed in inches, is in the lowest 16 percent of the population, and his weight, expressed in pounds, is in the highest 16 percent.

This concept is developed later, but before we discuss using the standard deviation to describe status or position in a group, we need to examine the normal distribution.

NORMAL DISTRIBUTION

The earliest mathematical analysis of the theory of probability dates to the eighteenth century. Abraham DeMoivre, a French mathematician, discovered that a mathematical relationship explained the probabilities associated with various games of chance. He developed the equation and the graphic pattern that describes it. During the nineteenth century, a French astronomer, LaPlace, and a German mathematician, Gauss, independently arrived at the same principle and applied it more broadly to areas of measurement in the physical sciences. From the limited applications made by these early mathematicians and astronomers, the theory of probability, or the curve of distribution of error, has been applied to data

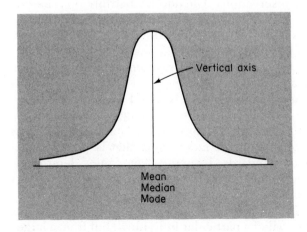

FIGURE 7–2 The normal curve.

gathered in the areas of biology, psychology, sociology, and other sciences. The theory describes the fluctuations of chance errors of observation and measurement. It is necessary to understand the theory of probability and the nature of the curve of normal distribution in order to comprehend many important statistical concepts, particularly in the area of standard scores, the theory of sampling, and inferential statistics.

The law of probability and the normal curve that illustrates it are based upon the law of chance or the probable occurrence of certain events. When any body of observations conforms to this mathematical form, it can be represented by a bell-shaped curve with definite characteristics (see Figure 7–2).

1. The curve is symmetrical around its vertical axis.
2. The terms cluster around the center (the median).
3. The mean, median, and the mode of the distribution have the same value.
4. The curve has no boundaries in either direction, for the curve never touches the base line, no matter how far it is extended. The curve is a curve of probability, not of certainty.

The operation of chance prevails in the tossing of coins or dice. It is believed that many human characteristics respond to the influence of chance. For example, if certain limits of age, race, and gender were kept constant, such measures as height, weight, intelligence, and longevity would approximate the normal distribution pattern. But the normal distribution does not appear in data based upon observations of samples. There just are not enough observations. The normal distribution is based upon an infinite number of observations beyond the capability of any observer; thus there is usually some observed deviation from the symmetrical pattern. But for purposes of statistical analysis, it is assumed that many characteristics do conform to this mathematical form within certain limits, providing a convenient reference.

The concept of measured intelligence is based upon the assumption that intelligence is normally distributed throughout limited segments of the population. Tests are so constructed (standardized) that scores are normally distributed in the large group that is used for the determination of norms or standards. Insurance companies determine their premium rates by the application of the curve of probability. Basing their expectation on observations of past experience, they can estimate the probabilities of survival of a man from age 45 to 46. They do not purport to predict the survival of a particular individual, but from a large group they can predict the mortality rate of all insured risks.

The total area under the normal curve may be considered to approach 100 percent probability. Interpreted in terms of standard deviations, areas between the mean and the various standard deviations from the mean under the curve show these percentage relationships (Figure 7–3).

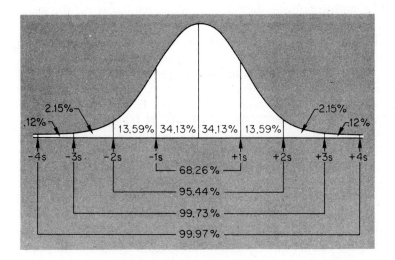

FIGURE 7–3 Percentage of frequencies in a normal distribution falling within a range of a given number of standard deviations from the mean.

Note the graphic conformation of the characteristics of the normal curve:

1. It is symmetrical—the percentage of frequencies is the same for equal intervals below or above the mean.
2. The terms "cluster" or "crowd around the mean"—note how the percentages in a given standard deviation are greatest around the mean and decrease as one moves away from the mean.

$$\overline{X} \text{ to } \pm1.00z \qquad 34.13\%$$
$$\pm1.00 \text{ to } \pm2.00z \qquad 13.59\%$$
$$\pm2.00 \text{ to } \pm3.00z \qquad 2.15\%$$
$$z = \text{standard deviation}$$
$$\text{distance from the mean}$$

3. The curve is highest at the mean—the mean, median, and mode have the same value.
4. The curve has no boundaries—a small fraction of 1 percent of the space falls outside of ±3.00 standard deviations from the mean.

The normal curve is a curve that also describes probabilities. For example, if height is normally distributed for a given segment of the population, the chances are $\frac{34.13}{100}$ that a person selected at random will be between the mean and one standard deviation above the mean in height, and $\frac{34.13}{100}$ that the person selected will be between the mean and one standard deviation below the mean in height—or $\frac{68.26}{100}$ that the selected person will be within one standard deviation (above or below) the mean in height. Another interpretation is that 68.26 percent of this population segment will be between the mean and one standard deviation above or below the mean in height.

An example may help the reader understand this concept. IQ (intelligence quotient) is assumed to be normally distributed. The Wechsler Intelligence Scale for Children–Revised (WISC-R) has a mean of 100 and a standard deviation of 15. Thus, a WISC-R IQ score that is one standard deviation above the mean is 115, and a score of 85 is one standard deviation below the mean. From this information we know that approximately 68 percent of the population should have WISC-R scores between 85 and 115.

For practical purposes the curve is usually extended to ± 3 standard deviations from the mean ($\pm 3z$). Most events or occurrences (or probabilities) will fall between these limits. The probability is $\frac{99.74}{100}$ that these limits account for observed or predicted occurrences. This statement does not suggest that events or measures could not fall more than three standard deviations from the mean but that the likelihood would be too small to consider when making predictions or estimates based upon probability. Statisticians deal with probabilities, not certainty, and there is always a degree of reservation in making any prediction. Statisticians deal with the probabilities that cover the normal course of events, not the events that are outside the normal range of experience.

Nonnormal distributions

As mentioned earlier in our discussions of parametric and nonparametric data and the relative usefulness of the mean and median, not all distributions, particularly of sample data, are identical to or even close to a normal curve. There are two other types of distributions that can occur: *skewed* and *bimodal*. With skewed distributions, the majority of scores are near the high or low end of the range, with relatively few scores at the other end. The distribution is considered skewed in the direction of the tail (fewest scores). In Figure 7–4, distribution A is skewed positively and distribution B is skewed negatively. Skewed distributions can be caused by a number of factors, including a test that is too easy or hard, or an atypical sample (very bright or very low intelligence).

Bimodal distributions have two modes (see distribution C in Figure

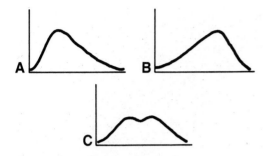

FIGURE 7-4   Nonnormal distributions.

7-4) rather than the single mode of normal or skewed distributions. This often results from a sample that consists of persons from two populations. For instance, the height of American adults would be bimodally distributed, females clustering around a mode of about 5 feet 4 inches, and males around a mode of about 5 feet 9 inches.

Interpreting the Normal Probability Distribution

When scores are normally or near normally distributed, a normal probability table is useful. The values presented in the normal probability table in Appendix B (page 341) are critical because they provide data for normal distributions that may be interpreted in the following ways:

1. The percentage of total space included between the mean and a given sigma distance (z) from the mean
2. The percentage of cases, or the number when N is known, that fall between the mean and a given sigma distance from the mean
3. The probability that an event will occur between the mean and a given sigma distance (z) from the mean

z = number of standard deviations from the mean

$$z = \frac{X - \bar{X}}{\sigma}$$

Figure 7-5 demonstrates how the area under the normal curve can be divided.
In a normal distribution the following characteristics hold true:

1. The space included between the mean and +1.00z is .3413 of the total area under the curve.
2. The percentage of cases that fall between the mean and +1.00z is .3413.

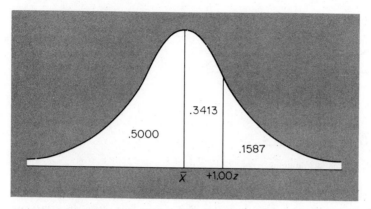

FIGURE 7–5 The space included under the normal curve between the mean and ±1.00z

3. The probability of an event occurring (observation) between the mean and +1.00z is .3413.

4. The distribution is divided into two equal parts; one half above the mean and the other half below the mean.

5. Because one half of the curve is above the mean and .3413 of the total area is between the mean and +1.00z, the area of the curve that is above +1.00z is .1587.

Because the normal probability curve is symmetrical, the shape of the right side (above the mean) is identical to the shape of the left side (below the mean). As the values for each side of the curve are identical, only one set of values is presented in the probability table, expressed to one-hundredth of a sigma (standard deviation) unit.

		PROBABILITY
above the mean	.5000	50/100
below the mean	.5000	50/100
above +1.96z	.5000 − .4750 = .0250	2.5/100
below + .32z	.5000 + .1255 = .6255	62.5/100
below − .32z	.5000 − .1255 = .3745	37.5/100

Practical Applications of the Normal Curve

In the field of educational research the normal curve has a number of practical applications:

1. To calculate the percentile rank of scores in a normal distribution.

2. To normalize a frequency distribution, an important process in standardizing a psychological test or inventory.

3. To test the significance of observed measures in experiments, relating them to the chance fluctuations or errors that are inherent in the process of sampling and generalizing about populations from which the samples are drawn.

MEASURES OF RELATIVE POSITION: STANDARD SCORES

Standard scores provide a method of expressing any score in a distribution in terms of its distance from the mean in standard deviation units. The utility of this conversion of a raw score to a standard score will become clear as each type is introduced and illustrated. Three types of standard scores are considered.

1. Sigma Score (z)
2. T Score (T)
3. College Board Score (Z_{cb})

Remember that the distribution is assumed to be normal when using any type of standard score.

The Sigma Score (z).   In describing a score in a distribution, its deviation from the mean—expressed in standard deviation units—is often more meaningful than the score itself. The unit of measurement is the standard deviation.

$$z = \frac{X - \overline{X}}{\sigma} \text{ or } \frac{x}{\sigma}$$

where X = raw score
$\overline{X}$ = mean
σ = standard deviation
$x = (X - \overline{X})$ score deviation from the mean

EXAMPLE A	EXAMPLE B
$X = 76$	$X = 67$
$\overline{X} = 82$	$\overline{X} = 62$
$\sigma = 4$	$\sigma = 5$

$$z = \frac{76 - 82}{4} = \frac{-6}{4} = -1.50 \qquad z = \frac{67 - 62}{5} = \frac{5}{5} = +1.00$$

The raw score of 76 in Example A may be expressed as a sigma score of -1.50, indicating that 76 is 1.5 standard deviations below the mean. The score of 67 in Example B may be expressed as a sigma score of +1.00, indicating that 67 is one standard deviation above the mean.

In comparing or averaging scores on distributions where total points may differ, the use of raw scores may create a false impression of a basis for comparison. A sigma score (z) makes possible a realistic comparison of scores and may provide a basis for equal weighting of the scores. On the sigma scale, the mean of any distribution is converted to zero and the standard deviation is equal to 1.

For example, a teacher wishes to determine a student's equally weighted average (mean) achievement on an algebra test and on an English test.

SUBJECT	TEST SCORE	MEAN	HIGHEST POSSIBLE SCORE	STANDARD DEVIATION
Algebra	40	47	60	5
English	84	110	180	20

It is apparent that the mean of the two raw test scores would not provide a valid summary if the student's performance for the mean weighted overwhelmingly in favor of the English test score. The conversion of each test score to a sigma score makes them equally weighted and comparable, for both test scores have been expressed on a scale with a mean of zero and a standard deviation of one.

$$z = \frac{X - \bar{X}}{\sigma}$$

$$\text{Algebra } z \text{ score} = \frac{40 - 47}{5} = \frac{-7}{5} = -1.40$$

$$\text{English } z \text{ score} = \frac{84 - 110}{20} = \frac{-26}{20} = -1.30$$

On an equally weighted basis, the performance of the student was fairly consistent: 1.40 standard deviations below the mean in algebra and 1.30 standard deviations below the mean in English.

Because the normal probability table describes the percentage of area lying between the mean and successive deviation units under the normal curve (see Appendix B), the use of sigma scores has many other useful applications to hypothesis testing, determination of percentile ranks, and probability judgments.

The T score (T).

$$T = 50 + 10 \frac{(X - \bar{X})}{\sigma} \text{ or } 50 + 10z$$

Although the sigma score (z) is most frequently used, it is some-times awkward to have negatives or scores with decimals. Therefore, another version of a standard score, the T score, has been devised to avoid some confusion resulting from negative z scores (below the mean) and also to eliminate decimal values.

Adding 50 to the mean and multiplying the z score by 10 results in a scale of positive whole number values. Using the scores in the previous example, $T = 50 + 10z$:

Algebra $T = 50 + 10(-1.40) = 50 + (-14) = 36$

English $T = 50 + 10(-1.30) = 50 + (-13) = 37$

T scores are always rounded to the nearest whole number. A sigma score of $+1.27$ would be converted to a T score of 63.

$$T = 50 + 10(+1.27) = 50 + (+12.70) = 62.70 = 63$$

The College Board score (Z_{cb}). The College Entrance Examination Board and several other testing agencies use another conversion that provides a more precise measure by spreading out the scale (see Figure 7–6).

$$Z_{cb} = 500 + 100 \frac{(X - \bar{X})}{\sigma} = 500 + 100z$$

The mean of this scale is 500.
The standard deviation is 100.
The range is 200–800.

Percentile rank. Often useful to describe a score in relation to other scores, the percentile rank is the point in the distribution below which a given percentage of scores fall. If the eightieth percentile rank is a score of 65, 80 percent of the scores fall below 65. The median is the fiftieth percentile rank, for 50 percent of the scores fall below it.

When N is small, the definition needs an added refinement. To be completely accurate, the percentile rank is the score in the distribution below which a given percentage of the scores fall, plus one half the percentage of space occupied by the given score.

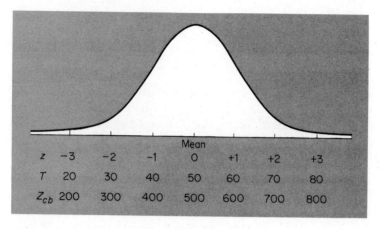

z	−3	−2	−1	0	+1	+2	+3
T	20	30	40	50	60	70	80
Z_{cb}	200	300	400	500	600	700	800

FIGURE 7–6   A comparison of three types of standard scores.

This point can be demonstrated by a rather extreme example.

SCORES
50
47
43
——
39
30

Upon inspection it is apparent that 43 is the median, or occupies the fiftieth percentile rank. Fifty percent of the scores should fall below it, but in fact only two out of five scores fall below 43. That would indicate 43 has a percentile rank of 40. But by adding the phrase "plus one half the percentage of space occupied by the score," we reconcile the calculation:

40% of scores fall below 43: each score occupies 20% of the total space

$$40\% + 10\% = 50 \text{ (true percentile rank)}$$

When N is large, this qualification is unimportant because percentile ranks are rounded to the nearest whole number, ranging from the highest percentile rank of 99 to the lowest of zero.

High schools frequently rate their graduating seniors in terms of rank in class. Because schools vary so much in size, colleges find these rankings of limited value unless they are converted to some common basis for comparison. The percentile rank provides this basis by converting class rank into a percentile rank.

$$Percentile\ rank = 100 - \frac{(100RK - 50)}{N}$$

where RK = rank from the top

Jones ranks twenty-seventh in his senior class of 139 students. Twenty-six students rank above him, 112 below him. His percentile rank is:

$$100 - \frac{(2700 - 50)}{139} = 100 - 19 = 81$$

In this formula, 50 is subtracted from $100RK$ to account for half the space occupied by the individual's score.

MEASURES OF RELATIONSHIP

Correlation. Correlation is the relationship between two or more paired variables or two or more sets of data. The degree of relationship may be measured and represented by the coefficient of correlation. This coefficient may be identified by either the letter r, the Greek letter *rho* (ρ), or other symbols depending upon the data distributions and the way the coefficient has been calculated.

Students who have high intelligence quotients tend to receive high scores in mathematics tests, whereas those with low IQs tend to score low. When this type of relationship is obtained, the factors of measured intelligence and scores on mathematics tests are said to be positively correlated.

Sometimes variables are negatively correlated when a large amount of one variable is associated with a small amount of the other. As one increases, the other tends to decrease.

When the relationship between two sets of variables is a pure-chance relationship, we say that there is no correlation.

These pairs of variables are usually positively correlated: As one increases the other tends to increase.

1. Intelligence   Academic achievement
2. Productivity per acre Value of farm land
3. Height   Shoe size
4. Family income   Value of family home

These variables are usually negatively correlated: As one increases the other tends to decrease.

1. Academic achievement   Hours per week of TV watching
2. Total corn production   Price per bushel
3. Time spent in practice   Number of typing errors
4. Age of an automobile   Trade-in value

There are other traits that probably have no correlation.

1. Body weight   Intelligence
2. Shoe size   Monthly salary

The degree of linear correlation can be represented quantitatively by the coefficient of correlation. A perfect positive correlation is +1.00. A perfect negative correlation is −1.00. A complete lack of relationship is zero (0). Rarely, if ever, are perfect coefficients of correlations of +1.00 or −1.00 encountered, particularly in relating human traits. Although some relationships tend to appear fairly consistently, there are variations or exceptions that reduce the measured coefficient from either a −1.00 or a +1.00 toward zero.

A definition of *perfect positive correlation* specifies that for every unit increase in one variable there is a proportional unit increase in the other. The *perfect negative correlation* specifies that for every unit increase in one variable there is a proportional unit decrease in the other. That there can be no exceptions explains why coefficients of correlation of +1.00 or −1.00 are not encountered in relating human traits. The sign of the coefficient indicates the direction of the relationship, and the numerical value its strength.

The scattergram and linear regression line.   When the relationship between two variables is plotted graphically, paired variable values are plotted against each other on the X and Y axis.

The line drawn through, or near, the coordinate points is known as the "line of best fit," or the *regression line*. On this line the sum of the deviations of all the coordinate points has the smallest possible value. As the coefficient approaches zero (0) the coordinate points fall further from the regression line (see Figure 7–7 for examples of different correlations' scattergrams).

When the coefficient of correlation is either +1.00 or −1.00, all of the coordinate points fall on the regression line, indicating that, when $r = +1.00$, for every increase in X there is a proportional increase in Y; and when $r = -1.00$, for every increase in X there is a proportional decrease in Y. There are no individual exceptions. If we know a person's score on one measure, we can determine his or her exact score on the other measure.

The slope of the regression line, or line of best fit, is not determined

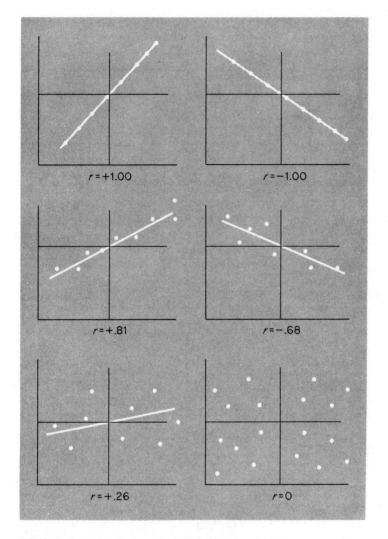

FIGURE 7-7   Scatter diagrams illustrating different coefficients of correlation.

by guess or estimation but by a geometric process that w:_. be described later.

There are actually two regression lines. When $r = +1.00$ or -1.00, the lines are superimposed and appear as one line. As r approaches zero, the lines separate further.

Only one of the regression lines is described in this discussion, the Y on X (or Y from X) line. It is used to predict unknown Y values from known X values. The X values are known as the predictor variable, and the Y values, the predicted variable. The other regression line (not de-scribed here) would be used to predict X from Y.

Plotting the slope of the regression line. The slope of the regression (Y from X) line is a geometric representation of the coefficient of correla-tion and is expressed as a ratio of the magnitude of the *rise* (if r is $+$) to the run, or as a ratio of the *fall* (if r is $-$) to the run, expressed in standard deviation units.

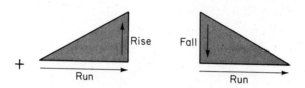

For example, if $r = +.60$, for every sigma unit increase (run) in X, there is a .60 sigma unit increase (rise) in Y.

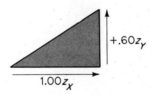

If $r = -.60$, for every sigma unit increase (run) in X, there is a .60 sigma unit decrease (fall) in Y.

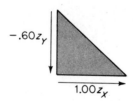

The geometric relationship between the two legs of the right trian-gle determines the slope of the hypotenuse, or the regression line.

Because all regression lines pass through the intersection of the mean of X and the mean of Y lines, only one other point is necessary to determine the slope. By measuring one standard deviation of the X dis-tribution on the X axis and a .60 standard deviation of the Y distribution on the Y axis, the second point is established (see Figures 7–8 and 7–9).

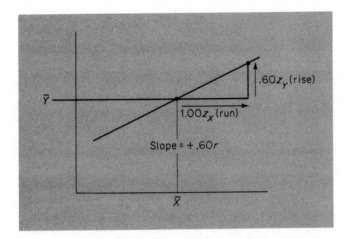

FIGURE 7–8   A positive regression line, $r = +.60$.

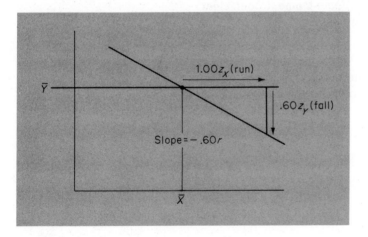

FIGURE 7–9   A negative regression line, $r = -.60$.

The regression line (r) involves one awkward feature: all values must be expressed in sigma scores (z) or standard deviation units. It would be more practical to use actual scores to determine the slope of the regression line. This can be done by converting to a slope known as b. The slope of the b regression line Y on X is determined by the formula:

$$b = r \frac{\sigma_Y}{\sigma_X}$$

For example, if $r = +.60$

$$\sigma_Y = 6$$

and

$$\sigma_X = 5$$

$$b = +.60\frac{6}{5} = \frac{3.60}{5} = +.72$$

Thus an r of $+.60$ becomes $b = +.72$. Now the ratio of the rise to the run has another value and indicates a different slope of the regression line (Figure 7–10).

Pearson's Product-Moment Coefficient of Correlation (r)

The most often used and most precise coefficient of correlation is known as the *Pearson product-moment coefficient (r)*. This coefficient may be calculated by converting the raw scores to sigma scores and finding the mean value of their cross-products.

$$r = \frac{\Sigma(z_x)(z_y)}{N}$$

z_x	z_y	$(z_x)(z_y)$
+1.50	+1.20	+1.80
+2.00	+1.04	+2.08
−.75	−.90	+.68
+.20	+.70	+.14
−1.00	+.20	−.20
−.40	+.30	−.12
+1.40	+.70	+.98
+.55	+.64	+.35
−.04	+.10	−.00
−.10	+.30	−.03

$$\Sigma(z_x)(z_y) = 5.68$$

$$r = \frac{+5.68}{10} = +.568$$

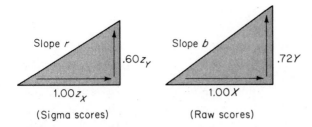

FIGURE 7–10 Two regression lines, *r* and *b*. An *r* of +.60 is converted to a *b* of +.72 by the formula

$$b = r\frac{\sigma_Y}{\sigma_X}$$

If most of the negative z values of X are associated with negative z values of Y, and positive z values of X with positive z values of Y, the correlation coefficient will be positive. If most of the paired values are of opposite signs, the coefficient will be negative.

positive correlation $(+)(+) = +$ high on X, high on Y
$(-)(-) = +$ low on X, low on Y

negative correlation $(+)(-) = -$ high on X, low on Y
$(-)(+) = -$ low on X, high on Y

The z score method is not often used in actual computation because it involves the conversion of each score into a sigma score. Two other methods, a deviation method and a raw score method, are more convenient, more often used, and yield the same result.

The deviation method uses the following formula and requires the setting up of a table with seven columns.

$$r = \frac{\Sigma\ xy}{\sqrt{(\Sigma\ x^2)(\Sigma\ y^2)}}$$

where $\Sigma\ x^2 =$ the sum of the $\bar{X}$ subtracted from each X score squared $(X - \bar{X})^2$
$\Sigma\ y^2 =$ the sum of the $\bar{Y}$ subtracted from each Y score squared $(Y - \bar{Y})$
$\Sigma\ xy =$ the cross-products of the mean subtracted from that score $(X - \bar{X})(Y - \bar{Y})$

Using the data from Table 7–4, with reading scores being the X variable and arithmetic scores being the Y variable, we calculate r like this:

VARIABLES

X	Y	x	x²	y	y²	xy
95	76	20	400	1	1	+20
90	78	15	225	3	9	+45
85	77	10	100	2	4	+20
80	71	5	25	-4	16	-20
75	75	0	0	0	0	0
70	79	-5	25	4	16	-20
65	73	-10	100	-2	4	+20
60	72	-15	225	-3	9	-45
55	74	-20	400	-1	1	+20

$\Sigma X = 675$ $\Sigma Y = 675$ $\Sigma x = 1500$ $\Sigma y = 60$ $\Sigma xy = 130$
$\bar{X} = 75$ $\bar{Y} = 75$

$$r = \frac{130}{\sqrt{(1500)(60)}} = \frac{130}{\sqrt{90,000}} = \frac{130}{300} = .433$$

The raw score method requires the use of five columns as illustrated below using the same data.

$$r = \frac{N \Sigma XY - (\Sigma X)(\Sigma Y)}{\sqrt{N \Sigma X^2 - (\Sigma X)^2}\sqrt{N \Sigma Y^2 - (\Sigma Y)^2}}$$

where ΣX = sum of the X scores
        ΣY = sum of the Y scores
        ΣX^2 = sum of the squared X scores
        ΣY^2 = sum of the squared Y scores
        ΣXY = sum of the products of paired X and Y scores
        N = number of paired scores

VARIABLES

X	Y	X²	Y²	XY
95	76	9025	5776	7220
90	78	8100	6084	7020
85	77	7225	5929	6545
80	71	6400	5041	5680
75	75	5625	5625	5625
70	79	4900	6241	5530
65	73	4225	5329	4745
60	72	3600	5184	4320
55	74	3025	5476	4070

$\Sigma X = 675$ $\Sigma Y = 675$ $\Sigma X^2 = 52,125$ $\Sigma Y^2 = 50,685$ $\Sigma XY = 50,755$

$$r = \frac{9(50,755) - (675)(675)}{\sqrt{9(52,125) - (675)^2} \, \sqrt{9(50,685) - (675)^2}}$$

$$r = \frac{456,795 - 455,625}{\sqrt{469,125 - 455,625} \, \sqrt{456,165 - 455,625}}$$

$$r = \frac{1170}{\sqrt{13,500} \, \sqrt{540}}$$

$$r = \frac{1170}{(116.19)(23.24)}$$

$$r = \frac{1170}{2700.26} = .433$$

Rank Order Correlation (ρ)

A particular form of the Pearson product-moment correlation that can be used with ordinal data is known as the Spearman rank order coefficient of correlation. The paired variables are expressed as ordinal values (ranked) rather than as interval or ratio values. It lends itself to an interesting graphic demonstration.

In the following example, the students ranking highest in IQ rank highest in mathematics, and those lowest in IQ, lowest in mathematics.

Pupil	IQ rank	Achievement in mathematics rank
A	1	1
B	2	2
C	3	3
D	4	4
E	5	5

Perfect positive coefficient of correlation

$$\rho = +1.00$$

In the following example, the students ranking highest in time spent in practice rank lowest in number of errors.

Pupil	Time spent in practice rank	Number of typing errors rank
A	1	5
B	2	4
C	3	3
D	4	2
E	5	1

Perfect negative coefficient of correlation

$$\rho = -1.00$$

In the following example, there is probably little more than a pure chance relationship (due to sampling error) between height and intelligence.

Pupil	*Height rank*	*IQ rank*
A	1	3
B	2	4
C	3	2
D	4	1
E	5	5

Very low coefficient of correlation

$$\rho = +.10$$

To compute the Spearman rank order coefficient of correlation, this rather simple formula is used:

$$\rho = 1 - \frac{6\Sigma\ D^2}{N(N^2 - 1)}$$

where D = the difference between paired ranks
   $\Sigma\ D^2$ = the sum of the squared differences between ranks
   N = number of paired ranks

If we converted the previously used data to ranks and calculated Spearman's ρ, it would look like this:

PUPIL	RANK IN READING	RANK IN ARITHMETIC	D	D²
Arthur	1	4	-3	9
Betty	2	2	0	0
John	3	3	0	0
Katherine	4	9	-5	25
Charles	5	5	0	0
Larry	6	1	5	25
Donna	7	7	0	0
Edward	8	8	0	0
Mary	9	6	3	9

$$\Sigma\ D^2 = 68$$

$$\rho = 1 - \frac{6(68)}{9(81 - 1)} = 1 - \frac{408}{9(80)}$$

$$\rho = 1 - \frac{408}{720} = 1 - .567$$

$$\rho = +.433$$

As we have just demonstrated, Spearman's ρ and Pearson's r yielded the same result. This is the case when there are no ties. When there are ties, the results will not be identical, but the difference will be insignificant.

The Spearman rank order coefficient of correlation computation is quick and easy. It is an acceptable method if data are available only in ordinal form. Teachers will find this computation method useful when conducting studies using a single class of students as subjects.

Phi Correlation Coefficient (ϕ)

The data are considered dichotomous when there are only two choices for scoring a variable (e.g., pass-fail or female-male). In these cases, each person's score usually would be represented by a 0 or 1, although sometimes 1 and 2 are used instead. The Pearson product-moment correlation, when both variables are dichotomous, is known as the *phi* (ϕ) coefficient. The formula for ϕ is simpler than for Pearson's r but algebraically identical. Because we rarely have two dichotomous variables of interest of which we want to know the relationship, we will not present the formula here. This brief mention of ϕ is to make the reader aware of it. Those wishing more detail should refer to one of the many statistics texts available (e.g., Ferguson, 1981; Glass & Hopkins, 1984).

INTERPRETATION OF A CORRELATION COEFFICIENT

Two circumstances can cause a higher or lower correlation than usual. First, when one person or relatively few people have a pair of scores that differ markedly from the rest of the sample's scores, the resulting r may be spuriously high. When this occurs, the researcher needs to decide whether to remove this individual's pair of scores (known as an *outlier*) from the data analyzed. Second, when all other things are equal, the more homogeneous a group of scores, the lower their correlation will be. That is, the smaller the range of scores, the smaller r will be. Researchers need to consider this potential problem when selecting samples that may be highly homogeneous. However, if the researcher knows the standard deviation of the heterogeneous group from which the homogeneous group was selected, Glass and Hopkins (1984) and others describe a formula that corrects for the restricted range and provides the correlation for the heterogeneous group.

There are a number of ways to interpret a correlation coefficient or adjusted correlation coefficient depending upon the researcher's purpose and the circumstances that may influence the correlation's magnitude. One method that is frequently presented is to use a crude criterion for evaluating the magnitude of a correlation:

COEFFICIENT (r)	RELATIONSHIP
.00 to .20	Negligible
.20 to .40	Low
.40 to .60	Moderate
.60 to .80	Substantial
.80 to 1.00	High to very high

Another interpretive approach is a test of statistical significance of the correlation, based upon the concept of sampling error described in the next chapter. The *test of significance*, simply put, is a test of the null hypothesis: that is, the correlation found is not different from zero. In other words, if the correlation is statistically significant, it is evidence that the variables are actually related, although the magnitude of the relationship may or may not be large. Appendix C gives a table that can be used to determine the significance of a given correlation, with only the correlation itself and the sample size required. This table is based on the probability of sampling error, which decreases as the size of the sample increases; thus, with a sample of 10, a correlation must be greater than .716 at the .01 probability level, and with a sample of 1000, a correlation need be only greater than .074 to be significant at the .01 probability level.

Still another way of interpreting a correlation coefficient is in terms of variance. The variance of the measure that we want to predict can be divided into the part that is explained by, or due to, the predictor variable and the part that is explained by other factors (generally unknown) including sampling error. We find this percent of explained variance by calculating r^2, known as the *coefficient of determination*. The percent of variance not explained by the predictor variable is then $1 - r^2$.

An example may help the reader understand this important concept. In combining studies using IQ to predict general academic achievement, Walberg (1984) found the overall correlation between these variables to be .71. We can use this correlation to find $r^2 = .50$. This means that 50 percent of the variance in academic achievement (how well or poorly different students do) is predictable from the variance of IQ. This also obviously means that 50 percent of the variance of academic achievement is due to factors other than IQ, such as motivation, home environment, school attended, test error, and so forth. Walberg also found that the correlation of IQ with science achievement was .48. This means that only 23 percent (r^2) of variance in science achievement is predictable by IQ and that 77 percent is due to other factors, some of which are known and some of which are not known.

There are additional techniques, too advanced for this introductory text, that allow researchers to use more than one variable. Thus it is possible, for example, to use a combination of IQ, self-concept scores, a measure of motivation, and a socioeconomic scale to predict academic achievement. This multiple correlation would increase the correlation, which would in turn increase the percent of variance of academic achievement that is explained by known factors.

Misinterpretation of the Coefficient of Correlation

Several fallacies and limitations should be considered in interpreting the meaning of a coefficient of correlation. The coefficient does not imply a cause-and-effect relationship between variables. High positive correlations have been observed between the number of stork's nests and the number of human births in northwestern Europe, and between the number of ordinations of ministers in the New England colonies and the consumption of gallons of rum. These high correlations obviously do not imply causality. As population increases, both good and bad things are likely to increase in frequency.

Similarly, a zero (or even negative) correlation does not necessarily mean that no causation is possible. Glass and Hopkins (1984) point out that "some studies with college students have found no correlation between hours of study for an examination and test performance. . . . [This is likely due to the fact that] some bright students study little and still achieve average scores, whereas some of their less gifted classmates study diligently but still achieve an average performance. A controlled experimental study would almost certainly show some causal relationship" (p. 106).

Prediction

An important use of the coefficient of correlation and the Y on X regression line is for prediction of unknown Y values from known X values. Because it is a method for estimating future performance of individuals on the basis of past performance of a sample, prediction is an inferential application of correlational analysis. It has been included in this chapter to illustrate one of the most useful applications of correlation.

Let us assume that a college's admissions officers wish to predict the likely academic performance of students considered for admission or for scholarship grants. They have built up a body of data based upon the past records of a substantial number of admitted college students over a period of several years. They have calculated the coefficient of correlation between their high school grade-point averages and their college freshman grade-point averages. They can now construct a regression line and predict the future college freshman GPA for any prospective student, based upon his or her high school GPA.

Let us assume that the admissions officers found the coefficient of correlation to be +.52. The slope of the line could be used to determine any Y values for any X value. This process would be quite inconvenient, however, for all grade-point averages would have to be entered as sigma (z) values.

A more practicable procedure would be to construct a regression line with a slope of b so that any college grade-point average (Y) could be predicted directly from any high school grade-point average. The b regression line and a carefully drawn graph would provide a quick method for prediction. For example:

$$\text{If:} \quad r = +.52 \quad \text{Then:} \quad b = r\frac{(S_Y)}{(S_X)}$$

$$S_Y = .50 \qquad\qquad b = +.52\frac{(.50)}{(.60)}$$

$$S_X = .60 \qquad\qquad b = +.43$$

X_A is student A's high school GPA, $\hat{Y}_A$ his predicted college GPA.
X_B is student B's high school GPA, $\hat{Y}_B$ her predicted college GPA.

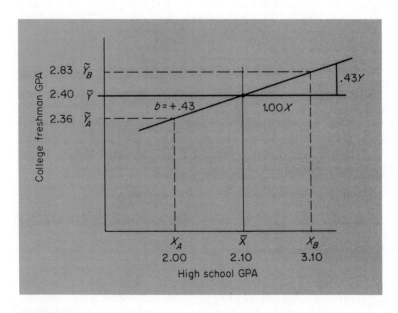

FIGURE 7–11 A regression line used to predict college freshman GPA from high school GPA.

Another, and perhaps more accurate, alternative for predicting unknown Ys from known Xs is to use the regression equation rather than the graph. The formula for predicting Y from X is:

$$\hat{Y} = a + bx$$

$\hat{Y}$ = The predicted score (e.g., college freshman GPA)
x = The predictor slope (e.g., high school GPA)
b = Slope
a = Constant, or Y intercept

We have already seen that $b = S_Y/S_X$. We can find a by $a = \overline{Y} - b\overline{X}$. Given the following data, we can then find the most likely freshman GPA for two students.

b = .43 (found earlier)
$\overline{X}$ = 2.10
$\overline{Y}$ = 2.40
$a = 2.40 - 2.10(.43) = 2.40 - .90 = 1.50$
X_a (student A's high school GPA) = 2.00
X_b (student B's high school GPA) = 3.10

$\hat{Y}_a = 1.50 + .43(X_a)$
$\hat{Y}_a = 1.50 + .43(2.00)$
$\hat{Y}_a = 1.50 + .86$
$\hat{Y}_a = 2.36$

$\hat{Y}_b = 1.50 + .43(X_b)$
$\hat{Y}_b = 1.50 + .43(3.10)$
$\hat{Y}_b = 1.50 + 1.33$
$\hat{Y}_b = 2.83$

For student A, whose high school GPA was below the mean, the predicted college GPA was also below the mean. For student B, whose high school GPA was well above the mean, the predicted GPA was substantially above the mean. These results are consistent with a positive coefficient of correlation in general: high in X, high in Y; low in X, low in Y.

STANDARD ERROR OF ESTIMATE

When the coefficient of correlation based upon a sufficient body of data has been determined as ±1.00, there will be no error of prediction. Perfect correlation indicates that for every increase in X, there is a proportional increase (when +) or proportional decrease (when −) in Y. There are no exceptions. But when the magnitude of r is less than +1.00 or −1.00, error of prediction is inherent because there have been exceptions to a consistent, orderly relationship. The regression line does not coincide or pass through all of the coordinate values used in determining the slope.

A measure for estimating this prediction error is known as the *standard error of estimate* (S_{est}).

$$S_{est_Y} = S_Y\sqrt{1 - r^2}$$

As the coefficient of correlation increases, the prediction error decreases. When $r = \pm 1.00$

$$S_{est_Y} = S_Y\sqrt{1 - r^2} = S_Y\sqrt{1 - (1)^2} = S_Y(0) = 0$$

When $r = 0$

$$S_{est_Y} = S_Y\sqrt{1 - (0)^2} = S_Y(1) = S_Y$$

When $r = 0$ (or when the coefficient of correlation is unknown), the best blind prediction of any Y from any X is the mean of Y. This is true because we know that most of the scores in a normal distribution cluster around the mean and that about 68 percent of them would probably fall within one standard deviation from the mean. In this situation the standard deviation of Y may be thought of as the standard error of estimate. When $r = 0$, $S_{est_Y} = S_Y$.

If the coefficient of correlation is more than zero, this blind prediction can be improved upon in two ways:

1. By plotting Y from a particular X from the regression line
2. By reducing the error of prediction of Y by calculating how much S_Y is reduced by the coefficient of correlation

For example, when $r = \pm .60$

$$S_{est_Y} = S_Y\sqrt{1 - (r)^2} = S_Y\sqrt{1 - (.60)^2} = S_Y\sqrt{1 - .36}$$
$$= S_Y\sqrt{.64} = .80S_Y$$

Thus the estimate error of Y has been reduced from S_Y to $.80S_Y$. Interpretation of the standard error of estimate is similar to the interpretation of the standard deviation. If $r = \pm .60S_Y$, the standard error of estimate of Y will be $.80S_Y$. An actual performance score of Y would probably fall within a band of $\pm .80S_Y$ from the predicted Y in about 68 of 100 predic-

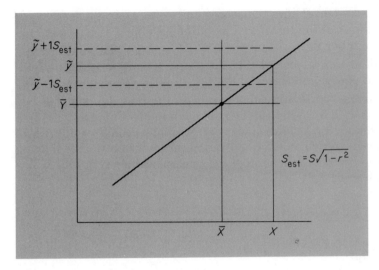

FIGURE 7–12 A predicted *Y* score from a given *X* score, showing the standard error of estimate.

tions. In other words, the probability is that the predicted score would not be more than one standard error of estimate from the actual score in about 68 percent of the predictions.

In addition to the applications described, the coefficient of correlation is indispensable to psychologists who construct and standardize psychological tests and inventories. A few of the basic procedures are briefly described.

Computing the coefficient of correlation is the usual procedure used to evaluate the degree of validity and reliability of psychological tests and inventories.

The coefficient of validity. A test is said to be valid to the degree that it measures what it claims to measure, or, in the case of predictive validity, to the extent that it predicts accurately such types of behavior as academic success or failure, job success or failure, or stability or instability under stress. Tests are usually validated by correlating test scores against some outside criteria, which may be scores on tests of accepted validity, successful performance or behavior, or the expert judgment of recognized authorities.

The coefficient of reliability. A test is said to be reliable to the degree that it measures accurately and consistently, yielding comparable results when administered a number of times. There are a number of ways of using the process of correlation to evaluate reliability:

1. Test-retest—correlating the scores on two or more successive administrations of the test (administration number 1 versus administration number 2)
2. Equivalent forms—correlating the scores when groups of individuals take equivalent forms of the test (form L versus form N)
3. Split halves—correlating the scores on the odd items of the test (numbers 1, 3, 5, 7, etc.) against the even items (numbers 2, 4, 6, 8, etc.). This method yields lower correlations because of the reduction in size to two tests of half the number of items. This may be corrected by the application of the Spearman-Brown prophecy formula.

$$r = \frac{2r}{1 + r}$$

If $r = \pm.60$,

$$r = \frac{1.20}{1 + .60} = +.75$$

A NOTE OF CAUTION

Statistics is an important tool of the research worker, and an understanding of statistical terminology, methodology, and logic is important for the consumer of research. A number of limitations, however, should be recognized in using statistical processes and in drawing conclusions from statistical evidence.

1. Statistical process, a servant of logic, only has value if it verifies, clarifies, and measures relationships that have been established by clear, logical analysis. Statistics is a means, never an end, of research.
2. A statistical process should not be employed in the analysis of data unless it adds clarity or meaning to the analysis of data. It should not be used as window dressing to impress the reader.
3. The conclusions derived from statistical analysis will be no more accurate or valid than the original data. To use an analogy, no matter how elaborate the mixer, a cake made of poor ingredients will be a poor cake. All the refinement of elaborate statistical manipulation will not yield significant truths if the data result from crude or inexact measurement. In computer terminology, this is known as GI–GO, "garbage in–garbage out."

4. All treatment of data must be checked and double-checked frequently to minimize the likelihood of errors in measurement, recording, tabulation, and analysis.

5. There is a constant margin of error wherever measurement of human beings is involved. The error is increased when qualities or characteristics of human personality are subjected to measurement or when inferences about the population are made from measurements derived from statistical samples.

When comparisons or contrasts are made, a mere number difference is not in itself a valid basis for any conclusion. A test of statistical significance should be employed to weigh the possibility that chance in sample selection could have yielded the apparent difference. To apply these measures of statistical significance is to remove some of the doubt from the conclusions.

6. Statisticians and liars are often equated in humorous quips. There is little doubt that statistical processes can be used to prove nearly anything that one sets out to prove if the procedures used are inappropriate. Starting with false assumptions, using inappropriate procedures, or omitting relevant data, the biased investigator can arrive at false conclusions. These conclusions are often particularly dangerous because of the authenticity that the statistical treatment seems to confer.

Distortion may be deliberate or unintentional. In research, omitting certain facts or choosing only those facts favorable to one's position is as culpable as actual distortion, which has no place in research. The reader must always try to evaluate the manipulation of data, particularly when the report seems to be persuasive.

SUMMARY

This chapter deals with only the most elementary statistical concepts. For a more complete treatment the reader is urged to consult one or more of the references listed.

Statistical analysis is the mathematical process of gathering, organizing, analyzing, and interpreting numerical data, and is one of the basic phases of the research process. Descriptive statistical analysis involves the description of a particular group. Inferential statistical analysis leads to judgments about the whole population, to which the sample at hand is presumed to be related.

Data are often organized in arrays in ascending or descending numerical order. Data are often grouped into class intervals so that analysis is simplified and characteristics more readily noted.

Measures of central tendency (mean, median, and mode) describe data in terms of some sort of average. Measures of position, spread, or dispersion describe data in terms of relationship to a point of central tendency. The range, deviation, variances, standard deviation, percentile, and sigma score are useful measures of position, spread, or dispersion.

Measures of relationship describe the relationship of paired variables, quantified by a coefficient of correlation. The coefficient is useful in educational research in standardizing tests and in making predictions when only some of the data are available. Note that a high coefficient does not imply a cause-and-effect relationship but merely quantifies a relationship that has been logically established prior to its measurement.

Statistics is the servant, not the master, of logic; it is a means rather than an end of research. Unless basic assumptions are valid, unless the right data are carefully gathered, recorded, and tabulated, and unless the analysis and interpretations are logical, statistics can make no contribution to the search for truth.

EXERCISES

1. More than half the families in a community can have an annual income that is lower than the mean income for that community. Do you agree or disagree? Why?
2. The median is the midpoint between the highest and the lowest scores in a distribution. Do you agree or disagree? Why?
3. Compute the mean and the median of this distribution:
    74
    72
    70
    65
    63
    61
    56
    51
    42
    40
    37
    33
4. Determine the mean, the median, and the range of this distribution:
    88
    86
    85
    80
    80

77
75
71
65
60
58

5. Compute the variance (σ^2) and the standard deviation (σ) for this set of scores:

27
27
25
24
20
18
16
16
14
12
10
7

6. The distribution with the larger range is the distribution with the larger standard deviation. Do you agree or disagree? Why?

7. If five points were added to each score in a distribution, how would this change each of the following:
   a. the range
   b. the mean
   c. the median
   d. the mode
   e. the variance
   f. the standard deviation

8. Joan Brown ranked twenty-seventh in a graduating class of 367. What was her percentile rank?

9. In a coin-tossing experiment where $N = 144$ and P (probability) $= .50$, draw the curve depicting the distribution of probable outcomes of heads appearing for an infinite number of repetitions of this experiment. Indicate the number of heads for the mean, and at 1, 2, and 3 standard deviations from the mean, both positive and negative.

10. Assuming the distribution to be normal with a mean of 61 and a standard deviation of 5, calculate the following standard score equivalents:

X	x	z	T
66			
58			
70			
61			
52			

11. Using the normal probability table in Appendix B, calculate the following values:

   a. below −1.25z   _____ %
   b. above −1.25z   _____ %
   c. between −1.40z and +1.67z   _____ %
   d. between +1.50z and +2.50z   _____ %
   e. 65th percentile rank   _____ z
   f. 43rd percentile rank   _____ z
   g. top 1% of scores   _____ z
   h. middle 50% of scores   _____ z to _____ z
   i. not included between −1.00z and +1.00z   _____ %
   j. 50th percentile rank   _____ z

12. Assuming a normal distribution of scores, a test has a mean score of 100 and a standard deviation of 15. Compute the following scores:

   a. score that cuts off the top 10%   _____
   b. score that cuts off the lower 40%   _____
   c. percentage of scores above 90   _____%
   d. score that occupies the 68th percentile rank   _____
   e. score limits of the middle 68%   _____ to _____

13. Consider the following table showing the performance of three students in algebra and history:

	MEAN	σ	TOM	DONNA	HARRY
Algebra	90	30	60	100	85
History	20	4	25	22	19

Who had:

   a. the poorest score on either test?   _____
   b. the best score on either test?   _____
   c. the most consistent scores on both tests? _____
   d. the least consistent scores on both tests? _____
   e. the best mean score on both tests?   _____
   f. the poorest mean score on both tests?   _____

14. The coefficient of correlation measures the magnitude of the cause-and-effect relationship between paired variables. Do you agree or disagree? Why?

15. Using the Spearman rank order coefficient of correlation method, compute ρ.

	X VARIABLE	Y VARIABLE
Mary	1	3
Peter	2	4

Paul	3	1
Helen	4	2
Ruth	5	7
Edward	6	5
John	7	6

16. Two sets of paired variables are expressed in sigma (z) scores. Compute the coefficient of correlation between them.

z_X	z_Y
+.70	+.55
−.20	−.32
+1.50	+2.00
+1.33	+1.20
−.88	−1.06
+.32	−.40
−1.00	+.50
+.67	+.80
−.30	−.10
+1.25	+1.10
+.50	−.20

17. Using the Pearson product-moment raw score method, compute the coefficient of correlation between these paired variables:

X	Y	X^2	Y^2	XY
66	42			
50	55			
43	60			
8	24			
12	30			
35	18			
24	48			
20	35			
16	22			
54	38			

18. A class took a statistics test. The students completed all of the questions. The coefficient of correlation between the number of correct and the number of incorrect responses for the class was _____.

19. There is a significant difference between the slope of the regression line r and that of the regression line b. Do you agree? Why?

20. Compute the standard error of estimate of Y from X when:

$$S_Y = 6.20$$
$$r = +.60$$

21. Given the following information, predict the Y score from the given X, when $X = 90$, and:

a. $r = +.60$

$\overline{X} = 80 \quad S_X = 12$

$\overline{Y} = 40 \quad S_Y = 8$

b. $r = -.60$

REFERENCES

FERGUSON, G. A. (1981). *Statistical analysis in psychology and education* (5th ed.). New York: McGraw-Hill.

GLASS, G. V. & HOPKINS, K. D. (1984). *Statistical methods in education and psychology* (2nd ed.). Englewood Cliffs, NJ: Prentice-Hall.

GLASS, G. V., PECKHAM, P. D., & SANDERS, J. R. (1972). Consequences of failure to meet assumptions underlying the fixed effects analysis of variance and covariance. *Review of Educational Research, 42,* 237–288.

GUILFORD, J. P. & FRUCHTER, B. (1978). *Fundamental statistics in psychology and education.* New York: McGraw-Hill.

KIRK, R. E. (1982). *Experimental design: Procedures for the behavioral sciences.* Belmont, CA: Brooks/Cole.

LUNNEY, G. H. (1970). Using analysis of variance with a dichotomous dependent variable: An empirical study. *Journal of Educational Measurement, 7,* 263–269.

MANDEVILLE, G. K. (1972). A new look at treatment differences. *American Educational Research Journal, 9,* 311–321.

SIEGEL, S. (1956). *Nonparametric statistics for the behavioral sciences.* New York: McGraw-Hill.

WALBERG, H. J. (1984). Improving the productivity of America's schools. *Educational Leadership, 41,* 19–30.

WINER, B. J. (1971). *Statistical principles in experimental design.* New York: McGraw-Hill.

Chapter 8

Inferential
Data Analysis

In Chapter 1 we described the ultimate purpose of research as the discovery of general principles based upon observed relationships between variables. If it were necessary to observe all of the individuals in the population about which one wished to generalize, the process would be never-ending and prohibitively expensive. The practical solution is to select samples that are representative of the population of interest; then, through observations and analysis of the sample data, the researcher may infer characteristics of the population. (The reader may wish to refer to the discussion of types of samples and sampling procedures presented in Chapter 1.)

STATISTICAL INFERENCE

Many laypersons share the misconception that an adequate sample must be a miniature carbon copy, or have the identical characteristics, of the population under study. If a large number of researchers selected random samples of 100 teachers from the population of all teachers in California, the mean weight of the samples would not be identical. A few would be relatively high, a few relatively low, but most would tend to cluster around the population mean. This variation of sample means is due to what is known as *sampling error*. The term does not suggest any fault or mistake in the *sampling process* but merely describes the chance variations that are inevitable when a number of randomly selected sample means are computed.

Estimating or inferring a population characteristic (parameter) from a random sample (statistic) is not an exact process. It has been noted that successive means of randomly selected samples from the same population are not identical. Thus, if these means are not identical, it would be logical to assume that any one of them probably differs from the population mean. This would seem to present an insurmountable obstacle to statisticians, for they have only a sample to use as a basis for generalizations about a population. Fortunately, an advantage of random selection is that the sample statistic will be an unbiased estimate of the population parameter. Because the nature of the variations of random sample means is known, it is possible to estimate the degree or variation of sample means on a probability basis.

254

THE CENTRAL LIMIT THEOREM

An important principle, known as the *central limit theorem*, describes the characteristics of sample means.

If a large number of equal-sized samples (greater than 30 subjects) is selected at random from an infinite population:

1. The means of the samples will be normally distributed.
2. The mean value of the sample means will be the same as the mean of the population.
3. The distribution of sample means will have its own standard deviation. This is in actuality the distribution of the expected sampling error. Known as the *standard error of the mean*, it is computed from this formula:

$$S_{\bar{x}} = \frac{S}{\sqrt{N}}$$

where S = the standard deviation of individual scores
   N = the size of the sample
   $S_{\bar{x}}$ = the standard error of the mean

To illustrate the operation of the central limit theorem, let us assume that the mean of a sample is 180 and the standard deviation is 12. Figure 8–1 illustrates the relationship between the distribution of individual scores and the distribution of sample means when the sample size is 36. If $\bar{X} = 180$, $N = 36$, and $S = 12$:

$$S_{\bar{x}} = \frac{S}{\sqrt{N}} = \frac{12}{\sqrt{36}} = \frac{12}{6} = 2$$

The standard error of the mean has a smaller value than the standard deviation of individual scores. This is understandable, because in computing the means of samples, the extreme scores are not represented; means are middle score values. Note the difference between the range and standard deviation of individual scores and those of the sample means.

From the formula

$$S_{\bar{x}} = \frac{S}{\sqrt{N}}$$

it is apparent that as the size of the sample increases, the standard error of the mean decreases. To cite extreme cases as illustrations, as the

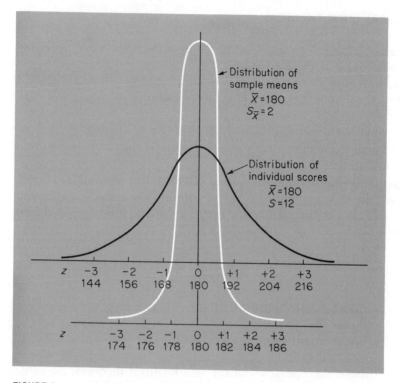

FIGURE 8–1   Normal distribution of individual scores and of sample means when $N = 36$.

sample N approaches infinity, the mean approaches the population mean and the standard error of the mean approaches zero.

$$S_{\bar{X}} = \frac{S}{\sqrt{\infty}} = \frac{S}{\infty} \doteq 0$$

As the sample is reduced in size and approaches one, the standard error of the mean approaches the standard deviation of the individual scores.

$$S_{\bar{X}} = \frac{S}{\sqrt{1}} = \frac{S}{1} = S$$

As sample size increases, the magnitude of the error decreases. Sample size and sampling error are negatively correlated (see Figure 8–2).

It may be generalized that, as the number of independent observations increases, the error involved in generalizing from sample values to population values decreases and accuracy of prediction increases.

To the statisticians who must estimate the population mean from a sample mean, their obtained sample mean would not be too far away

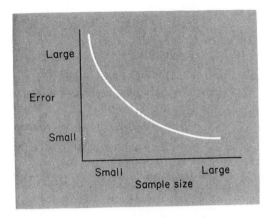

FIGURE 8–2   The relationship between sample size and the magnitude of sampling error.

from the unknown population mean. One might say that the population mean is "known only to God," but a particular mean calculated from a randomly selected sample can be related to the population mean in the following way.

The chances or probabilities are approximately

$\frac{68}{100}$ that the sample mean will not be farther than 1 $S_{\bar{x}}$ from the population mean

$\frac{95}{100}$ that the sample mean will not be farther than 1.96 $S_{\bar{x}}$ from the population mean

$\frac{99}{100}$ that the sample mean will not be farther than 2.58 $S_{\bar{x}}$ from the population mean

Thus the value of a population mean, inferred from a randomly selected sample mean, can be estimated on a probability basis. In the example presented in Figure 8–1, since $S_{\bar{x}} = 2$ points, there is approximately a $\frac{68}{100}$ probability that the mean of any randomly selected sample of $N = 36$ and $S = 12$ would not be more than 2 points away from the population mean, and $\frac{95}{100}$ probability that the sample mean would not be more than 3.92 points away ($\pm 1.96 S_{\bar{x}}$).

Knowing the mean and the standard error of the mean of a sample, we can easily determine the confidence interval, within which the "true" mean of the population most likely will be. To find the 95 percent confidence interval, the standard error of the mean is multiplied by 1.96 and the result is added to and subtracted from the mean. To find the 99 percent confidence interval, the standard error of the mean is multiplied by 2.58 and the result is added to and subtracted from the mean. Thus if we had a sample with a mean of 93, and a standard error of the mean ($S_{\bar{x}}$) of 3.2, the 95 percent confidence interval would be

$\mu_{95\%}$ (the population mean) = $93 \pm (1.96)\ S_{\bar{x}} = 93 \pm (1.96)\ 3.2 = 93 \pm 6.27$
$\mu_{95\%}$ = between 86.73 and 99.27

The 99 percent confidence interval would be

$\mu_{99\%} = 93 \pm (2.58)\ S_{\bar{x}} = 93 \pm (2.58)\ 3.2 = 93 \pm 8.86$
$\mu_{99\%}$ = between 84.14 and 101.86

We could then say that 95 times out of 100 we would probably be correct in stating that the mean of the population is between 86.73 and 99.27; and correct 99 times out of 100 in stating that the mean of the population is between 84.14 and 101.86.

PARAMETRIC TESTS

Parametric tests are considered to be the most powerful tests and should be used if their basic assumptions can be met. These assumptions are based on the nature of the population distribution and on the way the type of scale is used to quantify the data observations. However, as we mentioned in Chapter 7, some parametric tests (the *t* test and analysis of variance, in particular) are quite robust and are appropriate even when some assumptions are violated (see Glass & Hopkins, 1984, for a more complete explanation). The assumptions for most parametric tests are the following:

1. The observations are independent. The selection of one case is not dependent upon the selection of any other case (there are specific parametric tests for nonindependent samples).
2. The samples have equal or nearly equal variances. This condition is particularly important to determine when samples are small.
3. The variables described are expressed in interval or ratio scales. Nominal measures (frequency counts) and ordinal measures (ranking) do not qualify for parametric treatment.

TESTING STATISTICAL SIGNIFICANCE

The Significance of the Difference Between the Means of Two Independent Groups

Because a mean is probably the most satisfactory measure for characterizing a group, researchers find it important to determine whether the difference between means of samples is significant. To illustrate the point, an example might be helpful.

Let us assume that an experiment is set up to compare the relative effectiveness of two methods of teaching reading. A sample is randomly selected and the subjects randomly assigned to either the experimental group or the control group.

The experimental group is taught by the initial alphabet method and the control group by the traditional alphabet. At the end of a year a standardized reading test is administered and the mean score of each group is computed. The effectiveness of the experimental group method as compared to the effectiveness of the control group method is the issue, with the end-of-year mean scores of each group the basis for comparison.

A mere quantitative superiority of the experimental group mean score over the control group mean score is not conclusive proof of its superiority. Because we know that the means of two groups randomly drawn from the same population are not necessarily identical, any difference that appeared at the end of the experimental cycle could possibly be attributed to sampling error or chance. To be statistically significant, the difference must be greater than that reasonably attributed to sampling error. Determining whether a difference is significant always involves discrediting a sampling error explanation. The test of the significance of the difference between two means is known as a *t test*. It involves the computation of the ratio between experimental variance (observed difference between two sample means) and error variance (the sampling error factor).

$$t = \frac{\overline{X}_1 - \overline{X}_2}{\sqrt{\dfrac{S_1^2}{N_1} + \dfrac{S_2^2}{N_2}}}$$

$\overline{X}_1$ = mean of experimental sample
$\overline{X}_2$ = mean of control sample
N_1 = number of cases in experimental sample
N_2 = number of cases in control sample
S_1^2 = variance of experimental sample
S_2^2 = variance of control sample

If the value of the numerator in this ratio is not significantly greater than the denominator, it is likely that sampling error—not the effect of the treatment or experimental variable—is indicated. But before we discuss the quantitative criteria that determines the statistical significance of the difference between means, two additional concepts should be considered:

1. The null hypothesis (H_0)
2. The level of significance

The Null Hypothesis (H_0)

A null hypothesis states that there is no significant difference or relationship between two or more parameters. It concerns a judgment as to whether apparent differences or relationships are true differences or relationships or whether they merely result from sampling error. The experimenter formulates for statistical purposes a null hypothesis, a no-difference or relationship hypothesis. The experimenter hypothesizes that any apparent difference between the mean achievement of the experimental and control sample groups at the end of the experimental cycle is simply the result of sampling error, as explained by the operation of the central limit theorem. It should be noted that, although the null hypothesis is needed for statistical purposes, most actual hypotheses are alternatives to the null; that is, hypotheses that propose that differences will exist.

The use of the null hypothesis is not restricted to experimental studies. It may be used when inferring generalizations about populations from sample data in descriptive research studies.

Students have complained that the statement of a null hypothesis sounds like double talk. They are understandably puzzled about the reasons for the negative statement that the researcher attempts to reject. The explanation is somewhat involved, but the logic is sound. Verification of one consequence of a positive hypothesis does not prove it to be true. Observed consequences that may be consistent with a positive hypothesis may also be compatible with equally plausible but competing hypotheses. Verifying a positive hypothesis provides a rather inconclusive test.

Rejecting a null or negative hypothesis provides a stronger test of logic. Evidence that is inconsistent with a particular negative hypothesis provides a strong basis for its rejection. Before a court of law, a defendant is assumed to be not guilty until the not-guilty assumption is discredited or rejected. In a sense, the not-guilty assumption is comparable to the null hypothesis.

If the difference between the mean achievement of the experimental and the control groups is too great to attribute to the normal fluctuations that result from sampling error, the experimenter may reject the null hypothesis, saying in effect that it is probably not true that the difference is merely the result of sampling error. The means no longer behave as random sample means from the same population. Something has happened to, or affected, the experimental group in such a way that it behaves like a random sample from a different or changed population. Thus the researcher may conclude that the experimental variable or treatment probably accounted for the difference in performance, as measured by the mean test scores. The experimenter is using a statistical test to discount chance or sampling error as an explanation for the difference.

If the difference between means was not great enough to reject the null hypothesis, the researcher fails to reject it. He or she concludes that there was no significant difference and that chance or sampling error probably accounted for any observed difference.

The Level of Significance

The rejection or acceptance of a null hypothesis is based upon some level of significance (alpha level) as a criterion. In psychological and educational circles, the 5 percent (.05) alpha (α) level of significance is often used as a standard for rejection. Rejecting a null hypthesis at the .05 level indicates that a difference in means as large as that found between experimental and control group would have resulted from sampling error in less than 5 out of 100 replications of the experiment. This suggests a 95 percent probability that the difference was due to the experimental treatment rather than to sampling error.

A more rigorous test of significance is the 1 percent (.01) α level. Rejecting a null hypothesis at the .01 level would suggest that as large a difference between experimental and control mean achievement would have resulted from sampling error in less than 1 in 100 replications of the experiment.

When samples are large (more than 30 in size) the t critical value approaches the z (sigma) score. In these cases, if the z value equals or exceeds 1.96, we may conclude that the difference between means is significant at the .05 level. If the z value equals or exceeds 2.58, we may conclude that the difference between means is significant at the .01 level.

Using the example of the reading experiment previously described, let us supply the data and test the null hypothesis that there was no significant difference between the mean reading achievement of the initial-teaching alphabet experimental group and the traditional alphabet control group.

EXPERIMENTAL   CONTROL
ITA GROUP   TRADITIONAL ALPHABET GROUP

$N_1 = 32$ $N_2 = 34$
$\overline{X}_1 = 87.43$ $\overline{X}_2 = 82.58$
$S_1^2 = 39.40$ $S_2^2 = 40.80$

$$t = \frac{\overline{X}_1 - \overline{X}_2}{\sqrt{\dfrac{S_1^2}{N_1} + \dfrac{S_2^2}{N_2}}} = \frac{87.43 - 82.58}{\sqrt{\dfrac{39.40}{32} + \dfrac{40.80}{34}}}$$

$$= \frac{4.85}{\sqrt{1.23 + 1.20}} = \frac{4.85}{\sqrt{2.43}} = \frac{4.85}{1.56} \quad t = 3.11$$

Because a *t* value of 3.11 exceeds 2.58, the null hypothesis may be rejected at the .01 level of significance. If this experiment were replicated with random samples from the same population, the probability is that a difference between mean performance as great as that observed would result from sampling error in fewer than 1 out of 100 replications. This test would indicate rather strong evidence that the treatment would probably make a difference in the teaching of reading when applied to similar populations of pupils.

DECISION MAKING

Statistical decisions about parameters based upon evidence observed in samples always involve the possibility of error. Statisticians do not deal with decisions based upon certainty. They merely estimate the probability or improbability of occurrences of events.

Rejection of a null hypothesis when it is really true is known as a *Type I error.* The level of significance (alpha) selected determines the probability of a Type I error. For example, when the researcher rejects a null hypothesis at the .05 level, he or she is taking a 5 percent risk of rejecting what should be a sampling error explanation when it is probably true.

Not rejecting a null hypothesis when it is really false is known as a *Type II error.* This decision errs in accepting a sample error explanation when it is probably false.

Setting a level of significance as high as the .01 level minimizes the risk of a Type I error. But this high level of significance is more conservative and increases the risk of a Type II error. The researcher sets the level of significance based upon the relative seriousness of making a Type I or a Type II error.

Two-Tailed and One-Tailed Tests of Significance

If a null hypothesis was proposed that there was no difference (other than in sampling error) between the mean IQs of athletes and nonathletes, we would be concerned only with a difference and not with the superiority or inferiority of either group.

> There is no difference between the mean IQs of athletes and nonathletes. In this situation we apply a two-tailed test.

If we changed the null hypothesis to indicate the superiority or inferiority of either group it might be stated:

> Athletes do not have higher IQs than nonathletes.
> or
> Athletes do not have lower IQs than nonathletes.

Each of these hypotheses indicates a direction of difference. When researchers are hypothesizing a direction of difference, rather than the mere existence of a difference, they use a one-tailed test.

For a large sample two-tailed test, the 5 percent area of rejection is divided between the upper and lower tails of the curve (2.5 percent at each end), and it is necessary to go out to ±1.96 on the sigma (z) scale to reach the area of rejection (Figure 8–3).

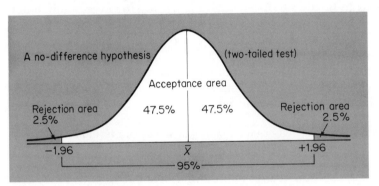

FIGURE 8–3   A two-tailed test at the .05 level (2.5 percent at each end).

For a one-tailed test, since the 5 percent area of rejection is either at the upper tail or at the lower tail of the curve, the t critical value is lower, for it is not necessary to go as far out on the sigma scale to reach the area of rejection (Figure 8–4). The t critical value in such a case is ±1.645.

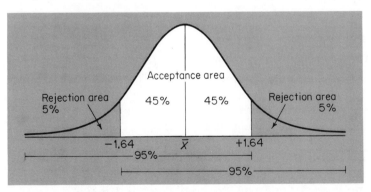

FIGURE 8–4   A one-tailed test at the .05 level (5 percent at one end or 5 percent at the other end).

Large Sample *t* Critical Values for
Rejection of the Null Hypothesis

	.05 level	.01 level
Two-tailed test	1.96	2.58
One-tailed test	1.64	2.33

A similar pair of curves would illustrate the difference between *t* critical areas of rejection at the 1 percent level of significance. The *t* values must equal or exceed these *t* critical values for the rejection of a null hypothesis.

Because the *t* values needed to reject a null hypothesis are smaller for a one-tailed test, and because most researchers would like to reject the null hypothesis, it is tempting always to propose a directional hypothesis so as to be able to use a one-tailed test. However, a one-tailed test should only be used when a directional hypothesis is actually proposed for logical and/or theoretical reasons prior to the collection of even preliminary data. Hypotheses that athletes would have higher or lower IQs than nonathletes are probably inappropriate for one-tailed tests. A better example of a directional hypothesis, for which a one-tailed test would be appropriate, would be:

> Children will score higher on a reading achievement test after first grade than they did prior to first grade.

The test of the significance of the difference between two independent means to this point has concerned large samples, and the critical *t* values for rejection of the null hypothesis have been found in the normal probability table.

When small samples are used to infer population differences, a different set of *t* critical values is used. But before discussing small sample tests, an important concept known as degrees of freedom should be considered.

Degrees of Freedom

The number of degrees of freedom in a distribution is the number of observations or values that are independent of each other, that cannot be deduced from each other. Although this concept has been puzzling to students of statistics, several analogies and their application to estimation or prediction may help to clarify it.

1. Let us assume that a coin is tossed in the air. The statistician predicts that a head will turn up. If a head comes up, he or she has made one correct, independent prediction. But if the statistician predicted that a head would turn up and a tail would face down, he or she has made two predictions. Only one prediction, however, is an independent prediction, for the other can be deduced from the first. The second added no new information. In this case there was one degree of freedom, not two.

   The strength of a prediction is increased as the number of independent observations or degrees of freedom is increased.

2. When a mean is computed from a number of terms in a distribution, the sum is calculated and divided by N.

$$\overline{X} = \frac{\Sigma X}{N}$$

But in computing a mean, 1 degree of freedom is used up or lost, and subsequent calculations of the variance and the standard deviation will be based on $N - 1$ independent observations or $N - 1$ degrees of freedom. An example of the loss of a degree of freedom follows.

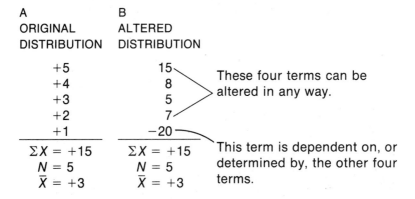

A ORIGINAL DISTRIBUTION	B ALTERED DISTRIBUTION	
+5	15	These four terms can be
+4	8	altered in any way.
+3	5	
+2	7	
+1	−20	
$\Sigma X = +15$	$\Sigma X = +15$	This term is dependent on, or
$N = 5$	$N = 5$	determined by, the other four
$\overline{X} = +3$	$\overline{X} = +3$	terms.

In the altered distribution, the fifth term must have a value of −20 for the sum to equal +15, the mean to be +3, and the sum of the deviations from the mean to equal zero. Thus, four terms are independent and can be altered, but one is dependent or fixed and is deduced from the other four. There are $N - 1$ (5 − 1) or 4 degrees of freedom.

The strength of a prediction or the accuracy of an inferred value increases as the number of independent observations (sample size) is increased. Because large samples may be biased, sample size is not the only important determinant; but if unbiased samples are selected randomly from a population, large samples will provide a more accurate basis than will smaller samples for inferring population values.

Standard deviation for samples (S). In Chapter 7 we described the variance and standard deviation for a population. Because most of the time we use samples selected from the population, it is necessary to introduce the formulas for the variance (S^2) and the standard deviation (S) of a sample. The sample formulas differ only slightly from the population formulas. As we will see, instead of dividing by N in the deviation formula and by N^2 in the raw score formula, the sample formulas divide by $n - 1$ and $n(n - 1)$, respectively. This is done to correct for the probability that the smaller the sample, the less likely it is that extreme scores will be included. Thus the formula for σ, if used with a sample, would underestimate the standard deviation of the population. Dividing by $n - 1$ or $n(n - 1)$ corrects for this bias more or less depending upon the sample's size. This makes the standard deviation of the sample more representative of the population. In a small sample, say $N = 5$, the correction is rather large, dividing by 4 instead of 5—a reduction of 20 percent in the denominator. In a large sample, say $N = 100$, the correction is insignificant, dividing by 99 instead of 100—a reduction of 1 percent in the denominator.

The two formulas for sample standard deviation with the deviation and the raw score methods of computation, respectively, are:

$$S = \sqrt{\frac{(X - \bar{X})^2}{n - 1}} \text{ or } \sqrt{\frac{X^2}{n - 1}}$$

and

$$S = \sqrt{\frac{N\Sigma X^2 - (X)^2}{n(n - 1)}}$$

No doubt the reader can see that the only changes are in the denominator. Thus, if we substitute $n(n - 1)$ for N^2 and calculate S^2 and S using the previous data, we would find the following:

$$S^2 = \frac{9(52,125) - (675)^2}{9(8)} = \frac{469,125 - 455,625}{72}$$

$$S^2 = \frac{13,500}{72} = 187.50$$

$$S = \sqrt{187.50} = 13.69$$

These results are quite a change from $\sigma^2 = 166.67$ (change of $+20.83$) and $\sigma = 12.91$ (change of $+0.78$). These relatively large differences from the population formula to the sample formula are due to the small sample size ($n = 9$), which made a relatively large correction necessary. The correction for calculating the variance and standard deviation is important because unless the loss of a degree of freedom is considered, the calculated sample variance or standard deviation is likely to underestimate the population variance or standard deviation. This is true because the mean of the squared deviations from the mean of any distribution is the smallest possible value, and probably would be smaller than the mean of the squared deviation from any other point in the distribution. Because the mean of the sample is not likely to be identical to the population mean (because of sampling error), the use of the number of degrees of freedom, rather than N in the denominator, tends to correct for this underestimation of the population variance or standard deviation.

The strength of a prediction or the accuracy of an inferred value increases as the number of independent observations (sample size) is increased. Because large samples may be biased, sample size is not the only important determinant, but if unbiased samples are selected randomly from a population, large samples will provide a more accurate basis than will smaller samples for inferring population values.

STUDENT'S DISTRIBUTION (*t*)

When small samples are involved, the *t* table is used to determine statistical significance, rather than the normal probability table. This concept of small sample size was developed around 1915 by William Sealy Gosset, a consulting statistician for Guinness Breweries of Dublin, Ireland. Because his employer's rules prohibited publication under the researcher's name, he signed the name "Student" when he published his findings.

Gosset determined that the distribution curves of small sample means were somewhat different from the normal curve. Small sample distributions were observed to be lower at the means and higher at the tails or ends of the distributions.

Gossett's *t* critical values, carefully calculated for small samples, are reproduced in the *t* distribution table in Appendix D. The *t* critical values necessary for rejection of a null hypothesis are higher for small samples at a given level of significance (see Figure 8–5). Each *t* critical

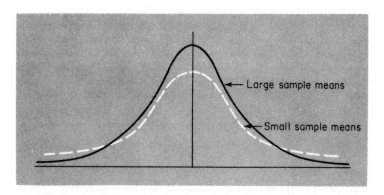

FIGURE 8–5 Distribution of large and small sample means.

value for rejection is based upon the appropriate number of degrees of freedom.

As the sample sizes increase, the t critical values necessary for rejection of a null hypothesis diminish and approach the z values of the normal probability table.

Significance of the Difference between Two Small Sample Independent Means

When the samples are small and their variances are equal or nearly equal, the method of pooled variances provides the appropriate test of the significance of the difference between two independent means.

The formula is a bit more involved than the one previously illustrated, but it provides a more precise test of significance. The appropriate t critical value for rejection of the null hypothesis would be found for $N + N - 2$ degrees of freedom, using the t distribution table.

$$t = \frac{\bar{X}_1 - \bar{X}_2}{\sqrt{\frac{(N_1 - 1)S_1^2 + (N_2 - 1)S_2^2}{N_1 + N_2 - 2}\left(\frac{1}{N_1} + \frac{1}{N_2}\right)}}$$

For example, in comparing the significance of the mean IQ difference between samples of 8 athletes and 10 nonathletes, the number of degrees of freedom would be $N + N - 2 = 8 + 10 - 2 = 16$. From the t distribution table at 16 degrees of freedom, the t critical values necessary for the rejection of the null hypothesis would be:

	LEVEL OF SIGNIFICANCE	
16 DEGREES OF FREEDOM	.05	.01
Two-tailed test	2.120	2.921
One-tailed test	1.746	2.583

HOMOGENEITY OF VARIANCES

In t tests for small samples, one condition must be met to justify the method of pool variances. This condition is known as equality or *homogeneity of variance*. It does not literally mean that the variances of the samples to be compared must be identical, but only that they do not differ by an amount that is statistically significant. Differences that would be attributed to sampling error do not impair the validity of the process.

To determine whether the samples meet the criterion of equality of variances an F_{max} test is used.

$$F = \frac{S^2 \text{ (largest variance)}}{S^2 \text{ (smallest variance)}}$$

This F ratio is never less than one, for the largest variance is always divided by the smallest. To test for homogeneity of variance, an F distribution table is used in much the same way as the t distribution table. F critical values are presented for determining the statistical significance of the calculated F critical ratio, based upon the appropriate rows and columns, each at $N - 1$ degrees of freedom.

A few .05-level-of-significance values from the F_{max} distribution table are presented in Table 8–1. The degrees of freedom for the largest group is used if the samples differ in size. With t tests, there will only be two variances. For Analysis of Variance (discussed later in this chapter), there will be more than two variances.

Unless the calculated F equals or exceeds the appropriate F critical value, it may be assumed that the variances are homogeneous and the difference is not significant.

For example, if two samples with 10 degrees of freedom (greater variance 38.40) and 12 degrees of freedom (smaller variance 18.06) were subjected to the test of homogeneity:

$$F = \frac{38.40}{18.06} = 2.13$$

An F critical value of 3.28 must be equaled or exceeded to determine that the difference between variances is significant at the .05 level. In this example, since $2.13 < 3.28$, the researcher would conclude that the variances fulfilled the condition of homogeneity and that the method of pooled variances is appropriate. An example using small samples illustrates the process of calculating the F ratio to test homogeneity of variance and then calculating the appropriate t test.

The mean score of 10 delinquent boys on a personal adjustment inventory was compared with the mean score of 12 nondelinquent boys,

TABLE 8–1   Distribution of F (.05 level)

NUMBER OF VARIANCES

		2	3	4
Degrees of	9	4.03	5.34	6.31
freedom for	10	3.72	4.85	5.67
largest group	12	3.28	4.16	4.79
$(N - 1)$	15	2.86	3.54	4.01

both groups selected at random. Test the null hypothesis that there is no statistically significant difference between the mean test scores at the .01 level of significance.

DELINQUENT BOYS   NONDELINQUENT BOYS

$\bar{X}_2 = 9$ $\bar{X}_1 = 14$
$S_2^2 = 20.44$ $S_1^2 = 19.60$
$N_2 = 10$ $N_1 = 12$

$$F = \frac{20.44}{19.60} = 1.04 \text{ (the variances are homogeneous)}$$

$$df = 10 + 12 - 2 = 20$$

$$t = \frac{\bar{X}_1 - \bar{X}_2}{\sqrt{\frac{(N_1 - 1)S_1^2 + (N_2 - 1)S_2^2}{N_1 + N_2 - 2}\left(\frac{1}{N_1} + \frac{1}{N_2}\right)}}$$

$$t = \frac{14 - 9}{\sqrt{\frac{11(19.60) + 9(20.44)}{12 + 10 - 2}\left(\frac{1}{12} + \frac{1}{10}\right)}}$$

$$t = \frac{5}{\sqrt{\frac{215.60 + 183.96}{20}\left(\frac{11}{60}\right)}}$$

$$t = \frac{5}{\sqrt{19.98\left(\frac{11}{60}\right)}} = \frac{5}{\sqrt{3.66}}$$

$$t = \frac{5}{1.96} = 2.62$$

Because this is a two-tailed test, the t critical value for rejection of the null hypothesis at the .01 level of significance for 20 degrees of freedom is 2.831.

Because the calculated value is 2.62, it does not equal or exceed the t critical value necessary for rejection of the null hypothesis at the .01 level for 20 degrees of freedom; the hypothesis is not rejected, and we conclude that there is no significant difference.

Had we used the .05 level of significance for 20 degrees of freedom, the t critical value necessary for rejection would be 2.086, and we could have rejected the null hypothesis, for our calculated t critical ratio of 2.62 exceeds the 2.086 t table value.

By using the data from a previous example, comparing reading achievement of a group using the ITA reading method with that of the control group, we can see that this formula gives us the same result as did the formula used in that example:

ITA CONTROL

$N_1 = 32$ $\quad$ $N_2 = 34$
$\bar{X}_1 = 87.43$ $\quad$ $\bar{X}_2 = 82.58$
$S_1^2 = 39.40$ $\quad$ $S_2^2 = 40.80$

$$F = \frac{40.80}{39.40} = 1.04 \text{ (the variances are homogeneous)}$$

$$df = 32 + 34 - 2 = 64$$

$$t = \frac{\bar{X}_1 - \bar{X}_2}{\sqrt{\frac{(N_1 - 1)\, S_1^2 + (N_2 - 1)\, S_2^2}{N_1 + N_2 - 2} \left(\frac{1}{N_1} + \frac{1}{N_2} \right)}}$$

$$t = \frac{87.43 - 82.58}{\sqrt{\frac{31\ (39.4) + 33\ (40.8)}{64} \left(\frac{1}{32} + \frac{1}{34} \right)}}$$

$$t = \frac{4.85}{\sqrt{\frac{1231.4 + 1346.4}{64} \left(\frac{34}{1088} + \frac{32}{1088} \right)}}$$

$$t = \frac{4.85}{\sqrt{80.52 \left(\frac{66}{1088} \right)}}$$

$$t = \frac{4.85}{\sqrt{2.44}} = \frac{4.85}{1.56}$$

$$t = 3.11$$

Thus the two formulas presented in this chapter for comparing the means of two independent samples are actually equivalent.

Significance of the Difference between the Means of Two Matched or Correlated Groups (Nonindependent Samples)

The two previous examples of testing the significance of the difference between two independent means assume that the individuals were randomly assigned to the control and experimental groups. There are situations when it is appropriate to determine the significance of the difference between means of groups that are not randomly assigned. Two such situations are:

1. When the pairs of individuals who make up the groups have been matched on one or more characteristics—IQ, reading achievement, identical twins, or on some other basis for equating the individuals.
2. When the same group of individuals takes a pretest, is exposed to a treatment, and then is retested to determine whether the influence of the treatment has been statistically significant, as determined by mean gain scores.

Because the groups are not independent samples, it is necessary to calculate the coefficient of correlation between:

1. the posttest scores of the matched pairs sample; or
2. the pretest and posttest scores of the participants in the experiment.

Using the coefficient of correlation, the appropriate *t* test would be based upon this formula:

$$t = \frac{\bar{X}_1 - \bar{X}_2}{\sqrt{\dfrac{S_1^2}{N_1} + \dfrac{S_2^2}{N_2} - 2r\left(\dfrac{S_1}{\sqrt{N_1}}\right)\left(\dfrac{S_2}{\sqrt{N_2}}\right)}}$$

The number of degrees of freedom would be the number of pairs minus one. Two examples illustrate situations A and B:

Example A. Two groups, each made up of 20 fifth-grade students, were matched on the basis of IQs. Filmstrips were used to teach the experimental group; the control group was exposed to a conventional "read and discuss" method.

The researcher wished to treat the null hypothesis that there was no difference between the mean achievement of the two groups (a two-tailed test) at the .05 level.

X	C
$N_1 = 20$	$N_2 = 20$
$S_1^2 = 54.76$	$S_2^2 = 42.25$
$\bar{X}_1 = 53.20$	$\bar{X}_2 = 49.80$
$r = +.60$	$df = 19$

$$F = \frac{54.76}{42.25} = 1.30 \text{ (variances are homogeneous)}$$

$$t = \frac{53.20 - 49.80}{\sqrt{\dfrac{54.76}{20} + \dfrac{42.85}{20} - 2(+.60)\left(\dfrac{7.40}{4.47}\right)\left(\dfrac{6.50}{4.47}\right)}}$$

$$t = \frac{3.40}{\sqrt{2.74 + 2.14 - 1.20(1.66)(1.45)}}$$

$$t = \frac{3.40}{\sqrt{4.84 - 2.89}}$$

$$t = \frac{3.40}{\sqrt{1.95}} = \frac{3.40}{1.40} = 2.43$$

Because the *t* value of 2.43 exceeds the *t* critical value of 2.093 for a two-tailed test at the .05 level at 19 degrees of freedom, the null hypothesis may be rejected.

Example B. A typing teacher wished to determine the effectiveness of 10 minutes of transcendental meditation upon the speed and accuracy of his class of 30 students. He administered a timed speed/accuracy test and recorded the score for each student. The next day, after 10 minutes of class participation in a TM exercise, he administered a similar timed speed/accuracy test.

He computed the mean scores for the pretest and the scores obtained after the TM experience and calculated the coefficient of correlation between the pairs of scores to be +.84.

He then tested the null hypothesis that the TM experience would not improve the proficiency in speed and accuracy of typing of his class. He chose the .01 level of significance, using a one-tailed test.

PRETEST   TEST AFTER TM

$N_2 = 30$ $N_1 = 30$
$S_2^2 = 37.21$ $S_1^2 = 36.10$
$\bar{X}_2 = 44.80$ $\bar{X}_1 = 49.10$
$r = +.84$ $df = 29$

$$F = \frac{37.21}{36.10} = 1.03 \text{ (variances are homogeneous)}$$

$$t = \frac{49.10 - 44.80}{\sqrt{\dfrac{37.21}{30} + \dfrac{36.10}{30} - 2(+.84)\left(\dfrac{6.10}{5.48}\right)\left(\dfrac{6.01}{5.48}\right)}}$$

$$t = \frac{4.30}{\sqrt{1.24 + 1.20 - 1.68(1.11)(1.10)}}$$

$$t = \frac{4.30}{\sqrt{2.44 - 2.05}} = \frac{4.30}{\sqrt{.39}}$$

$$t = \frac{4.30}{.62} = 6.94$$

Because the *t* value of 6.94 exceeds the *t* critical value of 2.462 for a one-tailed test at the .01 level for 29 degrees of freedom, he rejected the null hypothesis, concluding that the mediation experience did improve performance proficiency.

Statistical Significance of a Coefficient of Correlation

Throughout this chapter on inferential data analysis, the idea of statistical significance and its relationship to the null hypothesis have been emphasized. An observed coefficient of correlation may result from chance or sampling error, and a test to determine its statistical significance is appropriate. In small sample correlations, chance could yield what might appear to be evidence of a genuine relationship.

The null hypothesis (H_0) states that the coefficient of correlation is zero. Only when chance or sampling error has been discredited on a probability basis can a coefficient of correlation be accepted as statistically significant. The test of the significance of *r* is determined by the use of the formula:

$$t_r = \frac{r\sqrt{N - 2}}{\sqrt{1 - r^2}}$$

With $N - 2$ degrees of freedom a coefficient of correlation is judged as statistically significant when the *t* value equals or exceeds the *t* critical value in the *t* distribution table.

$$\text{If } r = .40$$
$$N = 25$$
$$t = \frac{.40\sqrt{23}}{\sqrt{1 - (.40)^2}} = \frac{1.92}{.92} = 2.09$$

Using a two-tailed test at the .05 level with 23 degrees of freedom, the null hypothesis is rejected, exceeding the *t* critical value of 2.07. As sample size is decreased, the probability of sampling error increases. For a smaller sample, the coefficient must be larger to be statistically significant.

If $r = .40$
$N = 18$

$$t = \frac{.40\sqrt{16}}{\sqrt{1 - (.40)^2}} = \frac{1.60}{.92} = 1.74$$

At 16 degrees of freedom the observed value of 1.74 fails to equal or exceed the t critical value of 2.12 at the .05 level of significance, and the null hypothesis would not be rejected. Thus, with a sample N of 18, a coefficient of correlation of .40 would not be large enough for the rejection of the null hypothesis, a sampling error explanation.

The reader should remember from Chapter 7, however, that the interpretation of a correlation involves more than just its statistical significance. A low correlation, for example $r = .20$, is statistically significant if a large sample, 200 subjects, was used. Despite its statistical significance, this correlation, .20, is still a low correlation with the two variables only having .04 of their variance in common.

ANALYSIS OF VARIANCE (ANOVA)

We have noted that the t test is employed to determine, after treatment, whether the means of two random samples were too different to attribute to chance or sampling error. The analysis of variance is an effective way to determine whether the means of *more than two samples* are too different to attribute to sampling error.

It would be possible to use a number of t tests to determine the significance of the difference between five means, two at a time, but it would involve ten separate tests. The number of necessary pair-wise comparisons of N things is determined by the formula:

$$\frac{N(N-1)}{2}$$

If $N = 5$

$$\frac{5(5-1)}{2} = \frac{20}{2} = 10$$

Analysis of variance makes it possible to determine whether the five means differ significantly with a single test, rather than ten. Another advantage lies in the fact that computing a number of separate t tests will increase the overall Type I error rate for the experiment. For instance, if we calculated ten t tests (for comparing five means) and accepted .05 as our significance level, we would have ten times .05, or .50, as the probability that we would reject at least one null hypothesis when it is really true (Type I error). Thus we would have an unacceptably high error rate for the total experiment. Analysis of variance takes care of this by comparing all five means simultaneously in a single test.

In *single classification*, or *one-way analysis of variance*, *the relationship between one independent and one dependent variable is examined*. For example:

> A test of abstract reasoning is administered to three randomly selected groups of students in a large state university majoring in mathematics, philosophy, and chemistry. Are the mean test scores of each of the three groups significantly different from one another?

The analysis of variance consists of these operations:

1. The variance of the scores for three groups are combined into one composite group, known as the *total groups variance* (V_t).
2. The mean value of the variances of each of the three groups, computed separately, is known as the *within-groups variance* (V_w).
3. The difference between the total groups variance and the within-groups variance is known as the *between-groups variance* $(V_t - V_w = V_b)$.
4. The F ratio is computed

$$F = \frac{V_b}{V_w} = \frac{\text{between-groups variance}}{\text{within-groups variance}}$$

The logic of the F ratio is as follows. The within-groups variance represents the sampling error in the distributions and is also referred to as the error variance or residual. The between-groups variance represents the influence of the variable of interest or the experimental variable. If the *between-groups variance* is not substantially greater than the *within-groups variance*, the researcher would conclude that the difference between the means is probably only a reflection of sampling error. If the F ratio were substantially greater than one, it would seem that the ratio of the *between-groups variance* and the *within-groups variance* was probably too great to attribute to sampling error.

The significance of the F ratio (named for Sir Ronald Fisher) is found in an F table, which indicates the critical values necessary to test the null hypothesis at selected levels of significance.

As can be seen in the F table presented in Appendix F, there are two different degrees of freedom, one for V_b (the numerator) and one for V_w (the denominator). The degrees of freedom for the within-groups variance (V_w) is determined in the same way as it is for the t test—that is, the sum of the subjects for all of the groups minus the number of groups.

We can use K to represent the number of groups and $N_1 + N_2 + \cdots - K$ to represent the degrees of freedom for the within-groups variance. In the above example, if we had ten students in each of the three groups, we would have $10 + 10 + 10 - 3$, or 27, degrees of freedom for the within-groups variance. The degrees of freedom for the between-groups variance (V_b) is determined by the number of groups minus one $(K - 1)$. In the above example, there are three groups, thus, two degrees of freedom. The above example then has two degrees of freedom for the numerator and 27 for the denominator, for a total of 29, one less than the total number of subjects.

The calculation of F involves finding the mean of the deviations from the mean, squared. Thus the between-groups variance (V_b) is more commonly referred to as the mean squared between (MS_b), and the within-groups variance (V_w) is more commonly referred to as the mean squared within (MS_w). The formula then becomes:

$$F = \frac{MS_b}{MS_w}$$

Given the data in Table 8–2, we would calculate F as follows. The first step is to find the sum of the squared deviations of each person's score for the mean of all of the subjects (x). This is known as the total sum of squares (SS_t) and can be found by using the following formula:

$$SS_t = \Sigma X^2 - \frac{(\Sigma X)^2}{N}$$

TABLE 8–2 Sample Data for Calculating Analysis of Variance

GROUP 1 MATHEMATICS MAJORS		GROUP 2 PHILOSOPHY MAJORS		GROUP 3 CHEMISTRY MAJORS	
X_1	X_1^2	X_2	X_2^2	X_3	X_3^2
18	324	26	676	18	324
22	484	27	729	14	196
18	324	18	324	15	225
23	529	22	484	14	196
19	361	23	529	19	361
24	576	19	361	21	441
20	400	27	729	17	289
21	441	26	676	17	289
19	361	24	576	18	324
25	625	26	676	19	361
$\Sigma X_1 = 209$	$\Sigma X_1^2 = 4425$	$\Sigma X_2 = 238$	$\Sigma X_2^2 = 5760$	$\Sigma X_3 = 172$	$\Sigma X_3^2 = 3006$
$\bar{X}_1 = 20.9$		$\bar{X}_2 = 23.8$		$\bar{X}_3 = 17.2$	

$\bar{\bar{X}} = 20.63$ $\Sigma X^2 = \Sigma X_1^2 + \Sigma X_2^2 + \Sigma X_3^2 = 13{,}191$

In our example this would be:

$$SS_t = 13{,}191 - \frac{(619)^2}{30} = 13{,}191 - 12{,}772.03 = 418.97$$

The next step is to divide the total sum of squares into the between-groups sum of squares (SS_b) and the within-groups sum of squares (SS_w). We determine SS_b using the formula:

$$SS_b + \frac{(\Sigma X_1)^2}{n_1} + \frac{(\Sigma X_2)^2}{n_2} + \cdots \cdots - \frac{(\Sigma X)^2}{N}$$

n = the number of subjects in a group
N = the number of subjects for all the groups combined

In our example this would be

$$SS_b = \frac{(209)^2}{10} + \frac{(238)^2}{10} + \frac{(172)^2}{10} - \frac{(619)^2}{30}$$
$$SS_b = 4368.1 + 5664.4 + 2958.4 - 12{,}772.03$$
$$SS_b = 218.87$$

The within-groups sum of squares (SS_w) can be calculated in two ways. First, we can calculate it directly using the formula:

$$SS_w = \Sigma X_1^2 - \frac{(\Sigma X_1)^2}{n_1} + \Sigma X_2^2 - \frac{(\Sigma X_2)^2}{n_2} \cdots + \frac{(\Sigma X_i)^2}{n_i} - \frac{(\Sigma X_i)^2}{n_i}$$

In our example this would be

$$SS_w = 4425 - 4368.1 + 5760 - 5664.4 + 3006 - 2958.4$$
$$SS_w = 200.1$$

SS_w can also be found by subtracting SS_b from SS_t:

$$SS_w = SS_t - SS_b$$
$$SS_w = 418.97 - 218.87 = 200.1$$

By using both methods of calculating SS_w, we can check our results for computational errors.

To find the mean square between (MS_b) and mean square within (MS_w), we divide the sum of squares between (SS_b) and the sum of squares within (SS_w) by their respective degrees of freedom (df).

$$F = \frac{MS_b}{MS_w} = \frac{SS_b/df_b}{SS_w/df_w}$$

$$F = \frac{MS_b}{MS_w} = \frac{218.87/2}{200.1/27}$$

$$F = \frac{109.44}{7.41} = 15.41$$

Table 8–3 shows what a typical summary table for this analysis of variance would look like. The F of 15.41 is statistically significant at the .01 level. That is, there is less than 1 chance in 100 that the observed differences among these three group means is due to sampling error. We can reject the null hypothesis with this degree of confidence.

However, this significant F does not pinpoint exactly where the differences are in a pair-wise way. That is, the three groups differ significantly, but does Group 1 differ from Group 2 and/or Group 3? Does Group 2 differ from Group 3? These questions can be answered by still further analysis of the data using one of the several *post hoc* analyses available (e.g., Scheffe, Tukey, Neuman-Keuls, Duncan). The reader should consult one of several fine texts (e.g., Glass & Hopkins, 1984; Kirk, 1982; Winer, 1971) for more information regarding the use and calculation of these *post hoc* tests.

In *multiple classification* or *factorial analysis of variance, both the independent and interactive effects of two or more independent variables on one dependent variable may be analyzed.* Not only may the effect of several independent variables be tested, but their interaction (how they may combine in a significant way) may be examined. Because human behavior and the factors influencing it are complex and can rarely be explained by single independent variable influences, this method of analysis is a powerful statistical tool of the behavioral researcher.

With computers so readily available, it is rarely necessary to calculate a factorial analysis of variance by hand. An example of a computer printout from such an analysis is included in Chapter 9.

In factorial designs, the total variance is divided into more than two parts. It is divided into one part for each independent variable (main effect), one part for each interaction of two or more independent variables, and one part for the residual, or within-group, variance. Thus, in a

TABLE 8–3 Summary of Three Group Analysis of Variance

SOURCE OF VARIANCE	SS	df	MS	F
Between groups (major)	218.87	2	109.44	15.41*
Within groups (error)	200.10	27	7.41	
Total	418.97			

* $p < .01$

design with two independent variables, the variance is divided into four parts. For example, in our previous example comparing the performance of mathematics, philosophy, and chemistry majors on a test of abstract reasoning, we could also divide each of the three groups into males and females. We then have a factorial design with two independent variables, student's major and sex. Because there are three conditions of student major and two conditions of sex, this is a 3 × 2 design. As shown in Chapter 9, this results in the variance's being divided into four parts: the main effect of student's major, the main effect of student's sex, the interaction effect of student's major with sex, and residual. From this, three separate *F*s are derived: one to test the difference among the three majors, one to test the difference between males and females, and one to test the interaction of students' sex and major. An example of a signification interaction was presented in Chapter 5 (see Figure 5–3).

With the aid of computers, analysis of variance can be used with any number of independent variables. The only limitations are in controlling for potentially confounding variables and interpreting complex interaction effects. Glass and Hopkins (1984), Kirk (1982), and Winer (1971) are excellent resources for the student wanting more information about analysis of variance designs and computation.

ANALYSIS OF COVARIANCE (ANCOVA) AND PARTIAL CORRELATION

Analysis of covariance and partial correlation are statistical techniques that can remove the effect of a confounding variable's influence from a study. *Partial correlation* is used to remove the effect of one variable on the correlation between two other variables. For example, if a correlation is desired between IQ and academic achievement and the subjects have a range of ages, we would not want the variable of chronological age to affect the correlation. Thus, we would partial out its effect on the other two variables, IQ and academic achievement. This is symbolized by $r_{12.3}$, the correlation of variables 1 and 2 with 3 removed. We can calculate the partial correlation using the following formula:

$$r_{12.3} = \frac{r_{12} - (r_{13})(r_{23})}{\sqrt{(1 - r_{13}^2)(1 - r_{23}^2)}}$$

An example from Glass and Hopkins (1984) may help to further clarify this concept. In this example a correlation between visual perception (X_1) and reading performance (X_2) is found to be .64 for children ranging in age (X_3) from six to fifteen years. Because of the wide age range, and because children's reading and visual perception both generally improve with age, it seems appropriate to partial out the effect of age. Given the following correlation coefficients, we can calculate the partial correlation of visual perception and reading performance with age removed.

r_{12} (correlation of visual perception (X_1)
and reading performance (X_2) = .64
r_{13} [correlation of X_1 and age (X_3)] = .80
r_{23} (correlation of X_2 and X_3) = .80

$$r_{12.3} = \frac{.64 - (.80)\,(.80)}{\sqrt{(1 - .80^2)\,(1 - .80^2)}} = \frac{.64 - .64}{.36} = .00$$

As Glass and Hopkins (1984) point out:

. . . one would estimate the value of R_{12} for children of the *same chronological age* to be zero. If enough children of the same chronological age were available, r could be calculated for them alone to check the previous result. The partial correlation coefficient serves the purpose of estimating r_{12} for a single level of chronological age even when there is an insufficient number of persons at any single chronological age to do the estimating by direct calculation. (p. 131)

Analysis of covariance uses the principles of partial correlation with analysis of variance. It is particularly appropriate when the subjects in two or more groups are found to differ on a pretest or other initial variable. In this case, the effects of the pretest and/or other relevant variables are partialed out and the resulting adjusted means of the post-test scores are compared. Analysis of covariance is a method of analysis that enables the researcher to equate the preexperimental status of the groups in terms of relevant variables. The initial status of the groups may be determined by pretest scores in a pretest-posttest study, or in post-test-only studies, by such measures as intelligence, reading scores, grade-point average, or previous knowledge of subject matter. Differences in the initial status of the groups can be removed statistically so that they can be compared as though their initial status had been equated. The scores that have been corrected by this procedure are known as *residuals*, for they are what remain after the inequalities have been removed.

Analysis of covariance, used with one or more independent variable and one dependent variable, is an important method of analyzing experiments carried on under conditions that otherwise would be unacceptable. The mathematical procedures are rather complicated, and there are many steps in computing their values. However, with the use of standard computer programs, the analysis of complex studies can be processed almost instantaneously.

It should be noted that analysis of covariance is not as robust as analysis of variance. That is, violation of the assumptions on which analysis of covariance is based may make its use inappropriate. In addition, as Glass and Hopkins (1984) point out, ANCOVA does not transform a quasi-experiment into a true (randomized) experiment. There is no substitute for randomization.

MULTIPLE REGRESSION AND CORRELATION

In Chapter 7, we discussed correlation and linear regression when only two variables are involved. We demonstrated the prediction (regression) equation for estimating the value of one variable from another: $\hat{Y} = a + bX$.

In many cases, it is better to use more than one predictor variable to predict an outcome, or dependent, variable. For example, a university may use a number of variables to predict college GPA in its admission process. High school grades and SAT or ACT scores are usually used. Ranks in high school graduating class could also be included.

Multiple regression is the term used for predicting $\hat{Y}$ (in the example above, college GPA) from two or more independent variables combined. The formula for multiple regression is just an extension of that for linear regression:

$$\hat{Y} = a + b_1X_1 + b_2X_2 + \ldots$$

$\hat{Y}$ = the variable to be predicted
a = the constant or intercept
b_1 = the slope of the first predictor
b_2 = the slope of the second predictor
X_1 = the score on the first predictor
X_2 = the score on the second predictor

An example may further clarify this procedure. In Chapter 7 we gave an example of predicting college GPA from high school GPA. We will use the data given in that example and add SAT score (combined verbal and quantitative).

$\hat{Y}$ = college GPA
X_1 = high school GPA
X_2 = SAT score
r_{12} = correlation of high school GPA and SAT score
r_{Y1} = correlation of college GPA and high school GPA
r_{Y2} = correlation of college GPA and SAT score

The data are as follows:

$$\hat{Y} = 2.40$$
$$S_y = 0.50$$
$$\overline{X}_1 = 2.10$$
$$S_{x1} = 0.60$$
$$\overline{X}_2 = 930.00$$
$$S_{x2} = 80.00$$
$$r_{12} = 0.22$$
$$r_{Y1} = 0.52$$
$$r_{Y2} = 0.66$$

The first step in finding b is to calculate the standardized beta weight (β):

$$\beta_1 = \frac{r_{y1} - (r_{y2})(r_{12})}{1 - r_{12}^2} \qquad \beta_2 = \frac{r_{y2} - (r_{y1})(r_{12})}{1 - r_{12}^2}$$

$$\beta_1 = \frac{.52 - (.66)(.22)}{1 - (.22)^2} = \frac{.375}{.952} = .394$$

$$\beta_2 = \frac{.66 - (.52)(.22)}{1 - (.22)^2} = \frac{.546}{.952} = .574$$

Using the standardized beta weights and the standard deviations, we can calculate the raw score beta weights (b):

$$b_1 = \beta_1 \frac{(S_y)}{S_{x1}} \qquad b_2 = \beta_2 \frac{(S_y)}{S_{x2}}$$

$$b_1 = .394 \left(\frac{.50}{.60}\right) = .338$$

$$b_2 = .574 \left(\frac{.50}{80}\right) = .004$$

The next step is to calculate the intercept, a, from the formula:

$$a = \overline{Y} - b_1\overline{X}_1 - b_2\overline{X}_2 - \dots$$

In this case:

$$a = 2.4 - .338(2.1) - .004(930)$$
$$a = 2.4 - .710 - 3.72 = -2.03$$

Finally, we can calculate the predicted college GPA for the two students in the example from Chapter 7:

$$X_{a1} = \text{(student A's high school GPA)} = 2.00$$
$$X_{a2} = \text{(student A's SAT score)} = 900.00$$
$$X_{b1} = \text{(student B's high school GPA)} = 3.10$$
$$X_{b2} = \text{(student B's SAT score)} = 1100.00$$

$$\hat{Y} = a + b_1 X_1 + b_2 X_{2...}$$
$$\hat{Y}_a = -2.03 + .338\,(2.00) + .004\,(900)$$
$$\hat{Y}_a = -2.03 + .688 + 3.6 = 2.25$$
$$\hat{Y}_b = -2.03 + .338\,(3.10) + .004\,(1100)$$
$$\hat{Y}_b = -2.03 + 1.05 + 4.4 = 3.42$$

Student A, with the below-average high school GPA and SAT score, is predicted to have a below-average college GPA, and student B, with the above-average high school GPA and SAT score, is expected to have an above-average college GPA. When we compare these findings with the regression results in Chapter 7, we see that the addition of a confirming score resulted in a prediction further above or below the average. That is, when we included an SAT score for student A that was to the same side of (below) the mean as his or her high school GPA, the result was a predicted college GPA further below the average than the one predicted by high school GPA alone (2.25 versus 2.36). Conversely, when we included an SAT score for student B that was above the mean, as was his or her high school GPA, the result was a predicted college GPA further above the average than the one predicted by high school GPA alone (3.42 versus 2.83).

If we had added a disconfirming SAT score to high school GPA, it would have the opposite effect described above. For example, if student A had an SAT of 1080 instead of 900, his or her predicted college GPA would be higher than that predicted with high school GPA alone.

$$\hat{Y}_a = -2.03 + .338\,(2.00) + .004\,(1080)$$
$$\hat{Y}_a = -2.03 + .68 + 4.32 = 2.97$$

In either case, confirming or disconfirming the addition of related variables to a prediction equation will result in more accurate predictions.

We should point out that when we write of "adding" a variable to the equation, we do not mean that the amount of the prediction from one variable is just added to by the amount of prediction from a second, and/ or subsequent, variable. The multiple regression equation controls for the overlap (relatedness) of the predictor variables. The result is that the second variable only "adds" the amount of prediction that it has independent of the first variable. This is necessary since other attributes (variables) may directly influence more than one of the predictor variables. For instance, in our example, high school grades and SAT scores are probably both influenced by IQ. Multiple regression controls for that part that SAT scores and high school grades have in common due to other factors such as IQ. This has the same effect as partial correlation.

Multiple correlation (R) is the correlation between the actual scores (Y) and the scores predicted $(\hat{Y})$ by two or more independent variables. It is most useful for determining the percent of the variance of the predicted scores that can be explained by the predictors. This was discussed as the coefficient of determination (r^2) in relation to the simple, bivariate correlation (r) in Chapter 7. For multiple correlation, R^2 is the percent of the variance of the predicted (dependent) variable that is due to, or explained by, the combined predictor (independent) variables. Conversely, $1 - R^2$ is the percent of the variance of the predicted variable that is due to factors other than the predictor variables.

In the previous multiple regression example, the multiple correlation (the correlation between actual college GPA and predicted college GPA) is $R = .583$. The percent of college GPA that is due to a combination of high school GPA and SAT scores is then $R^2 = .340$. Thirty-four percent of the variance of college GPA is explained by high school grades and SAT scores. Because $1 - R^2$ is .660, 66 percent of college GPA is due to other factors such as motivation, involvement in extracurricular activities, measurement error, and so on. This gives a good idea of just how accurate we can expect individual predictions to be. Given this data, we would expect to be able to predict broad categories such as "probable fail," "borderline," "probable pass," and probable high GPA. To expect to accurately predict a person's college GPA would be unrealistic.

For greater detail, the reader should consult a more advanced text that specializes on this topic (e.g., Cohen & Cohen, 1975; Neter & Wasserman, 1974). A computer analysis of a more intricate multiple regression is presented in Chapter 9.

NONPARAMETRIC TESTS

The parametric tests presented in this chapter are generally quite robust; that is, they are useful even when some of their mathematical assumptions are violated. However, sometimes it is necessary, or preferable, to use a nonparametric or distribution free test.

Nonparametric tests are appropriate when

1. The nature of the population distribution from which samples are drawn is not known to be normal.

2. The variables are expressed in nominal form (classified in categories and represented by frequency counts).
3. The variables are expressed in ordinal form (ranked in order, expressed as first, second, third, etc.).

Nonparametric tests, because they are based upon counted or ranked data rather than on measured values, are less precise, have less power than parametric tests, and are not as likely to reject a null hypothesis when it is false.

Many statisticians suggest that parametric tests be used, if possible, and that nonparametric tests be used only when parametric assumptions cannot be met. Others argue that nonparametric tests have greater merit than is often attributed to them because their validity is not based upon assumptions about the nature of the population distribution, assumptions that are so frequently ignored or violated by researchers employing parametric tests.

Of the many nonparametric tests, two of the most frequently used are described and illustrated here: the Chi square (χ^2) test, and the Mann-Whitney Test.

The Chi Square Test (χ^2)

The χ^2 test applies only to discrete data, counted rather than measured values. It is a test of independence, the idea that one variable is not affected by, or related to, another variable. The χ^2 is not a measure of the degree of relationship. It is merely used to estimate the likelihood that some factor other than chance (sampling error) accounts for the apparent relationship. Because the null hypothesis states that there is no relationship (the variables are independent), the test merely evaluates the probability that the observed relationship results from chance. As in other tests of statistical significance, it is assumed that the sample observations have been randomly selected.

The computed χ^2 value must equal or exceed the appropriate table's (see Appendix E) critical value to justify rejection of the null hypothesis or the assumption of independence at the .05 or the .01 level of significance.

A finding of a statistically significant χ^2 value doesn't necessarily indicate a cause-and-effect relationship, a limitation that was observed when interpreting a coefficient of correlation. A significant χ^2 finding indicates that the variables probably do not exhibit the quality of independence, that they tend to be systematically related, and that the relationship transcends pure chance or sampling error.

There are situations when the theoretical or expected frequencies must be computed from the distribution. Let us assume that 200 residents of a women's college dormitory are blonde, brunette, or redhead. Is the variable, hair color, related to the number of dates the women have in a three-week period? The null hypothesis would indicate that hair color is not related to frequency of dating—that the variables hair color and frequency of dating are independent.

Chi square observations should be organized in crossbreak form. In each category, the expected frequencies (fe), as contrasted to the observed frequencies (fo), is the number of cases that would appear if there were no systematic relationship between the variables, a pure chance relationship.

Number of Dates

	FEWER THAN 10	11–15	MORE THAN 15	TOTAL
Blondes	6(12)	60(56)	14(12)	80*
Brunettes	14(12)	48(56)	8(12)	80*
Redheads	10(6)	32(28)	8(6)	40*
Total	30**	140**	30**	200 grand total

f_e *Σf row **Σf column
numbers represent the actual observed frequencies f_o
numbers in parentheses represent the expected frequencies f_e

The expected frequency for each of the 9 cells is computed by the formula

$$f_e = \frac{(\Sigma f \text{ column})\,(\Sigma f \text{ row})}{\text{grand total}}$$

Computation of expected frequencies (fe):

$$\frac{(30)(80)}{200} = (12) \qquad \frac{(140)(80)}{200} = (56) \qquad \frac{(30)(80)}{200} = (12)$$

$$\frac{(30)(80)}{200} = (12) \qquad \frac{(140)(80)}{200} = (56) \qquad \frac{(30)(40)}{200} = (6)$$

$$\frac{(30)(40)}{200} = (6) \qquad \frac{(140)(40)}{200} = (28) \qquad \frac{(30)(40)}{200} = (6)$$

Computation of the χ^2 value:

$$\chi^2 = \Sigma \left(\frac{(f_o - f_e)^2}{f_e} \right)$$

$$\frac{(6-12)^2}{12} = 3 \qquad \frac{(60-56)^2}{56} = .28 \qquad \frac{(14-12)^2}{12} = .33$$

$$\frac{(14-12)^2}{12} = .33 \qquad \frac{(48-56)^2}{56} = 1.14 \qquad \frac{(8-12)^2}{12} = 1.33$$

$$\frac{(10-6)^2}{6} = 2.67 \qquad \frac{(32-28)^2}{28} = .57 \qquad \frac{(8-6)^2}{6} = .67$$

$$\chi^2 = 3 + .28 + .33 + .33 + 1.14 + 1.33 + 2.67 + .57 + .67 = 10.32$$

$$\text{degrees of freedom} = (\text{rows} - 1)(\text{columns} - 1)$$
$$= (3-1)(3-1) = (2)(2) = 4$$
χ^2 critical values for 4 degrees of freedom (see Appendix E).

.01	.05
13.28	9.49

$\chi^2 = 10.32$

The test indicates that there is a significant relationship between hair color and number of dates at the .05 but not at the .01 level of significance. If we wished to answer the question, "Is there a relationship between blond hair and number of dates?" we would combine the brunette and redhead categories and use a χ^2 table with 6 rather than 9 cells.

Number of Dates

	FEWER THAN 10	11–15	MORE THAN 15	TOTAL
Blondes	6(12)	6(56)	14(12)	80
Nonblondes	24(18)	80(84)	16(18)	120
Total	30	140	30	200

$$\frac{(30)(80)}{200} = (12) \qquad \frac{(140)(80)}{200} = (56) \qquad \frac{(30)(80)}{200} = (12)$$

$$\frac{(30)(120)}{200} = (18) \qquad \frac{(140)(120)}{200} = (84) \qquad \frac{(30)(120)}{200} = (18)$$

$$\frac{(6-12)^2}{12} = 3.00 \qquad \frac{(60-56)^2}{56} = .29 \qquad \frac{(14-12)^2}{12} = .33$$

$$\frac{(24-18)^2}{18} = 2.00 \qquad \frac{(80-84)^2}{84} = .19 \qquad \frac{(16-18)^2}{18} = .22$$

$$\chi^2 = 3.00 + .29 + .33 + 2.00 + .19 + .22 = 6.03 \quad \text{at } 2df:$$

.01	9.21
.05	5.99

The null hypothesis may be rejected at the .05 but not at the .01 level of significance.

In a 2 × 2 table (4 cells) with 1 degree of freedom, there is a simple formula that eliminates the need to calculate the theoretical frequencies for each cell.

$$\chi^2 = \frac{N[|AD - BC|]^2}{(A + B)(C + D)(A + C)(B + D)}$$

Terms in a 2 × 2 table

A	B
C	D

Let us use an example employing this formula. A random sample of auto drivers revealed the relationship between experiences of those who had taken a course in driver education and those who had not.

	REPORTED ACCIDENT	NO ACCIDENT	TOTAL
Had driver's education	44A	10B	54
No driver's education	81C	35D	116
Total	125	45	170

This is a 2 × 2 table with one degree of freedom.

$$\chi^2 = 170 \frac{[|(44 \times 35) - (10 \times 81)|]^2}{(54 + 10)(81 + 35)(44 + 81)(10 + 35)}$$

$$= 170 \frac{[|1540 - 810|]^2}{(54)(116)(125)(45)}$$

$$= \frac{170(730)^2}{35,235,000} = \frac{90,593,000}{35,235,000} = 2.57$$

The χ^2 value does not equal or exceed the critical χ^2 value (3.84) necessary to reject the null hypothesis at the .05 level of significance. There seems to be no significant relationship between completing the course in driver education and the number of individuals who had recorded auto accidents.

Yate's correction for continuity. In computing a *chi* square value for a 2 × 2 table with one degree of freedom, the formula is modified when any cell has a frequency count of fewer than 10. This formula differs from the previous formula.

$$\chi^2 = \frac{N\left[\,|AD - BC| - \dfrac{N}{2}\right]^2}{(A + B)(C + D)(A + C)(B + D)}$$

Example: A pharmaceutical company wished to evaluate the effectiveness of X–40, a recently developed headache relief pill.

Two randomly selected and assigned samples of patients who complained of headaches were given pills. The experimental group was given 6 X–40 pills daily and the control group was given 6 placebos (or sugar pills) daily, although they thought that they were receiving medication. After a week they repeated their experience.

	X–40 X	PLACEBO C	TOTAL
Headaches relieved	30_A	40_B	70
Headaches continued	4_C	10_D	14
Total	34	50	84

A χ^2 test using a 2 × 2 table at 1 degree of freedom was applied, with Yate's correction. Was the effectiveness of the X–40 medication significant at the .05 level?

$$\chi^2 = \frac{84[\,|(30 \times 10) - (40 \times 4)| - 4|2]^2}{(30 + 40)(4 + 10)(30 + 4)(40 + 10)} = \frac{84[300 - 160| - 42]^2}{(70)(14)(34)(50)}$$

$$= \frac{84(98)^2}{1,666,000} = \frac{84(9604)}{1,666,000} = \frac{806,736}{1,666,000}$$

$$\chi^2 = \frac{806,736}{1,666,000} = .48$$

The computed χ^2 is far below the χ^2 critical value (3.84) necessary for the rejection of the null hypothesis at the .05 level. The research concludes that the null hypothesis is not rejected: there is no significant relationship between the use of X–40 pills at this dosage and headache relief. Any apparent effectiveness was probably the result of sampling error.

The Mann-Whitney Test

The Mann-Whitney U test is designed to test the significance of the difference between two populations, using random samples drawn from the same population. It is a nonparametric equivalent of the parametric *t* test. It is more powerful than the median test and lends itself to one- or two-tailed tests of the null hypothesis. It may be considered a useful alternative to the *t* test when the parametric assumptions cannot be met and when the observations are expressed in at least ordinal scale values.

The basic computation is U_1, and in experiments using small samples, the significance of an observed *U* may be determined by the *U* critical values of the Mann-Whitney tables.

When the size of either of the groups is more than 20, the sampling distribution of *U* rapidly approaches the normal distribution, and the null hypothesis may be tested with the reference to the *z* critical values of the normal probability table.

The values of the combined samples, N_1 and N_2, are ranked from the lowest to the highest rank, irrespective of groups, rank 1 to the lowest score, rank 2 to the next lowest, and so forth. Then the ranks of each sample group are summed individually and represented as ΣR_1 and ΣR_2.

There are two *U*s calculated for the formulas:

a. $U_1 = N_1 N_2 + \dfrac{N_1(N_1 + 1)}{2} - \Sigma R_1$

b. $U_2 = N_1 N_2 + \dfrac{N_2(N_2 + 1)}{2} - \Sigma R_2$

N_1 = number in one group $\qquad \Sigma R_1$ = sum of ranks in one group
N_2 = number in second group $\qquad \Sigma R_2$ = sum of ranks in second group

Only one *U* need be calculated, for the other can be easily computed by the formula

$$U_1 = N_1 N_2 - U_2$$

It is the smaller value of *U* that is used when consulting the Mann-Whitney *U* table.

The *z* value of *U* can be determined by the formula

$$z = \frac{U - \dfrac{N_1 N_2}{2}}{\sqrt{\dfrac{(N_1)(N_2)(N_1 + N_2 + 1)}{12}}}$$

It does not matter which *U* (the larger or the smaller) is used in the computation of *z*. The sign of the *z* will depend on which is used, but the numerical value will be identical.

For example, a teacher wishes to evaluate the effect of two methods of teaching reading to two groups of 20 randomly assigned students, drawn from the same population.

TABLE 8–4   Performance Scores of Students Taught by Method A or by Method B

A	RANK	B	RANK
50	3	49	2
60	8	90	36
89	35	88	33.5
94	38	76	21
82	28	92	37
75	20	81	27
63	10	55	7
52	5	64	11
97	40	84	30
95	39	51	4
83	29	47	1
80	25.5	70	15
77	22	66	12
80	25.5	69	14
88	33.5	87	32
78	23	74	19
85	31	71	16
79	24	61	9
72	17	55	6
68	13	73	18
$N_1 = 20$	$\Sigma R_1 = 469.5$	$N_2 = 20$	$\Sigma R_2 = 350.5$

$$U_1 = N_1 N_2 + \frac{N_1(N_1 + 1)}{2} - \Sigma R_1$$

The null hypothesis proposed is that there is no significant difference between the performance of the students taught by Method A and the students taught by Method B.

After a period of four months' exposure to the two teaching methods, the scores of the students on a standardized achievement test were recorded. All scores were ranked from lowest to highest and the Mann-Whitney test was used to test the null hypothesis at the .05 level of significance.

$$U_1 = (20)(20) + \frac{20(21)}{2} - 469.50$$

$$= 400 + 210 - 469.50$$

$$= 140.50$$

$$U_2 = N_1 N_2 + \frac{N_2(N_2 + 1)}{2} - \Sigma R_2$$

$$= (20)(20) + \frac{20(21)}{2} - 350.50$$

$$= 400 + 210 - 350.50$$

$$= 259.50$$

Check: $$U_1 = N_1 N_2 - U_2$$

$$140.50 = 400 - 259.50$$

$$140.50 = 140.50$$

$$z = \frac{U_1 - \dfrac{N_1 N_2}{2}}{\sqrt{\dfrac{N_1 N_2 (N_1 + N_2 + 1)}{12}}}$$

$$z = \frac{140.50 - \dfrac{400}{2}}{\sqrt{\dfrac{(20)(20)(41)}{12}}} = -\frac{59.5}{\sqrt{1366.67}} = -\frac{59.50}{36.97}$$

$$z = -1.61$$

Because the observed z value of -1.61 did not equal or exceed the z critical value of 1.96 for a two-tailed test at the .05 level, the null hypothesis was not rejected. The difference was not significant, and the apparent superior performance of the Method A group could well have resulted from sampling error.

For further information on these and other nonparametric tests, we recommend Hollander and Wolfe (1973) and Siegel (1956).

SUMMARY

Statistics is an indispensable tool for researchers that enables them to make inferences or generalizations about populations from their observations of the characteristics of samples. Although samples do not duplicate the characteristics of populations, and although samples from the same population will differ from one another, the nature of their variation is reasonably predictable. The central limit theorem describes the nature of sample means and enables the researcher to make estimates about population means (parameters) with known probabilities of error.

The pioneering contributions of Sir Ronald Fisher and Karl Pearson to statistics and scientific method, and William Sealy Gosset to small-sampling theory, have made practical the analysis of many of the types of problems encountered in psychology and education as well as in agricultural and biological research, where they were first applied.

Parametric statistical treatment of data is based upon certain assumptions about the nature of distributions and the types of measures used. Nonparametric statistical treatment makes possible useful inferences without assumptions about the nature of data distributions. Each type makes a significant contribution to the analysis of data relationships.

Statistical decisions are not made with certainty but are based upon probability estimates. The central limit theorem, sampling error, variance, the null hypothesis, levels of significance, and one-tailed and two-tailed tests have been explained and illustrated. Although this treatment has been brief and necessarily incomplete, the presentation of concepts may help the consumer of research to understand many simple research reports. Students who aspire to significant research activity, or who wish to interpret complex research studies with understanding, will need additional background in statistics and experimental design. They will find it helpful to participate in research seminars and to acquire competence through apprenticeship with scholars who are making contributions to knowledge through their own research activities.

EXERCISES

1. Why is it stronger logic to be able to reject a negative hypothesis than to try to confirm a positive one?

2. A statistical test of significance would have no useful purpose in a purely descriptive study in which sampling was not involved. Do you agree? Why?

3. When a statistical test determines that a finding is significant at the .05 level, it indicates that there is $\frac{5}{100}$ probability that the relationship was merely the result of sampling error. Do you agree? Why?

4. Any hypothesis that can be rejected at the .05 level of significance can surely be rejected at the .01 level. Do you agree?

5. The t critical value necessary for the rejection of a null hypothesis (at a given level of significance and for a given number of degrees of freedom) is higher for a one-tailed test than it is for a two-tailed test. Do you agree? Why?

6. A manufacturer guaranteed that a particular type of steel cable had a mean tensile strength of 2000 pounds with a standard deviation of 200 pounds. In a shipment, 16 lengths of the cable were submitted to a test for breaking strength. The mean breaking strength was 1900 pounds. Using a one-tailed test at the .05 level of significance, determine whether the shipment met the manufacturer's specifications.

7. Two samples of mathematics students took a standardized engineering aptitude test. Using a two-tailed test at the .05 level of significance, determine whether the two groups were random samples from the same population.

GROUP A   GROUP B

$N = 25$ $N = 30$
$\overline{X} = 80$ $\overline{X} = 88$
$S = 8$ $S = 9$

8. An achievement test in spelling was administered to two randomly selected fifth-grade groups of students from two schools. Test the null hypothesis that there was no significant difference in achievement between
the two fifth-grade populations from which the samples were selected at
the .05 level of significance. Use the method of separate variances.

SCHOOL A   SCHOOL B

$N = 40$ $N = 45$
$\overline{X} = 82$ $\overline{X} = 86$
$S = 12.60$ $S = 14.15$

9. One group of rats was given a vitamin supplement while the other group
received a conventional diet. The rats were randomly assigned. Test the
hypothesis that the vitamin supplement did not result in increased weight
gain for the experimental group. Use a one-tailed test at the .05 level.

X   C

$N = 12$ $N = 16$
$S = 15.50$ g $S = 12.20$ g
$\overline{X} = 140$ g $\overline{X} = 120$ g

10. A consumer research agency tested two popular makes of automobiles
with similar weight and horsepower. Eleven car A's provided a mean miles
per gallon of 24.20 with an S of 1.40, while 11 car B's provided a mean
miles per gallon of 26.30 with an S of 1.74. Using a two-tailed test at the .05
level, test the null hypothesis that there was no significant difference
between the mean gasoline mileage of the two makes of cars.

11. Calculate the number of degrees of freedom when
    a. computing the statistical significance of a coefficient of correlation.
    b. determining the significance between two means.
    c. a 2 × 2 χ^2 table computation is involved.
    d. a 3 × 5 χ^2 table computation is involved.

12. In a survey to determine high school students' preference for a soft drink,
the results were:

	BRAND A	BRAND B	BRAND C
Boys	25	30	52
Girls	46	22	28

Was there any relationship between the brand preference and the gender
of the consumers?

13. A group of 50 college freshmen was randomly assigned to experimental
and control groups to determine the effectiveness of a counseling program upon academic averages. Use the Mann-Whitney test to test the null

hypothesis that there was no difference between the academic performance of the experimental and control groups at the .05 level of significance.

EXPERIMENTAL	CONTROL
2.10	2.01
3.00	2.69
1.96	3.07
2.04	2.14
3.27	2.82
3.60	2.57
3.80	3.44
2.75	4.00
1.98	3.01
2.00	2.55
2.98	2.77
3.10	3.09
3.69	2.72
2.66	3.34
2.56	2.81
2.50	3.05
3.77	2.67
2.40	1.90
3.20	1.70
1.71	1.57
3.04	1.39
2.06	2.09
2.86	3.68
3.02	2.11
1.88	2.83

14. Compute the *t* value of the coefficient of correlation:

$$r = +.30$$
$$N = 18$$

15. Calculate $\hat{Y}$ given the following information:

$$a = 11.2$$
$$b_1 = .2$$
$$b_2 = .4$$
$$b_3 = .3$$
$$X_1 = 70$$
$$X_2 = 60$$
$$X_3 = 82$$

REFERENCES

COHEN, J. & COHEN, P. (1975). *Applied multiple regression correlation analysis for the behavioral sciences*. Hillsdale, NJ: Lawrence Erlbaum.

GLASS, G. V. & HOPKINS, K. D. (1984). *Statistical methods in education and psychology* (2nd ed.). Englewood Cliffs, NJ: Prentice-Hall.

HOLLANDER, M. & WOLFE, D. A. (1973). *Nonparametric statistical methods*. New York: John Wiley.

KIRK, R. E. (1982). *Experimental design: Procedures for the behavioral sciences* (2nd ed.). Belmont, CA: Brooks/Cole.

NETER, J. & WASSERMAN, W. (1974). *Applied linear statistical models*. Homewood, IL: Richard D. Irwin, Inc.

SIEGEL, S. (1956). *Nonparametric statistics for the behavioral sciences*. New York: McGraw-Hill.

WINER, B. J. (1971). *Statistical principles in experimental design* (2nd ed.). New York: McGraw-Hill.

ADDITIONAL READINGS

COHRAN, W. G. (1977). *Sampling techniques* (3rd ed.). New York: John Wiley.

FERGUSON, G. A. (1981). *Statistical analysis in psychology and education* (5th ed.). New York: McGraw-Hill.

GUILFORD, J. P. & FRUCHTER, B. (1978). *Fundamental statistics in psychology and education*. New York: McGraw-Hill.

HOPKINS, K. D. & GLASS, G. V. (1978). *Basic statistics for the behavioral sciences*. Englewood Cliffs, NJ: Prentice-Hall.

NUNNALLY, J. C. (1975). *Introduction to statistics for psychology and education*. New York: McGraw-Hill.

NUNNALLY, J. C. (1967). *Psychometric theory*. New York: McGraw-Hill.

TATSUOKA, M. M. (1971). *Multivariate analysis*. New York: John Wiley.

YAMARE, T. (1967). *Elementary sampling theory*. Englewood Cliffs, NJ: Prentice-Hall.

Chapter 9

Computer
Data Analysis

The purpose of this chapter is to show how computers can be used in analyzing data. Computers can perform calculations in just a few seconds that human beings would need weeks to do by hand. Although computers, as we know them today, have only been in existence for approximately 40 years, all of our daily lives are affected by them.

The microchip has made possible small computers that are within the financial reach of many Americans. As the price of these small computers comes down and their capabilities increase, more homes and small businesses will have computers. The computer programs presented later in this chapter were all run using a large university "main frame" computer. However, comparable programs are already available for many of the microcomputers.

THE COMPUTER

The electronic digital computer is one of the most versatile and ingenious developments of the technological age. It is unlikely that complex modern institutions of business, finance, and government would have developed so rapidly without the contributions of the computer.

To the researcher, the use of the computer to analyze complex data has made complicated research designs practical. Performing calculations almost at the speed of light, the computer has become one of the most useful research tools in the physical and behavioral sciences as well as in the humanities.

An early predecessor of the modern computer was a mechanical device developed by Charles Babbage, a nineteenth-century English mathematician. Late in that century Herman Hollerith, a director of the U.S. Census Bureau, devised a hole-punched card to aid in the more efficient processing of census data. The punched card was a significant development, for it has been a very important part of modern computer data processing.

In the mid-1940s, an electrical impulse computer was devised with circuits employing thousands of vacuum tubes. These computers, which were very large and cumbersome, required a great deal of space. The heat generated by the vacuum tubes required extensive air-conditioning equipment to prevent heat damage, and the uncertain life of the vacuum tubes caused frequent malfunction.

With the development of transistorized components, replacement of the vacuum tubes, miniaturization, increased component reliability, elimination of heat dissipation problems, and other improvements, the computer has become a much more effective device for the storage, processing, and retrieval of information.

The most advanced current models have incorporated microcircuitry of even more compact size, improved storage capacity, and greater processing speed. Functions can be processed in nanoseconds, or billionths of a second.

Computer technology includes four basic functions: input, storage, control, and output. *Input* entails entering information or data into the computer. This is generally done through a cathode ray tube (CRT) terminal (similar to a television) that is connected to and interacts with the computer. Other possible input methods include the use of punched cards, optical scanning readers that translate printed page information, or magnetic tape. Once information is input, it is *stored* for eventual use on magnetic cores, tapes, or disks. *Control* of stored information, as well as new input, is achieved through programs written in one of several possible computer languages that are translated by the computer's controller to the computer's assembly (basic) language. FORTRAN, which has gone through several modifications over the years, is the prevailing language for statistical calculations. Such directions as *do, go to, read, call, write, if,* and *then* are FORTRAN language terms. Computer centers have many "canned" or preprepared programs to perform a variety of statistical procedures, so the researcher usually does not need to write his or her own. The *output* or retrieval process transfers the processed information or data from the computer to the researcher, using one of a number of devices to communicate the results. The output may be displayed on a CRT screen, printed on paper, or recorded on a tape or disk.

The computer can perform many statistical calculations easily and quickly. Computation of means, standard deviations, correlation coefficients, *t* tests, analysis of variance, analysis of covariance, multiple regression, factor analysis, and various nonparametric analyses are just a few of the programs and subprograms that are available at computer centers.

It has been said that the computer makes no mistakes, but program writers do make mistakes, and any directions given to the computer are faithfully executed. The computer doesn't think; it can only execute the directions of a thinking person. If poor data or faulty programs are introduced into the computer, the data analysis will be meaningless. The expression "garbage in, garbage out" describes the problem quite well.

It is critical when using canned programs to carefully follow the appropriate program syntax. If a comma or slash is missing, the program may stop processing the data or, worse yet, process the data incorrectly.

With the large "main frame" computers of university and large business computer centers, hundreds of users at different terminals can communicate with the computer at a single time. Computer programs (software) are available at these centers for many purposes, including statistical analyses. The canned programs include the *Statistical Package for the Social Sciences*[1] (versions include SPSS® and SPSS-X®), Statistical Analysis System[2] (SAS®) and others. Though the actual programs, input procedures (syntax), and output (printouts) differ for these package programs, they are similar in their capabilities and the variety of statistical analyses that can be performed using them. Perhaps the most widely used are those programs published by SPSS. Which set of programs is used, however, depends on the user's needs and preference. Examples of programs from SPSS, SPSS-X, and SAS systems—using the computer facilities of the University of Illinois at Chicago—will be presented later in this chapter.

Microcomputers include a wide range of equipment from small, low-cost computers for games and other purposes to computers that cost several thousands of dollars and can perform a variety of functions. Depending on the model and storage capabilities, there are programs available, SPSS among them, that can calculate any of the statistical analyses presented in this text, and many more.

DATA ORGANIZATION

Prior to the input stage of data analysis comes the organizing of data for proper input into the computer system. Regardless of the type of computer or program to be used, if data are poorly organized the researcher will have trouble analyzing their meaning.

The data must first be coded. Categorical data, such as a person's sex or occupation, need to be given a number to represent them. For instance:

SEX	OCCUPATION
1 = Female	1 = Farmer
2 = Male	2 = Service
	3 = Professional

[1] SPSS and SPSS-X are trademarks of SPSS, Inc. of Chicago, Ill., for its proprietary computer software.

[2] SAS is the registered trademark of SAS Institute, Inc., Cary, N.C.

The researcher may also want to convert interval or ratio data into categories and code them. For instance,

IQ LEVEL   INCOME

1 = 120 to 139   1 = 40,000 and over
2 = 100 to 119   2 = 30,000 to 39,999
3 = 80 to 99   3 = 20,000 to 29,999
4 = 60 to 79   4 = below 20,000

The next step is to assign each variable to the spaces in which it will always be placed. Most systems call for a maximum of 80 columns per line. Once the researcher knows how many spaces each variable will occupy, the variables can be assigned to their column numbers (from 1 to 80). If more than 80 spaces are needed for each subject, then two or more lines will need to be assigned. The first columns will usually be the individual subject identity (ID) number. If less than 100 subjects are included, two spaces starting with 01 will be needed. Sometimes a researcher may include one or more attributes into the ID number, thereby increasing the number of columns needed. For instance, in the data set used in the analysis of variance presented in this chapter, we use a four-digit ID. The first digit represents the student's major, the second the student's sex, and the third and fourth digits the distinctive ID number. Thus, subject number 2113 was a philosophy major, male, and the thirteenth subject coded. When a large number of variables are used in a study, separating the variables with spaces will make the data easier to comprehend and easier for use with some programs. In any case, the researcher needs to have a list that shows which variables are represented in which column numbers.

Figure 9–1 shows how the data used in the later example of regression was coded on to a form. Although only four variables are included in the regression example, the actual data set contained an ID number and fourteen variables. Note how the variables are separated from each other by a space left between them. Figure 9–2 is the list used to determine which columns contained the different variables.

Survey researchers frequently have a system for coding and recording their data prior to distributing the questionnaires. For example, the questionnaire may ask for the sex of the respondent, "1" for male or "2" for female. If data is precoded for all questions and the researcher knows into which columns each answer will be placed, the data may be input to the computer directly from the returned survey forms, thereby saving the time of transferring the data to coding forms.

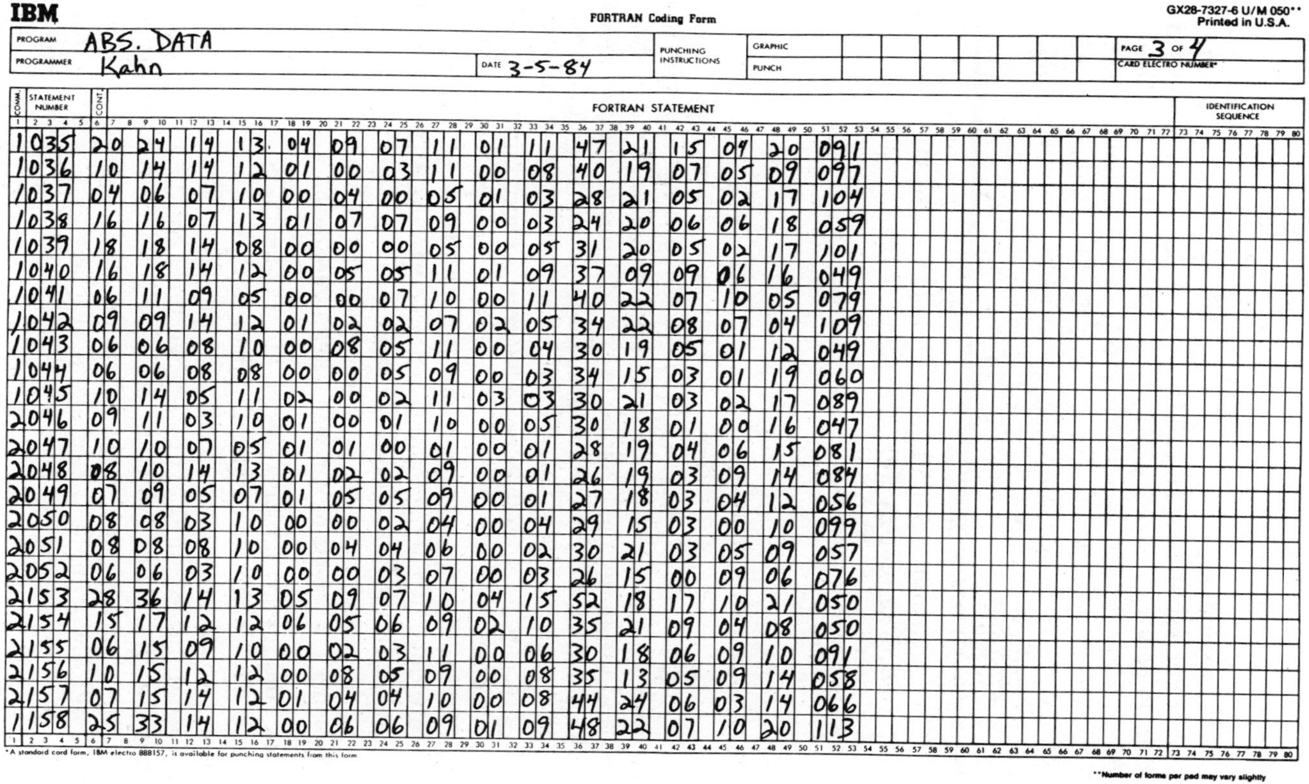

IBM FORTRAN Coding Form GX28-7327-6 U/M 050** Printed in U.S.A.

PROGRAM ABS. DATA
PROGRAMMER Kahn DATE 3-5-84
PUNCHING INSTRUCTIONS GRAPHIC PUNCH
PAGE 3 OF 4 CARD ELECTRO NUMBER*

COMM. STATEMENT NUMBER CONT. FORTRAN STATEMENT IDENTIFICATION SEQUENCE

1035	20	24	14	13	04	09	07	11	01	11	47	21	15	04	20 091
1036	10	14	14	12	01	00	03	11	00	08	40	19	07	05	09 097
1037	04	06	07	10	00	04	00	05	01	03	28	21	05	02	17 104
1038	16	16	07	13	01	07	07	09	00	03	24	20	06	06	18 059
1039	18	18	14	08	00	00	00	05	00	05	31	20	05	02	17 101
1040	16	18	14	12	00	05	05	11	01	09	37	09	09	06	16 049
1041	06	11	09	05	00	00	07	10	00	11	40	22	07	10	05 079
1042	09	09	14	12	01	02	02	07	02	05	34	22	08	07	04 109
1043	06	06	08	10	00	08	05	11	00	04	30	19	05	01	12 049
1044	06	06	08	08	00	00	05	09	00	03	34	15	03	01	19 060
1045	10	14	05	11	02	00	02	11	03	03	30	21	03	02	17 089
2046	09	11	03	10	01	00	01	10	00	05	30	18	01	00	16 047
2047	10	10	07	05	01	01	00	01	00	01	28	19	04	06	15 081
2048	08	10	14	13	01	02	02	09	00	01	26	19	03	09	14 084
2049	07	09	05	07	01	05	05	09	00	01	27	18	03	04	12 056
2050	08	08	03	10	00	00	02	04	00	04	29	15	03	00	10 099
2051	08	08	08	10	00	04	04	06	00	02	30	21	03	05	09 057
2052	06	06	03	10	00	00	03	07	00	03	26	15	00	09	06 076
2153	28	36	14	13	05	09	07	10	04	15	52	18	17	10	21 050
2154	15	17	12	12	06	05	06	09	02	10	35	21	09	04	08 050
2155	06	15	09	10	00	02	03	11	00	06	30	18	06	09	10 091
2156	10	15	12	12	00	08	05	09	00	08	35	13	05	09	14 058
2157	07	15	14	12	01	04	04	10	00	08	44	24	06	03	14 066
1158	25	33	14	12	00	06	06	09	01	09	48	22	07	10	20 113

*A standard card form, IBM electro 888157, is available for punching statements from this form

**Number of forms per pad may vary slightly

FIGURE 9–1 Coded data.

COLUMN NUMBER		COLUMN NUMBER	
1–4	ID Number	36–37	Independent
6–7	Expressive Language (EL)		Functioning (ABS1)
9–10	Receptive Language (RL)	39–40	Physical Develop-
12–13	Object Permanence (OP)		ment (ABS2)
15–16	Means-End (ME)	42–43	Language (ABS4)
18–19	Vocal Imitation (VI)	45–46	Self-direction
21–22	Gestural Imitation (GI)		(ABS8)
24–25	Causality	48–49	Mental Age (MA)
27–28	Spatial Relations	51–53	Chronological Age
30–31	Responsibility (ABS9)		(CA)
33–34	Socialization (ABS10)		

FIGURE 9–2   Variable list for coded data.

COMPUTER ANALYSIS OF DATA

Once the data is coded, it is ready to be stored in the computer. The researcher then must decide on the descriptive and inferential statistics desired and the program(s) that he or she will use to analyze the data. The selection of appropriate statistics will generally depend on the design of the study, and the specific program(s) to be used will depend upon the researcher's preference. Some researchers prefer one of the canned program packages and almost always use just that one. Others use different statistical programs from different packages. In the following we introduce two of the more popular statistical systems, presenting the control cards and output for two analyses from each.

Example 1: Analysis of Variance—SPSS Version 9

After the researcher has selected the program to be used, he or she must give the computer certain directions. These directions are provided on two types of control cards. Figure 9–3 presents the control cards for our first example. The first five lines are the job control language (JCL) cards that instruct the computer on such parameters as the maximum computer time to be allocated, the region (or memory) needed, and where and how to print the output; they also tell it that the SPSS system of programs will be used. These JCL cards are specific to the computer system being used and will vary somewhat from system to system. The rest of the control cards are specific to SPSS and are needed regardless of the computer system being used.

The data used in this example are identical to the data used in Chapter 8 on the analysis of variance (ANOVA), with one important

```
/*JOBPARM T=(,29),R=474
/*OUTPUT PRT FORMS=8500,DEST=LOCAL
// EXEC SPSS
//FT06F001 DD SYSOUT=(A,,PRT)
//SPSS.SYSIN DD *
RUN NAME          THREE BY TWO TWO-WAY ANOVA EXAMPLE
VARIABLE LIST     MAJOR SEX ABSTR
INPUT FORMAT      FIXED(2F1.0,3X,F2.0)
INPUT MEDIUM      CARD
VAR LABELS        ABSTR ABSTRACT REASONING/
                  MAJOR STUDENT'S MAJOR/
                  SEX STUDENT'S SEX
VALUE LABELS      MAJOR (1) MATHEMATICS
                        (2) PHILOSOPHY
                        (3) CHEMISTRY
                  SEX   (1) FEMALE
                        (2) MALE
ANOVA             ABSTR BY MAJOR (1,3) SEX (1,2)/
READ INPUT DATA
1101 18
1102 22
1103 18
1104 23
1105 19
1206 24
1207 20
1208 21
1209 19
1210 25
2111 26
2112 27
2113 18
2114 22
2115 23
2216 19
2217 27
2218 26
2219 24
2220 26
3121 18
3122 14
3123 15
3124 14
3125 19
3226 21
3227 17
3228 17
3229 18
3230 19
END INPUT DATA
FINISH
```

FIGURE 9–3   Control cards and data for analysis of variance example using SPSS Version 9.

difference. In the current example, the ten students in each college major are evenly divided into males and females. Thus, instead of the simple one-way analysis of variance presented in Chapter 8, the current example is a two-way analysis of variance.

The SPSS control cards begin with the RUN NAME, which gives the computer run a title, in this case: "Three by Two Two-way ANOVA Example." Next comes the VARIABLE LIST, which names the independent and dependent variables. The INPUT FORMAT tells the program where to find the variables named on the previous line. The variables—college major and sex—are in the first and second columns. The next three spaces are skipped, and abstract reasoning is in columns six and seven. The INPUT MEDIUM control card tells the program that the data will accompany the program in card image form. VAR LABELS allow the researcher to give more complete labels to the short names on the variable list card. With the VALUE LABELS card, a 1, 2, or 3 in the first column tells us the student's major—mathematics, philosophy, or chemistry, respectively; and a 1 or a 2 in the second column tells us whether the student is a female or a male. The next line tells the program two things. First, the program is told that of all SPSS statistical programs available, we want to use the analysis of variance (ANOVA) program. This line also specifies abstract reasoning as the dependent variable, college major as an independent variable with three levels, and sex as another independent variable with two levels. Second, the program is told to read the data. Each line of data is for one subject: The first column is the student's major; the second column is the student's sex; the third and fourth columns contain the student's ID number; and the sixth and seventh columns contain the student's score on the test of abstract reasoning.

Figure 9–4 shows the analysis of variance table that is printed as the output of the above described program. The sources of variation include (1) the total for the two main effects, (2) each of the two main effects (major and sex), (3) the interaction effect of the two independent variables, (4) the total of the main effects and interaction effect (EX-PLAINED), (5) the within-groups or error (RESIDUAL), and (6) the total. The sum of squares, degrees of freedom (df), and mean squared are presented for each of these sources of variation. F's and the significance of each F are presented for each of the effects.

Of particular interest are the F's for the three effects: college major, sex, and the major by sex interaction. The F for major was found to be 15.094. Significance levels are carried out to three decimal places. Thus a significance of 0.000 is less than 0.001—less than one chance in a thousand that the three groups of students with different majors were observed to differ because of sampling error. The F for sex was found to be 3.352. The significance level of 0.080 is not low enough (.05 being the highest acceptable error rate) for us to reject the null hypothesis for the main effect of sex. That is, any observed differences between females and males should be considered due to sampling error. Finally, the F for the interaction of major and sex was found to be 0.124 with a significance level of 0.884. Obviously, the null hypothesis for the interaction of these variables is also not rejected.

The reader may be interested in comparing the results of this 3 by 2 (major by sex) analysis of variance with the one-way analysis of variance

THREE BY TWO TWO-WAY ANOVA EXAMPLE   08/08/84
FILE   NONAME   (CREATION DATE = 08/08/84)

```
* * * * * * * * * * A N A L Y S I S   O F   V A R I A N C E * * * * * * * * * * *
          ABSTR      ABSTRACT REASONING
       BY MAJOR      STUDENT'S MAJOR
          SEX        STUDENT'S SEX
* * * * * * * * * * * * * * * * * * * * * * * * * * * * * * * * * * * * * *
```

SOURCE OF VARIATION	SUM OF SQUARES	DF	MEAN SQUARE	F	SIGNIF OF F
MAIN EFFECTS	243.167	3	81.056	11.180	0.000
MAJOR	218.867	2	109.433	15.094	0.000
SEX	24.300	1	24.300	3.352	0.080
2-WAY INTERACTIONS	1.800	2	0.900	0.124	0.884
MAJOR SEX	1.800	2	0.900	0.124	0.884
EXPLAINED	244.967	5	48.993	6.758	0.000
RESIDUAL	173.999	24	7.250		
TOTAL	418.966	29	14.447		

```
30 CASES WERE PROCESSED.
 0 CASES (  0.0 PCT) WERE MISSING.
```

FIGURE 9–4 Sample analysis of variance output.

(major) performed in Chapter 8 on the same data. The reader should note that the total sum of squares and the sum of squares for major are identical. However, because this example included an additional main effect and an interaction effect, the residual (within-groups) sum of squares is reduced by the amount explained by these two effects. Similarly, the degrees of freedom of the residual changes from 27 to 24, with (1) sex and (2) the interaction of sex and major taking up these three degrees of freedom. Finally, due to the changes in the residual, the F for major (the only one that could be calculated using a one-way ANOVA) was changed slightly from 15.41 to 15.09.

Example 2: Multiple Regression—SPSS-X

SPSS, Inc. has published ten versions of SPSS for main frame computers. The most recent version used in this example is called SPSS-X. The previous version (Version 9), still available at most computer centers, was used in Example 1 to show the reader some of the changes. SPSS-X differs from all of the previous versions by simplifying the control cards.

The current example uses data collected by the second author and partially presented in Figure 9–1. The multiple regression presented uses three Piagetian independent variables (object permanence, means-end, and vocal imitation) to predict a receptive language score (presented as an age in months) of 76 profoundly retarded children. The first four control cards in this example are the job control language cards. They tell the computer the maximum computer time to be allocated, the memory (region) required, that SPSS-X will be used, and that the data, called ABS.DATA, will come from a file stored on a disk (the third line).

The first SPSS-X control card (NUMBERED) tells the SPSS-X program to only read columns 1 to 72. This is because in this type of job the computer system uses columns 73 to 80 for information that would interfere with the program if read by it. Instead of RUN NAME, TITLE is used to name the job ("SPSSX Regression Example"). The DATA LIST card replaces both the VARIABLE LIST and INPUT FORMAT cards. This card (two lines are used) tells the program that the data is in a file named "ABSDATA," that each variable is always in the same column

```
/*JOBPARM T=(,29),R=474
//  EXEC SPSSX
//ABSDATA DD DSN=ED04001.ABS.DATA,DISP=SHR
//SYSIN DD *
NUMBERED
TITLE SPSSX REGRESSION EXAMPLE
DATA LIST FILE=ABSDATA FIXED
   /RL 9-10 OP 12-13 ME 15-16 VI 18-19
VARIABLE LABELS  RL 'RECEPTIVE LANGUAGE'
                 OP 'OBJECT PERMANENCE'
                 ME 'MEANS-END'
                 VI 'VOCAL IMITATION'
REGRESSION  DESCRIPTIVES=DEFAULTS SIG/
            VARIABLES=RL OP ME VI/
            STATISTICS= R COEF/
            DEPENDENT=RL/
            ENTER/
```

FIGURE 9–5 Control cards for regression example using SPSS-X.

(fixed), and gives the short name and column numbers for each variable (e.g., "RL" is in columns 9 and 10, "OP" in columns 12 and 13). The VARIABLE LABELS card assigns more complete labels to the initially short names. Finally comes REGRESSION command and its options on the next five lines. The first of these lines instructs SPSS-X to do a regression analysis and identifies the descriptive statistics that are desired (those automatically calculated plus significance levels). The second and third lines present the variables to be used in the regression equation and the regression statistics to be calculated ("R" requests the multiple correlation and "Coef" requests the regression coefficients and beta). The fourth and fifth lines specify the dependent variable ("RL") and request that all of the other variables—the remaining variables are the independent variables—be entered simultaneously into the prediction equation.

Figure 9–6 presents two pages of output produced by the above example. The first page shows the descriptive statistics requested. The mean and standard deviation of each variable and a correlation matrix—showing the Pearson r and its significance level for each pair of variables—are presented. The second page of output shows the multiple correlation coefficient (MULTIPLE R), its square (R SQUARE), the adjusted R square (which corrects R for sampling error), and the standard error of estimate for predicting a score using the regression equation. This page also contains a table that shows "B," "standard error of B," and "*Beta*" for each independent variable. The table also presents the constant intercept and a "T" and its significance level for the importance of each variable to the prediction of the dependent variable. These t tests show that only object-permanence and means-end add significantly to the prediction of receptive language.

We could use the information regarding the B weights and the constant in a multiple regression equation to predict a profoundly retarded person's receptive language age given his or her vocal imitation, object-permanence, and means-end scores.

$$\hat{Y} = a + b_1X_1 + b_2X_2 \ldots$$
$$\hat{Y}(RL) = -2.359 + .694 \, (VI) + .886 \, (OP) + .648 \, (ME)$$

The resulting prediction of receptive language would have a standard error of estimate of 5.966.

Example 3: Descriptive Statistics—SAS:CORR

SAS offers a number of descriptive statistics programs. The one presented here is called CORR because it includes correlations. The job control language cards (JCL) are very similar to those in the previous

```
08 AUG 84    SPSSX REGRESSION EXAMPLE
18:00:08     UNIV OF ILLINOIS AT CHICAGO    IBM 3081-D    OS/MVS              PAGE 1

                        * * * *   M U L T I P L E   R E G R E S S I O N   * * * *

VARIABLE LIST NUMBER 1    LISTWISE DELETION OF MISSING DATA

           MEAN   STD DEV  LABEL

RL        17.079   8.000   RECEPTIVE LANGUAGE
OP        11.487   3.542   OBJECT PERMANENCE
ME        11.237   2.250   MEANS-END
VI         2.855   2.832   VOCAL IMITATION

N OF CASES =    76

CORRELATION, SIGNIFICANCE:

            RL        OP        ME        VI

RL        1.000      .621      .581      .474
           .999      .000      .000      .000

OP         .621     1.000      .745      .379
           .000      .999      .000      .001

ME         .581      .745     1.000      .434
           .000      .000      .999      .000

VI         .474      .379      .434     1.000
           .000      .001      .000      .999




VARIABLE LIST NUMBER 1    LISTWISE DELETION OF MISSING DATA                    PAGE 2

EQUATION NUMBER 1    DEPENDENT VARIABLE.. RL    RECEPTIVE LANGUAGE

   DESCRIPTIVE STATISTICS ARE PRINTED ON PAGE    2

BEGINNING BLOCK NUMBER  1.  METHOD: ENTER

VARIABLE(S) ENTERED ON STEP NUMBER  1..    VI      VOCAL IMITATION
                                    2..    OP      OBJECT PERMANENCE
                                    3..    ME      MEANS-END


MULTIPLE R            .68263
R SQUARE              .46598
ADJUSTED R SQUARE     .44373
STANDARD ERROR       5.96640

F =    20.94201      SIGNIF F =  .0000


------------------- VARIABLES IN THE EQUATION -------------------

VARIABLE          B         SE B       BETA         T      SIG T

VI             .69437      .27128     .24580      2.560    .0126
OP             .88566      .29276     .39215      3.025    .0034
ME             .64807      .47341     .18229      1.369    .1753
(CONSTANT)   -2.35936     3.64187               -.648     .5191


FOR BLOCK NUMBER  1   ALL REQUESTED VARIABLES ENTERED.
```

FIGURE 9–6 Sample regression output.

SPSS-X example. JCL for most canned programs are very similar for the computer system being used. In this example, the first four cards are the JCL (see Figure 9–7). The third JCL statement informs the computer that the data to be used is stored on a disk. The same data set is used here as in the prior regression example.

```
/*JOBPARM T=(,29),R=370
// EXEC SAS
//SAS.INBCD DD DSN=ED04001.ABS.DATA,DISP=SHR
//SAS.SYSIN DD *
DATA; INFILE INBCD;
INPUT ID EL RL OP ME VI GI CAUS SPA ABS9 ABS10 ABS1 ABS4 ABS8
      ABS9 MA CA;
LABEL EL= EXPRESSIVE LANGUAGE RL = RECEPTIVE LANGUAGE
      OP = OBJECT PERMANENCE   ME = MEANS-END
      VI = VOCAL IMITATION     GI = GESTURAL IMITATION
      CAUS = CAUSALITY    ABS1 = INDEPENDENT FUNCTIONING
      ABS4 = LANGUAGE    ABS8 = SELF-DIRECTION
      ABS10 = SOCIALIZATION   CA = CHRONOLOGICAL AGE
      MA = MENTAL AGE;
PROC CORR;
VAR OP ME VI GI CAUS MA CA;
WITH EL RL ABS1 ABS4 ABS8 ABS10;
```

FIGURE 9–7 Control cards for descriptive statistics example using SAS.

SAS statements are separated from each other by semicolons (;). Thus DATA tells the program to read the data, and INFILE INBCD tells it to read that data from the file from the disk previously named by the JCL statement. The INPUT statement tells the program the names of the variables and where they are. Because the variables are separated by spaces, we inform the program where they are simply by naming them in the order they appear in the file. The next statement, LABEL, gives longer labels to the previously listed variables. PROC CORR tells the SAS system that the procedure known as "correlation" is to be used. The next two statements request correlation coefficients to be calculated and printed for only certain combinations. The VAR statement lists the variables desired on the top of the printed correlation matrix, and the WITH statement lists the variables desired on the side of the correlation matrix.

Figure 9–8 shows the output produced by this program. The number of subjects, mean, standard deviation, sum of the scores, the lowest score and the highest score for each of the variables is presented first. Below that is the correlation matrix—with the significance level for each correlation—for the VAR variables with the WITH variables. If the VAR and WITH statements had not been included, a correlation matrix consisting of all of the possible combinations (all 13 variables by all 13 variables) would have resulted.

Example 4: Charting—SAS:CHART

Both SPSS-X and SAS systems have very sophisticated graphing options including three-dimensional and, if the printer is capable, color graphics. The present example demonstrates the Chart procedure, a relatively simple one, from SAS.

The first six lines of the control cards presented in Figure 9–9 are the job control language cards. These cards, once again, inform the computer of the computer time to be allocated and memory required, the type and place of printing desired, that the SAS system will be used, and the name (CANONL. DATA) and location (disk) of the data set to be used. The next two lines include the first three SAS statements and are similar to the SAS statements used in Example 3. The next six lines present a series of "IF . . . THEN" statements. These statements convert two of the variables to categories. The first four statements deal with chronological age in months (CA). Those children with CAs from 30 to 59 months are assigned a score of 1; those with CAs from 60 to 83 months are assigned a score of 2; those with CAs from 84 to 107 months are assigned a score of 3; and those with CAs above 107 are assigned a score of 4. Because the first digit of the four-digit ID number represents the subject's sex, those children with IDs over 2000 are female (F) and those with IDs below 2000 are male (M). The next line creates the computer

11:23 THURSDAY, AUGUST 9, 1984   1

SAS

VARIABLE	N	MEAN	STD DEV	SUM	MINIMUM	MAXIMUM
OP	76	11.48684211	3.54210266	873.00000000	3.00000000	14.00000000
ME	76	11.23684211	2.25014619	854.00000000	5.00000000	13.00000000
VI	76	2.85526316	2.83174362	217.00000000	0	9.00000000
GI	76	6.18421053	3.39297520	470.00000000	0	9.00000000
CAUS	76	4.40789474	2.17977143	335.00000000	0	7.00000000
MA	76	15.61842105	4.19830793	1187.00000000	4.00000000	22.00000000
CA	76	72.53947368	21.55887492	5513.00000000	31.00000000	118.00000000
EL	76	12.94736842	6.75849044	984.00000000	4.00000000	30.00000000
RL	76	17.07894737	7.99960525	1298.00000000	6.00000000	36.00000000
ABS1	76	42.47368421	13.43872383	3228.00000000	24.00000000	74.00000000
ABS4	76	19.28947368	3.45182383	1466.00000000	6.00000000	24.00000000
ABS8	76	7.81578947	4.35035792	594.00000000	0	17.00000000
ABS10	76	9.63157895	5.52290287	732.00000000	1.00000000	22.00000000

CORRELATION COEFFICIENTS / PROB > |R| UNDER HO:RHO=0 / N = 76

	OP	ME	VI	GI	CAUS	MA	CA
EL EXPRESSIVE LANGUAGE	0.53967 0.0001	0.53127 0.0001	0.50260 0.0001	0.53768 0.0001	0.38975 0.0005	0.58526 0.0001	0.09601 0.4094
RL RECEPTIVE LANGUAGE	0.62117 0.0001	0.58116 0.0001	0.47374 0.0001	0.61006 0.0001	0.51732 0.0001	0.56307 0.0001	0.02008 0.8633
ABS1 INDEPENDENT FUNCTIONING	0.48415 0.0001	0.47950 0.0001	0.55576 0.0001	0.53844 0.0001	0.19359 0.0938	0.43784 0.0001	0.07868 0.4993
ABS4 LANGUAGE	0.39726 0.0004	0.34297 0.0024	0.11074 0.3409	0.21397 0.0635	0.23219 0.0436	0.21566 0.0613	0.10412 0.3707
ABS8 SELF-DIRECTION	0.54237 0.0001	0.48942 0.0001	0.68076 0.0001	0.53618 0.0001	0.34970 0.0020	0.45018 0.0001	0.16527 0.1536
ABS10 SOCIALIZATION	0.53887 0.0001	0.51567 0.0001	0.64959 0.0001	0.59851 0.0001	0.35266 0.0018	0.39696 0.0004	-0.00592 0.9595

FIGURE 9–8 Sample SAS PROC CORR output.

```
/*JOBPARM T=(,29),R=374
/*OUTPUT PRT FORMS=8502,DEST=U1
// EXEC SAS
//FT12F001 DD SYSOUT=(A,,PRT)
//SAS.INBCD DD DSN=ED04001.CANON1.DATA,DISP=SHR
//SAS.SYSIN DD *
DATA; INFILE INBCD;
INPUT ID A B C D E F G H I J K L M N Q CA;
IF CA>35 <60 THEN AGE=1;
IF CA>59 <84 THEN AGE=2;
IF CA>83 <108 THEN AGE=3;
IF CA >107 THEN AGE=4;
IF ID <2000 THEN SEX='M';
IF ID> 2000 THEN SEX='F';
PUT AGE  SEX ;
PROC FORMAT;
     VALUE AGE 1= 3 TO 4
               2= 5 TO 6
               3= 7 TO 8
               4= 9 TO 11;
PROC CHART; VBAR AGE/ DISCRETE SUBGROUP=SEX;
            FORMAT AGE AGE.;
PROC CHART; PIE AGE/DISCRETE ;
            FORMAT AGE AGE.;
```

FIGURE 9-9   Control cards for charting example using SAS.

space for the variables of age and sex created in the previous six statements. The PROC FORMAT and VALUE statements assign more meaningful values to the variable age. Thus, those children assigned a 1 for CAs from 30 to 59 months are 3 to 4 years old; those children assigned a 2 for CAs from 60 to 83 months are 5 to 6 years old; and so on.

The next two lines request the SAS procedure CHART, a vertical bar graph (VBAR) to be created using the variable age, and the number of children of each sex to be included in the bars of the graph. The next two lines request another graph using the same SAS procedure. This time a pie or circular graph in sections is to be created using the variable age. Figure 9-10 presents both of these graphs on what would be two pages of output.

The pie chart gives both the frequency (number of subjects) and the percent of the total sample in each age range. The bar chart shows the number of males and females and the total number of children in each age group.

The purpose of this chapter has been to present the reader with an introduction to the use of computers in the analyses of data. We have presented four examples that are relatively simple and hope they have helped the reader to understand the capabilities of computer analyses. These programs required less than 3 seconds each of computer time and approximately 30 minutes each from the command to execute until the printout was ready. This time difference is primarily a function of the backlog of printouts waiting at the printers and the time required for printing.

We suggest that students wishing to develop skills in computer data analysis consult their university computer center and the suggested readings at the end of this chapter.

SUMMARY

Technological advances in the past 25 years have made computers an integral part of the functioning of our society. Computers and sophisticated "canned" computer programs have become widely available.

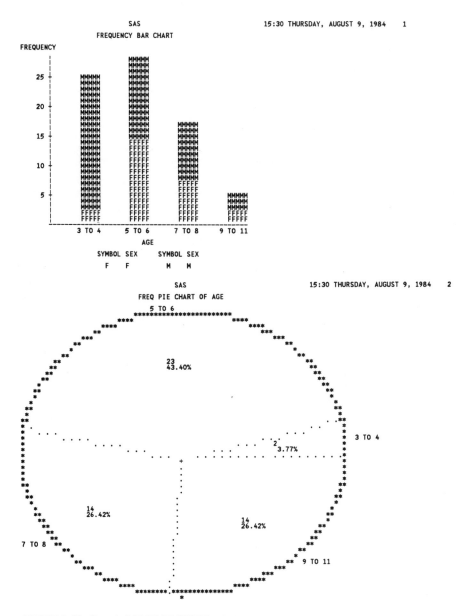

FIGURE 9–10 Sample SAS PROC CHART output.

The steps in using a computer to calculate statistical analyses are: (1) data organization and coding, (2) storing the data in the computer, (3) selection of appropriate descriptive and inferential statistics, (4) selection of appropriate programs for the desired statistics, (5) writing of control cards, and (6) execution of the computer program.

This chapter has presented four examples of control cards and output from "canned" programs. The statistics requested in these examples are relatively simple: a two-way analysis of variance, a multiple regression analysis, a descriptive statistics program, and two relatively simple graphics.

SUGGESTED READINGS

DIXON, W. D., BROWN, M. B., ENGLEMAN, L., FRANE, J. W., HILL, M. A., JEURICH, R. I., & TOPOREK, J. D. (Eds.). (1981). *BMDP statistical software.* Los Angeles, CA: University of California Press.

HULL, C. H. & NIE, N. H. (Eds.). (1981). *SPSS: Update 7–9.* New York: McGraw-Hill.

NIE, N. H., HULL, C. H., JENKINS, J. G., STEINBRENNER, K., & BRENT, D. H. (Eds.). (1975). *SPSS* (2nd ed.). New York: McGraw-Hill.

NORUSIS, M. J. (1983). *SPSS-X introductory statistics guide.* Chicago, IL: SPSS, Inc.

SAS user's guide: Basics. (1982). Cary, NC: SAS Institute.

SAS user's guide: Statistics. (1982). Cary, NC: SAS Institute.

SPSS-X user's guide. (1983). Chicago, IL: SPSS, Inc.

Chapter 10

The Research Report

Although research reports may differ considerably in scope of treatment, they are expected to follow a conventional pattern of style and form in academic circles. These matters of style and form may seem unduly arbitrary to the student. However, they are based upon principles of clear organization and presentation, and it is essential that graduate students in education be familiar with them if they are to communicate their ideas effectively.

STYLE MANUALS

Some graduate schools or departments have designated an official manual or have established their own style manual to which their theses or dissertations must conform. Students should find out which manual has been adopted officially by their institution or department. Beginning graduate students are disturbed when they discover that these manuals are not always in complete agreement on matter of typography or format. Careful examination, however, will reveal that differences concern minor details. In general, all style manuals are in basic agreement on the principles of correct presentation.

Regardless of which manual is used as a guide, it should be followed consistently in matters of form and style. The information in this chapter is consistent with one of the widely used style manuals, that of the American Psychological Association.

FORMAT OF THE RESEARCH REPORT

The research report, because of its relative brevity, differs somewhat from a thesis or dissertation. The following outline presents the sequence of topics covered in the typical research report prepared according to the American Psychological Association's (APA) *Publication manual* (1983):

   I. Title Page
      A. Title
      B. Author's name and affiliation

    C. Running head
    D. Acknowledgements (if any)
  II. Abstract
 III. Introduction (no heading used)
    A. Statement of the problem
    B. Background/review of literature
    C. Purpose and rationale/hypothesis
 IV. Method
    A. Subjects
    B. Apparatus or instrumentation (if necessary)
    C. Procedure
  V. Results
    A. Tables and figures (as appropriate)
    B. Statistical presentation
 VI. Discussion
    A. Support or nonsupport of hypotheses
    B. Practical and theoretical implications
    C. Conclusions
 VII. References
VIII. Appendix (if appropriate)

The APA style for typing a manuscript requires double spacing throughout the paper. Additional spaces may be used to set off certain elements, such as the running head on the title page, but single spacing should never be used. Leave margins of 1½ inches at the top, bottom, right, and left of every page. Number all pages, except the figures, beginning with the title page. The title page and the abstract are on separate pages (pages 1 and 2, respectively). A new page is begun for the introduction, for the references, for each table and figure, and for each appendix.

The first page of the report is the title page. This page includes the title, author's name, and author's affiliation near the top of the page, separated by double spaces. Toward the bottom of the page are the running head and acknowledgements, separated by a double space.

The title should be concise and should indicate clearly the purposes of the study. One should keep in mind its possible usefulness to the reader who may scan a bibliography in which it may be listed. The title should not claim more for the study than it actually delivers. It should not be stated so broadly that it seems to provide an answer that cannot be generalized, either from the data gathered or from the methodology employed. For example, if a simple, descriptive, self-concept study were made of a group of children enrolled in a particular inner-city elementary school, the title should not read, "The Self-Concepts of Inner-City Children." A more appropriate title would be "The Self-Concepts of a Group of Philadelphia Inner-City Children." The first title implies broader generalization than is warranted by the actual study.

The title should be typed in upper-case and lower-case letters, centered, and, when two or more lines are needed, double spaced. The running head, a shortened version of the title, should be a maximum of 50 characters including letters, punctuation, and spaces between words. The running head is typed near the bottom of the page in upper-case letters.

Acknowledgements appear as unnumbered footnotes near the bottom of the title page. Acknowledgements are used to indicate the basis of a study (e.g., doctoral dissertation), grant support, review of prior draft of the manuscript, and assistance in conducting the research and/or preparing the manuscript. They should be clearly and directly stated. Figure 10–1 illustrates a sample title page used in submitting a manuscript that was subsequently published (Kahn, 1982).

The abstract, on page 2 of the research report, describes the study in 100 to 150 words. Included in this summary are the problem under study, characteristics of the subjects, the procedures used (e.g., data-gathering techniques, intervention procedures), the findings of the study, and the conclusions reached by the researcher. A good abstract will increase the readership of the article because many persons start their reviews with abstracts.

Main Body of the Report

The main body of the research report is divided into four major sections: *introduction, method, results,* and *discussion.* The first of these sections, the *introduction,* begins a new page (page 3) and, because of its position, does not need or have a label.

A well-written introduction has three components. The researcher must give a clear and definitive statement of the problem. As described in Chapter 2 for research proposals, the problem must indicate the need for the research and give some indication of the expected outcome. It is also necessary to indicate why the problem is important in terms of theory and/or practice.

A review of previous literature on the topic is also an essential component of the introduction. The researcher must demonstrate an understanding of the existing literature pertinent to his or her study. However, although an exhaustive review is an appropriate part of a thesis or dissertation, it is not included in a research report. The author should assume that the reader has some knowledge of the field being investigated. Only research that is pertinent to the issue under investigation should be included. The author also needs to logically connect the previous body of literature with the current work.

Moral Reasoning in Irish Children and Adolescents

as Measured by the Defining Issues Test

James V. Kahn

University of Illinois at Chicago

This research was conducted while the author was a
Senior Fulbright—Hays Scholar at University College,
Cork, Ireland and on sabbatical leave from the
University of Illinois at Chicago. I wish to
acknowledge the assistance of the computer
facilities at both universities. I also wish to
thank the many children, teachers and administrators
at the various schools at which the data reported
were collected. I also wish to thank Rose Naputano
for her secretarial assistance and Larry Nucci for
his critical comments.

RUNNING HEAD: IRISH MORAL REASONING

FIGURE 10–1 Example of title page.

The final component of the introduction includes a clear rationale for the hypotheses to be proposed, definitions of the variables investigated and controlled, and a formal statement of each hypothesis. Each hypothesis must be stated so that it is clear how it will be tested. Terms must be clearly described, and predicted outcomes must be measurable. For example, an investigation of an early intervention program with children at high risk for mental retardation should not hypothesize that "the high-risk children in the experimental group will have greater gains in intelligence." We need to know *whom* the high-risk children will be surpassing, and we need to know how *intelligence* is conceptualized. A better hypothesis for this study would be, "high-risk children receiving the intervention program will have greater gains in IQ than will their control group peers."

The main body of the report continues with the *method* section, which follows the introduction. It includes two or more subsections and describes in great detail just what the investigator did. This allows the reader to determine how appropriate the procedures were and how much credence to give the results. A well-written method section is sufficiently detailed to enable a reader to replicate the components of the study. The method section is separated from the introduction by the centered heading, "Method." Generally, subsections are then labeled at the left margin and underlined.

The method section always should include at least two subsections: subjects and procedures. The subsection on *subjects* needs to identify the participants of the study, the number of persons included in the study, and the means by which the participants were selected. Major demographic characteristics, such as age, sex, socioeconomic status, and race, are included as they relate to the study. Sufficient information must be provided to permit the reader to be able to replicate the sample.

The *procedures* subsection describes the actual steps carried out in conducting the study. This includes the measurement devices, if no separate section is provided; the experimental treatments; the assignment of subjects to conditions; the order of assessments, if more than one; the time period, if pertinent; and any design features used to control potentially confounding variables. Again, enough information must be provided to permit replication. However, procedures that are published in detail elsewhere should only be summarized with the citation given for the other publication.

Additional subsections may be included as deemed necessary. For instance, if a battery of complex tests are to be used and described, a separate subsection on instrumentation would be appropriate. Complex designs also might be better described in a separate section.

The third section of the main body is *results*. The results section presents the data and the statistical analyses without discussing the implications of the findings. Individual scores or raw data are only presented in single-subject—or very small sample size—studies. All relevant findings are presented, including those that do not support the hypothesis. Tables and figures are useful to supplement textual material. They should be used when the data cannot readily be presented in a few sentences in the text. Data in the text and in tables or figures should not be redundant, rather they should be complementary. The test should indicate what the reader should expect to see in the tables and figures so as to clarify their meaning. The level of significance for statistical analyses should be presented.

Finally, the report's main body concludes with the *discussion* section. After presenting the results it is possible to determine the implications of the study, including whether the hypotheses were supported or should be rejected. It is appropriate to discuss both theoretical implications and practical applications of the study. A brief discussion of limitations of the present investigation and proposals for future research is appropriate. New hypotheses may be proposed if the data does not support the original hypotheses. The researcher should also include conclusions that reflect whether the original problem is better understood, or even resolved, as a result of this study.

References and Appendices

The reference section of the manuscript begins a new page with the label "References," centered. *References* consist of all documents, including journal articles, books, chapters, technical reports, computer programs, and unpublished works that are mentioned in the text of the manuscript. A reference section should not be confused with a bibliography: a bibliography contains everything that would be in the reference section *plus* other publications that are useful but were not cited in the manuscript. Bibliographies are not generally provided for research reports; only references are usually included.

References are arranged in alphabetical order by the last names of the first-named authors. When no author is listed, the first word of the title or sponsoring organization is used to begin the entry. Each reference starts at the left margin of the page, with subsequent lines double spaced and indented. No extra spaces separate the entries.

An *appendix* may be useful in providing detailed information that would seem inappropriate or too long for the main body of the paper. Each appendix begins on a new page with the label "Appendix" and its identifying letter, centered. Following this label is the centered title of the appendix and then the material. Materials that generally should be in an appendix include: a new computer program, unpublished tests, lengthy treatments that are not available elsewhere, and so on.

THE THESIS OR DISSERTATION

Research theses and dissertations follow the same outline as described for the research report. The major difference of the thesis and dissertation is length and comprehensiveness. Many institutions have their own style manuals for these major research papers; they may require a certain order of topics, the designating of each major (and some minor) sections as a chapter, bibliographies in place of reference sections, and more complete appendices. Since a goal of the thesis or dissertation is to demonstrate the student's knowledge in a particular field, it is more appropriate to be complete and comprehensive than concise and brief. Length is not an issue here as it is when submitting an article to a journal. It may even be appropriate to include raw data and computer printouts of the analyses performed. Students should read their institution's required style manual carefully before beginning their thesis or dissertation.

STYLE OF WRITING

The research report should be presented in a style that is creative, clear, and concise. Although the phraseology should be dignified and straightforward, it need not be dull or pedantic. Even the most profound ideas can best be explained in simple language and short, coherent sentences.

Slang, hackneyed or flippant phrases, and folksy style should be avoided. Because objectivity is the primary goal, there should be no element of exhortation or persuasion. The research report should describe and explain, rather than try to convince or move to action. In this respect the research report differs from an essay or feature article.

For years it was considered inappropriate for a researcher to use personal pronouns such as *I, me, we,* and so forth; people thought their use indicated a lack of objectivity. This changed, however, when the second edition of the APA's *Publication manual* was published in 1974. Personal pronouns should be used when they are appropriate. "I believe . . . ." is preferable to "The present author believes . . . ." The writer should, however, refrain from using plural personal pronouns (e.g., *we*) unless there are multiple authors.

Only the last names of cited authorities are used. Titles such as *professor, Dr., Mr.,* and *Dean* are omitted. The past tense should be used in describing research procedures that have been completed.

Abbreviations may be used only after their referrent has been spelled out, with the abbreviation following in parentheses. There are a few exceptions to this rule for well-known abbreviations such as *IQ*.

Discussion of quantitative terms. "*Few* in number" and "*less* in quantity" are the preferred forms of expression. Numbers beginning a sentence should always be spelled out. Fractions and numbers of less than ten should be spelled out. Use "one-half," but for all figures with fractions, use "4½" or "4.5." *Percent* (meaning "per hundred") is spelled out except in tables and figures. Use Arabic numerals with percent ("18 percent"), unless they begin a sentence. *Percentage* means "proportion." In numbers with more than three digits, commas should point off thousands or millions (1,324; 12,304,000). (Note, however, that publishers' styles may differ.)

Ordinarily, standard statistical formulas are not presented in the research report, nor are computations included. If a rather unusual formula is used in the analysis, it is appropriate to include it.

Of course, the ordinary rules of correct usage should prevail. A good dictionary, a spelling guide, a handbook of style, and a thesaurus are helpful references.

We have frequently found in our own students' work errors of spelling, nonagreement between subject and predicate, nonparallel construction, and inconsistent tense sequence. Students who have difficulty in written expression should have a competent friend or relative proofread their copy for correct usage before they type the final manuscript. Inability to write correctly is a serious limitation. Carelessness is an equally great fault.

Writing research reports effectively is not an easy task. Good reports are not written hurriedly. Even skillful and experienced writers revise many times before they submit a manuscript for publication.

TYPING THE REPORT

Many students type their own term papers or research reports. Anyone with reasonable proficiency and a willingness to learn proper procedures can do an acceptable job. In fact, typing a report is an excellent way to learn proper form.

Typographical standards for the thesis or dissertation are more exacting. Strikeovers, crossovers, insertions, and erasures are not permitted. Therefore, only typists with great proficiency should attempt to prepare thesis or dissertation copy. Although the expense of professional typing may seem high, the saving of time and excessive effort usually makes this arrangement the wise choice.

It is the writer's responsibility to present manuscript material to the professional typist in proper form. Except for minor typographical matters, the correction of major errors is not the responsibility of the typist.

After the material is received from the typist, the student should proof-read it carefully before it is turned in.

RULES OF TYPOGRAPHY

1. A good quality of bond paper, 8½″ by 11″ in size and of 13 to 16 pound weight should be used. Only one side of the sheet is used in typewritten manuscript.
2. The type must be clean and a black ribbon should be used. It is surprising what a new typewriter ribbon and clean type will do to produce effective copy. Special symbols not available on the type-writer keyboard should be carefully inserted, using black ink.
3. To facilitate the proper placement of copy on the page a guide sheet may be constructed, showing the proper margins, the center of the copy portion, and the number of lines for the top and bottom margins. This sheet should be ruled in black ink and placed beneath the first sheet, so that the markings show through. The use of the guide sheet takes much of the guesswork out of copy placement.
4. All margins should be 1½ inches—top, bottom, left, and right.
5. All material should be double spaced.
6. Words should not be divided at the end of the line unless completing them would definitely interfere with the margin. A few spaces of runover is preferable. In dividing words, consult a dictionary for correct syllabication.
7. Direct quotations not over three typewritten lines in length are included in the text and enclosed in quotation marks. Quotations of more than three lines are set off from the text in a double-spaced paragraph and indented five spaces from the left margin without quotation marks. Original paragraph indentations are retained.
8. Page numbers are given in parentheses at the end of a direct quotation.
9. Underlining words or letters informs the printer to set those words or letters in italics. For example, book titles are underlined in a typed manuscript and printed in italics in a journal or book.

REFERENCE FORM

References are cited in the text by giving the last name(s) of the author(s) and the year of the publication or, in the case of unpublished citations, the year the reference was written. If the author's name does not appear in the text, the name and year appear in parentheses, separated by a comma. If the author's name is used in the text, the year follows the name in parentheses. When more than one work is cited in parentheses, the references are separated by semicolons. Page number are only given, in parentheses, for direct quotations. See examples of this style of citation throughout this book.

All materials referred to in the text, and only those, are listed alphabetically in the reference section of the manuscript. The *Publication manual* of the American Psychological Association (1983) has specific guidelines for the format of various types of work. The following illustrates the form that different types of references should take.

1. Book:
    Vaizey, J. (1967). Education in the modern world. New York: McGraw-Hill.

2. Book with multiple authors:
    Barzun, J. & Graff, H. F. (1977). The modern researcher. New York: Harcourt, Brace, Jovanovich.

3. Book in subsequent edition:
    Hallahan, D. P. & Kauffman, J. M. (1982). Exceptional children (2nd ed.). Englewood Cliffs, NJ: Prentice-Hall.

4. Editor as author:
    Buros, O. K. (Ed.). (1979). The eighth mental measurement yearbook. Highland Park, NJ: Gryphon Press.

5. No author given:
    Prentice-Hall author's guide. (1978). Englewood Cliffs, NJ: Prentice-Hall.

6. Corporate or association author:
    American Psychological Association. (1983). Publication manual (3rd ed.). Washington, DC: Author.

7. Part of a series of books:
    Terman, L. M. & Oden, M. H. (1947). Genetic studies of genius series: Vol. 4. The gifted child grows up. Stanford, CA: Stanford University Press.

8. Chapter in an edited book:
    Kahn, J. V. (1984). Cognitive training and its relationship to the language of profoundly retarded children. In J. M. Berg (Ed.), Perspectives and progress in mental retardation. Baltimore: University Park Press.

9. Journal article:
    Seltzer, M. M. (1984). Correlates of community opposition to community residences for mentally retarded persons. American Journal of Mental Deficiency, 89, 1–8.

10. Magazine article:
    Meer, J. (1984, August). Pet theories. Psychology Today, pp. 60–67.

11.   Unpublished paper presented at a meeting:
       Schmidt, M., Kahn, J. V., and Nucci, L. (1984, May). Moral and
       social conventional reasoning of trainable mentally retarded
       adolescents. Paper presented at the annual meeting of the Amer-
       ican Association on Mental Deficiency, Minneapolis, MN.

12.   Thesis or dissertation (unpublished):
       Best, J. W. (1948). An analysis of certain selected factors underly-
       ing the choice of teaching as a profession. Unpublished doc-
       toral dissertation, University of Wisconsin, Madison.

13.   Unpublished manuscripts:
       Kahn, J. V., Jones, C., and Schmidt, M. (1984). Effect of object
       preference on sign learnability by severely and profoundly re-
       tarded children: A pilot study. Unpublished manuscript, Univer-
       sity of Illinois at Chicago.
       Kahn, J. V. (1984). Cognitive training and language learning. Manu-
       script submitted for publication.

14.   Journal article accepted for publication:
       Kahn, J. V. (in press). Evidence of the similar structure hypothe-
       sis controlling for organicity. American Journal of Mental Defi-
       ciency.

15.   Technical report:
       Kahn, J. V. (1981). Training sensorimotor period and language skills
       with severely retarded children. Chicago, IL: University of Illi-
       nois at Chicago. (ERIC Document Reproduction Service, No. ED
       204 941).

PAGINATION

Page numbers are assigned to each page of the paper or report. The title
page does not have a page number typed on it, but a number is allowed
for it in the series.

Page numbers are placed in the upper right-hand corner, one inch
below the top of the page and aligned with the right margin. Pages are
numbered consecutively from the title page, through the abstract, main
body of the paper, and references. After the references come the footnotes (if any), tables, figures, and appendices (if any), the numbering of
pages continuing in this order.

In addition, each page except the title page has a short title typed
above the page number (usually the first two or three words of the whole
title). This is so that if the pages are separated, they can be identified
with the appropriate manuscript.

TABLES

A table is a systematic method of presenting statistical data in vertical columns and horizontal rows, according to some classification of subject matter. Tables enable the reader to comprehend and interpret masses of data rapidly and to grasp significant details and relationships at a glance. Tables and figures should be used sparingly; too many will overwhelm the reader.

Good tables are relatively simple, concentrating on a limited number of ideas. Including too much data in a table minimizes the value of tabular presentation. It is often advisable to use several tables rather than to include too many details in a single one. It has been said that the mark of a good table is its effectiveness in conveying ideas and relationships independently of the text of the report.

Because each table is on a separate page following the references, the desired placement of the table is indicated by the following method.

Text references should identify tables by number, rather than by such expressions as "the table above," or "the following table." Tables should rarely be carried over to the second or third page. If the table must be continued, the headings should be repeated at the top of each column of data on each page.

Tables should not exceed the page size of the manuscript. Large tables that must be folded into the copy are always cumbersome and cannot be easily refolded and replaced. Large tables should be reduced to manuscript page size by photostat or some other process of reproduction. Tables that are too wide for the page may be turned sideways, with the top facing the left margin of the manuscript.

See Figure 10–2 for a sample of a properly presented table. The word *table* is centered between the page margins and typed in capital letters, followed by the table number in arabic numerals. Tables are numbered consecutively throughout the entire report or thesis, including those tables that may be placed in the appendix. The caption or title is placed one double space below the word *table* and centered. No terminal punctuation is used. The main title should be brief, clearly indicating the nature of the data presented. Occasionally a subtitle is used to supplement a briefer main title, denoting such additional information as sources of data and measuring units employed.

Column headings, or box heads, should be clearly labeled, describing the nature and units of measure of the data listed. If percentages are presented, the percentage symbol (%) should be placed at the top of the column, not with the numbers in the table.

TABLE 2

Occupations of Fathers of University
of Wisconsin Seniors Preparing to Teach*

Occupations	Men		Women	
	No.	%	No.	%**
Business proprietor	24	23	32	29
Skilled labor	19	18	10	9
Farming	17	17	19	17
Clerical–sales	16	16	18	16
Profession	15	15	20	18
Unskilled labor	6	6	6	5
No data	5	5	7	6
Total	102	100	112	100

* Adapted from John W. Best, An Analysis of Certain Selected
Factors Underlying the Choice of Teaching as a Profession
(Unpublished Doctoral Dissertation, University of Wisconsin,
Madison, 1948), 47.

** Percentages rounded to equal 100%.

FIGURE 10–2 A sample table.

If numbers are shortened by the omission of zeros, that fact should
be mentioned in the subtitle ("in millions of dollars"; "in thousands of
tons"). The "stub," or label, for the rows should be clear and concise,
parallel in grammatical structure, and if possible, no longer than two
lines.

Decimal points should always be carried out to the same place (e.g.,
tenths or hundreths) and aligned in the column. When no data are available for a particular cell, indicate the lack by a dash, rather than a zero.
When footnotes are needed to explain items in the table, small letters are
used. Numerical superscripts would be confused with the data contained in the table. Asterisks are used to indicate probability levels and
are also placed below the table.

FIGURES

A figure is a device that presents statistical data in graphic form. The term *figure* is applied to a wide variety of graphs, charts, maps, sketches, diagrams, and drawings. When skillfully used, figures present aspects of data in a visualized form that may be clearly and easily understood. Figures should not be intended as substitutes for textual description, but included to emphasize certain significant relationships.

Many of the qualities that were listed as characteristics of good tables are equally appropriate when applied to figures.

1. The title should clearly describe the nature of the data presented.
2. Figures should be simple enough to convey a clear idea and should be understandable without the aid of much textual description.
3. Numerical data upon which the figure is based should be presented in the text or an accompanying table, if they are not included in the figure itself.
4. Data should be presented carefully and accurately, so that oversimplification, misrepresentation, or distortion do not result.
5. Figures should be used sparingly. Too many figures detract from, rather than illuminate, the presentation.
6. Figures follow tables in the order of items in a manuscript. The placement desired in the text is indicated in the same manner used to indicate the placement of tables.
7. Figures should follow, not precede, the related textual discussion.
8. Figures are referred to by number, never as "the figure above" or "the figure below."
9. The title and number of the figure is placed on a separate page that precedes the figure in the manuscript.

The Line Graph

The line graph is useful in showing change in data relationships over a period of time. The horizontal axis usually measures the independent variable, the vertical axis the measured characteristic. Graphic arrangement should proceed from left to right on the horizontal axis, and from bottom to top on the vertical. The zero point should always be represented, and scale intervals should be equal. If a part of the scale is omitted, a set of parallel jagged lines should be used indicating that part of the scale is omitted (see Figure 10–3).

We have devised two figures, a line graph and a bar graph, that depict data relationships that were presented textually in two periodical articles (see Figures 10–4 and 10–5).

FIGURE 10-3   A line graph.

When coordinate graph paper is used, the lines connecting the intersecting points should be made heavy enough to distinguish them from the rulings on the paper. When several lines are drawn, they may be distinguished by using various types of lines—solid, dotted, or alternate dots and dashes. Black India ink is used.

A smoothed curve cannot be obtained by plotting any data directly.

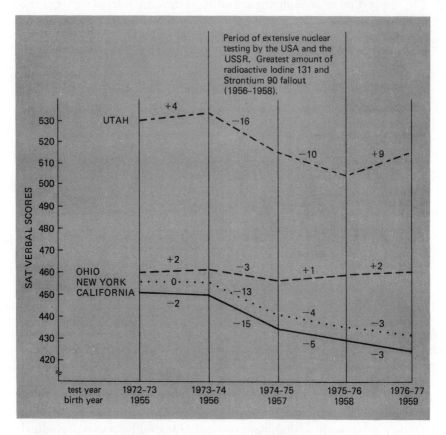

FIGURE 10-4   Mean verbal SAT scores, 1972–1977, in four selected states.

Graphic representation by the author, adapted from *Kappan* interview with Ernest Sternglass, "The Nuclear Radiation/SAT Score Decline Connection," *Phi Delta Kappan* 61 (Nov. 1979), 184.

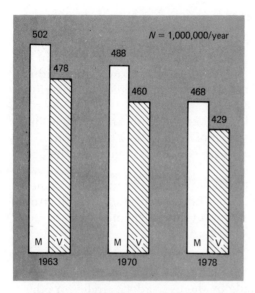

FIGURE 10–5   Decline of mean Scholastic Aptitude Test scores from 1963 to 1978. (Throughout the 1970s, verbal scores declined .04 standard deviations each year and mathematical scores declined .025 standard deviations.)

Adapted from Paul Copperman, "The Achievement Decline of the 1970s," *Phi Delta Kappan* 60 (June 1979), 736.

Only when infinite data are obtained will the lines connecting the points approach a curved line. The figure formed by the lines connecting the points is known as a *frequency polygon*.

The Bar Graph or Chart

The bar graph, which can be arranged either horizontally or vertically, represents data by bars of equal width, drawn to scale length. The numerical data may be lettered within the bar or outside it. A grid may be used to help quantify the graphic representation. A divided bar graph represents the components of a whole unit in one bar (see Figure 10–6).

In bar graphs, the bars are usually separated by space. If the graph contains a large number of items, the bars may be joined to save space.

Horizontal bar graphs are usually used to compare components at a particular time. Vertical bars are used when making comparisons at different times.

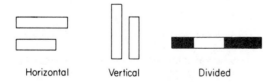

Horizontal   Vertical   Divided

FIGURE 10–6   Divided bars for graphs.

The Circle, Pie, or Sector Chart

Circle, pie, or sector charts show the division of a unit into its component parts. They are frequently used to explain how a unit of government distributes its share of the tax dollar, how an individual spends his or her salary, or any other type of simple percentage distribution.

The radius is drawn vertically, and components are arranged in a clockwise direction in descending order of magnitude. The proportion of data is indicated by the number of degrees in each segment of the 360-degree circle (see Figure 10–7).

This kind of data should be typed or printed within the segment if possible. If there is insufficient room for this identification, a small arrow should point from the identification term to the segment.

Maps

When geographic location or identification is important, maps may be used. Identification may be made by the use of dots, circles, or other symbols, and density or characteristics of areas can be represented by shading or crosshatching. A key or legend should always be supplied if shadings are used.

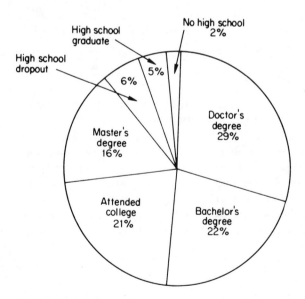

FIGURE 10–7   Educational backgrounds of 129 American celebrities listed in the *Current Biography 1966 Yearbook.*

Adapted from Adela Deming, "The Educational Attainments of Americans Listed in the Current Biography, 1966 Yearbook," (Unpublished report, Butler University, Indianapolis, Indiana, 1967), 7.

Organization Charts

To show staff functions, lines of authority, or flow of work within an organization, an organization chart is a helpful graphic device.

Units may be represented by circles, squares, or oblongs, with names lettered within the units. Distinctions between direct and indirect relationships may be indicated by the use of solid and dotted lines. Ordinarily, authority, supervision, or movement of materials flows from the top to the bottom of the chart, but variations can be indicated by the use of arrows.

EVALUATING A RESEARCH REPORT

Writing a critical analysis of a research report is a valuable experience for the student of educational research. Reports for this purpose may be taken from published collections and such periodicals as the *Educational Researcher,* the *Journal of Educational Research,* or one of the many other publications that publish reports of research in education or in the closely related fields of psychology or sociology. Unpublished research reports written by previous students of educational research are another source, as are the theses or dissertations found in the university library.

Through a critical analysis, the student may gain some insight into the nature of a research problem, the methods by which it may be attacked, the difficulties inherent in the research process, the ways in which data are analyzed and conclusions drawn, and the style in which the report is presented.

The following questions are suggested as a possible structure for the analysis:

1. The Title and Abstract
   a. Are they clear and concise?
   b. Do they promise no more than the study can provide?
2. The Problem (Introductory Section)
   a. Is it clearly stated?
   b. Is it properly delimited?
   c. Is its significance recognized?
   d. Are hypotheses clearly stated and testable?
   e. Are assumptions, limitations, and delimitations stated?
   f. Are important terms defined?
3. Review of Related Literature (Introductory Section)
   a. Is it adequately covered?
   b. Are important findings noted?

    c. Is it well organized?

    d. Is an effective summary provided?

    e. Is the literature cited directly relevant to the problem and hypotheses?

4. Method Section

    a. Is the research design described in detail?

    b. Is it adequate?

    c. Are the samples described in detail?

    d. Are relevant variables recognized?

    e. Are appropriate controls provided?

    f. Are data-gathering instruments appropriate?

    g. Are validity and reliability established?

    h. Can the sample and procedure be replicated based on the information and references given?

5. Results Section

    a. Is the statistical treatment appropriate?

    b. Is appropriate use made of tables and figures?

    c. Is the analysis of data relationships logical, perceptive, and objective?

6. Discussion Section

    a. Is the discussion clear and concise?

    b. Is the problem/hypothesis restated appropriately?

    c. Is the analysis objective?

    d. Are the findings and conclusions justified by the data presented and analyzed?

    e. Did the author(s) generalize appropriately or too much?

7. Overall Writing of Paper

    a. Is it clear, concise, and objective?

    b. Are the parts of the paper properly related to each other?

SUMMARY

The research report is expected to follow the conventional pattern of style and form used in academic circles. Although style manuals differ in some of the smaller details, students are expected to be consistent in following the pattern of style contained in the manual required by their institution or in the one that they are permitted to select.

    The style of writing should be clear, concise, and completely objective. Of course, the highest standards of correct usage are expected, and careful proofreading is necessary before the final report is submitted.

    Tables and figures may help to make the meaning of the data clear. They should be presented in proper mechanical form and should be carefully designed to present an accurate and undistorted picture.

The evaluation of a research project is a valuable exercise for students of educational research. Using analytical questions such as those suggested, the critiquing of another researcher's report helps students develop competency in their own research and reporting skills.

REFERENCES

American Psychological Association. (1983). *Publication manual* (3rd ed.). Washington, DC: Author.

KAHN, J. V. (1982). Moral reasoning in Irish children and adolescents as measured by the Defining Issues Test. *Irish Journal of Psychology, 2,* 96–108.

ADDITIONAL READINGS

CAMPBELL, W. G. AND BALLOU, S. V. (1974). *Form and style: Theses, reports, term papers.* Boston: Houghton Mifflin.

KOEFOD, P. E. (1964). *The writing requirements for graduate degrees.* Englewood Cliffs, NJ: Prentice-Hall.

PERRIN, P. G. (1972). *Reference handbook of grammar and usage.* New York: William Morrow.

Roget's international thesaurus (4th ed.). (1979). New York: Harper & Row.

STRUNK, W. & WHITE, E. B. (1962). *The elements of style.* New York: Macmillan.

TURABIAN, K. L. (1973). *A manual for writers of term papers, theses, and dissertations.* Chicago: University of Chicago Press.

University of Chicago (1969). *A manual of style* (rev. ed.). Chicago: University of Chicago Press.

Statistical Formulas and Symbols

STATISTICAL FORMULAS

1. $>$ is greater than
   $<$ is less than

2. Mean $\overline{X}$

$$\overline{X} = \frac{\Sigma X}{N}$$

3. Mode M_0

4. Percentile rank P_r

$$P_r - 100 - \frac{(100R - 50)}{N}$$

5. Variance σ^2
   Standard deviation σ

$$\sigma^2 = \frac{\Sigma x^2}{N} \qquad x = (X - \overline{X})$$

$$\sigma = \sqrt{\frac{\Sigma x^2}{N}}$$

(deviation computation)

$$\sigma = \frac{N\Sigma X^2 - (\Sigma X)^2}{N^2}$$

$$\sigma = \sqrt{\frac{N\Sigma X^2 - (\Sigma X)^2}{N^2}}$$

(raw score computation)

6. Variance S^2
   Standard deviation S

$$S^2 = \frac{\Sigma x^2}{N - 1}$$

$$S = \sqrt{\frac{\Sigma x^2}{N - 1}}$$

GLOSSARY OF STATISTICAL SYMBOLS

$a > b$ a is greater than b
$b < a$ b is less than a

$\overline{X}$ arithmetic average
Σ sum of
X, Y scores
N number of scores

M_0 mode: score that occurs most frequently in a distribution

P_r percentage of scores that fall below a given value, plus $\frac{1}{2}$ the percentage of space occupied by that score

R rank from the top of a distribution

σ^2 population variance: mean value of the squared deviations from the mean

σ population standard deviation: positive square root of the variance $x = (X - M)$ deviation from the mean

S^2 variance of a population estimated from a sample

S standard deviation of population estimated from a sample

STATISTICAL FORMULAS

GLOSSARY OF STATISTICAL SYMBOLS

(deviation computation)

$$S^2 = \frac{N\Sigma X^2 - (\Sigma X)^2}{N(N-1)}$$

$$S = \sqrt{\frac{N\Sigma X^2 - (\Sigma X)^2}{N(N-1)}}$$

(raw score computation)

Variance (S_{DV}^2) or standard deviation (S_{DV}) of a dichotomous variable

Dichotomous variable
an outcome is either-or: plus or minus, true or false, heads or tails
N number of events
P probability of an outcome

$$S_{DV}^2 = \frac{NP(1-P)}{1}$$
$$S_{DV} = \sqrt{NP(1-P)}$$

$$S_{DV}^2 = \frac{N}{4}$$

(general formula)

$$S_{DV} = \sqrt{\frac{N}{4}}$$

(when $P = .50$)

7. Standard error of the mean ($S_{\bar{x}}$)

$$S_{\bar{x}} = \frac{S}{\sqrt{N}} \qquad \sigma_{\bar{x}} = \frac{\sigma}{\sqrt{N}}$$

8. Standard scores z, Z, Z_{cb}

z sigma score
$Z(T)$ standard score
Z_{cb} College Board standard score

$$z = \frac{X - \bar{X}}{\sigma} \quad or \quad \frac{x}{\sigma}$$

$$T = 50 + 10\frac{(X - \bar{X})}{\sigma}$$
$$or \; T = 50 + 10z$$
$$Z_{cb} = 500 + 100z$$

9. Coefficient of correlation (r)

$$r = \frac{\Sigma(z_x)(z_y)}{N}$$

r Pearson product-moment coefficient of correlation

$$r = \frac{N\Sigma XY - (\Sigma X)(\Sigma Y)}{\sqrt{N\Sigma X^2 - (\Sigma X)^2}\sqrt{N\Sigma Y^2 - (\Sigma Y)^2}}$$

STATISTICAL FORMULAS

$$\rho(rho) = 1 - \frac{6\Sigma D^2}{N(N^2 - 1)}$$

10. Statistical significance of r/ρ

$$t = \frac{r\sqrt{N-2}}{\sqrt{1-r^2}}$$

$$t = \frac{\rho\sqrt{N-2}}{\sqrt{1-\rho^2}}$$

11. Regression line slope

$$r = \frac{rise}{run} = \frac{z_Y}{z_X}$$

$$b = \frac{rise}{run} = \frac{Y}{X} \qquad b_Y = r\left(\frac{z_Y}{z_X}\right)$$

$$b_X = r\left(\frac{z_X}{z_Y}\right)$$

12. Regression equations

$$\hat{Y} = b_Y(X - \bar{X}) + \bar{Y}$$

$$\hat{X} = b_X(Y - \bar{Y}) + \bar{X}$$

13. Standard error of estimate S_{est}

$$S_{est} = S\sqrt{1 - r^2}$$

14. Standard error of the difference between two means (independent variances; when variances are not equal)

$$S_{\bar{x}_1 - \bar{x}_2} = \sqrt{\frac{s_1^2}{N_1} + \frac{s_2^2}{N_2}}$$

(pooled variances; when variances are equal)

$$S_{\bar{x}_1 - \bar{x}_2} = \sqrt{\frac{(N_1 - 1)S_1^2 + (N_2 - 1)S_2^2}{N_1 + N_2 - 2}\left(\frac{1}{N_1} + \frac{1}{N_2}\right)}$$

15. Significance of the difference between two means

$$t = \frac{difference\ between\ means}{standard\ error\ of\ the\ difference}$$

GLOSSARY OF STATISTICAL SYMBOLS

$\rho(rho)$　Spearman difference in ranks coefficient of correlation

D　difference between each pair of ranks

Test of the statistical significance of a coefficient of correlation

r　the slope expressed in sigma (z) units

b　the slope of the line expressed in raw scores.

Predicting a Y from a known X when the coefficient of correlation is known
$\hat{Y}$ predicted Y
$\hat{X}$ predicted X

STATISTICAL FORMULAS

$$t = \frac{\bar{X}_1 - \bar{X}_2}{\sqrt{\dfrac{(N_1 - 1)S_1^2 + (N_2 - 1)S_2^2}{N_1 + N_2 - 2}\left(\dfrac{1}{N_1} + \dfrac{1}{N_2}\right)}}$$

(uncorrelated or unmatched groups)

$$t = \frac{\bar{X}_1 - \bar{X}_2}{\sqrt{\dfrac{S_1^2}{N_1} + \dfrac{S_2^2}{N_2} - 2r\left(\dfrac{S_1}{\sqrt{N_1}}\right)\left(\dfrac{S_2}{\sqrt{N_2}}\right)}}$$

16. Chi square χ^2

$$\chi^2 = \Sigma \frac{(f_o - f_e)^2}{f_e}$$

$df = (f \text{ rows} - 1)(f \text{ columns} - 1)$

$$\chi^2 = \frac{N\left[|AD - BC| - \dfrac{N}{2}\right]^2}{(A + B)(C + D)(A + C)(B + D)}$$

f_o observed frequencies
f_e expected frequencies
df degrees of freedom

A	B
C	D

Computation for a 2 × 2 table

17. Median test

$$\chi^2 = + \frac{N\left[|AD - BC| - \dfrac{N}{2}\right]^2}{(A + B)(C + D)(A + C)(B + D)}$$

Statistical significance of the difference between the medians of two independent groups: at or above common median and below common median

18. Mann-Whitney test $(N > 20)$

$$U_1 = (N_1)(N_2) + \frac{N_1(N_1 + 1)}{2} - \Sigma R_1$$

$$U_2 = (N_1)(N_2) + \frac{N_2(N_2 + 1)}{2} - \Sigma R_2$$

$$z = \frac{U - \dfrac{(N_1)(N_2)}{2}}{\sqrt{\dfrac{(N_1)(N_2)(N_1 + N_2 + 1)}{12}}}$$

N_1 number in one group
N_2 number in second group
ΣR_1 sum of ranks of one group
ΣR_2 sum of ranks of second group
The significance of U is read from the U critical table. When $N > 20$, the z computation may be used with the normal probability table values.

STATISTICAL FORMULAS

19. Sign test (matched pairs)

$$z = \frac{(0 \pm .50) - \dfrac{N}{2}}{\sqrt{\dfrac{N}{4}}}$$

20. Wilcoxon matched-pairs signed ranks test

$$z = \frac{T - \dfrac{N(N + 1)}{4}}{\sqrt{\dfrac{N(N + 1)(2N + 1)}{24}}}$$

GLOSSARY OF STATISTICAL SYMBOLS

O number of signs of interest. When $O < N/2$, use $(O + .50)$; when $O > N/2$, use $(O - .50)$

N number of pairs ranked
T sum of the ranks of the smaller of the like-signed numbers

Percentage of Area Lying between the Mean and Successive Standard Deviation Units under the Normal Curve

$z\left(\dfrac{x}{\sigma}\right)$	.00	.01	.02	.03	.04	.05	.06	.07	.08	.09
.0	.0000	.0040	.0080	.0120	.0160	.0199	.0239	.0279	.0319	.0359
.1	.0398	.0438	.0478	.0517	.0557	.0596	.0636	.0675	.0714	.0753
.2	.0793	.0832	.0871	.0910	.0948	.0987	.1026	.1064	.1103	.1141
.3	.1179	.1217	.1255	.1293	.1331	.1368	.1406	.1443	.1480	.1517
.4	.1554	.1591	.1628	.1664	.1700	.1736	.1772	.1808	.1844	.1879
.5	.1915	.1950	.1985	.2019	.2054	.2088	.2123	.2157	.2190	.2224
.6	.2257	.2291	.2324	.2357	.2389	.2422	.2454	.2486	.2517	.2549
.7	.2580	.2611	.2642	.2673	.2704	.2734	.2764	.2794	.2823	.2852
.8	.2881	.2910	.2939	.2967	.2995	.3023	.3051	.3078	.3106	.3133
.9	.3159	.3186	.3212	.3238	.3264	.3290	.3315	.3340	.3365	.3389
1.0	.3413	.3438	.3461	.3485	.3508	.3531	.3554	.3577	.3599	.3621
1.1	.3643	.3665	.3686	.3708	.3729	.3749	.3770	.3790	.3810	.3830
1.2	.3849	.3869	.3888	.3907	.3925	.3944	.3962	.3980	.3997	.4015
1.3	.4032	.4049	.4066	.4082	.4099	.4115	.4131	.4147	.4162	.4177
1.4	.4192	.4207	.4222	.4236	.4251	.4265	.4279	.4292	.4306	.4319
1.5	.4332	.4345	.4357	.4370	.4383	.4394	.4406	.4418	.4429	.4441
1.6	.4452	.4463	.4474	.4484	.4495	.4505	.4515	.4525	.4535	.4545
1.7	.4554	.4564	.4573	.4582	.4591	.4599	.4608	.4616	.4625	.4633
1.8	.4641	.4649	.4656	.4664	.4671	.4678	.4686	.4693	.4699	.4706
1.9	.4713	.4719	.4726	.4732	.4738	.4744	.4750	.4756	.4761	.4767
2.0	.4772	.4778	.4783	.4788	.4793	.4798	.4803	.4808	.4812	.4817
2.1	.4821	.4826	.4830	.4834	.4838	.4842	.4846	.4850	.4854	.4857
2.2	.4861	.4864	.4868	.4871	.4875	.4878	.4881	.4884	.4887	.4890
2.3	.4893	.4896	.4898	.4901	.4904	.4906	.4909	.4911	.4913	.4916
2.4	.4918	.4920	.4922	.4925	.4927	.4929	.4931	.4932	.4934	.4936
2.5	.4938	.4940	.4941	.4943	.4945	.4946	.4948	.4949	.4951	.4952
2.6	.4953	.4955	.4956	.4957	.4959	.4960	.4961	.4962	.4963	.4964
2.7	.4965	.4966	.4967	.4968	.4969	.4970	.4971	.4972	.4973	.4974
2.8	.4974	.4975	.4976	.4977	.4977	.4978	.4979	.4979	.4980	.4981
2.9	.4981	.4982	.4982	.4983	.4984	.4984	.4985	.4985	.4986	.4986
3.0	.4987									

Example: Between the mean and $+1.00z$ is 34.13% of the area.
Between the mean and $-.50z$ is 19.15% of the area.

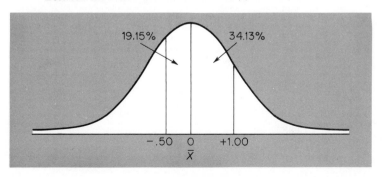

Appendix C[a]

Critical Values for Pearson's Product-Moment Correlation (r)

n	$\alpha_2 = .10$	$\alpha_2 = .05$	$\alpha_2 = .02$	$\alpha_2 = .01$
3	.988	.997	.9995	.9999
4	.900	.950	.980	.990
5	.805	.878	.934	.959
6	.729	.811	.882	.917
7	.669	.754	.833	.874
8	.622	.707	.789	.834
9	.582	.666	.750	.798
10	.549	.632	.716	.765
11	.521	.602	.685	.735
12	.497	.576	.658	.708
13	.476	.553	.634	.684
14	.458	.532	.612	.661
15	.441	.514	.592	.641
16	.426	.497	.574	.623
17	.412	.482	.558	.606
18	.400	.468	.542	.590
19	.389	.456	.528	.575
20	.378	.444	.516	.561
21	.369	.433	.503	.549
22	.360	.423	.492	.537
23	.352	.413	.482	.526
24	.344	.404	.472	.515
25	.337	.396	.462	.505
26	.330	.388	.453	.496
27	.323	.381	.445	.487
28	.317	.374	.437	.479
29	.311	.367	.430	.471
30	.306	.361	.423	.463
35	.282	.333	.391	.428
40	.264	.312	.366	.402
45	.248	.296	.349	.381
50	.235	.276	.328	.361
60	.214	.254	.300	.330
70	.198	.235	.277	.305
80	.185	.220	.260	.286
90	.174	.208	.245	.270
100	.165	.196	.232	.256
150	.135	.161	.190	.210
200	.117	.139	.164	.182
250	.104	.124	.147	.163
300	.095	.113	.134	.148
400	.082	.098	.115	.128
500	.074	.088	.104	.115
1,000	.052	.062	.074	.081

n	$\alpha_2 = .10$	$\alpha_2 = .05$	$\alpha_2 = .02$	$\alpha_2 = .01$
5,000	.0233	.0278	.0329	.0364
10,000	.0164	.0196	.0233	.0258

[a] This table is abridged from Table 13 in *Biometrika Tables for Statisticians,* vol. 1, 2nd ed. New York: Cambridge, 1958. Edited by E. S. Pearson and H. O. Hartley. Reproduced with the kind permission of the editors and the trustees of Biometrika.

Critical Values of Student's Distribution (t)

df	Two-tailed test level of significance		One-tailed test level of significance	
	.05	.01	.05	.01
1	12.706	63.557	6.314	31.821
2	4.303	9.925	2.920	6.965
3	3.182	5.841	2.353	4.541
4	2.776	4.604	2.132	3.747
5	2.571	4.032	2.015	3.365
6	2.447	3.707	1.943	3.143
7	2.365	3.499	1.895	2.998
8	2.306	3.355	1.860	2.896
9	2.262	3.250	1.833	2.821
10	2.228	3.169	1.812	2.764
11	2.201	3.106	1.796	2.718
12	2.179	3.055	1.782	2.681
13	2.160	3.012	1.771	2.650
14	2.145	2.977	1.761	2.624
15	2.131	2.947	1.753	2.602
16	2.120	2.921	1.746	2.583
17	2.110	2.898	1.740	2.567
18	2.101	2.878	1.734	2.552
19	2.093	2.861	1.729	2.539
20	2.086	2.845	1.725	2.528
21	2.080	2.831	1.721	2.518
22	2.074	2.819	1.717	2.508
23	2.069	2.807	1.714	2.500
24	2.064	2.797	1.711	2.492
25	2.060	2.787	1.708	2.485
26	2.056	2.779	1.706	2.479
27	2.052	2.771	1.703	2.473
28	2.048	2.763	1.701	2.467
29	2.045	2.756	1.699	2.462
30	2.042	2.750	1.697	2.457
40	2.021	2.704	1.684	2.423
60	2.000	2.660	1.671	2.390
120	1.980	2.617	1.658	2.358
∞	1.960	2.576	1.645	2.326

Abridged Table of Critical Values for CHI Square

df	Level of significance	
	.05	.01
1	3.84	6.64
2	5.99	9.21
3	7.82	11.34
4	9.49	13.28
5	11.07	15.09
6	12.59	16.81
7	14.07	18.48
8	15.51	20.09
9	16.92	21.67
10	18.31	23.21
11	19.68	24.72
12	21.03	26.22
13	22.36	27.69
14	23.68	29.14
15	25.00	30.58
16	26.30	32.00
17	27.59	33.41
18	28.87	34.80
19	30.14	36.19
20	31.41	37.57
21	32.67	38.93
22	33.92	40.29
23	35.17	41.64
24	36.42	42.98
25	37.65	44.31
26	38.88	45.64
27	40.11	46.96
28	41.34	48.28
29	42.56	49.59
30	43.77	50.89

Critical Values of the F Distribution

DF FOR DE-NOMI-NATOR	χ	\multicolumn{12}{c}{DF FOR NUMERATOR}
		1	2	3	4	5	6	7	8	9	10	11	12
1	.10	39.9	49.5	53.6	55.8	57.2	58.2	58.9	59.4	59.9	60.2	60.5	60.7
	.05	161	200	216	225	230	234	237	239	241	242	243	244
2	.10	8.53	9.00	9.16	9.24	9.29	9.33	9.35	9.37	9.38	9.39	9.40	9.41
	.05	18.5	19.0	19.2	19.2	19.3	19.3	19.4	19.4	19.4	19.4	19.4	19.4
	.01	98.5	99.0	99.2	99.2	99.3	99.3	99.4	99.4	99.4	99.4	99.4	99.4
3	.10	5.54	5.46	5.39	5.34	5.31	5.28	5.27	5.25	5.24	5.23	5.22	5.22
	.05	10.1	9.55	9.28	9.12	9.01	8.94	8.89	8.85	8.81	8.79	8.76	8.74
	.01	34.1	30.8	29.5	28.7	28.2	27.9	27.7	27.5	27.3	27.2	27.1	27.1
4	.10	4.54	4.32	4.19	4.11	4.05	4.01	3.98	3.95	3.94	3.92	3.91	3.90
	.05	7.71	6.94	6.59	6.39	6.26	6.16	6.09	6.04	6.00	5.96	5.94	5.91
	.01	21.2	18.0	16.7	16.0	15.5	15.2	15.0	14.8	14.7	14.5	14.4	14.4
5	.10	4.06	3.78	3.62	3.52	3.45	3.40	3.37	3.34	3.32	3.30	3.28	3.27
	.05	6.61	5.79	5.41	5.19	5.05	4.95	4.88	4.82	4.77	4.74	4.71	4.68
	.01	16.3	13.3	12.1	11.4	11.0	10.7	10.5	10.3	10.2	10.1	9.96	9.89
6	.10	3.78	3.46	3.29	3.18	3.11	3.05	3.01	2.98	2.96	2.94	2.92	2.90
	.05	5.99	5.14	4.76	4.53	4.39	4.28	4.21	4.15	4.10	4.06	4.03	4.00
	.01	13.7	10.9	9.78	9.15	8.75	8.47	8.26	8.10	7.98	7.87	7.79	7.72
7	.10	3.59	3.26	3.07	2.96	2.88	2.83	2.78	2.75	2.72	2.70	2.68	2.67
	.05	5.59	4.74	4.35	4.12	3.97	3.87	3.79	3.73	3.68	3.64	3.60	3.57
	.01	12.2	9.55	8.45	7.85	7.46	7.19	6.99	6.84	6.72	6.62	6.54	6.47
8	.10	3.46	3.11	2.92	2.81	2.73	2.67	2.62	2.59	2.56	2.54	2.52	2.50
	.05	5.32	4.46	4.07	3.84	3.69	3.58	3.50	3.44	3.39	3.35	3.31	3.28
	.01	11.3	8.65	7.59	7.01	6.63	6.37	6.18	6.03	5.91	5.81	5.73	5.67
9	.10	3.36	3.01	2.81	2.69	2.61	2.55	2.51	2.47	2.44	2.42	2.40	2.38
	.05	5.12	4.26	3.86	3.63	3.48	3.37	3.29	3.23	3.18	3.14	3.10	3.07
	.01	10.6	8.02	6.99	6.42	6.06	5.80	5.61	5.47	5.35	5.26	5.18	5.11
10	.10	3.29	2.92	2.73	2.61	2.52	2.46	2.41	2.38	2.35	2.32	2.30	2.28
	.05	4.96	4.10	3.71	3.48	3.33	3.22	3.14	3.07	3.02	2.98	2.94	2.91
	.01	10.0	7.56	6.55	5.99	5.64	5.39	5.20	5.06	4.94	4.85	4.77	4.71
11	.10	3.23	2.86	2.66	2.54	2.45	2.39	2.34	2.30	2.27	2.25	2.23	2.21
	.05	4.84	3.98	3.59	3.36	3.20	3.09	3.01	2.95	2.90	2.85	2.82	2.79
	.01	9.65	7.21	6.22	5.67	5.32	5.07	4.89	4.74	4.63	4.54	4.46	4.40
12	.10	3.18	2.81	2.61	2.48	2.39	2.33	2.28	2.24	2.21	2.19	2.17	2.15
	.05	4.75	3.89	3.49	3.26	3.11	3.00	2.91	2.85	2.80	2.75	2.72	2.69
	.01	9.33	6.93	5.95	5.41	5.06	4.82	4.64	4.50	4.39	4.30	4.22	4.16
13	.10	3.14	2.76	2.56	2.43	2.35	2.28	2.23	2.20	2.16	2.14	2.12	2.10
	.05	4.67	3.81	3.41	3.18	3.03	2.92	2.83	2.77	2.71	2.67	2.63	2.60
	.01	9.07	6.70	5.74	5.21	4.86	4.62	4.44	4.30	4.19	4.10	4.02	3.96
14	.10	3.10	2.73	2.52	2.39	2.31	2.24	2.19	2.15	2.12	2.10	2.08	2.05
	.05	4.60	3.74	3.34	3.11	2.96	2.85	2.76	2.70	2.65	2.60	2.57	2.53
	.01	8.86	6.51	5.56	5.04	4.69	4.46	4.28	4.14	4.03	3.94	3.86	3.80
15	.10	3.07	2.70	2.49	2.36	2.27	2.21	2.16	2.12	2.09	2.06	2.04	2.02
	.05	4.54	3.68	3.29	3.06	2.90	2.79	2.71	2.64	2.59	2.54	2.51	2.48
	.01	8.68	6.36	5.42	4.89	4.56	4.32	4.14	4.00	3.89	3.80	3.73	3.67
16	.10	3.05	2.67	2.46	2.33	2.24	2.18	2.13	2.09	2.06	2.03	2.01	1.99
	.05	4.49	3.63	3.24	3.01	2.85	2.74	2.66	2.59	2.54	2.49	2.46	2.42
	.01	8.53	6.23	5.29	4.77	4.44	4.20	4.03	3.89	3.78	3.69	3.62	3.55

DF FOR NUMERATOR													DF FOR DE-NOMI-
15	20	24	30	40	50	60	100	120	200	500	∞	χ	NATOR
61.2	61.7	62.0	62.3	62.5	62.7	62.8	63.0	63.1	63.2	63.3	63.3	.10	1
246	248	249	250	251	252	252	253	253	254	254	254	.05	
9.42	9.44	9.45	9.46	9.47	9.47	9.47	9.48	9.48	9.49	9.49	9.49	.10	2
19.4	19.4	19.5	19.5	19.5	19.5	19.5	19.5	19.5	19.5	19.5	19.5	.05	
99.4	99.4	99.5	99.5	99.5	99.5	99.5	99.5	99.5	99.5	99.5	99.5	.01	
5.20	5.18	5.18	5.17	5.16	5.15	5.15	5.14	5.14	5.14	5.14	5.13	.10	3
8.70	8.66	8.64	8.62	8.59	8.58	8.57	8.55	8.55	8.54	8.53	8.53	.05	
26.9	26.7	26.6	26.5	26.4	26.4	26.3	26.2	26.2	26.2	26.1	26.1	.01	
3.87	3.84	3.83	3.82	3.80	3.80	3.79	3.78	3.78	3.77	3.76	3.76	.10	4
5.86	5.80	5.77	5.75	5.72	5.70	5.69	5.66	5.66	5.65	5.64	5.63	.05	
14.2	14.0	13.9	13.8	13.7	13.7	13.7	13.6	13.6	13.5	13.5	13.5	.01	
3.24	3.21	3.19	3.17	3.16	3.15	3.14	3.13	3.12	3.12	3.11	3.10	.10	5
4.62	4.56	4.53	4.50	4.46	4.44	4.43	4.41	4.40	4.39	4.37	4.36	.05	
9.72	9.55	9.47	9.38	9.29	9.24	9.20	9.13	9.11	9.08	9.04	9.02	.01	
2.87	2.84	2.82	2.80	2.78	2.77	2.76	2.75	2.74	2.73	2.73	2.72	.10	6
3.94	3.87	3.84	3.81	3.77	3.75	3.74	3.71	3.70	3.69	3.68	3.67	.05	
7.56	7.40	7.31	7.23	7.14	7.09	7.06	6.99	6.97	6.93	6.90	6.88	.01	
2.63	2.59	2.58	2.56	2.54	2.52	2.51	2.50	2.49	2.48	2.48	2.47	.10	7
3.51	3.44	3.41	3.38	3.34	3.32	3.30	3.27	3.27	3.25	3.24	3.23	.05	
6.31	6.16	6.07	5.99	5.91	5.86	5.82	5.75	5.74	5.70	5.67	5.65	.10	
2.46	2.42	2.40	2.38	2.36	2.35	2.34	2.32	2.32	2.31	2.30	2.29	.10	8
3.22	3.15	3.12	3.08	3.04	3.02	3.01	2.97	2.97	2.95	2.94	2.93	.05	
5.52	5.36	5.28	5.20	5.12	5.07	5.03	4.96	4.95	4.91	4.88	4.86	.01	
2.34	2.30	2.28	2.25	2.23	2.22	2.21	2.19	2.18	2.17	2.17	2.16	.10	9
3.01	2.94	2.90	2.86	2.83	2.80	2.79	2.76	2.75	2.73	2.72	2.71	.05	
4.96	4.81	4.73	4.65	4.57	4.52	4.48	4.42	4.40	4.36	4.33	4.31	.01	
2.24	2.20	2.18	2.16	2.13	2.12	2.11	2.09	2.08	2.07	2.06	2.06	.10	10
2.85	2.77	2.74	2.70	2.66	2.64	2.62	2.59	2.58	2.56	2.55	2.54	.05	
4.56	4.41	4.33	4.25	4.17	4.12	4.08	4.01	4.00	3.96	3.93	3.91	.01	
2.17	2.12	2.10	2.08	2.05	2.04	2.03	2.00	2.00	1.99	1.98	1.97	.10	11
2.72	2.65	2.61	2.57	2.53	2.51	2.49	2.46	2.45	2.43	2.42	2.40	.05	
4.25	4.10	4.02	3.94	3.86	3.81	3.78	3.71	3.69	3.66	3.62	3.60	.01	
2.10	2.06	2.04	2.01	1.99	1.97	1.96	1.94	1.93	1.92	1.91	1.90	.10	12
2.62	2.54	2.51	2.47	2.43	2.40	2.38	2.35	2.34	2.32	2.31	2.30	.05	
4.01	3.86	3.78	3.70	3.62	3.57	3.54	3.47	3.45	3.41	3.38	3.36	.01	
2.05	2.01	1.98	1.96	1.93	1.92	1.90	1.88	1.88	1.86	1.85	1.85	.10	13
2.53	2.46	2.42	2.38	2.34	2.31	2.30	2.26	2.25	2.23	2.22	2.21	.05	
3.82	3.66	3.59	3.51	3.43	3.38	3.34	3.27	3.25	3.22	3.19	3.17	.01	
2.01	1.96	1.94	1.91	1.89	1.87	1.86	1.83	1.83	1.83	1.80	1.80	.10	14
2.46	2.39	2.35	2.31	2.27	2.24	2.22	2.19	2.18	2.18	2.14	2.13	.05	
3.66	3.51	3.43	3.35	3.27	3.22	3.18	3.11	3.09	3.09	3.03	3.00	.01	
1.97	1.92	1.90	1.87	1.85	1.83	1.82	1.79	1.79	1.77	1.76	1.76	.10	15
2.40	2.33	2.29	2.25	2.20	2.18	2.16	2.12	2.11	2.10	2.08	2.07	.05	
3.52	3.37	3.29	3.21	3.13	3.08	3.05	2.98	2.96	2.92	2.89	2.87	.01	
1.94	1.89	1.87	1.84	1.81	1.79	1.78	1.76	1.75	1.74	1.73	1.72	.10	16
2.35	2.28	2.24	2.19	2.15	2.12	2.11	2.07	2.06	2.04	2.02	2.01	.05	
3.41	3.26	3.18	3.10	3.02	2.97	2.93	2.86	2.84	2.81	2.78	2.75	.01	

DF FOR DE-NOMI-NATOR	X	DF FOR NUMERATOR											
		1	2	3	4	5	6	7	8	9	10	11	12
17	.10	3.03	2.64	2.44	2.31	2.22	2.15	2.10	2.06	2.03	2.00	1.98	1.96
	.05	4.45	3.59	3.20	2.96	2.81	2.70	2.61	2.55	2.49	2.45	2.41	2.38
	.01	8.40	6.11	5.18	4.67	4.34	4.10	3.93	3.79	3.68	3.59	3.52	3.46
18	.10	3.01	2.62	2.42	2.29	2.20	2.13	2.08	2.04	2.00	1.98	1.96	1.93
	.05	4.41	3.55	3.16	2.93	2.77	2.66	2.58	2.51	2.46	2.41	2.37	2.34
	.01	8.29	6.01	5.09	4.58	4.25	4.01	3.84	3.71	3.60	3.51	3.43	3.37
19	.10	2.99	2.61	2.40	2.27	2.18	2.11	2.06	2.02	1.98	1.96	1.94	1.91
	.05	4.38	3.52	3.13	2.90	2.74	2.63	2.54	2.48	2.42	2.38	2.34	2.31
	.01	8.18	5.93	5.01	4.50	4.17	3.94	3.77	3.63	3.52	3.43	3.36	3.30
20	.10	2.97	2.59	2.38	2.25	2.16	2.09	2.04	2.00	1.96	1.94	1.92	1.89
	.05	4.35	3.49	3.10	2.87	2.71	2.60	2.51	2.45	2.39	2.35	2.31	2.28
	.01	8.10	5.85	4.94	4.43	4.10	3.87	3.70	3.56	3.46	3.37	3.29	3.23
22	.10	2.95	2.56	2.35	2.22	2.13	2.06	2.01	1.97	1.93	1.90	1.88	1.86
	.05	4.30	3.44	3.05	2.82	2.66	2.55	2.46	2.40	2.34	2.30	2.26	2.23
	.01	7.95	5.72	4.82	4.31	3.99	3.76	3.59	3.45	3.35	3.26	3.18	3.12
24	.10	2.93	2.54	2.33	2.19	2.10	2.04	1.98	1.94	1.91	1.88	1.85	1.83
	.05	4.26	3.40	3.01	2.78	2.62	2.51	2.42	2.36	2.30	2.25	2.21	2.18
	.01	7.82	5.61	4.72	4.22	3.90	3.67	3.50	3.36	3.26	3.17	3.09	3.03
26	.10	2.91	2.52	2.31	2.17	2.08	2.01	1.96	1.92	1.88	1.86	1.84	1.81
	.05	4.23	3.37	2.98	2.74	2.59	2.47	2.39	2.32	2.27	2.22	2.18	2.15
	.01	7.72	5.53	4.64	4.14	3.82	3.59	3.42	3.29	3.18	3.09	3.02	2.96
28	.10	2.89	2.50	2.29	2.16	2.06	2.00	1.94	1.90	1.87	1.84	1.81	1.79
	.05	4.20	3.34	2.95	2.71	2.56	2.45	2.36	2.29	2.24	2.19	2.15	2.12
	.01	7.64	5.45	4.57	4.07	3.75	3.53	3.36	3.23	3.12	3.03	2.96	2.90
30	.10	2.88	2.49	2.28	2.14	2.05	1.98	1.93	1.88	1.85	1.82	1.79	1.77
	.05	4.17	3.32	2.92	2.69	2.53	2.42	2.33	2.27	2.21	2.16	2.13	2.09
	.01	7.56	5.39	4.51	4.02	3.70	3.47	3.30	3.17	3.07	2.98	2.91	2.84
40	.10	2.84	2.44	2.23	2.09	2.00	1.93	1.87	1.83	1.79	1.76	1.73	1.71
	.05	4.08	3.23	2.84	2.61	2.45	2.34	2.25	2.18	2.12	2.08	2.04	2.00
	.01	7.31	5.18	4.31	3.83	3.51	3.29	3.12	2.99	2.89	2.80	2.73	2.66
60	.10	2.79	2.39	2.18	2.04	1.95	1.87	1.82	1.77	1.74	1.71	1.68	1.66
	.05	4.00	3.15	2.76	2.53	2.37	2.25	2.17	2.10	2.04	1.99	1.95	1.92
	.01	7.08	4.98	4.13	3.65	3.34	3.12	2.95	2.82	2.72	2.63	2.56	2.50
120	.10	2.75	2.35	2.13	1.99	1.90	1.82	1.77	1.72	1.68	1.65	1.62	1.60
	.05	3.92	3.07	2.68	2.45	2.29	2.17	2.09	2.02	1.96	1.91	1.87	1.83
	.01	6.85	4.79	3.95	3.48	3.17	2.96	2.79	2.66	2.56	2.47	2.40	2.34
200	.10	2.73	2.33	2.11	1.97	1.88	1.80	1.75	1.70	1.66	1.63	1.60	1.57
	.05	3.89	3.04	2.65	2.42	2.26	2.14	2.06	1.98	1.93	1.88	1.84	1.80
	.01	6.76	4.71	3.88	3.41	3.11	2.89	2.73	2.60	2.50	2.41	2.34	2.27
∞	.10	2.71	2.30	2.08	1.94	1.85	1.77	1.72	1.67	1.63	1.60	1.57	1.55
	.05	3.84	3.00	2.60	2.37	2.21	2.10	2.01	1.94	1.88	1.83	1.79	1.75
	.01	6.63	4.61	3.78	3.32	3.02	2.80	2.64	2.51	2.41	2.32	2.25	2.18

DF FOR NUMERATOR												χ	DF FOR DE-NOMI-NATOR
15	20	24	30	40	50	60	100	120	200	500	∞		
1.91	1.86	1.84	1.81	1.78	1.76	1.75	1.73	1.72	1.71	1.69	1.69	.10	17
2.31	2.23	2.19	2.15	2.10	2.08	2.06	2.02	2.01	1.99	1.97	1.96	.05	
3.31	3.16	3.08	3.00	2.92	2.87	2.83	2.76	2.75	2.71	2.68	2.65	.01	
1.89	1.84	1.81	1.78	1.75	1.74	1.72	1.70	1.69	1.68	1.67	1.66	.10	18
2.27	2.19	2.15	2.11	2.06	2.04	2.02	1.98	1.97	1.95	1.93	1.92	.05	
3.23	3.08	3.00	2.92	2.84	2.78	2.75	2.68	2.66	2.62	2.59	2.57	.01	
1.86	1.81	1.79	1.76	1.73	1.71	1.70	1.67	1.67	1.65	1.64	1.63	.10	19
2.23	2.16	2.11	2.07	2.03	2.00	1.98	1.94	1.93	1.91	1.89	1.88	.05	
3.15	3.00	2.92	2.84	2.76	2.71	2.67	2.60	2.58	2.55	2.51	2.49	.01	
1.84	1.79	1.77	1.74	1.71	1.69	1.68	1.65	1.64	1.63	1.62	1.61	.10	20
2.20	2.12	2.08	2.04	1.99	1.97	1.95	1.91	1.90	1.88	1.86	1.84	.05	
3.09	2.94	2.86	2.78	2.69	2.64	2.61	2.54	2.52	2.48	2.44	2.42	.01	
1.81	1.76	1.73	1.70	1.67	1.65	1.64	1.61	1.60	1.59	1.58	1.57	.10	22
2.15	2.07	2.03	1.98	1.94	1.91	1.89	1.85	1.84	1.82	1.80	1.78	.05	
2.98	2.83	2.75	2.67	2.58	2.53	2.50	2.42	2.40	2.36	2.33	2.31	.01	
1.78	1.73	1.70	1.67	1.64	1.62	1.61	1.58	1.57	1.56	1.54	1.53	.10	24
2.11	2.03	1.98	1.94	1.89	1.86	1.84	1.80	1.79	1.77	1.75	1.73	.05	
2.89	2.74	2.66	2.58	2.49	2.44	2.40	2.33	2.31	2.27	2.24	2.21	.01	
1.76	1.71	1.68	1.65	1.61	1.59	1.58	1.55	1.54	1.53	1.51	1.50	.10	26
2.07	1.99	1.95	1.90	1.85	1.82	1.80	1.76	1.75	1.73	1.71	1.69	.05	
2.81	2.66	2.58	2.50	2.42	2.36	2.33	2.25	2.23	2.19	2.16	2.13	.01	
1.74	1.69	1.66	1.63	1.59	1.57	1.56	1.53	1.52	1.50	1.49	1.48	.10	28
2.04	1.96	1.91	1.87	1.82	1.79	1.77	1.73	1.71	1.69	1.67	1.65	.05	
2.75	2.60	2.52	2.44	2.35	2.30	2.26	2.19	2.17	2.13	2.09	2.06	.01	
1.72	1.67	1.64	1.61	1.57	1.55	1.54	1.51	1.50	1.48	1.47	1.46	.10	30
2.01	1.93	1.89	1.84	1.79	1.76	1.74	1.70	1.68	1.66	1.64	1.62	.05	
2.70	2.55	2.47	2.39	2.30	2.25	2.21	2.13	2.11	2.07	2.03	2.01	.01	
1.66	1.61	1.57	1.54	1.51	1.48	1.47	1.43	1.42	1.41	1.39	1.38	.10	40
1.92	1.84	1.79	1.74	1.69	1.66	1.64	1.59	1.58	1.55	1.53	1.51	.05	
2.52	2.37	2.29	2.20	2.11	2.06	2.02	1.94	1.92	1.87	1.83	1.80	.01	
1.60	1.54	1.51	1.48	1.44	1.41	1.40	1.36	1.35	1.33	1.31	1.29	.10	60
1.84	1.75	1.70	1.65	1.59	1.56	1.53	1.48	1.47	1.44	1.41	1.39	.05	
2.35	2.20	2.12	2.03	1.94	1.88	1.84	1.75	1.73	1.68	1.63	1.60	.01	
1.55	1.48	1.45	1.41	1.37	1.34	1.32	1.27	1.26	1.24	1.21	1.19	.10	120
1.75	1.66	1.61	1.55	1.50	1.46	1.43	1.37	1.35	1.32	1.28	1.25	.05	
2.19	2.03	1.95	1.86	1.76	1.70	1.66	1.56	1.53	1.48	1.42	1.38	.01	
1.52	1.46	1.42	1.38	1.34	1.31	1.28	1.24	1.22	1.20	1.17	1.14	.10	200
1.72	1.62	1.57	1.52	1.46	1.41	1.39	1.32	1.29	1.26	1.22	1.19	.05	
2.13	1.97	1.89	1.79	1.69	1.63	1.58	1.48	1.44	1.39	1.33	1.28	.01	
1.49	1.42	1.38	1.34	1.30	1.26	1.24	1.18	1.17	1.13	1.08	1.00	.10	∞
1.67	1.57	1.52	1.46	1.39	1.35	1.32	1.24	1.22	1.17	1.11	1.00	.05	
2.04	1.88	1.79	1.70	1.59	1.52	1.47	1.36	1.32	1.25	1.15	1.00	.01	

Research Course Report Evaluation

RESEARCH REPORT EVALUATION FORM

Name_____Date_____Grade_____

+ adequate   − inadequate

TITLE

clear and concise_____

PROBLEM

clearly stated_____
specific questions raised_____
clear statement of hypothesis_____
testable hypothesis_____
significance recognized_____
properly delimited_____
assumptions stated_____
important terms defined_____

DATA ANALYSIS

perceptive recognition of data relation-
   ships_____
effective use of tables_____
effective use of figures_____
concise report of findings_____
appropriate statistical treatment_____
logical analysis_____

SUMMARY

problem restated_____
questions/hypothesis restated_____
procedures described_____
concisely reported_____
supporting data included_____
conclusions based on data analysis___

**REVIEW OF RELATED
LITERATURE**

adequately covered_____
well-organized_____
important findings noted_____
studies critically examined_____
effectively summarized_____

PROCEDURES

described in detail_____
adequate sample_____
appropriate design_____
variables controlled_____
effective data-gathering instruments or
   procedures_____

FORM AND STYLE

typing_____
spacing_____
margins_____
balance_____
table of contents_____
list of tables_____
list of figures_____
headings_____
pagination_____
citations/quotations_____
footnotes_____
tables_____
figures_____
bibliography_____
appendix_____
spelling_____
punctuation_____
sentence structure_____
proofreading_____
clear and concise style_____

Answers to Statistics Exercises

CHAPTER 7

1. Agree. The median could be lower than the mean if a large proportion of the families had low incomes.
2. Disagree. The median is that point in a distribution above and below which half of the scores fall. It may not be the midpoint between the highest and the lowest scores.
3. $M = 55.33$
   $Md = 58.50$
4. $M = 75$ Range $= 31$
   $Md = 77$
5.   Variance $= 41.33$
   Standard deviation $= 6.43$
6. Disagree. The range does not determine the magnitude of the variance or the standard deviation. These values indicate how all of the scores, not the most extreme, are clustered about the mean.
7. a. no change   d. +5
   b. +5   e. no change
   c. +5   f. no change
8. Percentile rank = 93.
9. $M = 72$ standard deviation $= 6$

z	-3	-2	-1	0	$+1$	$+2$	$+3$
heads	54	60	66	72	78	84	90

10.

X	x	z	Z
66	+5	+1.00	60
58	-3	-.60	44
70	+9	+1.80	68
61	0	0	50
52	-9	-1.80	32

11. a. 11%   f. $-.18_z$
    b. 89%   g. $+2.33_z$
    c. 87%   h. $-.67_z$ to $+ .67_z$
    d. 6%   i. 32%
    e. $+.39_z$ j. 0_z
12. a. 119   d. 107
    b. 96   e. 85 to 115
    c. 75%

13.

	TOM	DICK	HARRY
algebra z	−1.00	+.33	−.17
history z	+1.25	+.50	−.25

a. Tom   d. Tom
b. Tom   e. Dick
c. Harry   f. Harry

14. Disagree. The coefficient of correlation is an indication of the magnitude of the relationship, but does not necessarily indicate a cause-and-effect relationship.
15. $rho = +.61$
16. $r = +.65$
17. $r = +.53$
18. $r = -1.00$

most correct ⟶ most incorrect
least correct ⟶ least incorrect

19. Agree. $r = \dfrac{\text{rise}}{\text{run}}$ expressed in sigma units

$b = \dfrac{\text{rise}}{\text{run}}$ expressed in raw scores

The value of r cannot exceed ±1.00
The value of b can exceed ±1.00
20. $S_{est} = 4.96$
21. a. $\hat{Y} = 44$
    b. $\hat{Y} = 36$

CHAPTER 8

1. Confirming a positive hypothesis provides a weak argument, for the conclusion may be true for other reasons. It does not preclude the validity of alternative or rival hypotheses. Rejecting a negative hypothesis employs stronger logic.
2. Agree. A test of statistical significance provides a basis for accepting or rejecting a sampling error explanation on a probability basis. Only when a sampling process is involved is a test of significance appropriate.
3. Agree. The level of significance determines the probability of a sampling error, rather than a treatment variable explanation. When a researcher finds an observation significant at the .05 level, he or she is admitting that there is a 5/100 chance of a sampling error explanation.
4. Disagree. The .01 alpha level is a much more rigorous criterion than the .05 level. However, any hypothesis that can be rejected at the .01 level can surely be rejected at the .05 level of significance.
5. Disagree. The t critical value for a one-tailed test is lower. The area of rejection is one side of the normal curve and it is not necessary to go out as far to reach it.

	t CRITICAL VALUES FOR REJECTION	
	2t	1t
.05 level	1.96	1.64
.01 level	2.58	2.33

6. $t = -2.00$ Reject the null hypothesis. The cable did not meet the manufacturer's specifications.

7. $t = 3.49$ Reject the null hypothesis. The means do not behave as sample means from the same population.

8. $t = 1.38$ Do not reject the null hypothesis. There was no significant difference between the achievement of the two groups.

9. $t = 3.77$ Reject the null hypothesis. The weight gain for the experimental group was significant.

10. $t = 3.13$ Reject the null hypothesis. The difference in gasoline mileage was significant.

11.   a. $N - 1$
     b. $N - 2$
     c. $N + N - 2$
     d. 1
     e. 8

12. $\chi^2 = 14.06$ Reject the null hypothesis. There seems to be a significant relationship between gender and brand preference.

13. $z = .28$ Do not reject the null hypothesis. The effect of the counseling program did not seem to be statistically significant.

14. $t = 1.26$ Do not reject the null hypothesis. The coefficient of correlation was not statistically significant.

15. $\hat{Y} = 24.6$

Selected Indexes, Abstracts, and Reference Materials

References about References

There are a number of publications that identify specific references that cover particular areas of knowledge.

> *American Reference Books Annual.* **Bodhan S. Wynar, ed. Littleton, CO.: Libraries Unlimited, 1970–date.**

Most reference books published or distributed in the United States are reviewed. Reviews, written by more than 200 library specialists, vary in length from 75 to 300 words, and are not cumulated from year to year. This is probably the most complete and up-to-date reference on references available.

> *A Guide to Reference Books.* **Eugene P. Sheehy, compiler. Chicago: American Library Association, 1976.**

This comprehensive work lists, without evaluation, by subject area, by type, and by author or editor, the most important reference books printed in a number of languages. A section is devoted to education. Supplements appear every two or three years.

> **Wynar, Christine L.** *Guide to Reference Books for School Media Centers.* **Littleton, CO.: Libraries Unlimited, 1976. 475 pp.**

This guide includes 2575 entries with evaluative comments on reference books and selection tools for use in elementary schools, junior and senior high schools, and community and junior colleges. It is indexed by author, subject, and title.

> **Bell, Marion V. and Eleanor Swidan.** *Reference Books.* **Baltimore, MD.: Enoch Pratt Library, 1947–date.**

This brief annotated guide describes nearly a thousand reference books.

Reference Books Review Index. **Ann Arbor, MI.: Pierian Press, 1978.**

This annotated listing of references issues supplements quarterly.

Booklist. **Chicago: American Library Association, 1905–date.**

Published biweekly and cumulated every two years, this reference presents an unbiased critical analysis by expert librarians of atlases, encyclopedias, biographical works, dictionaries, and other reference materials in terms of their usefulness and reliability for libraries or homes. Every two years some of the more important reviews are published in a separate publication, titled

Reference and Subscription Books Reviews. **Chicago: American Library Association, 1956–date.**

Published every two years, critical reviews by expert librarians are cumulated from *Booklist.*

Cumulative Book Index. **New York: H. W. Wilson Co., 1898–date.**

This monthly publication, cumulated semiannually and in one- and two-year cumulations, indexes all books published in the English language by author, title, and subject. It is helpful in assuring the student that all pertinent books have been covered in his or her searches.

Books in Print
Subject Guide to Books in Print. **R. R. Bowker Co., 1948–date.**
Vol. I Authors
Vol. II Titles and Publishers

These two-volume comprehensive listings of in-print titles list names of publishers and other publication information.

New Serial Titles. **Washington, D.C.: Library of Congress, 1961–date.**

Issued monthly and indexed in the December issue, it lists periodicals, loose-leaf publications, government series, motion pictures, and filmstrips, both domestic and foreign. Also listed are holdings of the Library of Congress and hundreds of participating libraries.

The Standard Periodicals Directory. **New York: Oxbridge Publishing Co., 1964–date.**

Published every other year, this directory of over 30,000 entries covers every type of periodical, with the exception of local newspapers.

Periodicals are defined as publications appearing at least once every two years. Two hundred classifications are arranged by subject. An alphabetical index is provided.

> *Ulrich's International Periodicals Directory.* **New York: R. R. Bowker Co., 1966–date. 2 vols.**

This classified list of more than 57,000 foreign and domestic periodicals is arranged by subject and title. Publication information is provided.

> *Irregular Serials and Annuals. An International Directory: Excepting Periodicals Issued More Frequently than Once a Year.* **R. R. Bowker Co., 1972.**

Published biennially, this directory includes more than 20,000 publications.

> *Sources of Information in the Social Sciences.* **Chicago: American Library Association, 1973.**

Organized by subject area and indexed by author and title, this work contains a comprehensive listing and brief description of reference books, monographs, and scholarly journals.

> **Leidy, W. Philip.** *A Popular Guide to Government Publications.* **New York: Columbia University Press, 1976.**

This guide lists 119 alphabetically arranged subject headings. Only titles in print at time of publication are included.

> **Schorr, Alan E.** *Government Reference Books: A Biennial Guide to United States Government Publications.* **Littleton, CO.: Libraries Unlimited, 1968/69–date.**

This guide describes more than 1300 publications.

> **William L. Camp.** *Guide to Periodicals in Education.* **Metuchen, N.J.: Scarecrow Press, 1975.**

This reference, which indexes 449 periodicals, is particularly helpful to those who are planning to submit manuscripts for publication. Information is provided about editorial policies, type of readers, and how to submit manuscripts.

Indexes

A periodical index serves much the same purpose as the index of a book or the card file of a library. Usually listing articles alphabetically under subject, title, and author headings, the sources of periodical articles are indicated. Readers should read the directions for the use of an index before trying to locate references. Most indexes provide complete directions, as well as a list of the periodicals covered, the issue dates included, and a key to all abbreviations used.

Education Index. New York: H. W. Wilson Co., 1929–date. Published monthly (September through June), and cumulated annually.

Canadian Education Index. **Ottawa, Ontario: Canadian Council for Educational Research, 1965–date.**

Issued quarterly, this publication indexes periodicals, books, pamphlets, and reports published in Canada.

Current Contents: Education. **Philadelphia: Institute for Scientific Information and Encyclopedia Britannica Educational Corporation, 1969–date.**

Issued weekly, this publication reproduces the table of contents of more than 500 foreign and domestic educational periodicals. It contains an author index and address directory to facilitate writing for reprints of the articles and to identify the author's organization. Reprints are available directly from the Institute for Scientific Information.

Current Index to Journals in Education. **Phoenix, AZ.: Oryx Press, 1969– date.**

This index is issued monthly and cumulated semiannually and annually, and indexes approximately 20,000 articles each year from more than 700 education and education-related journals, a joint venture with the National Institute of Education.

Index of Doctoral Dissertations International. **Ann Arbor, MI.: Xerox University Microfilms, 1956–date.**

Published as the issue 13 of *Dissertation Abstracts International* each year, this work consolidates into one list all dissertations accepted by American, Canadian, and some European universities during the academic year, as well as those available in microfilm. It indexes by author and key words selected from dissertation titles.

Comprehensive Dissertation Index **(1861–1972). Ann Arbor, MI.: Xerox University Microfilms, 1974.**

This volume indexes by author name and key word 417,000 doctoral dissertations accepted at 362 accredited institutions from 1861–1972.

Research Studies in Education. **Bloomington, IN.: Phi Delta Kappa, 1953– date.**

This annual publication includes doctoral dissertations in education, both completed and in progress, author and subject indexes, and a research methods bibliography.

Bibliographic Index. **New York: H. W. Wilson Co., 1938–date.**

Issued semiannually, this guide indexes by subject current bibliographies containing more than 40 citations, including those published in books, pamphlets, and periodicals both in English and in foreign languages. More than 1500 periodicals are examined for bibliographic material.

Readers' Guide to Periodic Literature. **New York: H. W. Wilson Co., 1900– date.**

Issued twice each month, *Readers' Guide* indexes by subject and author articles of a popular and general nature. Prior to 1929, *Readers' Guide* covered many of the educational periodicals. By 1929, the number of educational periodicals had become so great that the *Education Index* was established as a more specialized guide. *Readers' Guide* may be helpful to students in education for finding references to articles in areas outside the field of professional education.

Abridged Readers' Guide to Periodic Literature. **New York: H. W. Wilson Co., 1935–date.**

Fifty-six selected periodicals most likely to be found in smaller libraries are indexed here.

New York Times Index. **New York, 1913–date.**

This index is published biweekly with annual cumulation, and it classifies material in the *New York Times* alphabetically and chronologically under subject, title, person, and organization name. It is also useful in locating materials in other newspapers because it gives a clue to the date of events. Complete issues of the *New York Times* are available in microfilm form in many libraries.

Subject Index to the Christian Science Monitor. **Boston: Christian Science Monitor, 1960–date.**

This publication is issued monthly with annual cumulations.

Social Sciences Index. **New York: H. W. Wilson Co., 1974–date.**

This guide indexes 263 periodicals.

Humanities Index. **New York: H. W. Wilson Co., 1974–date.**

Formerly published as *Social Sciences and Humanities Index* (1965–1973), the *Humanities Index* lists 260 periodicals. These two indexes, each issued quarterly and cumulated annually, index alphabetically by subject and title articles from more than 260 periodicals, including many published outside the United States.

Applied Science and Technology Index. **New York: H. W. Wilson Co., 1958–date.**

Formerly a part of the *Industrial Arts Index,* this subject index, issued monthly and cumulated annually, covers more than 225 periodicals in chemistry, physics, electricity, engineering, aerospace, metallurgy, machinery, and related subjects.

Business Periodicals Index. **New York: H. W. Wilson Co., 1958–date.**

Issued monthly and cumulated annually, this subject index covers more than 120 periodicals in the fields of business, accounting, labor and management, marketing, purchasing, office management, public administration, banking, finance, taxation, insurance, and related areas.

Air University Library Index. **Maxwell Field, AL.: Air University Library, United States Air Force, 1945–date.**

This work indexes quarterly and cumulates every three years more than 76 military periodicals published in the English language.

Music Index: The Key to Current Music Periodical Literature. **Detroit: Information Service, 1950–date.**

Issued monthly, cumulated annually, more than 300 periodicals are indexed.

Physical Education Index. **Cape Girardeau, MO.: Ben Oak Publishing Co., 1978–date.**

This quarterly indexes more than 130 domestic and foreign physical education journals by subject, title, and author.

Physical Education/Sports Index. Albany, N.Y.: Marathon Press, 1978–date.

This quarterly covers more than 100 journals. Since *Education Index* and *Current Index to Journals in Education* cover fewer than 10 physical education journals, these indexes provide an important additional source.

Art Index. New York: H. W. Wilson Co., 1929–date.

Published quarterly with cumulation annually and every two years, this publication indexes by author and subject 110 periodicals and museum bulletins, both foreign and domestic. Subjects included are archaeology, architecture, art history, arts and crafts, fine arts, graphic arts, industrial design, interior decoration, photography, planning, and landscape design.

Biological and Agricultural Index. New York: H. W. Wilson Co., 1916–date.

Formerly *Agricultural Index*, and issued monthly and cumulated annually, this work indexes by subject and title more than 190 periodicals in such fields of agriculture as chemicals, economics, engineering, animal husbandry, soil science, forestry, nutrition, biology, genetics, ecology, zoology, and veterinary medicine.

Occupational Index. Jaffrey, NH.: Personnel Services, 1936–date.

Issued quarterly, this work indexes more than 100 general and technical periodicals by subject, author, and title.

Cumulative Career Index. Moravia, NY.: Chronicle Guidance Publications, 1971–date.

This annual publication lists more than 1800 free and inexpensive materials on careers and work opportunities, listed by job titles.

Index to Legal Periodicals. New York: H. W. Wilson Co., 1908–date.

Issued monthly and cumulated annually, this index covers nearly 300 legal periodicals, indexed by subject with case notes.

Index Medicus. Washington, D.C.: National Library of Medicine, 1960.

Issued monthly, this index includes research reports from most medical journals, and is cumulated annually as:

Cumulated Index Medicus. **Chicago: American Medical Association, 1960–date.**

Abridged Index Medicus. **Washington, D.C.: National Library of Medicine and the A.M.A., Superintendent of Documents, 1970–date.**

Issued monthly, this work cross indexes articles from 118 English language medical journals by subject and author.

Hospital Literature Index. **Chicago: American Hospital Association, 1945–date.**

Issued semiannually with annual and five-year cumulations, this publication covers more than 180 periodicals in the United States and the British Commonwealth dealing with public health, nursing, hospital administration, gerontology, and medicine.

Cumulative Index to Nursing Literature. **Glendale, CA.: Seventh Day Adventist Hospital Assn., 1961–date.**

Issued quarterly with annual cumulation, this work indexes most nursing periodicals.

International Nursing Index. **Philadelphia: American Journal of Nursing, 1966–date.**

This index is issued quarterly with annual cumulation, with citations from more than 200 nursing journals; it lists doctoral dissertations in nursing.

Rehabilitation Literature. **Chicago: The National Society for Crippled Children and Adults, 1940–date.**

Published monthly, this index lists material on the physically handicapped.

Index to Religious Periodical Literature. **Chicago: American Theological Library Association, McCormick Seminary, 1949–date.**

This index to more than 100 religious periodicals is issued every two years.

Catholic Periodical and Literature Index. **Haverford, PA.: Catholic Library Association, 1930–date.**

The quarterly publication indexes more than 135 Catholic periodicals, books, newspapers, and bulletins.

Index to Jewish Periodicals. **Cleveland: Cleveland College of Jewish Studies, 1963–date.**

This index is issued quarterly, and lists by subject and author articles from Jewish periodicals.

Public Affairs Information Service Bulletin. **New York: Public Affairs Information Service, 1915–date.**

Published weekly and cumulated quarterly and annually, this publication lists by subject articles in books, pamphlets, government publications, periodicals, and society publications dealing with social, political, and economic affairs throughout the world.

Book Review Index. **Detroit: Gale Research Co., 1965–date.**

This biweekly publication with quarterly cumulations lists book reviews by author from more than 250 periodicals.

Mental Health Book Review Index. **New York: Research Center for Mental Health, 1956–date.**

Published annually and indexed by author, this work lists reviews from more than 200 English language journals.

Microforms in Print
Subject Guide to Microforms in Print. **Washington, D.C.: Microcard Editions Books, 1961–date.**

These annual cumulative guides to microfilms and microfiche do not include theses and dissertations.

Selected United States Government Publications. **Washington, D.C.: Superintendent of Documents, 1928–date.**

Issued biweekly, this small publication, available without cost, lists government books and pamphlets soon after publication.

Index to U.S. Government Periodicals. **Chicago: Infordot International, 1972–date.**

Issued quarterly and cumulated annually, this is a computer-generated guide to selected titles from over 100 major government periodicals.

International Guide to Educational Documentation. **Paris: UNESCO.**

Published every five years, this guide indexes annotated bibliographies covering major publications, bibliographies, and national directories, written in English, French, and Spanish.

United Nations Document Index. **New York: United Nations Library, 1950– date.**

All U.N. publications are listed by subject and issuing body in this monthly publication.

Abstracts

Another type of reference guide is the abstract, review, or digest. In addition to providing a systemized list of reference sources, it includes a summary of the contents. Usually the summaries are brief, but in some publications they are presented in greater detail.

Dissertation Abstracts International. **Ann Arbor, MI.: Xerox University Microfilms, 1955–date.**

Issued monthly and indexed annually, *Dissertation Abstracts* is divided into:

A. Humanities and Social Sciences
B. Sciences and Engineering

Dissertations accepted by all universities in the United States and Canada and some in foreign countries are indexed by author and key word. Libraries or individuals may purchase complete xerographic or microfiche copies of any dissertation.

Master's Abstracts. **Ann Arbor, MI.: Xerox University Microfilms, 1962– date.**

Issued semiannually, this guide abstracts those master's degree theses that are available on microfilm.

Resources in Education. **Washington, D.C.: Superintendent of Documents, Government Printing Office, 1966–date.**

This monthly abstract journal prepared by the National Institute of Education reports new and completed research projects gathered by the 16 Educational Research Information Centers (ERIC).

Completed Research in Health, Physical Education and Recreation Including International Sources. **Washington, D.C.: American Alliance for Health, Physical Education and Recreation, 1958–date.**

Issued annually, this work indexes by subject and title abstracts of studies conducted throughout the world.

Child Development Abstracts and Bibliography. **Chicago: University of Chicago Press, 1927–date.**

Issued every four months and cumulated every three years, this publication abstracts more than 20 journals.

Review of Child Development Research. **New York: Russell Sage Foundation, 1964–date.**

Research Relating to Children. **Washington, D.C.: Department of Health, Education and Welfare, Children's Bureau, 1948–date.**

Published annually, these abstracts of studies related to the welfare of children are indexed by subject, author, and title.

Research Related to Emotionally Disturbed Children. **Washington, D.C.: Department of Health, Education and Welfare, Children's Bureau, 1968.**

These abstracts are issued irregularly.

Exceptional Child Education Resources. **Arlington, VA.: Council for Exceptional Children, 1969–date.**

Issued quarterly, this publication indexes and abstracts books, periodicals, and government documents.

Deafness, Speech and Hearing Abstracts. **Washington, D.C.: Deafness, Speech and Hearing Publications, 1960–date.**

This quarterly publication abstracts more than 1800 articles each year from over 250 domestic and foreign journals.

Selected RAND Abstracts. **Santa Monica, CA.: RAND Corporation, 1963–date.**

Issued quarterly, these abstracts cover books and reports published by the corporation, many of which deal with education and other social sciences.

College Student Personnel Abstracts. **Claremont, CA.: College Student Personnel Institute, 1965–date.**

Issued quarterly, the abstracts cover more than 275 periodicals. Summaries deal with research practices and developments relating to college students and student services.

Psychological Abstracts. **Washington, D.C.: American Psychological Association, 1927–date.**

Issued bimonthly and indexed annually by subject and author, this publication has excellent signed summaries of psychological research reports. The December issue provides annual cumulative author and subject indexes. Beginning in 1963, each issue is also indexed by both subject and author. Libraries may also provide a cumulative subject index (1927–1960) and a cumulative author index (1927–1963).

Annual Review of Psychology. **Palo Alto, CA.: Annual Reviews, 1950–date.**

Each issue of this annual volume contains critical reviews of the literature in some 15 topical areas of contemporary psychology. Each review is written by a recognized authority on the topic. Although different authors writing in different years may vary considerably in their interpretation and handling of the same topic, all aim for comprehensive coverage of new developments.

Psychological Bulletin. **Washington, D.C.: American Psychological Association, 1904–date.**

Issued bimonthly, the *Bulletin* evaluates reviews of research literature and methodology.

Sociological Abstracts. **San Diego, CA.: Sociological Abstracts, Inc., 1952–date.**

Issued five times a year and cumulated annually, the *Abstracts* cover all areas of sociology, including educational sociology. The work abstracts articles and presents book reviews from several hundred periodicals, both domestic and foreign.

Social Work Research and Abstracts. **New York: National Association of Social Workers, 1965–date.**

Published quarterly, this volume indexes by subject, title, and author. It combines published research with the previously published journal, *Abstracts for Social Workers.*

New Studies: A Guide to Recent Publications in the Social and Behavioral Sciences. **Beverly Hills, CA.: Sage Publications, 1966–date.**

Published as part of the bimonthly journal *American Behavioral Scientist,* this guide abstracts approximately 100 items in each issue from more than 400 journals, reviews, books, and pamphlets, both foreign and domestic.

Crime and Delinquency Abstracts. **Rockville, MD.: National Institute of Mental Health, 1966–1972.**

These abstracts cover published material on delinquency, crime, and penology.

Research Annual on Intergroup Relations. **New York: Anti-Defamation League of B'nai B'rith, 1965–date.**

This annual abstracts major studies in interracial and interfaith relations.

Religious and Theological Abstracts. **Youngstown, OH.: Theological Abstracts, 1957–date.**

The quarterly publication abstracts articles on various phases of religion, including religious education.

Women Studies Abstracts. **Rush, N.Y.: Women Studies Abstracts, 1972–date.**

Issued quarterly, these abstracts cover articles and studies from many journals.

National School Law Reporter. **New London, CT.: Croft Educational Services, 1955–date.**

The biweekly publication abstracts court decisions on school law.

Book Review Digest. **New York: H. W. Wilson Co., 1905–date.**

Issued monthly and cumulated annually, this publication digests reviews of more than 6000 books each year taken from over 70 periodicals.

Research-oriented periodicals

There are many publications in education and in closely related areas that report research activity. Some of these publications are exclusively research-oriented. Others present both research reports and feature-type articles. It is possible that beginning researchers may not be familiar with many of the specialized publications that deal with a problem area selected. Browsing through these periodicals provides an effective introduction to the field. It is also possible that the student may find recent and current reports that have not yet appeared in the appropriate index.

The following list of periodicals may be helpful to those who are planning a research project.

EDUCATION

Administrative Science Quarterly
Adolescence
Adult Education
Adult Jewish Education
Alberta Journal of Educational Research
American Association of University Professors Bulletin
American Behavioral Scientist
American Biology Teacher
American Education
American Educational Research Journal
American Vocational Journal
Arbitration in the Schools
Arithmetic Teacher
Audio-Visual Communications Review
Audio-Visual Language Journal
Black Scholar
Bulletin of the National Association of Secondary Schools Principals
Business Education Forum
Business Education Quarterly
California Journal of Educational Research
Catholic Educational Review
Character Education Journal
Child Care Quarterly
Child Development
Child Study Journal
Child Welfare
Children Today
Childhood Education
Civil Rights Digest
Clearing House
College Board Review

Colorado Journal of Educational Research
Community and Junior College Journal
Comparative Education
Comparative Education Review
Computers and Education
Continuing Education
Convergence
Education and Urban Society
Educational Administration Quarterly
Educational Forum
Educational Leadership
Educational Record
Educational Researcher
Educational Research Quarterly
Educational Technology
Elementary School Journal
Evaluation Quarterly
Harvard Educational Review
High School Journal
History of Education Quarterly
Home Economics Research Journal
Human Development
Independent School Bulletin
Illinois School Research
Indian Historian
Integrated Education
International Journal of Aging and Human Development
International Journal of Educational Science
Jewish Education
Journal for Research in Mathematics Education
Journal for the Study of Religion

Journal of Afro-American Issues
Journal of Alcohol and Drug Education
Journal of American Indian Education
Journal of Business Education
Journal of Communication
Journal of Computer-Based Instruction
Journal of Creative Behavior
Journal of Drug Education
Journal of Educational Data Processing
Journal of Educational Measurement
Journal of Educational Research
Journal of Educational Statistics
Journal of Experimental Education
Journal of Higher Education
Journal of Home Economics
Journal of Industrial Teacher Education
Journal of Law and Education
Journal of Legal Education
Journal of Leisure Research
Journal of Library Research
Journal of Negro Education
Journal of Religion
Journal of Research and Development in Education
Journal of Research in Mathematics Education
Journal of Research in Music Education
Journal of Research in Science Teaching
Journal of Social Studies Research
Journal of Teacher Education
Junior College Journal
Kappa Delta Pi Record
Library Resources and Technical Services
Library Quarterly
Mathematics Teacher
Measurement in Education
Merrill Palmer Quarterly
Microfilm Review
Modern Language Journal
Multivariate Behavioral Research
National Business Education Quarterly
National Catholic Educational Association Bulletin

National Elementary Principal
National Education Association Research Bulletin
National Society for Programmed Instruction Journal
Negro Educational Review
New England Association Quarterly
North Central Association Quarterly
Outlook
Peabody Journal of Education
Phi Delta Kappan
Phylon
Pollution Abstracts
Practical Application of Research
Programmed Instruction
Psychometrika
Public Opinion Quarterly
Religion Teachers Journal
Religious Education
Research in Higher Education
Research in the Teaching of English
Review of Educational Research
Review of Religious Research
School and Society
School Law Journal
School Law Reporter
School Review
School Science and Mathematics
Science
Science Education
Science and Children
Science Teacher
Social Education
Social Science Research
Speech Monographs
Speech Teacher
Teachers College Record
Times Educational Supplement
Theory and Research in Social Education
Theory into Practice
UCLA Educator
Visual Education
Young Children

SOCIOLOGY

American Anthropologist
American Behavioral Scientist
American Journal of Sociology
American Sociological Review

Ethnology
Federal Probation
Human Relations
Journal of American Indian Education

Journal of Applied Behavioral Science
Journal of Correctional Education
Journal of Educational Sociology
Journal of Experimental Social Psychology
Journal of Marriage and the Family
Journal of Research in Crime and Delinquency
Rural Sociology
Social Behavior and Personality
Social Case Work
Social Education
Social Forces

Social Problems
Social Psychology
Social Work
Sociological Methods and Research
Sociological Record
Sociology of Education
Sociology and Social Research
Sociometry
Teaching Sociology
Urban Education
Urban Review

PSYCHOLOGY

American Journal of Orthopsychiatry
American Journal of Psychiatry
American Journal of Psychology
American Psychologist
Applied Psychological Measurement
Behavioral Disorders
British Journal of Psychology
British Journal of Educational Psychology
Catholic Psychological Record
Cognitive Psychology
Contemporary Educational Psychology
Educational and Psychological Measurement
Genetic Psychology Monographs
Journal of Abnormal Psychology
Journal of Abnormal Child Psychology
Journal of Applied Psychology
Journal of Autism and Childhood Schizophrenia
Journal of Clinical Psychology
Journal of Comparative and Physiological Psychology
Journal of Consulting and Clinical Psychology
Journal of Counseling Psychology
Journal of Creative Behavior
Journal of Educational Psychology
Journal of Experimental Child Psychology
Journal of General Psychology
Journal of Genetic Psychology

Journal of Humanistic Psychology
Journal of Mental and Nervous Disease
Journal of Personality
Journal of Personality and Social Psychology
Journal of Personal Assessment
Journal of Psychiatric Research
Journal of Psychology
Journal of Research in Personality
Journal of School Psychology
Journal of Social Psychology
Journal of Verbal Learning and Behavior
Learning and Motivation
Mental Hygiene
Pastoral Psychology
Perceptual and Motor Skills
Personnel Psychology
Psychiatry
Psychoanalytic Quarterly
Psychological Abstracts
Psychological Bulletin
Psychological Monographs
Psychological Record
Psychological Reports
Psychological Review
Psychology in the Schools
Psychology of Women Quarterly
Small Group Behavior
Transactional Analysis Journal

HEALTH AND PHYSICAL EDUCATION

American Journal of Nursing
American Journal of Occupational Therapy

American Journal of Physical Medicine
American Journal of Public Health

Athletic Journal
Health and Education Journal
Health Education
Journal of the American Dietetic Association
Journal of the American Medical Association
Journal of the American Physical Therapy Association
Journal of Clinical Nutrition
Journal of Continuing Education in Nursing
Journal of Drug Education
Journal of Health and Social Behavior
Journal of Health, Physical Education and Recreation
Journal of Medical Education
Journal of Mental Health

Journal of Nursing Education
Journal of Nutrition
Journal of Pediatrics
Journal of Rehabilitation
Journal of School Health
Nursing Mirror
Nursing Outlook
Nursing Times
Nutrition Today
Quarterly Review of Pediatrics
Registered Nurse
Research Quarterly of the American Alliance for Health, Physical Education and Recreation
School Health Review

GUIDANCE AND COUNSELING

American Vocational Journal
British Journal of Guidance and Counseling
California Personnel and Guidance Association Journal
Canadian Counsellor
Counselor Education and Supervision
Elementary School Guidance and Counseling

Focus on Guidance
Guidance Clinic
Measurement and Evaluation in Guidance
Personnel and Guidance Journal
School Counselor
School Guidance Worker
Vocational Guidance Quarterly

SPECIAL EDUCATION

Academic Therapy
American Annals of the Deaf
American Journal of Mental Deficiency
Braille Book Review
Digest of the Mentally Retarded
Education and Training of the Mentally Retarded
Education of the Visually Handicapped
Exceptional Children
Exceptional Child Education Abstracts
Exceptional Parent
Focus on Exceptional Children
Gifted Child Quarterly
Gifted Pupil
Hearing and Speech Action
International Journal for the Education of the Blind

Journal of Learning Disabilities
Journal of Mental Deficiency Research
Journal of Special Education
Journal of Speech and Hearing Disorders
Journal of Speech and Hearing Research
Language, Speech and Hearing Services in Schools
Learning Disorders
Mental Retardation
Mental Retardation Abstracts
New Outlook for the Blind
Sight Saving Review
Special Education
Teacher of the Blind
Teaching Exceptional Children
Training School Bulletin
Volta Review

READING

American Journal of Optometry	*Journalism Quarterly*
Elementary English	*Reading Horizons*
English Journal	*Reading Improvement*
Initial Teaching Alphabet Bulletin	*Reading Quarterly*
Journal of the Association for the Study of Perception	*Reading Research Quarterly*
	Reading Teacher
Journal of Reading	*Reading World*
Journal of Reading Behavior	

Index

AUTHOR INDEX

Ahmann, J. S., 107
Alevizos, P. N., 203
Alberson, L. G., 203
Anastasia, A., 149, 202
Anderson, C., 108
Anderson, D. B., 100, 107
Anderson, R. B., 130, 142
Appel, M., 27
Aydelotte, W. O., 65, 76

Babbie, E. R., 83, 107, 178, 202
Backstrom, H., 108
Ballou, S. V., 335
Barton, M., 104, 107
Barzun, J., 28, 77
Bellack, A. A., 58
Berkmans, T. R., 187, 202
Bernoff, R., 27
Best, J. H., 60, 76
Billington, R. A., 60, 76
Bogardus, E. S., 193, 202
Bonney, M. F., 203
Branscombe, A., 107
Brent, D. H., 314
Brickman, W. W., 77
Broadbeck, M., 28
Brown, M. B., 314
Burns, G. P., 130, 142
Buros, O. K., 158, 202
Burstein, L., 108

Campbell, D. T., 118–19, 122, 124, 129,
     142, 203
Campbell, E. Q., 107
Campbell, W. G., 335
Cannell, C. F., 187, 202–3
Carr, H., 77
Cartwright, C. A., 203
Cartwright, G. P., 203
Cayton, H. R., 94, 107
Chall, J., 108
Charters, W. W., 85, 107
Chave, E. J., 180, 203
Cohen, J., 285, 297
Cohen, P., 285, 297
Cohran, W. G., 297
Coleman, J. S., 102–3, 107–8

Combs, J., 89, 107–8
Conant, J. B., 28
Cook, T. D., 118, 124, 129, 142
Cooley, W. W., 89, 107–8
Copperman, P., 108
Crandall, R., 57
Crane, R., 107
Cremin, L., 63, 76
Cronbach, L. J., 149, 155, 202
Crowson, R., 85, 96, 107

Davies, A. P., 71, 76
Dewey, J., 4, 8, 27–28
Diener, E., 57
Diethorn, B. C., 62, 77
Dillon, H. J., 88, 107
Dixon, W. D., 314
Drake, S. C., 94, 107

Ebel, R. L., 28, 203
Edgerton, H. E., 77
Edwards, A. L., 181, 202
Elam, S. M., 83, 107
Engleman, L., 314
Ennis, H., 108
Ennis, R., 57

Feigl, H., 28
Fenlason, A., 203
Ferguson, G. A., 205, 239, 252, 297
Finley, M. I., 65, 76
Fisher, R. A., 13, 27
Flannigan, J. C., 108
Frane, J. W., 314
Frank, G., 28
Fruchter, B., 205, 252, 297

Gabel, D. L., 9, 27
Gage, N. L., 57
Garraghan, G. J., 77
Gebhard, P. H., 107
Gesell, A., 161, 202
Glass, G. V., 104–5, 107–8, 118, 130, 139,
     142, 205, 208, 239, 241, 252, 258, 279–
     82, 297

Goertzwitz, J. E., 108
Goldberg, M. L., 109
Gottschalk, L. R., 60, 65, 76–77
Graff, H. F., 77
Gronlund, N. E., 203
Guenzel, P. J., 187, 202
Guilford, J. P., 205, 252, 297

Hakel, M., 170, 203
Hall, H. V., 133, 142, 159, 203
Hare, V. C., 127, 142
Harns, D. B., 108, 165, 203
Hartshorne, H., 193, 203
Hawkins, G. S., 73–74, 77
Hays, W. L., 28, 118, 142
Hechinger, F. M., 85, 107
Hechinger, G., 85, 107
Helmstadter, G. C., 28
Henderson, K. B., 108
Henry, T. R., 94, 108
Herriott, R. E., 203
Hess, R. D., 109
Hill, M. A., 314
Hirschi, T., 109
Hobson, C. J., 107
Hockett, H. C., 60, 74, 77
Hodges, W. L., 131, 142
Hollander, M., 293
Hollingshead, A. B., 94, 107
Hopkins, K. D., 118, 139, 142, 203, 205,
    239, 241, 252, 258, 279–82, 297
House, E. L., 130, 142
Howe, A., 27
Hull, C. H., 314
Hursch, D., 108
Hurwitz, E., 85, 96, 107
Husen, T., 107
Hyman, H. H., 109, 203

Iwamoto, D., 130, 142

Jackson, G., 109
Jenkins, J. G., 314
Jeurich, R. I., 314
Jones, W. T., 28

Kahn, J. V., 9, 27, 114, 142, 318
Kahn, R. L., 203
Kamii, C., 9, 27
Kaplan, A., 28
Karplus, R., 9, 27
Kenney, K. C., 181, 202
Kerlinger, F. N., 118, 142, 203
Kinsey, A. C., 81, 107

Kirk, R. E., 118, 139, 142, 205, 252, 279–
    80, 297
Kish, L., 203
Klein, A., 77
Koefod, P. E., 335
Kuhn, T. S., 28

Lannie, V. L., 62, 77
Larson, R., 107
Lavatelli, C. S., 9, 27
Lawson, A. E., 27
Lesser, S., 109
Levin, S. B., 100, 107
Lohnes, P. R., 108
Lomax, R. G., 127, 142
Lucas, R. A., 94, 107
Lunney, G. H., 208, 252
Lunt, P. S., 94, 108
Lynd, H. M., 94, 107
Lynd, R. S., 94, 107

Mandeville, G. K., 208, 252
Martin, C. E., 107
Massey, R. H., 142, 203
May, M. A., 193, 203
Mayo, E., 113, 142
McKay, H. D., 82, 108
McLean, L. D., 130, 142
McPortland, J., 107
Mead, M., 96, 107
Mees, C. E. K., 4, 27
Mill, J. S., 111–12, 142
Minton, J. M., 100, 107
Mitchell, J. V., 158, 203
Moehlman, A., 77
Mood, A. M., 107
Mooney, R. L., 153, 203
Moreno, J. L., 203
Morris, V. C., 85, 96–97, 107
Mosteller, F., 104, 107
Moynihan, D. P., 104, 107
Myrdal, G., 81, 107

Neill, G., 108
Neter, J., 285, 297
Nevins, A., 66, 77
Nie, N. H., 314
Nordin, V. D., 77
Norusis, M. J., 314
Nucci, L. P., 138–39, 142
Nucci, M. S., 138–39, 142
Nunnaly, J. C., 203, 297

Oppenheim, A. N., 203
Osgood, C. E., 183, 203
Overholt, G. E., 109

Passow, A. H., 109
Peckham, P. D., 208, 252
Peizer, S. B., 142, 203
Perrin, P. G., 335
Peterson, C. S., 77
Piaget, J., 9, 27, 109
Polsky, R. M., 109
Pomeroy, W. B., 107
Popham, W. J., 109
Porter-Gehrie, C., 85, 96, 107
Price, A. B., 142, 203
Proper, E. C., 130, 142

Raph, J. B., 109
Reagan, M. D., 28
Rogers, J. M., 109
Rusch, J. J., 27
Ryans, D. G., 109

St. John, N., 109
St. Pierre, R. G., 130, 142
Sanders, J. R., 109, 208, 252
Schwartz, R. D., 203
Scott, W. R., 109
Search, P. W., 62, 77
Searls, D., 107
Sechrest, L., 203
See, H. W., 177, 203
Selvin, H. C., 109
Shaw, C. R., 82, 108
Sherman, M., 94, 108
Shinedling, M., 142, 203
Siegel, S., 205, 252, 293, 297
Skinner, B. F., 28
Slavin, R. E., 28
Smith, M. L., 104, 107
Snow, C. P., 28
Snow, R. E., 9, 27
Stake, R. E., 109
Stallings, E. W., 109
Stanley, J. C., 118–19, 122, 124, 142, 203
Staver, J. R., 9, 27
Stebbins, C. L., 77
Stebbins, L. B., 130, 142
Steinbrenner, K., 314
Stephenson, W., 188, 203
Strunk, W., 335

Suci, G. J., 183, 203
Sullivan, F., 27
Summers, G. F., 203

Tannenbaum, P. H., 183, 203
Tatsuoka, M. M., 297
Thursfield, R. E., 63, 77
Thurstone, L. L., 180, 203
Toporek, J. D., 314
Torgerson, W. S., 203
Torney, J. V., 109
Torsten, H., 84, 108
Travers, R. M., 57
Turabian, K. L., 335
Turner, W. L., 77

Vandermyn, G., 108

Walberg, H. J., 240, 252
Walker, D. F., 130, 142
Waples, D., 85, 107
Ward, A. W., 58
Warner, W. L., 94, 108
Warren, D. R., 60, 77
Wasserman, W., 285, 297
Watanabe, P., 127, 142
Webb, E. J., 203
Weinfeld, F. D., 107
West, J., 94, 108
Westbury, I., 58
White, E. B., 335
White, J. B., 77
Wilson, S., 109
Winer, B. J., 118, 139, 142, 205, 252, 279–80, 297
Wisler, C. E., 130, 142
Witty, P., 81, 108
Wolfe, D. A., 293, 297
Wolinsky, G. F., 9, 27
Wolman, W., 27
Worthen, B. R., 108–9
Wynn, R., 58

Yamare, T., 297
Yates, F., 13, 27
York, R. L., 107

Zigler, E., 58
Zirkel, P. A., 77

SUBJECT INDEX

Academic research problem (project), 31–37
Achievement tests, 150–51
Action research, 21–22
Activity analysis, 85
Alpha level, 261–62
American Journal of Education, 63
American Psychological Association, Committee on Ethical Standards, 43–44
American Psychological Association's *Publication Manual*, 316–18, 322, 325–26
Analysis of covariance (ANCOVA), 117–18, 280–82
Analysis of variance (ANOVA), 275–80
  between groups variance, 276–78
  computer program, 304–7
  within groups variance, 276–78
Appendices, 321
Applied research, 21
Aptitude tests, 151–52
Area or cluster sample, 15–16
Aristotle, 3–4
Artificiality of experimental setting, 122
Assessment, 23, 79–88
Assumptions, 38–39
Attribute variable, 115

Bacon, Francis, 3–4
Belmont Report: Ethical Principles and Guidelines for the Protection of Human Subjects on Research, 42
Beta weights, 283–84
Bias:
  experimenter, 121–22
  selection, 120–21
  test, 152
Bibliography card, 50–51
Blind, 121
Boyle's Law, 112

Case study, 92–95
Causal-comparative research, 24, 98
Central limit theorem, 255–58
Charles' Law, 112
Chi square test, 286–90
  Yate's correction, 289–90

Coleman Report (*Equality of Educational Opportunity Study*), 102–4
Community study, 94
Computer, 299–301
  mainframe, 301
  microcomputers, 301
Computer data analysis, 304–13
Confounding variable, 115–16
Consent, informed, 44
Constant or Y intercept, 243, 282–84
Constructs, 7
Content or document analysis, 90–92
Control group, 113–14
Correlation, 229–30
  interpretation of, 239–43
  misinterpretation of, 241
  Pearson product-moment, 234–37
  phi, 239
  rank order, 237–39
  use in prediction, 241–43
Counterbalanced designs, 136
Current Index to Journals in Education, 46

Dalton plan, 62
Darwin, Charles, 4
Data organization, 194–200, 209–10, 301–4
  array, into an, 209–10
  for computer use, 301–4
  ranking and weighting, 199
  sorting and tabulating, 196–98
Dead Sea Scrolls, 71–73
Deductive-inductive reasoning, 4
Deductive reasoning, 3, 5–6
Degrees of freedom, 264–65
Delimitations, 38–39
Dependent variable, 115
Descriptive research, 23–25, 79–80, 90–98
Descriptive statistics, 205–48
  computer program, 308–10
  measures of central tendency, 211–15
  (*See also* Mean; Median; Mode)
  measures of relationship, 229–43 (*See also* Correlation)

Descriptive statistics (cont.)
 measures of spread or dispersion, 215–
  19 (*See also* Range; Standard deviation; Variance)
 overview, 210–11
 standard scores, 225–29 (*See also* Z; T
  Score)
Dewey, John, 4, 61
Dissertation Abstracts International, 46
Document or content analysis, 90–92
Double blind, 121

Educational research, 24–25
*Educational Research Information Cen-
 ters* (ERIC), 46–47
Education Index, 46
*Equality of Educational Opportunity
 Study* (Coleman Report), 102–4
Equivalent materials, pretest-posttest
 design, 133–35
Equivalent time-samples design, 132–33
Essay on Population, 4
*Ethical Principles in the Conduct of
 Research with Human Participants*
 (APA), 43
Ethics in human experimentation, 41–45
 confidentiality, 45
 informed consent, 44
 invasion of privacy, 44–45
 knowledge of outcome, 45
 protection from stress, harm, or danger,
  45
Ethnographic studies, 95–98
Evaluating a research report, 333–34
Evaluation, 23–24, 79, 86–88
Exceptional Child Education Resources,
 46
Experimental designs, 123–40
Experimental group, 113–14
Experimental mortality, 121
Experimental research, defined, 25
Experimental validity, 118–23
 external, 119, 122–23
 internal, 118–22
 threats to, 119–23
Experimenter bias, 121–22
Explanatory observational research, 24,
 98–101
Ex post facto research, 24, 98–101, 104–5,
 122, 140
External validity, experimental, 119, 122–
 23
Extraneous variable, 116
 control of, 116–18

F ratio (Analysis of variance), 275–80
Factorial designs, 137–39
Figures, 329–33
 bar graph or chart, 331

Figures (cont.)
 circle, pie, or sector chart, 332
 computer program for bar and pie
  charts, 310–13
 line graph, 329–31
 maps, 332
 organizational chart, 333
Fisher, R. A., 112–13
Follow Through Planned Variation Study,
 129–31
Follow-up study, 88–90
Format of a research report, 316–17
Fortran, 300
Fundamental or basic research, 21

Hawthorne effect, 113–14
Historical criticism, 70–74
 external, 70
 internal, 70–71
Historical research, 24, 60–75
 definition, 24
 difficulties, 67–68
 generalization, 64–66
 hypothesis, 66–67
 sources of data, 68–70
 writing the report, 74–75
History of American education, 61–63
History of Education Quarterly, 63
History (threat in experimental research),
 119–20
Homoegeneity of variance (F_{max}), 268–71
Hypotheses, 4–5, 9
 null, 11
 research, 10, 40–41

Independent variable, 114–15
Index to Doctoral Dissertations, 46
Inductive reasoning, 3–4, 5
Inferential data analysis, 208–9, 254–94
 (*See also* Analysis of covariance;
  Analysis of variance; Chi square;
  Mann-Whitney; Multiple regression;
  Standard error of the mean; *t* test)
Inquiry forms, 166–85 (*See also*
 Opinionaire; Questionnaire)
Interaction effect, 138–39
Interest inventories, 152
Interference of prior treatment, 122
Internal validity, experimental, 118–22
International Association for the Evalua-
 tion of Educational Achievement, 84–
 85
Interval scale, 146
Intervening variable, 115
Interview, 186–88

Library, use of, 46–51
Likert method, 181–83
Limitations, 38–39

Main body of a report, 318, 320–21
Major premise, 3
Malthus, Thomas, 4
Mann-Whitney test, 290–93
Matching, 117
Maturation, 119
Mean, 211–12
Median, 212–14
Meta-analysis (research synthesis or research integration), 104
Method, research, 41
Microfiche, super-microfiche, ultra-microfiche, 47
Minor premise, 3
Mode, 214–15
Mortality, experimental, 121
Multiple correlation, 285
Multiple regression, 282–85
   computer program, 307–8

National Assessment of Educational Progress (NAEP), 23, 79, 84
Nominal scale, 145–46
Nonnormal distributions, 222–23
   bimodal, 222–23
   skewed, 222–23
Nonparametric data, 207–8
   appropriate statistical analyses, 207–8
   statistical tests for use with, 285–93
Nonprobability samples, 16
Normal distribution, 219–22 (*See also* Nonnormal distributions)
   interpretation of, 223–24
   practical applications, 224–25
Note card, illustrated, 49
Note taking, 47–50
Novum Organum, 3
Null hypothesis, 11, 260–61

Observation, data gathering by, 158–65
   characteristics of good, 165
   reliability, 161–62
   validity, 161–62
One-group, pretest-posttest design, 125
One-shot case study, 124–25
Operational definitions, 38–39, 118
Opinionnaire, 179–85
   Likert method, 181–83
   semantic differential, 183–85
   Thurstone technique, 180
Ordinal scale, 146
Organismic variable, 115

Pagination, 326
Parameter, 11

Parametric data, 207–8
   appropriate statistical analyses, 207
   statistical tests for use with, 258–85
Partial correlation, 280–82
Percentile rank, 227–29
Personality inventories, 152–53
Placebo, 113–14
Population, 11–12
Post hoc analyses, 279
Post hoc fallacy, 104–5
Posttest-only, equivalent groups design, 126–27
Pre-experimental designs, 124–26
Pretest-posttest equivalent groups design, 127–28
Pretest-posttest nonequivalent groups design, 129
Probability sampling, 83
Problem selection, 32–37
Procedures, 41
Programmatic research, 5
Progressive education, 63
Projective devices, 153–54
Project Talent, 89–90
Proposal, research, 37–41
Psychological Abstracts, 46
Psychological tests and inventories, 148–58
   achievement, 150–51
   aptitude, 151–52
   bias, 152
   interest, 152
   personality, 152–53
   projective, 153–54
   qualities of good, 154–58
   reliability, 154–55
   validity, 155–57
Public opinion surveys, 82–84
Pueblo plan, 62

Q methodology, 188–90
Qualitative studies, 147–48
Quantitative studies, 145–47
Quasi-experimental designs, 128–36
Questionnaire, 166–79
   characteristics of a good, 175–76
   preparing and administering, 176–78
   reliability, 178–79
   validity, 178–79
Quota sampling, 83

Randomization, 116–17
Randomness, 12–14
Random numbers, 13–14
Random sample (simple), 12–13
Range, 216

Ratio scale, 146–47
References, 321
  form of, 324–26
References, basic sources, 46
  Current Index to Journals in Education, 46
  Dissertation Abstracts International, 46
  Education Index, 46
  Index to Doctoral Dissertations, 46
  Psychological Abstracts, 46
  Resources in Education, 46
Regression line, linear, 230–34
  slope of, 232–34, 242–43
Related literature:
  finding, 46–47
  review of, 39–40
Reliability of research tools and methods, 144–45
  coefficient of, 245–46
  interview, 187–88
  observation, 161–62
  questionnaires, 178–79
  test or inventory, 154–55
Replication and secondary analysis, 101–4
Research, 17–21
  action, 21–22
  applied, 21
  causal-comparative, 24
  descriptive, 23–25, 79–80, 90–98
  educational, 24–25
  experimental, 25
  explanatory observational, 24
  ex post facto, 24
  fundamental or basic, 21
  historical, 24, 60–75
Research proposal, 37–41
  definitions, assumptions, limitations, delimitations, 38–39
  to funding agency, 54–55
  hypothesis, 40–41
  methods, 41
  review of related literature, 39–40
  significance of the problem, 38
  statement of the problem, 37–38
  time schedule, 41
Research topics used by students in a beginning graduate course, 52–54
Resources in Education, 46
Review of related literature, 39–40 (*See also* Related literature, finding)

Sample size, 16–17
Sampling, 11–17
  area or cluster sample, 15
  error, 12, 117
  nonprobability, 16
  probability, 83
  quota, 83

Sampling (cont.)
  random, 12–13
  size, 16–17
  stratified random, 15
  systematic, 14–15
Scattergram, 230–31
School surveys, 86–87
Science, 5–8
Scientific method, 4–5, 6, 17–18
Seat belt research, 98
Selection bias, 120–21
Selection and maturation, interaction of, 121
Selection and treatment, interaction of, 123
Semantic differential, 183–85
Sesame Street studies, 100–101
Significance (alpha) level, 261–62
  Type I error, 262
  Type II error, 262
Slope of a regression line, 232–34, 242–43, 282–84
Social scaling, 190–94
  sociogram, 191–92
  sociometry, 190–91
Social surveys, 81–82
Solomon four-group design, 128
Sources of historical data:
  primary, 68–69
  secondary, 68–70
Standard deviation:
  population, 217–19
  sample, 265–67
Standard error of estimate, 243–46
Standard error of the mean, 255–58
Statement of the problem:
  defined, 37–38
  selection, 32–37
  significance, 38
Static-group comparison design, 125–26
Statistic, 11
Statistical Analysis System (SAS), 301, 308–13
Statistical inference, 254 (*See also* Inferential data analysis)
Statistical Package for the Social Sciences (SPSS), 301, 304–8
Statistical regression, 120
Statistics:
  definition, 206
  descriptive analysis, 208
  inferential analysis, 208–9
Stonehenge, 73–74
Stratified random sample, 15
Student's distribution, 267–68 (*See also* *t* test)
Style manuals, 316
Subjects, 41

Surveys:
  public opinion, 82–84
  school, 86–87
  social, 81–82
Syllogism, 3
  conclusion, 3
  major premise, 3
  minor premise, 3
Systematic sample, 14–15

T score, 227
t test (Student's *t*), 258–59, 261–64, 267–68
  correlation, of a, 274–75
  distribution for, 267–68
  matched or correlated groups, 271–74
  one-tailed, 262–64
  small samples, 268
  two-tailed, 262–64
Tables, 327–28
Terman, L. M., 32
Testing effect, 120
  interaction of, 122
Theory, 5–6
  defined, 8–9
Thesis or dissertation, 322
Threats to experimental validity, 119–23
Thurstone technique, 180
Time-series design, 132
Title page, example, 319
Treatment verification, 123
Trend studies, 85–86
True experimental designs, 126–28
Type I and Type II error, 262
Typing a report, 323–24

Unstable instrumentation, 120

Validity:
  experimental, 118–23
  interview, 187–88
  observation, 161–62
  questionnaires, 178–79
  test or inventory, 155–57
    coefficient of, 245
    construct, 156
    content, 156
    criterion-related, concurrent, 156–57
    criterion-related, predictive, 156
  threats to, 119–23
Variables, 114–16
  attribute, 115
  confounding, 115–16
  dependent, 115
  extraneous, 116
  independent, 114–15
  intervening, 115
  organismic, 115
Variance:
  between groups, 276–78
  population parameter, 216–17
  sample statistic, 265–67
  within groups, 276–78

Winnetka plan, 62
Writing style, 322–23

z score, 225–26